MOUS Essentials Excel 97 Expert

Jane Calabria

Dorothy Burke

Que E&T

An Imprint of Macmillan Computer Publishing

MOUS Essentials: Excel 97 Expert

Library of Congress Catalog No: 98-066767

ISBN: 1-58076-055-4

01 00 99 4 3

Interpretation of the printing code: the rightmost double-digit number is the year of the book's printing; the rightmost single-digit number, the number of the book's printing. For example, a printing code of 98-1 shows that the first printing of the book occurred in 1998.

Screens reproduced in this book were created using Collage Plus from Inner Media, Inc., Hollis, NH.

Composed in *Stone Serif* and *MCPdigital* by Que® Education and Training

Publisher:
Robert Linsky

Executive Editor:
Randy Haubner

Acquisitions Editor:
Jon Phillips

Director of Product Marketing:
Susan L. Kindel

Managing Editor:
Caroline Roop

Development Editor:
Nancy D. Warner

Project Editor:
Susan Hobbs

Acquisitions Assistant:
Ken Schmidt

Technical Editor:
Ed Metzler

Cover Designer:
Nathan Clement

Book Designer:
Louisa Kluznick

Production Team:
Cheryl Lynch
Megan Wade

Indexer
Chris Barrick

About the Authors

Jane Calabria has authored 13 Macmillan Computer Publishing books. As a consultant, Jane works on a national level with large corporations and training organizations, developing user training programs and modeling help desk support structures. As a trainer, Jane teaches Microsoft desktop applications, operating systems, and Lotus Notes and Domino. She is a Certified Lotus Notes Professional (Principal level) and a Certified Microsoft User Specialist.

Jane and Dorothy Burke have teamed up successfully on several MCP books, including the *Certified Microsoft Office User Exam Guide for Microsoft Word 97, Microsoft Excel 97,* and *Microsoft Power Point 97*. They also co-authored *Microsoft Works 6-in-1, Microsoft Windows 95 6 in 1, Microsoft Windows 98 6 in 1, Using Microsoft Word 97,* and several Lotus Notes books.

Dorothy Burke has traveled a few career paths before becoming a computer instructor and consultant. She has worked as a magazine editor for an engineering trade magazine, in customer service and management in the home medical equipment industry, and in a management consulting firm as an office manager and editor of its newsletter and catalogs. Dorothy is a Certified Lotus Instructor and a Certified Lotus Professional in Lotus Notes. With a strong background in graphics and desktop publishing, Dorothy develops applications in Lotus Notes and for Domino Web sites. Writing with Jane Calabria, she has contributed to the *10 Minute Guide to Lotus Notes Mail 4.5* and *Lotus Notes 4.5 and the Internet 6-in-1* published by Que Corporation. She is also a contributing author to Que's *Special Edition Using PowerPoint 97* and is the co-author of the *10 Minute Guide to Lotus Notes Mail 4.6, 10 Minute Guide to Lotus Notes 4.6, Microsoft Works 4.5 6 in 1, Microsoft Windows 95 6 in 1, PowerPoint 97 Exam Guide, Word 97 Exam Guide, Excel 97 Exam Guide,* and *Using Microsoft Word 97.*

Trademark Acknowledgments

All terms mentioned in this book that are known to be trademarks or service marks have been appropriately capitalized. Que Education and Training cannot attest to the accuracy of this information. Use of a term in this book should not be regarded as affecting the validity of any trademark or service mark.

Preface

Que Education and Training is the educational publishing imprint of Macmillan Computer Publishing, the world's leading computer book publisher. Macmillan Computer Publishing books have taught more than 20 million people how to be productive with their computers.

This expertise in producing high-quality computer tutorial and reference books is evident in every Que Education and Training title we publish. The same tried-and-true writing and product-development process that makes Macmillan Computer Publishing books bestsellers is used to ensure that educational materials from Que Education and Training provide the most accurate and up-to-date information. Experienced and respected computer application instructors write and review every manuscript to provide class-tested pedagogy. Quality-assurance editors check every keystroke and command in Que Education and Training books to ensure that instructions are clear, accurate, and precise.

Above all, Macmillan Computer Publishing and, in turn, Que Education and Training have years of experience in meeting the learning demands of students across all disciplines.

The "MOUS Essentials" of Hands-On Learning

The *MOUS Essentials* are appropriate for use in both corporate training and college classroom settings. They can be used effectively as computer-lab applications modules to accompany any of Que Education and Training's computer concepts text or as stand-alone texts for an applications-only course. The *MOUS Essentials* workbooks enable users to become self-sufficient quickly; encourage self-learning after instruction; maximize learning through clear, complete explanations; and serve as future references.

The *MOUS Essentials* series uses the following elements to get the most out of the material:

Objectives list what students do and learn from the project.

Required Activities are the objectives as they relate to the Microsoft Office User Specialist exams.

"Why Would I Do This?" shows students why the material is essential.

Step-by-Step Tutorials simplify the procedures with large screen shots, captions, and annotations.

If you have problems... anticipates common pitfalls and advises students accordingly.

Inside Stuff provides tips and shortcuts for more effective applications.

Key Terms are highlighted in the text and defined in the margin when they first appear, as well as in an end-of-book glossary.

Jargon Watch offers a layperson's view of "technobabble" in easily understandable terms.

Exam Notes provide information and insight on topics that are covered on the MOUS exam and that should be reviewed carefully.

Checking Your Skills provides true/false, multiple choice, matching, and completion exercises.

Applying Your Skills contains directed, hands-on Practice exercises to check comprehension and reinforce learning, as well as self-directed Challenge exercises requiring students to use critical thinking skills.

CD-ROM contains files for the text's step-by-step tutorials and end of project exercises

Annotated Instructor's Edition

If you have adopted this text for use in a college classroom, you will receive, upon request, an Annotated Instructor's Edition at no additional charge. The manual contains suggested curriculum guides for courses of varying lengths, teaching tips, answers to exercises in Checking Your Skills and Applying Your Skills sections, test questions and answers, and data files and solutions for each tutorial and exercise. Please contact your local representative or write to us on school or business letterhead at Macmillan Computer Publishing, 201 West 103rd Street, Indianapolis, IN 46290-1097, Attention: Que Education and Training Sales Support.

Microsoft Office User Specialist Exams

In order to validate your skills using Office, Microsoft has created the Microsoft Office User Specialist program. The Specialist Program is available for many Office 95 and Office 97 applications at both Proficient and Expert User levels.

The Specialist designation distinguishes you from your peers as knowledgeable in using Office products, which can also make you more competitive in the job market.

The *Microsoft Office User Specialist exams* are for anyone who:

- Wants to expand their skills.
- Is seeking certification in a particular software.
- Wants to learn or reference tasks in short, concise lessons.
- Is an instructor or trainer preparing groups of people for the Microsoft Exams.

Que Education & Training Certification Resource Center

To keep up to date on the Microsoft Office User Specialist program exams, check the following Web sites:

```
www.queet.com/certification
www.mous.net
www.microsoft.com/office/train_cert
```

MOUS PinPoint® Training and Testing Software

MOUS PinPoint training and testing software is designed to supplement the projects in this book. It aids you in your preparation for taking and passing the *Microsoft Office User Specialist* exams. The MOUS PinPoint software consists of:

- Trainers
- Evaluations

Each **trainer** asks you to perform specific tasks that were covered in a particular project of this book. If you don't know how to perform a particular task, you can watch a demonstration (**SHOW ME**) of the task. Immediate feedback (concerning the correctness of performance) is given after each task in each trainer. Each **evaluation** consists of the same questions that were given in the trainer. However, with an evaluation, you may not view demonstrations and you do not receive feedback after trying each task. After performing a **trainer** or **evaluation**, you can view a report of your overall performance.

Preparing to Install the MOUS PinPoint Training and Testing Software

To install the MOUS PinPoint training and testing software, we recommend following these steps:

1. Check to see if your computer meets the minimum requirements (see Table I.1).
2. Perform a full installation of Office 97 on your computer if you have not already done so (see the section "Installing Office 97").
3. Install the MOUS PinPoint testing and training software (see the section "Installing the MOUS PinPoint Training and Testing Software").

Using the MOUS PinPoint Training and Testing Software

To use the MOUS PinPoint training and testing software, we recommend following these steps.

Study the projects in this book. After reading each project:

1. Run the **trainer** for the project (see the section "Running the MOUS PinPoint Software"). Then view a report on your performance (see the section "Viewing Reports").
2. Run the **evaluation** for the project (see the section "Running the MOUS PinPoint Software"). Then view a report on your performance (see the section "Viewing Reports"). Note: Some projects may not have a corresponding MOUS PinPoint trainer and evaluation.

After you have finished reading this book, take the MOUS PinPoint Final Exam:

1. Run the **evaluation** for the Final Exam Part 1. Final Exam Part 1 covers material included in the first half of this book.
2. Run the **trainer** for the Final Exam Part 1. Only the items missed in the trainer will be set to run.
3. Run the **evaluation** for the Final Exam Part 1 (again) as a final check.
4. Repeat the 1–3 given for Final Exam Part 2. Final Exam Part 2 covers material from roughly the second half of this book.
5. When you are finished using the MOUS PinPoint software, you can remove it from your computer (see the section "Removing the MOUS PinPoint Training and Testing Software").

Running MOUS PinPoint Testing and Training Software Requirements

The system components in Table I.1 are required to run the MOUS PinPoint Testing and Training Software.

Table I.1 System Component Requirements

Component	Minimum	Recommended
CPU	Pentium 90	Higher than Pentium 90
Operating System	Windows 95 or NT 4.0 Note: You must have an Administrator's or Power User's login if you are working on a Windows NT workstation.	N/A
Installed Apps	Office 97 (full installation)	N/A
RAM	16 MB	32 MB or higher

continues

Table I.1 (continued)		
Component	Minimum	Recommended
Hard Drive	Adequate space for installation, Office 97, and for MOUS PinPoint training and testing software.	N/A
CD-ROM Drive	2X speed	4X speed or faster
Pointing Device	Windows-compatible mouse or pointing device.	N/A
Video	Color VGA video display	N/A

Installing Office 97

Important: It is necessary to do a complete installation of Office 97. This means installing *all* components.

To perform a full installation of Office 97, complete the following steps:

1. Start Windows 95 or Windows NT 4.0 and close any applications that are running (other than Windows).
2. Insert the Office 97 CD and run **setup.exe**.
3. Click on the **Add/Remove** button, as shown in Figure I.1 (if a previous installation of Office 97 is already on your computer). If you do not have a previous installation of Office 97 on your computer, select **Custom** installation from a different screen.

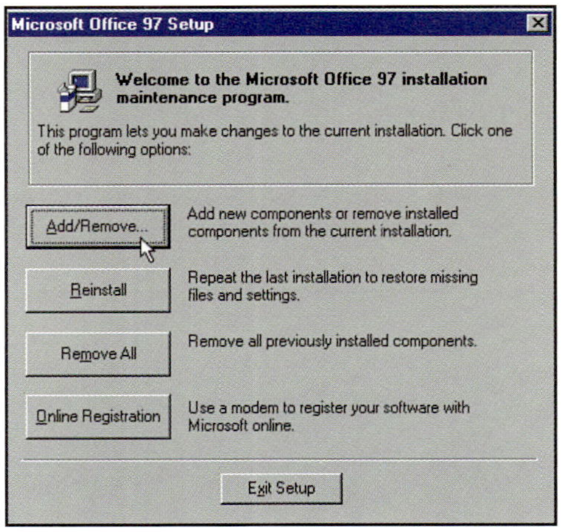

Figure I.1
The Microsoft Office 97 Setup dialog box.

4. Click on the **Select All** button (see Figure I.2).
5. Click on the **Continue** button.
6. Continue with the installation until it is finished.

Figure I.2
Choosing the Select All button will install *all* Office 97 components to the system.

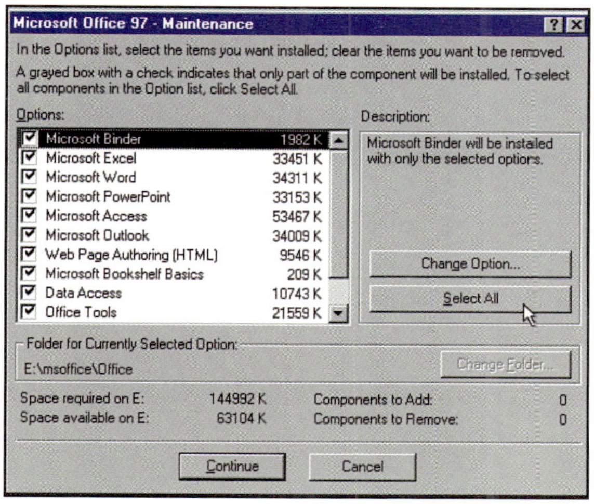

Installing the MOUS PinPoint Training and Testing Software

To install and run MOUS PinPoint trainers and evaluations on a single-user computer, you must first install the MOUS PinPoint **Launcher** by running a setup program from the MOUS PinPoint CD.

Installing the MOUS PinPoint Launcher

To run the setup program for the MOUS PinPoint Launcher:

1. Start Windows 95 or Windows NT 4.0 and insert the MOUS PinPoint CD into the CD-ROM drive.
2. Select **Start/Run** from the Windows desktop.
3. Enter (or browse to) **[Drive Letter]:\SETUP.EXE** (where **[Drive Letter]** is the assigned drive letter of the CD-ROM (see Figure I.3).

Figure I.3
Indicating the location of the setup.exe executable.

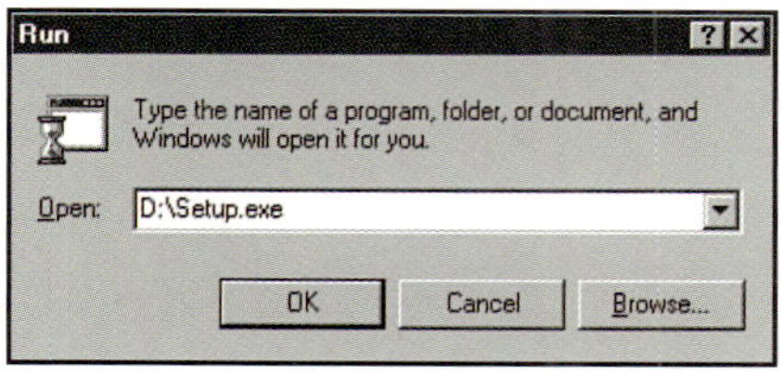

4. Click on **OK**. The setup program runs.
5. Answer the questions that appear during the installation.
6. When the dialog box in Figure I.4 displays, choose **Normal Single-User Installation**.

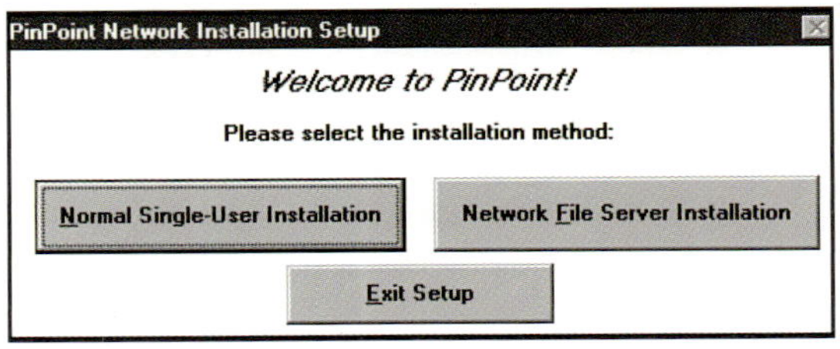

Figure I.4
The MOUS PinPoint Network Installation Setup dialog box

7. Click **Yes** when you are asked if you want to install MOUS PinPoint modules to your hard disk. The dialog box in Figure I.5 appears. The installation program is getting ready to install the **Launcher** to your computer. It needs to know the directory where you would like it installed.

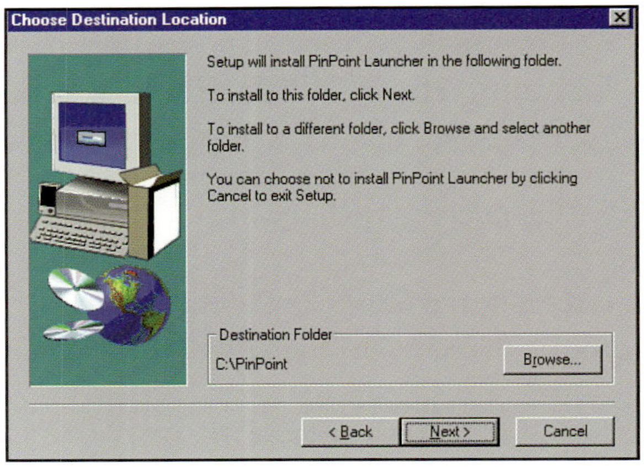

Figure I.5
The default location Destination Folder is shown.

8. To install the **Launcher** to the default location, click on the **Next** button. Otherwise, enter a new path for the **Launcher** and then click on the **Next** button.
9. Confirm the installation location by clicking on **Yes** in the dialog box in Figure I.6.

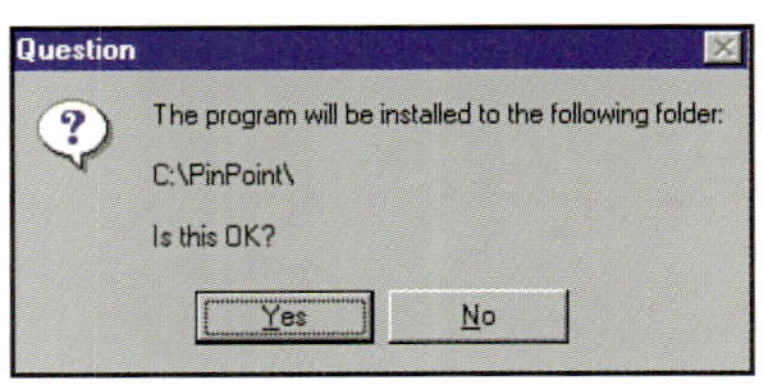

Figure I.6
The destination folder requires confirmation.

10. When Figure I.7 appears, click on Next.

A **PinPoint Training** group window is created (see Figure I.8). You can close this window. It is not necessary to use this window to start the PinPoint Launcher in the future since you can always select Start/Programs/PinPoint Training/PinPoint Training from your desktop.

Figure I.7
Creation of the Program Folder.

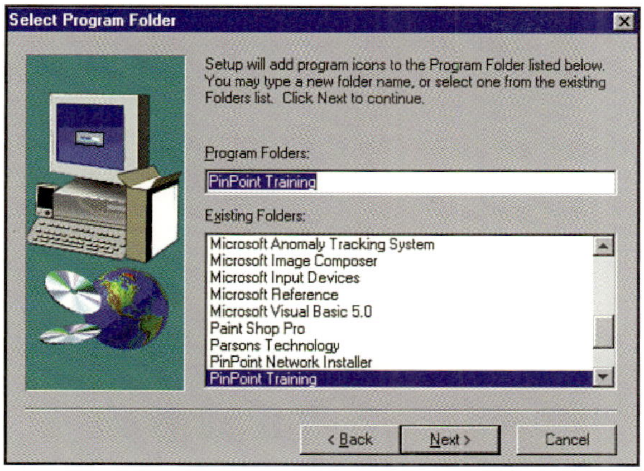

Figure I.8
The PinPoint Training group window that is created.

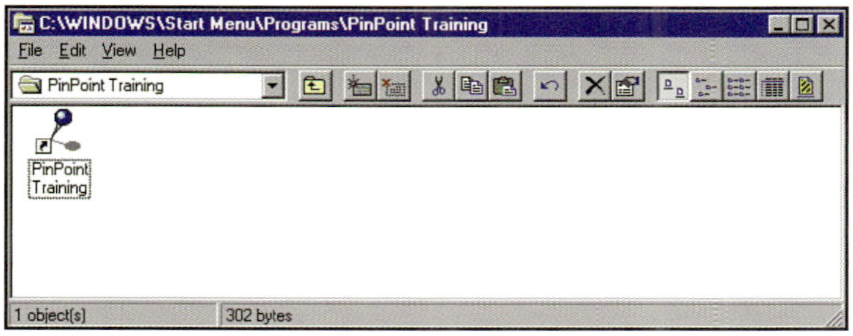

The PinPoint **Launcher** is used to:

- logon with your **UserID** and **Password**.
- install your MOUS PinPoint training and testing software for *an exam*.
- run your MOUS PinPoint training and testing software for *an exam*.
- view reports after you have run the MOUS PinPoint training and testing software.

To install the MOUS PinPoint training and testing software for *an exam*, continue with the next section.

Installing the MOUS PinPoint Software

To install the MOUS PinPoint training and testing software:

1. Start the Launcher by selecting Start/Programs/PinPoint Training/PinPoint Training (see Figure I.9).
2. Click on the **Installer** button (see Figure I.10).
3. Install your MOUS PinPoint software by selecting the specific module (for example, **Microsoft Excel 97 Proficiency Custom ME**) from the **Available Modules** list box and clicking on the **Install** button. (Do not install the **Launcher**. It's already installed!)
4. Answer the questions that appear during installation. You are asked to verify the location where the MOUS PinPoint software will install to your hard drive (see Figure I.11).

Figure I.9
The Home screen of the Launcher.

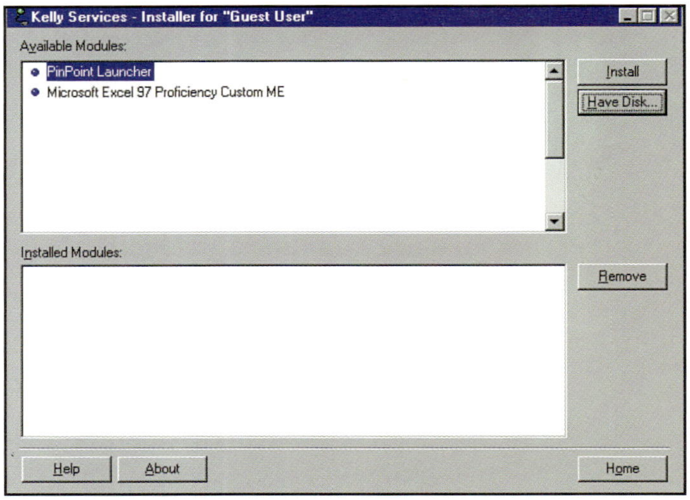

Figure I.10
The **Installer** screen.

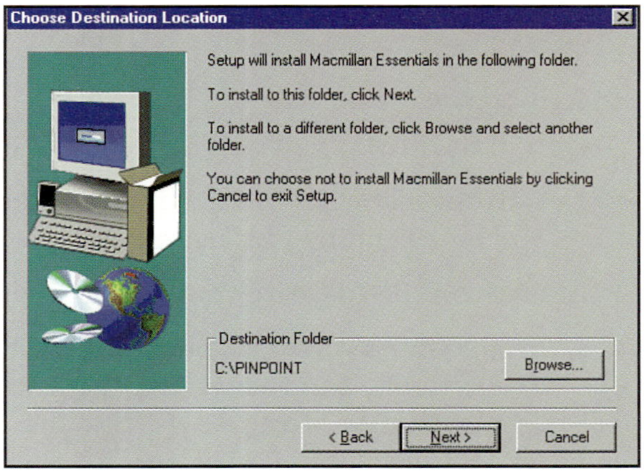

Figure I.11
The default location Destination Folder is shown.

5. Make changes as necessary by clicking on **Browse** and selecting a different destination folder. Important: The MOUS PinPoint software for *the specific exam* and the PinPoint **Launcher** must be installed under the same main directory (for example, **C:\PinPoint**) in order to work properly.

6. Click on **Next**.
7. Accept the subdirectory (for example, **xl8prome**) where the MOUS PinPoint software will be placed. You do not have a choice concerning the name of this subdirectory.

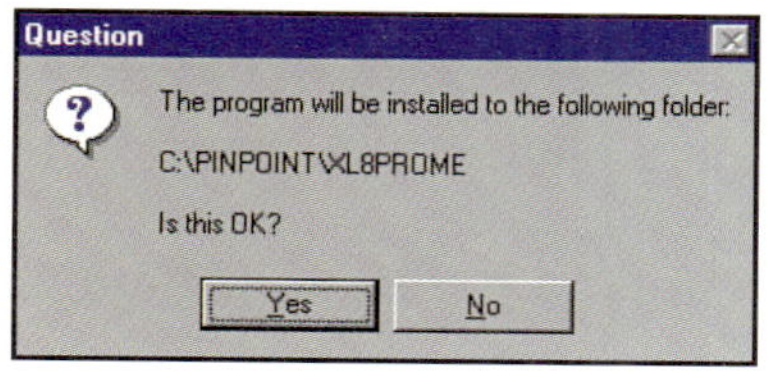

Figure I.12
The destination folder requires confirmation.

8. Click on **Yes**.
9. If you would like to view a README file concerning MOUS PinPoint software, click on **Yes** in the dialog box in Figure I.13. Otherwise, click on No.

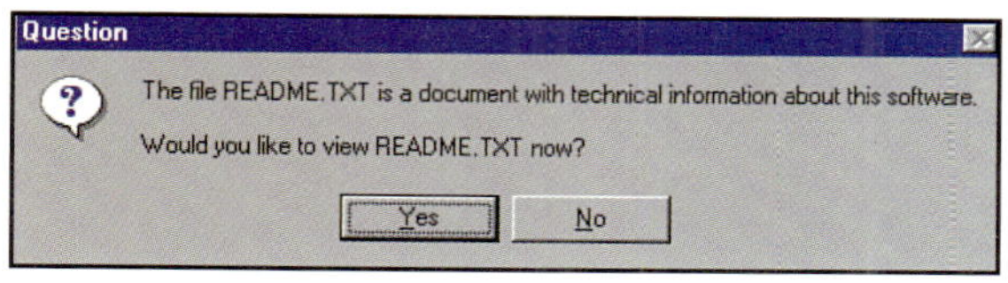

Figure I.13
Specify whether you want to review the README.txt file.

A PinPoint Training group window is created (see Figure I.14).

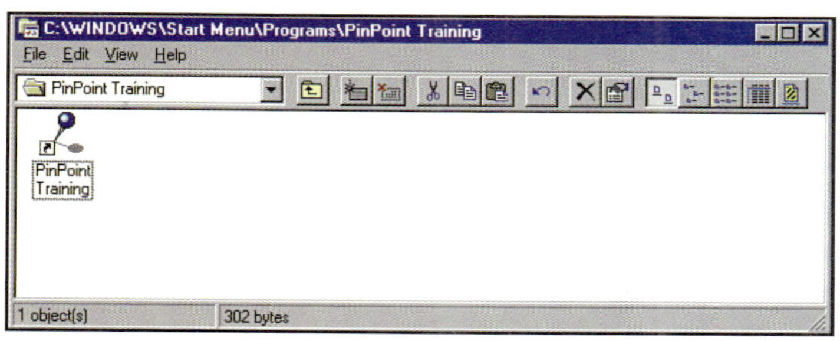

Figure I.14
The PinPoint Training group window that is created.

Close this window. It is not necessary to use this window to start the PinPoint **Launcher** in the future since you can always select Start/Programs/PinPoint Training/PinPoint Training from your desktop.

If you want to run the MOUS PinPoint software that you just installed, don't exit from the **Launcher**. Continue on with step 3 in the next section.

To exit from the **Launcher** to Windows, click on the **Exit** button.

Running the MOUS PinPoint Software

To run the MOUS PinPoint software, it is necessary to start the PinPoint **Launcher**. Important: Shut down all applications.

To run the MOUS PinPoint software:

1. Shut down all applications (except Windows and the Launcher) that are running, including any shortcut bars (such as Microsoft Office

shortcut bar). If the Office 97 exam application is running, shut it down.

2. Start the Launcher by selecting Start/Programs/PinPoint Training/PinPoint Training from the Windows desktop.
3. Click on the User Logon button (see Figure I.15). Logging on under your name allows the **Launcher** to keep track of your personal progress. This enables the **Launcher** to reconfigure a module the next time you take it. It also enables the **Launcher** to create a report containing information about your training or evaluation sessions.

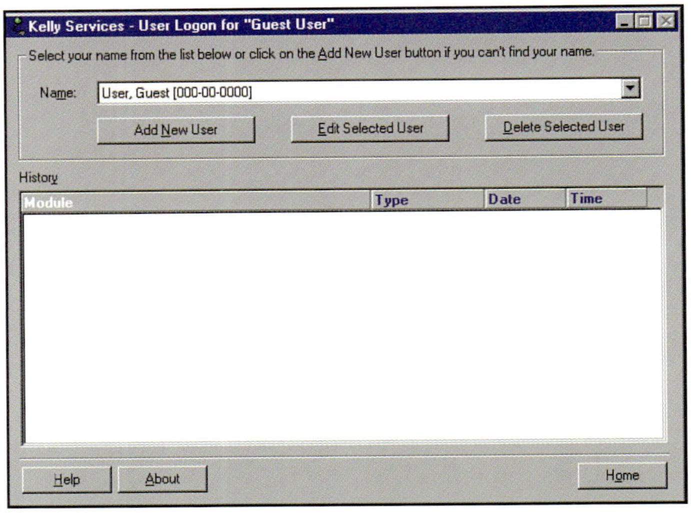

Figure I.15
The **User Logon** screen.

4. Select your name from the drop-down list in the **Name** combo box in Figure I.16:
   - You may need to use the scroll bar to find your name.
   - If your name is not in the list, go to step 5.
   - If you found your name, skip to step 8.

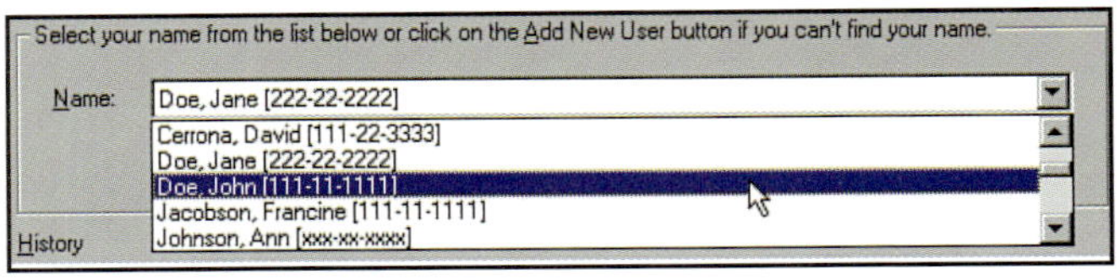

Figure I.16
Specify your logon name.

5. If this is your first time running MOUS PinPoint software, your name will not be in the list. If that is the case, create a user account for yourself by clicking on the **Add New User** button.
6. Enter your personal data, tabbing between fields in Figure I.17:
   - Enter all five data items. If one or more of the data items are missing, the **OK** button will remain grayed out (disabled).
   - Your **User ID** and **Password** may both consist of up to fourteen characters and are both case sensitive.

- After entering your **Password** in the **Password** field, you must confirm this **Password** by entering the identical **Password** again in the **Confirm Password** field.

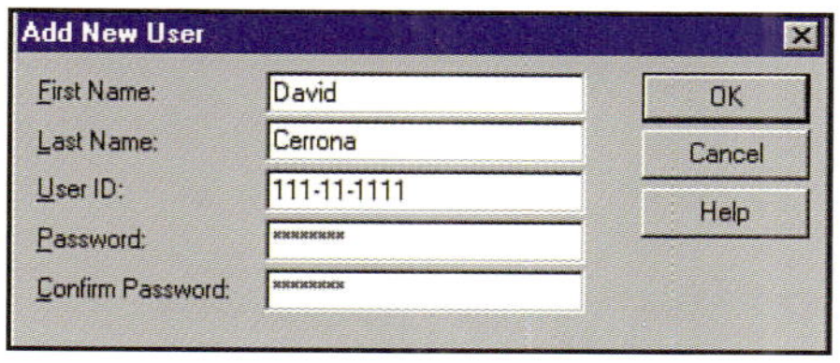

Figure I.17
The Add New User dialog box.

7. Click on **OK**. Your account is created and you are logged on. You are ready to move to the **Training & Testing** screen.
8. Click on the **Home** button to move to the **Home** screen.
9. Click on the **Training & Testing** button (see Figure I.18).

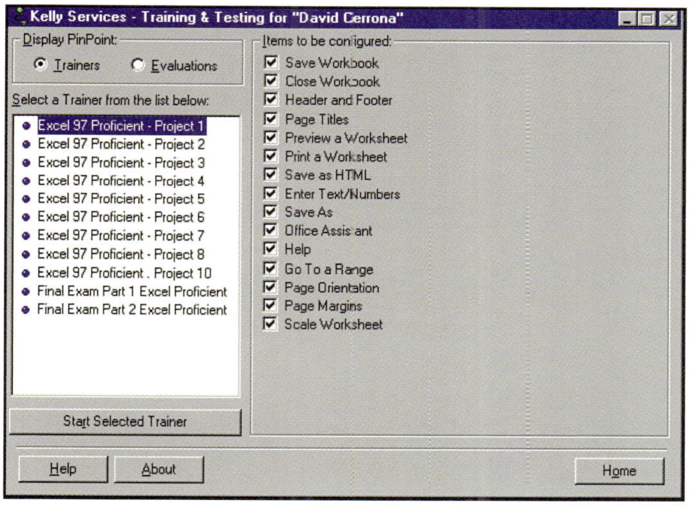

Figure I.18
The **Training & Testing** screen.

10. Select **Trainers** (or **Evaluations**), depending on which you would like to run (see Figure I.19). A list of trainers (or evaluations) displays.

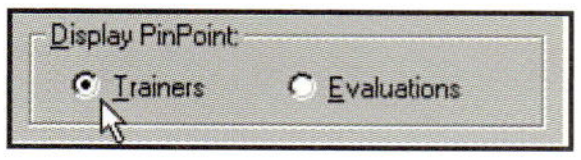

Figure I.19
Selecting trainers or evaluations.

11. Select the particular trainer or evaluation that you would like to run. Each trainer and evaluation is named by the project that it covers. Trainers may be configured. That means you can select the tasks that you would like to run. The first time you run a trainer, all tasks will automatically be selected. (Note: Evaluations may not be configured.)

12. If you are running a trainer, configure it by selecting or deselecting tasks in the **Items to be configured** section:

- A check indicates that the task will run.
- No check indicates that the task will not run.

You are now ready to start (launch) the trainer or evaluation for the project.

Figure I.20
Select the tasks you want to configure.

13. Click on the **Start Selected Trainer** button if you are starting a trainer or the **Start Selected Evaluation** button if you are starting an evaluation. Before the trainer or evaluation runs, you are asked to confirm (see Figure I.21).

Figure I.21
Confirm the running of the trainer or evaluation.

14. Click on **Yes** to confirm. While running the trainer or evaluation, you may use the controls in Figure I.22.

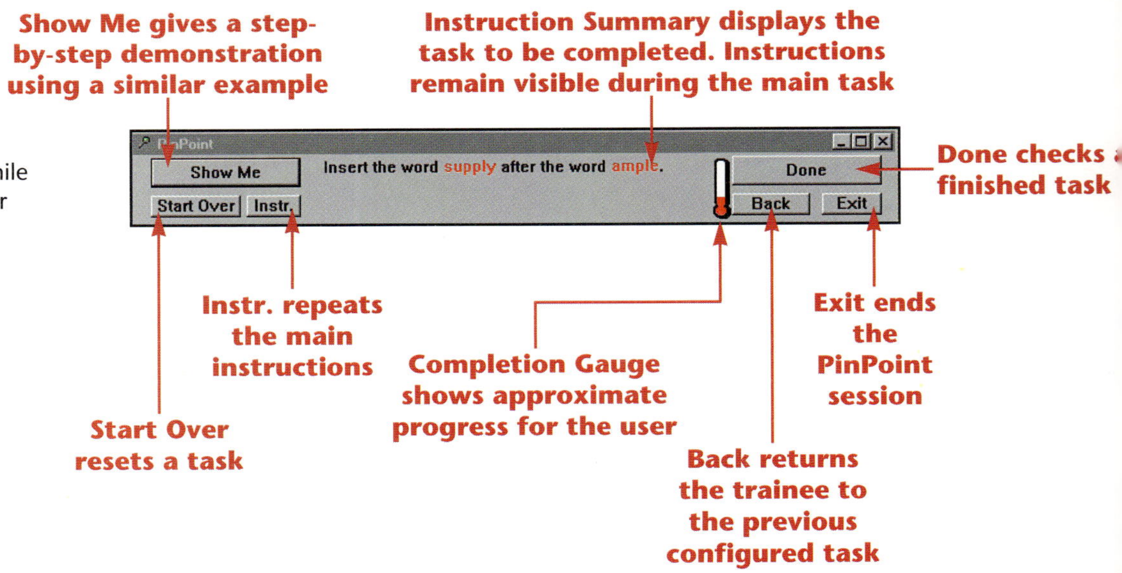

Figure I.22
Controls available while running the trainer or evaluation.

After running a trainer or evaluation, the **Training and Testing** screen reappears. You can continue to run other trainers or evaluations for other projects. When you are finished studying the whole book, you can also run the trainers and evaluations for the final exams.

To view reports for each trainer or evaluation that you ran, click on the **Reports** button (see the section "Running the MOUS PinPoint Software").

To exit from the **Launcher**, first move to the **Home** screen by clicking on the **Home** button. Then click on the **Exit** button.

Viewing Reports

In the **Launcher**, you can view two kinds of reports after running a MOUS PinPoint trainer or evaluation:

To display reports in the Launcher:

1. Start the **Launcher** and log on.
2. Click on the **Reports** button (see Figure I.23). This report displays a line (record) of data for each instance that you have run a MOUS PinPoint trainer or evaluation:
   - **Accuracy** is the number of tasks you performed correctly
   - **Maximum** is the total number of tasks that were configured to run
   - **Time** is the total elapsed time in minutes (from the moment you started running the trainer or evaluation to the moment that you exited the trainer or evaluation)

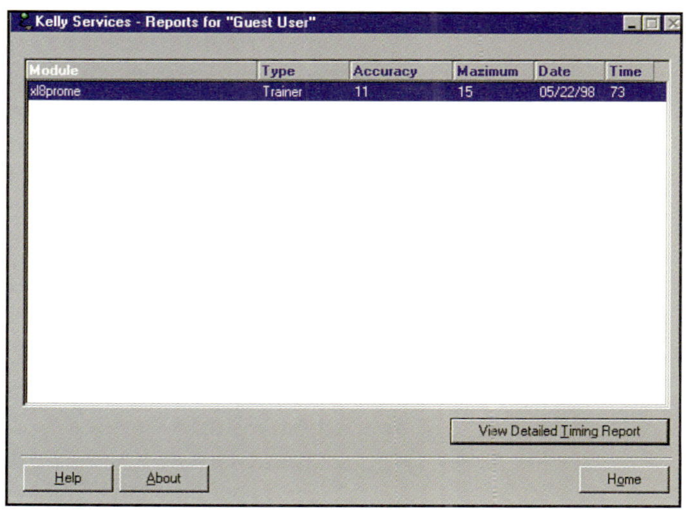

Figure I.23
The Reports screen appears, displaying the first kind of report.

3. The second kind of report is the **Detailed Timing Report** (see Figure I.24). If you wish to view this report, select the record for which you would like the timing report and click on the **View Detailed Timing Report** button.

Figure I.24
Select the specific record.

Module	Type	Accuracy	Maximum	Date	Time
xl8prome	Trainer	11	15	05/22/98	73

Figure I.25
The **Detailed Timing Report**.

Timing results of xl8prome for Guest User

Item No.	Item	Actual	Optimal	Correct	Did Show Me
1	Save Workbook	2	10	No	No
1	Save Workbook	8	10	Yes	No
2	Close Workbook	2	10	Yes	No
21	Header and Footer	130	30	No	No
21	Header and Footer	1	30	No	Yes (1)
26	Page Titles	23	25	No	No
26	Page Titles	21	25	No	Yes (1)
26	Page Titles	29	25	Yes	Yes (1)
35	Preview a Worksheet	8	20	No	No
35	Preview a Worksheet	24	20	No	Yes (1)
35	Preview a Worksheet	7	20	No	Yes (1)
35	Preview a Worksheet	7	20	No	Yes (1)
35	Preview a Worksheet	1	20	No	Yes (1)
36	Print a Worksheet	26	20	No	Yes (1)
41	Save as HTML	12	45	No	Yes (1)
44	Enter Text/Numbers	58	30	No	No
44	Enter Text/Numbers	66	30	Yes	No
45	Save As	12	30	Yes	No
49	Office Assistant	24	25	Yes	No
50	Help	13	30	Yes	No
51	Go To a Range	10	10	Yes	No
53	Page Orientation	12	15	Yes	No
54	Page Margins	27	20	Yes	No
55	Scale Worksheet	36	10	Yes	No

Close   Print

4. To print the **Detailed Timing Report**, click on the **Print** button:

   - **Actual** is the time, in seconds, you used to complete the task. This time is considered the "involved time," the time that was taken from the moment that you clicked with the mouse (or entered something on the keyboard) to the moment that you clicked on the **Done** button. It does not count the "thinking time" before you first moved the mouse (or used the keyboard), and it does not count the time used to run and view a SHOW ME demonstration.
   - **Optimal** is a reasonable amount of time, in seconds, required to perform a task by an efficient method
   - **Correct** - **Yes**, if the you performed the task correctly; **No** if you did not perform the task correctly
   - **Did Show Me** - **Yes**, if you viewed a SHOW ME demonstration for the task; **No**, if you did not view a SHOW ME demonstration for the task. The **Did Show Me** column appears only if the timing report contains data for a **trainer** and not for an **evaluation**. (Evaluations do not have SHOW MEs.)

5. Close the **Detailed Timing Report** window by clicking on the **Close** button. The **Reports** screen of the **Launcher** returns.

Removing the MOUS PinPoint Training and Testing Software

When you are finished using the MOUS PinPoint training and testing software, you can remove it. Be sure to follow the following procedure.

To remove your MOUS PinPoint training and testing software:

1. Start the **Launcher**.
2. Click on the **Installer** button.
3. Select the exam module from the **Installed Modules** list.

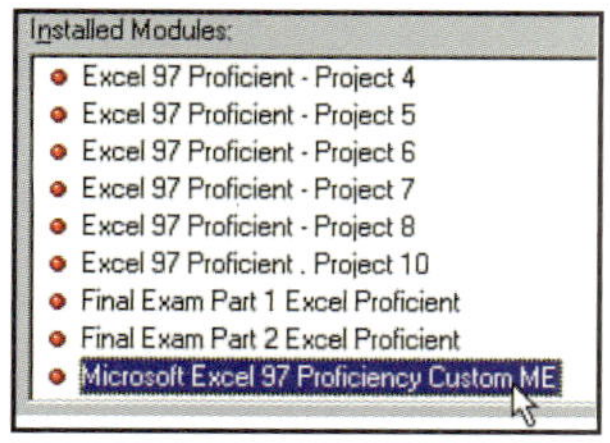

Figure I.26
Choose from the **Installed Modules** available.

4. Click the **Remove** button.
5. When the **Confirmation** dialog box appears, click **Yes**.
6. When the **Remove** dialog box appears, click the **Yes** button.
7. An **"Uninstall complete"** message appears.
8. Find the MOUS PinPoint directory on your computer and delete it.

Troubleshooting

Table I.2 lists a few problems that can arise while running the MOUS PinPoint training and testing software. For each problem, a solution or explanation is given.

Table I.2 MOUS PinPoint Training and Testing Software Problems and Solutions

Problem	Explanation or Action
A task is grayed out and not selected on the Training and Testing screen in the Launcher program (see Figure I.27).	A particular component has not been installed. Exit the Launcher and perform a full installation of Office 97 (see section "Installing Office 97").

Your computer crashes (locks up or exits ungracefully) while running the MOUS PinPoint training or testing.	Start you computer again and rerun the desired MOUS PinPoint training or testing. Exit the trainer or evaluation in the normal way. It is important to do this, even if you have no desire to run a trainer or evaluation. By running any trainer or evaluation, you will insure that your computer's registry is reset to normal.

Figure I.27
An example of a grayed out option.

continues

Table I.2 (continued)	
Problem	Explanation or Action
You see a message that says **"program was left in an unfinished state"** AND you have deleted the MOUS PinPoint directory (or one of its key components).	The problem is that your Windows Registry was changed by running the registry and needs to be set back to the state it was in before you started the MOUS PinPoint training and testing. Do the following: 1.Go to the **Windows** directory and find the following files: **OFC97.PIN** **OFC971.PIN** **OFC972.PIN** **OFC973.PIN** **OFC974.PIN** 2. Delete the **OFC97.PIN** file. 3. Rename the other four **.PIN** files so that they have a **.REG** extension. 4. Double-click on each of the .REG files to run them. This will reset your Registry.

Microsoft Excel Expert Specialist User Skills

The skill areas covered in the exam and the required tasks for those skill areas are listed in Table I.3.

Table I.3 Expert User Skills

Skill Set	Required Activity	Project	Lesson
Format worksheets	Apply formats (accounting, fraction, and scientific)	1	1
	Create custom formats	1	1
	Use styles and AutoFormats	2	3
Use lists	Sort data	8	3
	Query from a list	8	4
Print workbooks	Preview workbooks	4	7
	Print workbooks	4	7
Audit a worksheet	Check and review data	13	2
	Find cells referred to in a specific formula	13	2
	Find formulas that refer to a specific cell	13	2
	Find errors	13	1

Skill Set	Required Activity	Project	Lesson
Use advanced functionality	Query databases	8	4
	Extract data	8	5
	Use filters	8	5
	Use data analysis and pivot tables	11	1-5
		12	1-7
		13	1-7
	Use data map	2	6
	Use data validation	13	7
	Use conditional formatting	1	4
	Perform multi-level sorts	8	3
Use macros	Create and record macros	7	2
	Edit macros	7	4
	Run macros	7	3
Import and export data	Import from other applications	6	6
	Export to other applications	6	2,3, 4,5
Use templates	Work with existing templates	9	8
	Create templates	9	7
	Edit templates	9	9
Use multiple workbooks	Link workbooks	4	4
	Use multiple workbooks	4	8
Use workgroup functions	Cell tips	4	8
	Share lists	14	1,2
	Track changes	14	3
	Resolve conflicts	14	3
	Show history of changes	14	3
	Merge workbooks	14	4

Table of Contents at a Glance

Table of Contents

Conventions Used in This Book

The *MOUS Essentials* series uses the following conventions to make it easier for you to understand the material:

- Text that you are to type or that appears onscreen appears in a `special font and color`.
- Underlined letters in menu names, menu commands, and dialog-box options are the shortcut keys. Examples are the File menu, the Open command, and the File name list box.
- Key terms in *italic* the first time they are discussed and are defined in the margin as soon as they are introduced.

Project One 1

Advanced Formatting

Making Your Sales Figures Readable and Attractive

In this Project, you learn how to:

Objectives	Required Activities
➤ Apply Number Formats	Apply Formats (Accounting, Fraction, and Scientific)
➤ Create Custom Formats	Create Custom Formats
➤ Use Styles and AutoFormats	Use Styles and Autoformats
➤ Using Conditional Formatting	Use Conditional Formatting

Excel

Why Would I Do This?

Being able to use labels, values, and formulas to display and manipulate data with Microsoft Excel adds to your productivity and efficiency. There are times, however, when you want to share the results of your work. You may be using some formatting to help you read your worksheets, but now you have to consider how others view them. When you share your worksheets—by sharing files or by printing copies for others—you need to make them readable and attractive. This requires formatting.

In this project, you learn about number formats, custom formats you create for your specific needs, styles for consistent formatting, using the AutoFormats supplied by Excel, and using conditional formatting to highlight data that meets specified criteria.

Lesson 1: Apply Number Formats

Excel applies the General number format to the numbers (values) you enter in your worksheets, unless you specify otherwise. When you enter numbers in your worksheet, you can add a dollar sign ($) or percent sign (%) to indicate that you're working with currency or a percentage, or you can simply type in the numbers. However, if you want your numbers to all have a specific number of decimal places, currency signs, thousand separators, or appear as dates, times, percentages, or fractions, you need to apply a *format* to the cells. Table 1.1 describes the types of number formats available in Excel.

Format
The appearance of a cell, value, or text.

These formats do not change how Excel uses the numbers to calculate. Calculations are based on the original values, so even if you limit a value like 0.125695 to display only two decimal places (such as 12.57%), Excel still uses the entire value in calculations.

Table 1.1 Number Formats

Number Format	Examples	Description
General	10.6 $456,908.00	Excel displays your value as you enter it. In other words, this format displays currency or percent signs only if you enter them yourself.
Number	3,400.50 (120.39)	The default Number format has two decimal places and a comma for a thousand separator. Negative numbers appear in red and in parentheses, preceded by a minus sign.
Currency	$3,400.50 ($3,400.50)	The default Currency format has two decimal places, a comma for the thousands separator, and a dollar sign. Negative numbers appear in red and in parentheses.

Number Format	Examples	Description
Accounting	$3,400.00 $978.21	Use this format to align dollar signs and decimal points in a column. The default Accounting format has two decimal places and a dollar sign. It places a comma as the thousands separator.
Date	11/7	The default Date format is the month and day separated by a slash; however, you can select from numerous other formats.
Time	10:00	The default Time format is the hour and minutes separated by a colon; however, you can opt to display seconds, AM, or PM.
Percentage	99.50%	The default Percentage format has two decimal places. Excel multiplies the value in a cell by 100 and displays the result with a percent sign.
Fraction	1/2	The default Fraction format is up to one digit on either side of the slash. Use this format to display the number of digits you want on either side of the slash and the fraction type (such as halves, quarters, eighths, and so on).
Scientific	3.40E+03	The default Scientific format has two decimal places. Use this format to display numbers in scientific notation.
Text	135RV90	Use Text format to display both text and numbers in a cell as text. Excel displays the entry exactly as you type it.
Special	02110	This format is specifically designed to display zip codes, phone numbers, and social security numbers correctly so that you don't have to enter any special characters, such as hyphens.
Custom	111-xxx	Use Custom format to create your own number format. You can use any of the format codes in the Type list and then make changes to those codes. The # symbol represents a number placeholder, and 0 represents a zero placeholder.

This lesson shows you how to apply several types of number formats to an existing workbook.

To Apply Number Formats

1 From the Project-01 folder on the CD, open the Proj0101 file. Save the file as `Sales`.

This workbook contains the worksheets you need for most of this project.

2 Select the `Potential Sales` worksheet tab if it's not already selected.

This worksheet lists all the states and their population figures. The Potential Sales column shows the possible sale if each person in the state purchased $50 worth of goods. Column E, the Percent of Potential, compares the actual sales to the potential by displaying the percentage of the potential sales represented by the actual sales. The formulas have all been entered in the worksheet, but the numbers have not been formatted.

3 Click E5.

In this cell, you see the result written as `1.31E-05` (see Figure 1.1). If you don't specify the format for a cell, Excel applies the General format. With the General format, the numbers you type appear exactly as you type them. However, when you have calculations that involve numbers with several zeroes or decimal places, the General format uses the same notation as the Scientific format. The number is shown with two decimal places, followed by E (which stands for "exponent"), and then by a number which is the exponent of 10. Therefore, 1.31E-05 is 1.31 multiplied by 10^{-5} or 0.0000131.

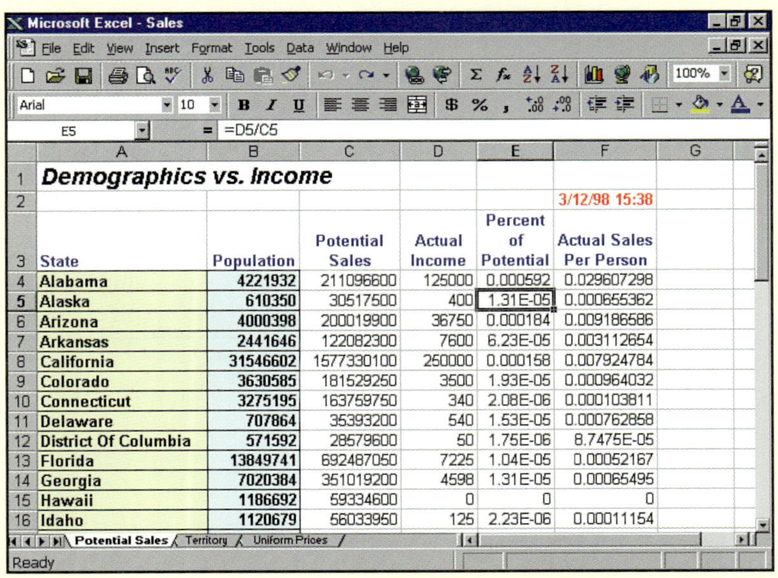

	A	B	C	D	E	F	G
1	*Demographics vs. Income*						
2						3/12/98 15:38	
3	State	Population	Potential Sales	Actual Income	Percent of Potential	Actual Sales Per Person	
4	Alabama	4221932	211096600	125000	0.000592	0.029607298	
5	Alaska	610350	30517500	400	1.31E-05	0.000655362	
6	Arizona	4000398	200019900	36750	0.000184	0.009186586	
7	Arkansas	2441646	122082300	7600	6.23E-05	0.003112654	
8	California	31546602	1577330100	250000	0.000158	0.007924784	
9	Colorado	3630585	181529250	3500	1.93E-05	0.000964032	
10	Connecticut	3275195	163759750	340	2.08E-06	0.000103811	
11	Delaware	707864	35393200	540	1.53E-05	0.000762858	
12	District Of Columbia	571592	28579600	50	1.75E-06	8.7475E-05	
13	Florida	13849741	692487050	7225	1.04E-05	0.00052167	
14	Georgia	7020384	351019200	4598	1.31E-05	0.00065495	
15	Hawaii	1186692	59334600	0	0	0	
16	Idaho	1120679	56033950	125	2.23E-06	0.00011154	

Figure 1.1
In the General and Scientific formats, numbers that have several decimal places are reduced to two decimals and an exponent.

Several other entries in Column E are also displayed in the scientific format. However, this column should be displayed as percentages. You therefore need to change the format of the numbers.

4 Click E4. Then click the Percent Style button on the Formatting toolbar.

The number in E4 now appears as `0%`. This doesn't provide enough information. You need to see more decimal places.

5 Click the Increase Decimal button on the Formatting toolbar three times.

The number in E4 now appears as `0.059%`. Each time you clicked the Increase Decimal button, an additional decimal place appeared. Now you need to apply that same format to the remainder of the column.

6 Click the Format Painter button on the Standard toolbar and then select the range E5:E54.

The Format Painter copies any format from a selected cell or range to another cell or range.

7 Click B4 and then the Comma Style button on the Formatting toolbar.

The Comma Style button adds a comma as the thousands separator. If you see ######### in the cell, just widen the column until the complete number appears. The Comma Style button also adds two decimal places to the number (see Figure 1.2). For population figures, you don't need the decimal places.

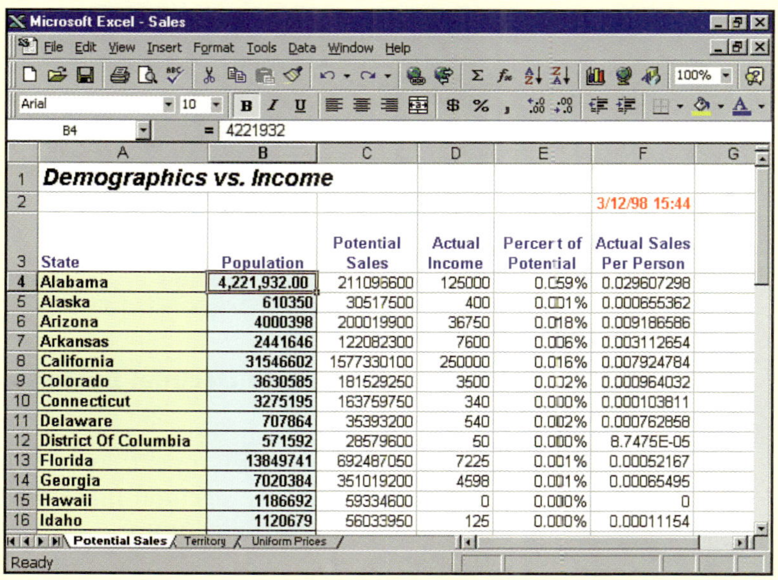

Figure 1.2
The Comma Style button adds commas as thousand separators and two decimal places.

8 Click the Decrease Decimal button on the Formatting toolbar twice.

The decimal places disappear, as each click of the Decrease Decimal button removes one decimal place.

continues

To Apply Number Formats (continued)

9 Click the Format Painter button on the Standard toolbar and select the range B5:B54.

The comma format with zero decimal places is copied to all the cells in the range. Now turn your attention to Column C, where the numbers for potential sales need to appear with dollar signs and commas.

10 Click C4 and then the Currency Style button on the Formatting toolbar.

The Currency Style button adds a dollar sign, commas as thousands separators, and two decimal places. As a result your number may appear as #########, so you have to widen the column until you see the entire number (see Figure 1.3). Because the figures in Column C are whole numbers, you don't need the two decimal places.

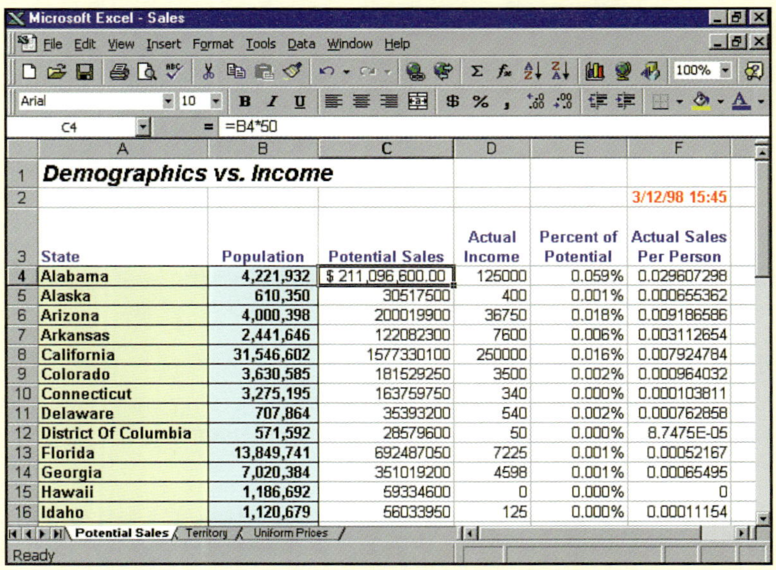

Figure 1.3
The Currency Style button adds a dollar sign, commas to separate the thousands, and two decimal places.

11 Click the Decrease Decimal button on the Formatting toolbar twice.

The decimal places disappear, as each click of the Decrease Decimal button removes one decimal place. In the next step, apply this format to the rest of the column.

12 Click the Format Painter button on the Standard toolbar and select the range C5:C54.

Note that the dollar signs for the values in Column C all align to the left side of the cell, and the decimal points align one below the other. When you click the Currency Style button, Excel applies the Accounting format to the cell. If you don't want the dollar signs and decimal points to align in this fashion, you need to use the Currency format.

13 Select the range D4:D54. Then choose Format, Cells from the menu. Select the Number tab.

In the Format Cells dialog box (see Figure 1.4), select a number format from the Category list. Then choose the specifics of the format on the right side of the dialog box.

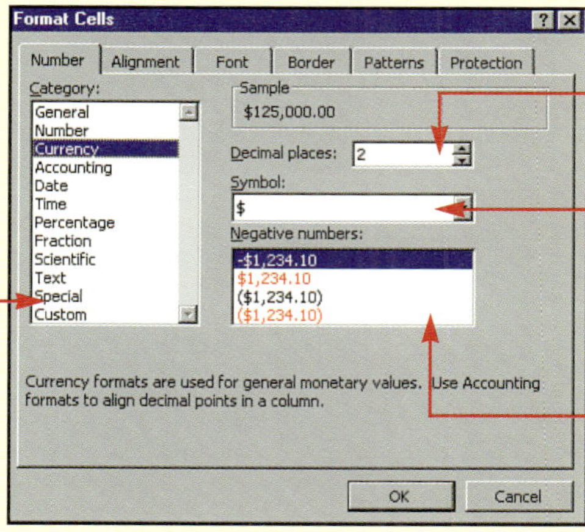

Figure 1.4
Set the type of number format you want and then select the format specifications such as number of decimal places.

14 Select Currency from the Category list. Type 2 in the Decimal places box. Choose OK.

The dollar signs appear just before the first digit in the number but the decimal points do line up. When you use the Format Cells dialog box to select a format, you have the option to set the number of decimal places.

15 Select the range F4:F54. Choose Format, Cells from the menu. Select the Number tab. Select Accounting from the Category list. Set the number of Decimal places to 3. Then choose OK.

The dollar signs align on the left side of the cells (see Figure 1.5).

16 Click F2. Choose Format, Cells. Click the Number tab.

Cell F2 shows the date and time, so Date is automatically selected as the Category.

17 From the Type list, select March 4, 1997. Choose OK.

The date shows the new format (you may have to widen the column to see it). In the next step, you apply different formats to other worksheets.

18 Select the Territory worksheet tab.

19 Click D13. Then hold down Ctrl and click on D25, D33, D41, D51, D58, and D65.

To select cells that are not next to each other, you hold down Ctrl and click on each cell.

continues

To Apply Number Formats (continued)

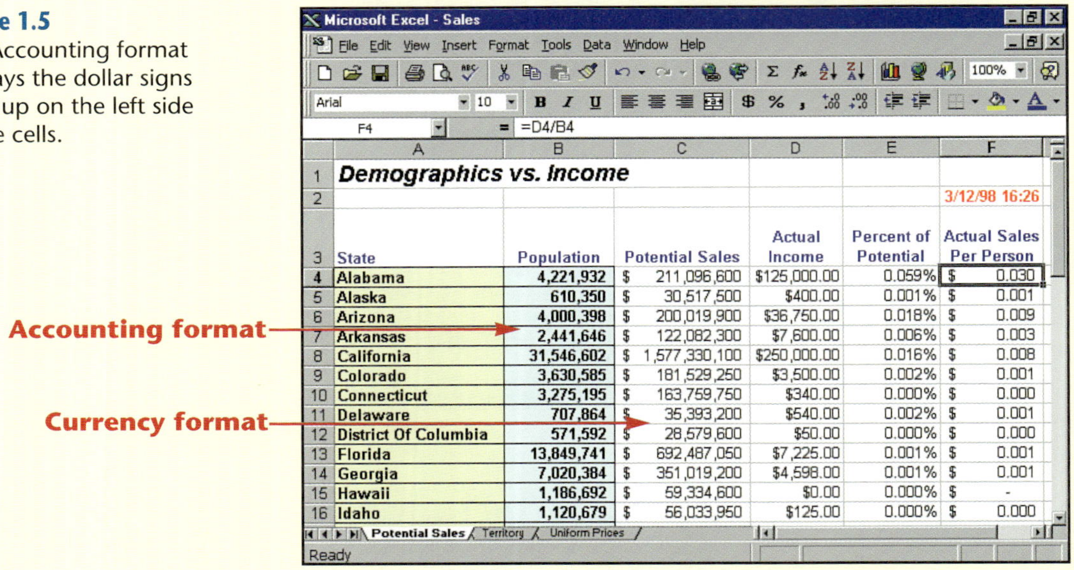

Figure 1.5
The Accounting format displays the dollar signs lined up on the left side of the cells.

20 **Choose Format, Cells and select the Number tab.**

21 **Select Fraction from the Category list and then Up to two digits from the Type list. Choose OK.**

The decimals are now displayed as fractions (see Figure 1.6).

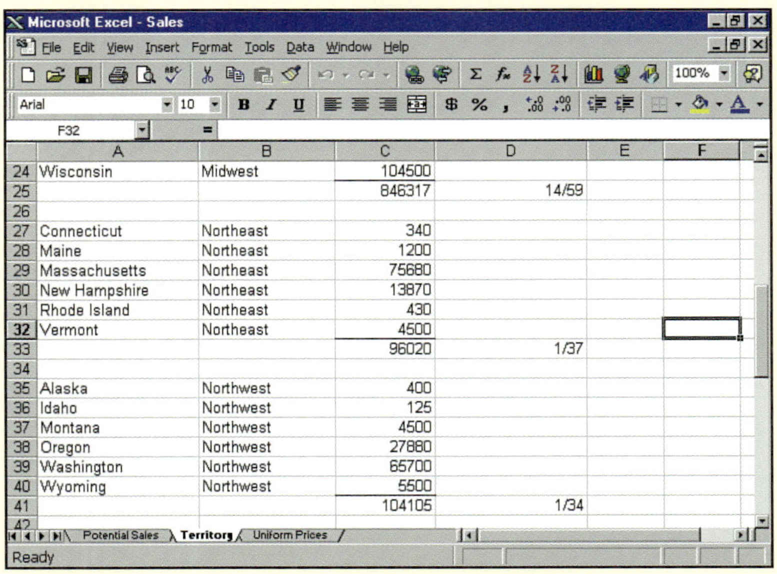

Figure 1.6
The Fraction format converts the decimals to fractions.

22 **Save the workbook and leave it open for the next lesson.**

Lesson 2: Create Custom Formats

Although Excel provides a wide variety of number formats, you may need one for special circumstances. A custom format could be used for account numbers or inventory numbers. For example, suppose your account numbers look like this:

10-20190-109

You could create a format like this:

##-#####-###

Then when you enter the number, 9089212098, for example, Excel formats it for you, adding the hyphens where needed:

90-89212-098

In this lesson, you create a custom format for product numbers.

To Create a Custom Format

1 In the `Sales` workbook, click the `Uniform Prices` worksheet tab.

This worksheet (see Figure 1.7) displays a list of different uniforms for domestic help and their prices. Each uniform has a model number. In the inventory system of this company, all products begin with a department number, followed by a dash and then the individual product number. You are going to make a custom format to apply to the model numbers in this worksheet.

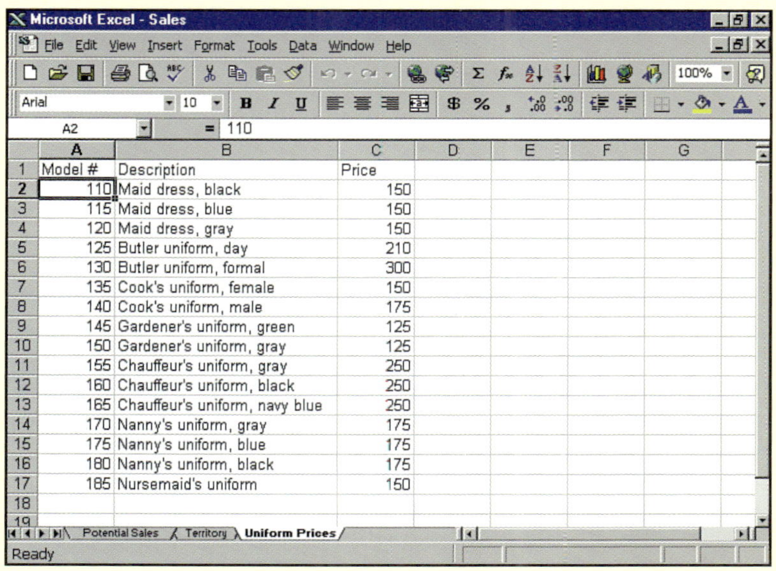

Figure 1.7
The model numbers in this worksheet need to be reformatted.

2 Select A2:A17 and then choose Format, Cells from the menu.

continues

To Create a Custom Format (continued)

3 Click the Number tab in the Format Cells dialog box (see Figure 1.8).

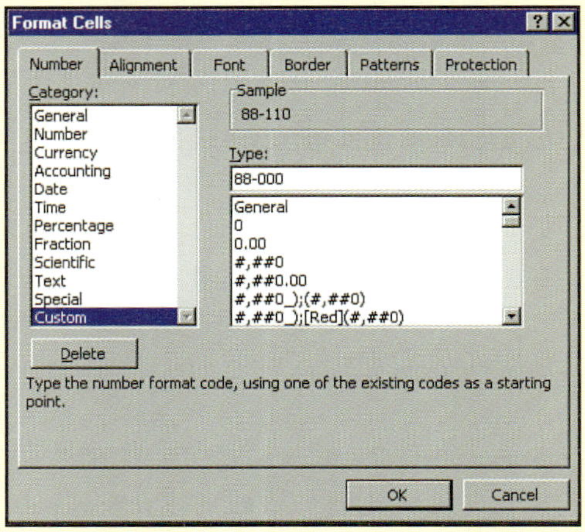

Figure 1.8
Enter your custom format in the Type text box, using zeroes to represent the numbers entered in the worksheet.

4 Choose Custom from the Category list.

A list of format possibilities appears in the Type list. If none of these is satisfactory, enter your own format in the text box.

5 Click in the text box and delete the text that is there.

The department number for uniforms is 88, so each number in this custom format begins with 88 and ends with a dash and the model number.

6 Type `88-000`.

In the sample box, you'll see the result of your new custom format is `88-110`.

7 Choose OK.

All the model numbers begin with 88- and end with the numbers that were originally entered in Column A.

8 Save the `Sales` workbook and leave it open for the next lesson.

Lesson 3: Use Styles and AutoFormats

Formatting a worksheet can involve a number of steps—setting the font, picking the font size, setting the font color, choosing the alignment, and so on. When you find yourself frequently combining the same set of steps together, it's time to create a *style*. A style collects the format components together under one name, and when you apply the style all the formats are applied together.

Style
A collection of formats that you define and save as a group, and then later apply to other cells. One style could combine font, font size, border, shading, and number format together.

AutoFormat
A collection of predefined formats that you apply to a range of data. Excel determines which rows include summary detail and adjusts the format accordingly.

To format an entire list or other large range that has distinct elements—for example, column and row labels, summary totals, and detail data—you can apply a built-in table design, called an *autoformat*. The design uses distinctive formats for the various elements of the table.

In this lesson, you create and apply styles and apply AutoFormats.

To Use Styles and AutoFormat

1. **Select the `Potential Sales` worksheet tab of the `Sales` workbook.**

   This worksheet already has quite a bit of formatting applied to the labels and to the numbers. In order to use the same formatting on other worksheets, you create some styles that you can apply on other sheets.

2. **Click E3 and choose Format, Style from the menu.**

   The Style dialog box opens (see Figure 1.9). The formatting already applied to E3 appears in the dialog box. Deselect any options for formatting you don't want to include in the style or click Modify to make changes to the formatting.

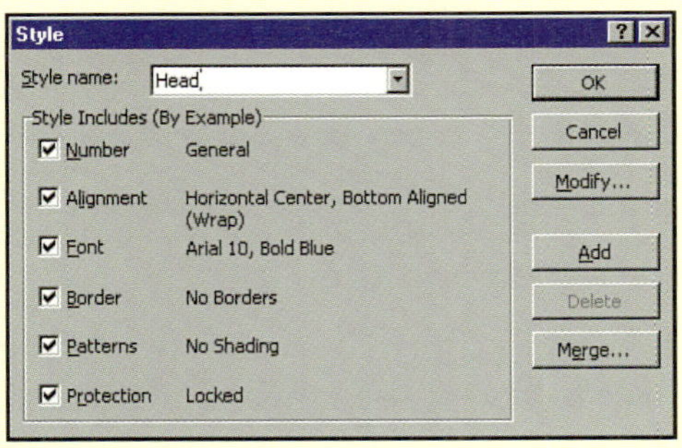

Figure 1.9
Enter the Style name and select which options you want included in the style.

3. **Type `Head` in the Style name box and click Add. Then choose OK.**

   You have created a style for the column head labels based on the formatting in cell E3. Now you apply that style to the Territory worksheet.

4. **Select the worksheet tab.**

5. **Select the range A1:D1. Choose Format, Style.**

6. **Choose Head from the Style name drop-down list and choose OK.**

   The column labels now match the ones on the Potential Sales worksheet. You can also modify the format choices as you create the style.

7. **Click on the `Potential Sales` sheet tab and then click C4.**

   This cell has an Accounting number format with zero decimal places.

continues

To Use Styles and AutoFormat (continued)

8 Choose Format, Style. In the Style name box, type `CurrencyA`**.**

9 Click Font to deselect it and then click Modify.

The Format Cells dialog box appears (see Figure 1.10). To make the numbers stand out, apply a color and boldface to the style.

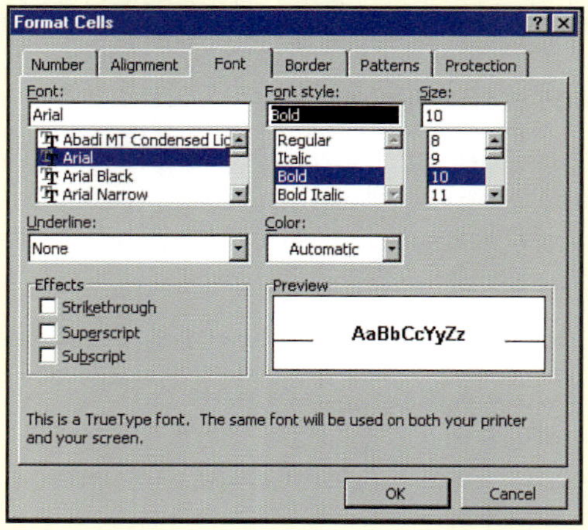

Figure 1.10
Select the font choices you want included in your style.

10 Click the Font tab, if it's not already selected. Choose Bold from the Font style list and Green (fourth color box in the second row) from the Color drop-down list.

11 Choose OK.

12 Choose Add and then OK.

You need to apply your new style to the remainder of the column as well as to one of the ranges on the Territory worksheet.

13 Select the range C5:C54. Choose Format, Style. From the Style name box, choose CurrencyA. Then choose OK.

14 Select the `Territory` **sheet tab. Select the range C2:C67. Choose Format, Style. From the Style name box, choose CurrencyA. Then choose OK.**

The CurrencyA style is applied to both ranges. To make your job easier, try using Excel's AutoFormats.

Inside Stuff

After you've created a style or set of styles, wouldn't it be nice to be able to use them in another workbook? Open the workbook that has the styles in it that you want to copy. Then open the workbook to which you want to copy the styles. Choose Format, Style from the menu to open the Style dialog box. Click Merge to open the Merge Styles dialog box. From the list in the Merge styles from box, double-click the name of the workbook that contains the styles you want to copy. If the active workbook already has some styles with the same names, Excel will ask if you want to replace them with the new styles. Click Yes to replace them; click No to keep the styles you have in the current workbook. This warning applies to any and all of the styles; you won't receive another warning for the next style name conflict.

15 **Select the** `Uniform Prices` **worksheet tab. Click A1.**

16 **Choose Format, AutoFormat from the menu.**

Excel automatically selects all the cells in your worksheet that have values, formulas, or labels in them. The AutoFormat dialog box appears (see Figure 1.11).

Figure 1.11
Select the table format you want to apply to your worksheet.

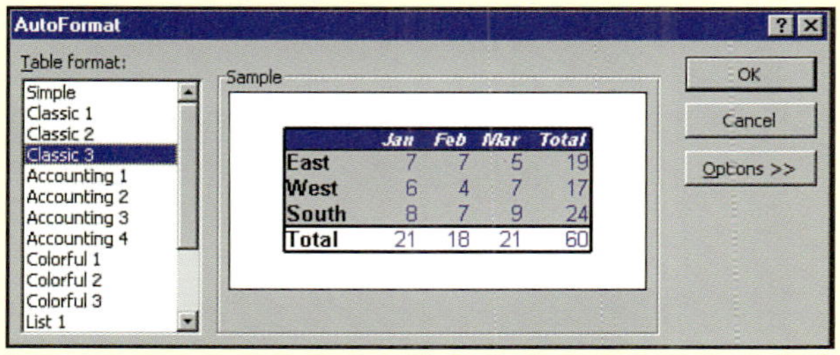

17 **From the Table format list, select the format you want to use.**

A preview of the selected format appears in the Sample box.

18 **Choose OK.**

The AutoFormat is applied to the selected range.

19 **Save the workbook and leave it open for the next lesson.**

Inside Stuff

You don't have to apply all the aspects of the AutoFormat to your worksheet. When you have the AutoFormat dialog box open, click Options. The dialog box becomes longer, including a series of check boxes for the Formats to apply. Deselect any format you don't want to use, such as number, border, font, patterns, alignment, or width/height.

Lesson 4: Using Conditional Formatting

Using formats to emphasize cells in a worksheet can call attention to specific data. When you format a cell, however, the formatting remains in effect even if the data changes. If you want to accent a cell depending on the value of the cell, you can use conditional formatting.

Conditional formats return a result based on whether or not the value in the cell meets a specified criteria. For example, in a worksheet tracking monthly sales, you may want to accent a monthly total only if it is less than the previous month's total or if it is greater than the target sales figure you have set.

In this lesson, you use conditional formatting to mark actual sales that exceed $100,000.

To Use Conditional Formatting

1 Click the `Potential Sales` worksheet tab of the Sales workbook.

2 Select the range D4:D54.

This selects the cells that contain the actual income per state.

3 Choose Format, Conditional Formatting from the menu.

The Conditional Formatting dialog box appears (see Figure 1.12).

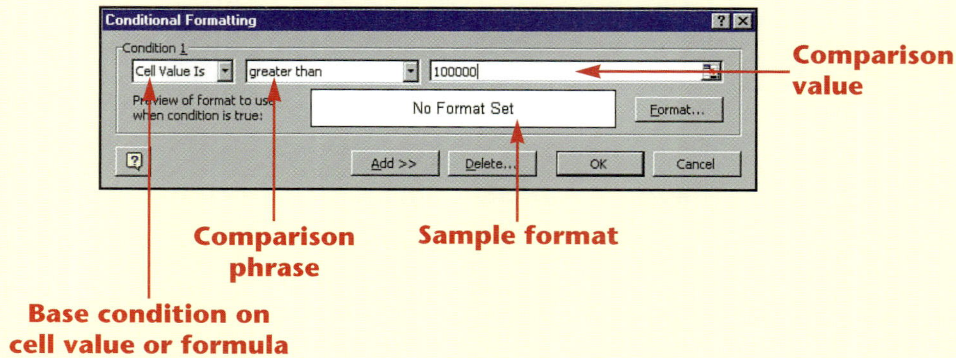

Figure 1.12
In the Conditional Formatting dialog box, you specify the comparison type and values needed to apply a particular format.

If you have problems...

If the Office Assistant opens, click No, don't provide help now to close the Office Assistant.

4 Under Condition 1, select Cell Value Is from the first drop-down list box and press Tab.

Because the condition for your formatting is an actual sales value over $100,000, you are basing your condition on the cell value.

Inside Stuff

If you choose Formula Is in the first text box, the formula you enter must result in a true or false value (so use an IF statement). For example, if you want to format some cells based on whether or not a corresponding value in Column C is more than 200% of the actual sales (D4), you could use this formula:

```
=IF(C4>200%*D4, TRUE, FALSE)
```

5 From the comparison phrase drop-down list (the second text box), select greater than and then press Tab.

This identifies the type of comparison you want to use, such as between, not between, equal to, not equal to, less than, greater than, greater than or equal to, or less than or equal to.

6 Type `100000` as the comparison value.

The conditional statement now tells Excel that if the cell value is greater than 100000, then apply the specified formatting.

7 Click the Format button.

Excel displays the Format Cells dialog box (see Figure 1.13) where you set the font, border, and shading characteristics you want to use for the conditional format.

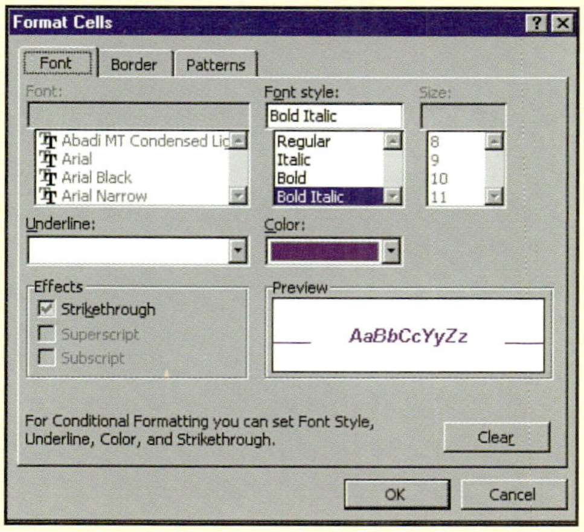

Figure 1.13
Select the font, border, and pattern attributes you want assigned to the conditional format.

8 Select the Font tab and choose Bold from the Font style list. Then choose Violet (last row, fifth color) from the drop-down Color palette.

9 Select the Patterns tab and click the Yellow color box (fourth row, third box). Choose OK.

A preview of the format appears in the sample box. If the color combinations aren't appealing, click Format and choose a different set of attributes.

10 Choose OK.

The formatting is applied to all values that meet the conditions you set (see Figure 1.14).

11 Save the workbook and print two copies of it. Then close the file.

If you have completed your session on the computer, exit Excel and Windows 95 before turning off the computer. Otherwise, continue with the "Checking Your Skills" and "Applying Your Skills" sections at the end of this project.

continues

To Use Conditional Formatting (continued)

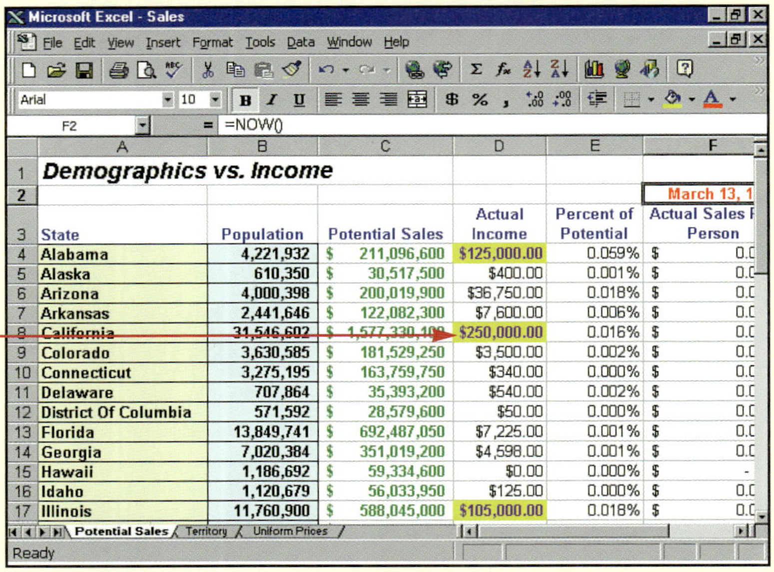

Figure 1.14
All the cells in Column D that meet the conditions now have bold, violet type with yellow shading.

Conditional formatting applied

Inside Stuff

You can set up to three conditions that must be met in order for the formatting to be applied. Simply click Add in the Conditional Formatting dialog box to display another set of Condition text boxes. Use the Delete button to remove one or more conditions.

Project Summary

To	Do This
Apply a number format	Select the cell or range, choose Format, Cells from the menu, and then click the Number tab of the Format Cells dialog box. Select a number type from the Category list, enter the number of Decimal places (if that is available) or set other specifications, and choose OK.
Create a custom format	Select the cell or range, choose Format, Cells from the menu, and then click the Number tab of the Format Cells dialog box. Select a Custom from the Category list, enter the format in the Type box, and choose OK.
Create a style	Apply the formatting for your style to a cell in the worksheet. Select that cell and choose Format, Style from the menu. Enter a name for the style in the Style name box. Select the types of formatting you want included in the style. Click Modify to add or change any of the formatting. Click Add. Then choose OK.

To	Do This
Apply a style	Select the cell or range to which you want to apply the style. Choose Format, Style from the menu. Select the style you want from the Style name drop-down list and then choose OK.
Use an AutoFormat	Click in a cell of the worksheet or select a range. Choose Format, AutoFormat from the menu. Select the format you want to use from the Table format list. Choose OK.
Apply conditional formatting	Select a cell or range and then choose Format, Conditional Formatting from the menu. Select the type of comparison and enter the comparison values. Click the Format button and choose the formatting attributes; then choose OK. Choose OK again.

Checking Your Skills

True/False

For each of the following statements, check *T* or *F* to indicate whether the statement is true or false.

__T __F **1.** All numbers entered in Excel worksheets are automatically formatted as currency.

__T __F **2.** You reduce the number of decimal places displayed in a number by clicking the Decrease Decimal button on the Formatting toolbar

__T __F **3.** When the dollar signs line up on the left sides of the cells, the number format is currency.

__T __F **4.** An AutoFormat applies a set of table formats to your worksheet.

__T __F **5.** You can set up to four conditions that must be met in order for conditional formatting to be applied.

__T __F **6.** Click the Currency Style button on the Formatting toolbar to apply the Currency format to the selected cell.

__T __F **7.** When you click the Comma Style button on the Formatting toolbar, it adds a comma as the thousands separator and two decimal places.

__T __F **8.** Excel uses the number as it is displayed on the screen when it performs calculations.

__T __F **9.** You cannot change a style once you've created it.

__T __F **10.** You use the Special number format for social security numbers.

Multiple Choice

Circle the letter of the correct answer for each of the following.

1. If the number in a cell reads 1.25E+2, what is the number?
   a. 12,500
   b. 0.0125
   c. 125
   d. 125,000

2. To have the numbers you enter break at specific points for hyphens (such as 10-345-9876), which format should you use?
   a. Scientific
   b. Special
   c. Fixed
   d. Custom

3. When you want to be able apply similar formatting to other text in your workbook, what should you create?
   a. Custom format
   b. Style
   c. AutoFormat
   d. Format painter

4. When setting conditional formatting, what items must you specify to base the condition on the cell value?
   a. Cell address, comparison phrase, and comparison value
   b. Formula, comparison phrase, and comparison value
   c. Limit, comparison phrase, and comparison value
   d. "Cell value is" and the comparison phrase and comparison value

5. What are the style buttons on the Formatting toolbar?
   a. Currency Style, Percent Style, Comma Style.
   b. Bold, Italic, Underline
   c. Left, Center, Right
   d. Increase Decimal, Decrease Decimal, Currency Style

6. When formatted as Percentage with 0 decimals, which of the following values will appear as 100%?
   a. 100
   b. 10.00
   c. 1.0
   d. 0.1

7. What command should you choose to remove a number from a cell and the formatting assigned to that number?
   a. Edit, Delete
   b. Edit, Clear, Contents
   c. Edit, Clear, All
   d. Press Del

8. Which of the following is not included in a style?
   a. Font
   b. Width
   c. Border
   d. Protection

9. When using AutoFormat to apply a table format to your worksheet, you don't have to accept all the formatting involved. Which of the following can't you turn off?
   a. Font
   b. Width
   c. Border
   d. Protection

10. What's the easiest way to copy the formatting from one cell to another?

a. Select the cell with the formatting, click the Format Painter on the Standard toolbar, and then click the other cell.

b. Create a style from the cell format and apply that style to the other cell.

c. Select the cell, choose Edit, Copy, then click the other cell and choose Edit, Paste.

d. Select the cell, click the Cut button on the Standard toolbar, then click the other cell, and click the Paste button on the Standard toolbar.

Completion

In the blank provided, write the correct answer for each of the following statements.

1. The number format to use when you want to display zip codes, phone numbers or social security number is _______________.
2. A collection of formats that you define and save as a group and later apply to other cells is a _______________.
3. A(n) _______________ is a collection of predefined formats that you apply to a range of data.
4. To copy the formatting in a cell or range to another cell or range, use the _______________.
5. The default Date format is the month and day separated by a _______________.
6. The number format that lines up the dollar signs on the left side of the cell is _______________.
7. To create a style from existing formatting, select the cells containing the desired formatting and choose _______________ from the menu.
8. When you don't need dollar signs for your numbers but you do want the thousands separators, click the _______________ button on the Formatting toolbar.
9. To remove the number formatting from selected cells but leave the values, choose _______________ from the menu.
10. When you want to center a title across the top of your worksheet, select the cells you want to center it in and click _______________ on the Formatting toolbar.

Excel

Matching

In the blank next to each of the following terms or phrases, write the letter of the corresponding term or phrase. (Note that some letters may be used more than once.)

a. Align Right
b. Merge and Center
c. Comma
d. General
e. Patterns
f. Format
g. Fraction
h. Style
i. Format, AutoFormat
j. Increase Decimal

_____ 1. This number format displays the number exactly as you type it, displaying currency or percentage signs only if you type them. It does change large values to numbers plus exponents

_____ 2. The appearance of a cell, value, or text

_____ 3. Click this button to make the text in a selected cell move to the right side

_____ 4. To add zeroes or more decimal places after the decimal point of a value, click this button

_____ 5. The number format you would use to display the value 0.5 as ½

_____ 6. The thousand separator is this character

_____ 7. When you want to create a style from an existing cell, click this in the Style dialog box to not add the shading as part of the style

_____ 8. Click this button to center text in the middle of selected cells

_____ 9. Command to apply a predefined table format to your worksheet

_____ 10. A collection of formats you define and save as a group and then later apply to other cells

Applying Your Skills

Practice

The following exercises enable you to practice the skills that you have learned in this project. Take a few minutes to work through these exercises now.

Applying Number Formats

The salespeople at Betsy's Baked Goodies are very competitive. They want to know who is ahead in sales and how much commission they will make each period. In this project, you format the numbers in the worksheet to make it more readable.

To make a sales commission worksheet readable, follow these steps:

1. From the Project-01 folder on the CD, open the file Proj0102. Save it as `Commissions.` Activate the `Quarter1` worksheet.
2. Apply the Accounting number format to the cells C5:F5, C17:F17, I5, and I17. Have all the numbers display two decimal places. Widen the columns as necessary.
3. Apply the Comma number format with two decimal places to the cells C6:C15 and I6:I15.
4. Apply the Percent format with one decimal place to the cells H5:H15.
5. Apply the Fraction format (up to two digits) to the range G5:G15.
6. Apply the Scientific format, with two decimal places, to the range J5:J15.
7. Save the changes to the worksheet. Print two copies if requested by your instructor.

Creating Custom Formats

Because Betsy's Baked Goodies stored its data in a database and then imported it into a worksheet, some of it needs reformatting. One column of data in particular—the Employee Number—needs to be reformatted so the numbers appear with hyphens, such as xx-xxx-x. To add that type of formatting to numbers, you need to create a custom format.

To create a custom format, follow these steps:

1. With the `Quarter1` worksheet of the workbook open, select the cells A5:A15.
2. Create a custom format so the numbers in the selected cells appear with hyphens in an xx-xxx-x format.
3. Save the workbook. Print two copies if your instructor requests them.

Using Styles

Only the Quarter1 worksheet of the Commissions workbook has been formatted. You need to create a series of styles that you can apply to the remaining worksheets.

To create and apply styles, follow these steps:

1. Open the `Quarter1` worksheet of the `Commissions` workbook, if it's not already on your screen.
2. Select **Betsy's Baked Goodies** (cell A1) and create a style called `Title`.
3. Select `Sales Commissions` and create a style called `Subtitle`.
4. Select the column heading in A4 and create a style called `Heading`.

5. Select the range A5:A15 and create a style called `EmplNumber`.
6. Switch to the `Quarter2` worksheet. Apply the newly created styles to the appropriate cells in the `Quarter2` worksheet to make the title, subtitle, all column headings, and all employee numbers look as they do in the `Quarter1` worksheet.
7. Save the file. Print two copies if requested by your instructor.

Using AutoFormats

Applying styles to each necessary range in all the worksheets can be tedious. Try applying one of Excel's pre-defined formats to one of the worksheets.

To apply an AutoFormat, follow these steps:

1. Open the `Quarter3` worksheet of the `Commissions` workbook.
2. Apply the Colorful2 table format to the range A4:J17.
3. Save the file. Print two copies if requested by your instructor.

Using Conditional Formatting

The salespeople like to see who is among the top sellers of baked goods in one month. To make the figures visible, you want to highlight the high sales figures with different coloring by using conditional formatting.

To apply conditional formatting, follow these steps:

1. Open the `Quarter1` worksheet of the `Commissions` workbook.
2. Select the range C5:E15.
3. Specify conditional formatting. Where the cell value is greater than 20,000, make the font bold and red. Where the cell value is between 15,000 and 19,999, make the font italic and blue.
4. Save the file and print two copies (if requested by the instructor). Then close the file and exit Excel.

Challenge

The following challenges enable you to use your problem-solving skills. Take time to work through these exercises now.

Applying Number Formats

The office manager where you work has created a workbook for tracking the prices, part numbers, and discounts that you get from the local office supply company. After adding the basic information, the manager has asked you to improve the appearance and readability of the workbook. From the

Project-01 folder on the CD, open the Proj0103 file and rename it `Price List`. Display the `Office Supplies` worksheet. On this worksheet, there are two immediate tasks you need to perform—format the unit prices as currency and format the quantity discounts as percentages. Then center the information in the Discount Amount column and in the Unit column.

Creating Custom Formats

In the Price List workbook, the part numbers on the `Office Supplies` worksheet need to be reformatted so the current values are preceded by `98-`. Create and apply a custom format for these part numbers that will provide that style of numbering. Then apply the same custom format to the part numbers on the `Computer Supplies` and `Books and Magazines` worksheets.

Using Styles and AutoFormats

On the `Office Supplies` worksheet, the title `Price List`, the subtitle (`Office Supplies`), and the headings in row 4 all have formatting applied to them. Create a title style, a subtitle style, and a heading style. Then apply those styles to the remaining worksheets. Using the Format Painter, copy the number format you applied to the Unit Price column and the Quantity Discount column to the remaining worksheets.

Because your office manager wants to post the book prices on the bulletin board, you need to dress it up a little more. Select the range A4:F11 and apply the List 1 table format to the selection.

Using Conditional Formatting

Because the office manager wants to emphasize the high cost of supplies, apply conditional formatting to the Office Supplies worksheet that highlights any prices over $5.00.

PinPoint Assessment

PinPoint Training

You have completed the project and the associated lessons, as well as the "Checking Your Skills" and "Applying Your Skills" sections. Now use the PinPoint software evaluation mode to assess your comprehension of the specific exam tasks you have just learned. You can also use the PinPoint Trainer Mode and the Show Me tutorials to practice these specific exam tasks.

Project Two 2

Using Charts and Maps

Charting Expenses and Mapping Office Sites

In this Project, you learn how to:

Objectives	Required Activities
➤ Create a Chart	
➤ Format Text in a Chart	
➤ Change the Chart Type	
➤ Enhance a Chart	
➤ Print a Chart	
➤ Create a Data Map	Use Data Map

Why Would I Do This?

After you create a worksheet, you may want to show the information to someone else. You can simply print the worksheet if you need only numerical detail, or you can transform the information in the worksheet into a chart. With Excel, you can also chart geographical information with maps. Charts and maps are great for visually representing relationships between numerical values while improving the appearance of a presentation.

This project shows you how to use sample data to create and enhance various types of charts. You also learn how to add a map to a worksheet.

Lesson 1: Creating a Chart

Embedded chart
A graphical representation of worksheet data created within the worksheet rather than as a separate worksheet.

In Excel, you can create an embedded chart directly on the worksheet. An *embedded chart* is a graphic **object**—a picture of the data—that appears on the worksheet along with your worksheet data. You can also add a chart of the data on a separate worksheet.

To create a chart, you select the data you want to use in the chart; then choose Insert, Chart or click the Chart Wizard button on the Standard toolbar. The Chart Wizard provides step-by-step assistance through a series of dialog boxes to choose a chart type and specify chart options, and then automatically creates the chart from the selected data and places it in a box (frame). You can then change or enhance the chart. Now try creating a chart to help you analyze your monthly office expenses.

To Create a Chart

1 From the Project-02 folder on the CD, open the file Proj0201 and save it as Expenses**.**

This is the workbook file you use in this project.

2 Select cells A2 through G7.

This is the data range you use to create the chart. You can create a chart by using any of the information in the worksheet. The range you selected here lets you see how your expense costs change over the course of six months. Note that the data range does not include the totals.

3 Click the Chart Wizard button on the Standard toolbar.

Excel displays the Chart Wizard - Step 1 of 4 - Chart Type dialog box, as shown in Figure 2.1. This dialog box contains two tabs, Standard Types and Custom Types, which contain chart types from which to make your selection.

Figure 2.1
The Chart Wizard - Step 1 of 4 - Chart Type dialog box enables you to choose a chart type and subtype.

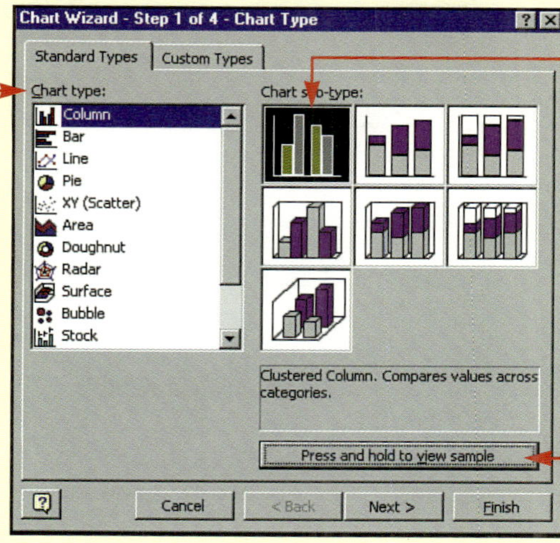

4 **In the Chart type list, click Column, if it is not already selected.**

For this example, the default chart type, Column, is acceptable. Otherwise, you could select a different chart type. Now you can choose a chart subtype. In this case, you use the default clustered column subtype for the column chart.

5 **Make sure the Clustered Column subtype from the Chart subtype list is selected. Check the area above the Press and hold to view sample button to see the description of the selected subtype.**

6 **Point to the Press and hold to view sample button and then click and hold down the left mouse button.**

A sample of your chart is displayed in the Sample box.

7 **Release the mouse button; then click the Next button.**

The chart type and subtype are accepted and the Chart Wizard - Step 2 of 4 - Chart Source Data dialog box appears, as shown in Figure 2.2. A sample of the chart you are creating is displayed in the Data Range tab of the dialog box. If necessary, you can change the way the **data series** is displayed from rows to columns, but for this example the default settings are fine. The Series tab allows you to add or remove a series or change the ranges being used for the names and values of each chart series.

8 **Click the Next button.**

The defaults are accepted and the Chart Wizard - Step 3 of 4 - Chart Options dialog box appears. Here, the tabs are displayed so that you can choose to add chart **titles**, label the **axes**, add **gridlines**, hide or change the placement of the **legend**, add **data labels**, or show the **data table**.

continues

To Create a Chart (continued)

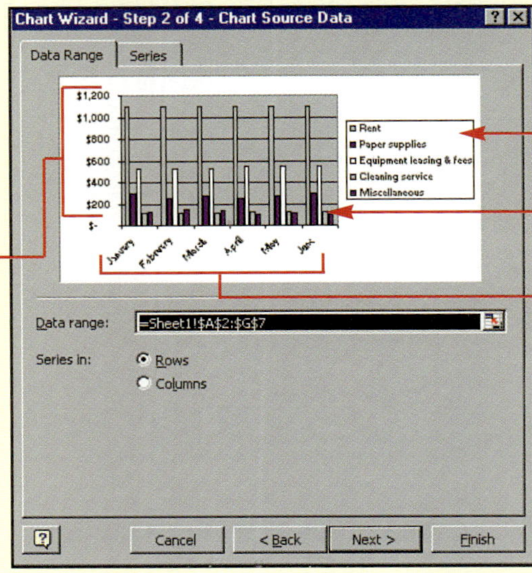

Figure 2.2
The Chart Wizard - Step 2 of 4 - Chart Source Data dialog box enables you to change the display of the data series.

9 **Click the Titles tab, and then the Chart title text box. Type** `Office Expenses` **and press Tab.**

Excel adds the title to the chart and moves the insertion point to the Category (X) axis text box.

10 **Type** `Months` **in the Category (X) axis text box, press Tab, and then type** `Dollars` **in the Value (Y) axis text box.**

Excel labels the axes on the chart. The Chart Wizard - Step 3 of 4 - Chart Options dialog box should now look like the one shown in Figure 2.3.

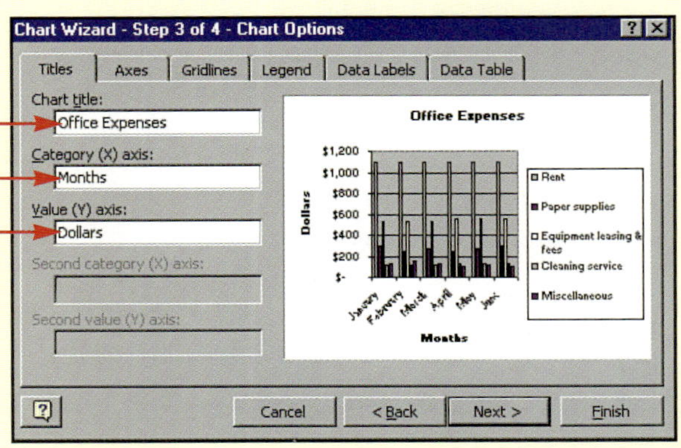

Figure 2.3
In the Chart Wizard - Step 3 of 4 - Chart Options dialog box, you can change the standard options for the selected chart type.

11 **Click the Next button.**

The Chart Wizard - Step 4 of 4 - Chart Location dialog box appears, as shown in Figure 2.4. If you want to see the chart displayed next to its source data, you can embed it as an object on the worksheet. If you prefer to work with the chart separately, place it on its own sheet and Excel automatically sizes it to fill an entire page.

Figure 2.4
The Chart Wizard - Step 4 of 4 - Chart Location dialog box enables you to specify the location of your chart.

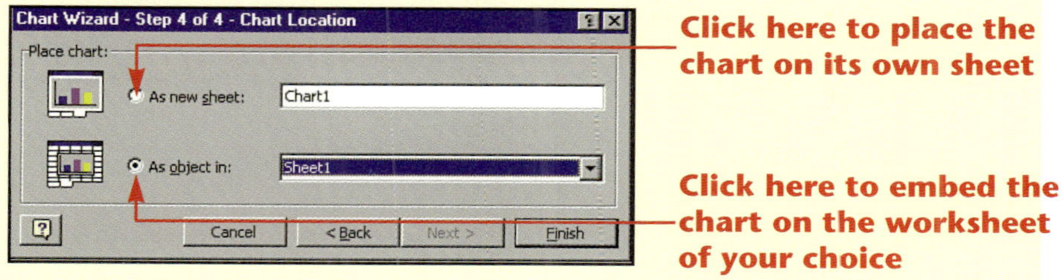

Handles
The small, black squares around a selected object. You use these squares to drag, size, or scale the object.

⓬ **Click Finish.**

Excel creates the chart and displays it with eight black squares called *handles* surrounding the box, as shown in Figure 2.5. The Chart toolbar, which you can use to edit the chart, should automatically appear. If it does not, choose View, Toolbars, Chart to display it.

With the chart selected, selection handles are displayed, and you can drag the chart to a new position below the worksheet.

Figure 2.5
Excel creates the chart and embeds it as an object in the current worksheet.

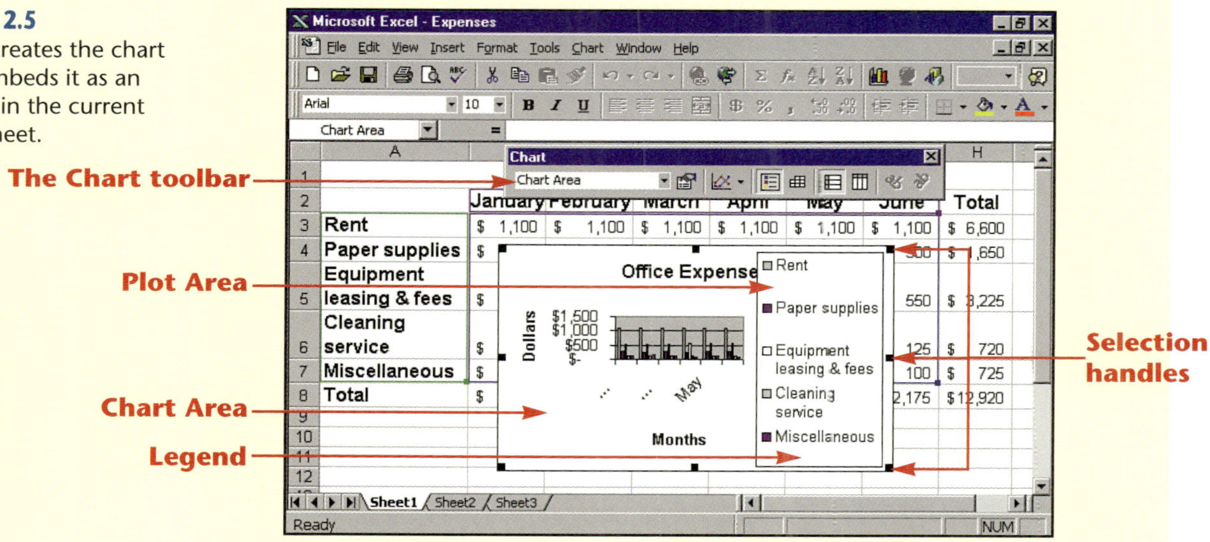

⓭ **Click inside the chart area (in any blank area) and drag the chart so that the upper-left corner is positioned in cell A10.**

As you drag the chart, the pointer changes to a four-headed arrow. The chart is repositioned, but it needs resizing. It is important to resize the chart before you format it. If you don't resize first, the formatting and added enhancements will be out of proportion with the chart.

continues

To Create a Chart (continued)

14. **Point to the selection handle in the lower-right corner of the chart.**

    The pointer changes to a two-headed diagonal arrow.

15. **Drag this selection handle down and to the right until the chart expands through cell G25.**

    The chart now fills cells A10:G25.

16. **Save your work and keep the** Expenses **worksheet open for the next lesson, where you learn how to format and enhance the appearance of the chart.**

Jargon Watch

Charts and maps are considered to be **objects** in Excel. An object is an item that has its own frame or box and that can be selected, moved, copied, sized, and formatted independently of the worksheet cells behind it. Other objects in Excel include text boxes and clip art.

Charts consist of a number of elements, most of which you can modify or delete. An axis, for example, is a line that serves as a major reference for plotting data on a chart; **axes** is the plural of axis. In a two-dimensional chart, there are two axes: One is the y-axis or Value Axis where the numbers appear and the other axis is the x-axis or Category Axis where the labels define the categories into which the values fall. The two axes normally meet at the value 0. On a 3-D chart, a second Value axis (z-axis) is included.

The data in your worksheet is plotted against the axes; each value for each category is represented by a data point. A row or column of worksheet data that produces a line on a line chart, a set of columns or bars that share a color on column or bar charts, or an area in an area chart is called a **data series**.

To help a user understand the value of the data points on a chart, you can display **gridlines**. These are lines that extend from the tick marks on an axis through the plot area to make it easier to evaluate data points. There are also axis labels (either values or categories) to help the user understand the chart.

Charts also include text elements. A **chart title** is the text that appears above the chart and defines what the chart is or shows. You can also add axis labels to explain the values or categories displayed. A **legend** is a key that identifies the patterns, colors, or symbols associated with the markers of a data series by the series name. **Data labels** are optional labels that appear at the data points on the chart; they can show the value, category, or percentage of the data point. A **data table** appears with the chart and shows the original values and labels from the worksheet, which is useful if you print the chart separately from the worksheet.

Inside Stuff

You can move a selected chart or its elements (such as the legend and titles) on the chart by dragging them to a new location. You can also resize a selected chart or element by positioning the mouse pointer over any one of the chart box handles until the pointer changes to a two-headed arrow. Drag the handle away from the center of the chart box to enlarge the box or toward the center of the box to reduce it.

When you drag a handle on the middle of one side of the box, you change the size horizontally or vertically. When you drag a corner handle, you change the vertical and horizontal dimensions at the same time. If you hold down ⇧Shift while dragging a corner handle, you maintain the original proportions of the chart.

Be careful when increasing the size of a chart because data series proportions can be misleading. For example, if you stretch the height of a chart without maintaining the original proportions, you visually exaggerate the numerical differences in the data, which can change the impact of the information.

If you want to delete a chart, simply select the chart and press Del.

You can create a chart on its own sheet in the default (2-D column) chart type by selecting the data and pressing F11 or the Alt + F1 key combination. You can then modify the chart by using the chart commands.

Lesson 2: Formatting Text in a Chart

After you create a chart, you can format chart text to enhance the chart's title, axes labels, or legend. You can even change the emphasis of the chart's details. You can change text in a chart simply by clicking the text area you want to modify and then making the change, or by formatting the text in the entire chart area at the same time.

You change the format of the text in Excel charts by using the same methods you use to format text in worksheet cells. Now try formatting text in the chart you created in Lesson 1.

To Format Text in a Chart

1 In the Expenses **worksheet, scroll up until you can see the top of the chart. If the handles are not displayed, click somewhere in the chart area.**

The selected chart can be edited and formatted. The Chart Objects text box in the Chart toolbar shows that the Chart Area is selected.

If you cannot see the Chart toolbar on your screen, choose View, Toolbars, and then click the Chart option.

continues

To Format Text in a Chart (continued)

2 Click the Format Chart Area button on the Chart toolbar.

The Format Chart Area dialog box is displayed.

3 Click the Font tab.

This displays the Font options used to change the appearance of text in a chart, as shown in Figure 2.6.

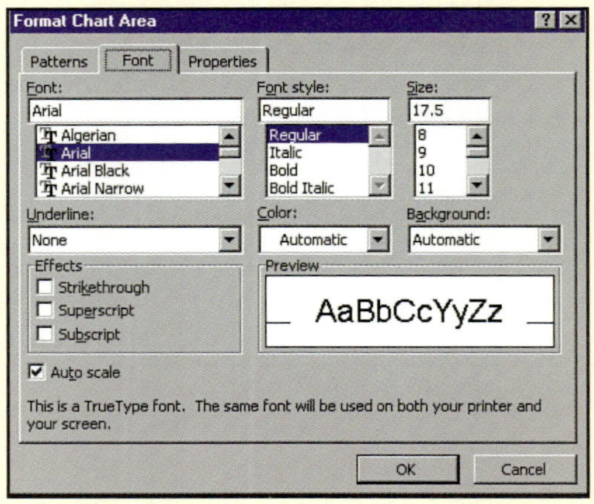

Figure 2.6
The Font tab of the Format Chart Area dialog box enables you to change the appearance of the chart text.

4 In the Font list, select Times New Roman. In the Font style list, select Bold. In the Size list, select 8. Then click OK.

This changes all of the text in the chart to the Times New Roman font with bold style and reduces the font size to eight points.

5 Double-click the chart's title.

A selection box appears around the chart's title and the Format Chart Title dialog box appears.

6 Click the Font tab if it is not displayed.

7 In the Size list box, select 24; then click OK.

This increases the size of the chart's title to 24 points and closes the dialog box.

8 Scroll down the worksheet until the bottom of the chart appears; then double-click any Category (x) axis label.

The Format Axis dialog box appears. Now you will change the orientation (direction) of the text for the Category (x) axis. From the Chart toolbar, you can rotate text up or down 45 degrees; however, if you want the text to be rotated 90 degrees, you need to use the Alignment tab in this dialog box.

9 Click the Alignment tab of the Format Axis dialog box.

The alignment options are displayed, as shown in Figure 2.7.

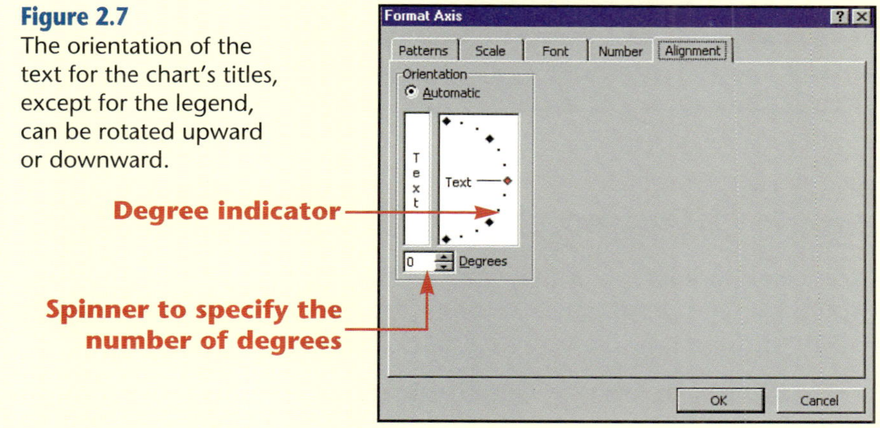

Figure 2.7
The orientation of the text for the chart's titles, except for the legend, can be rotated upward or downward.

10 Drag the degree indicator up until 90 degrees is displayed in the Degrees box; click OK.

The Format Axis dialog box closes. Now view the completed chart in its own window. This eliminates scrolling through the worksheet to view a chart, and chart editing can be done while the chart is open in the window.

11 Choose View, Chart Window.

The entire chart appears in a chart window that is the same size as the chart on your worksheet, as shown in Figure 2.8.

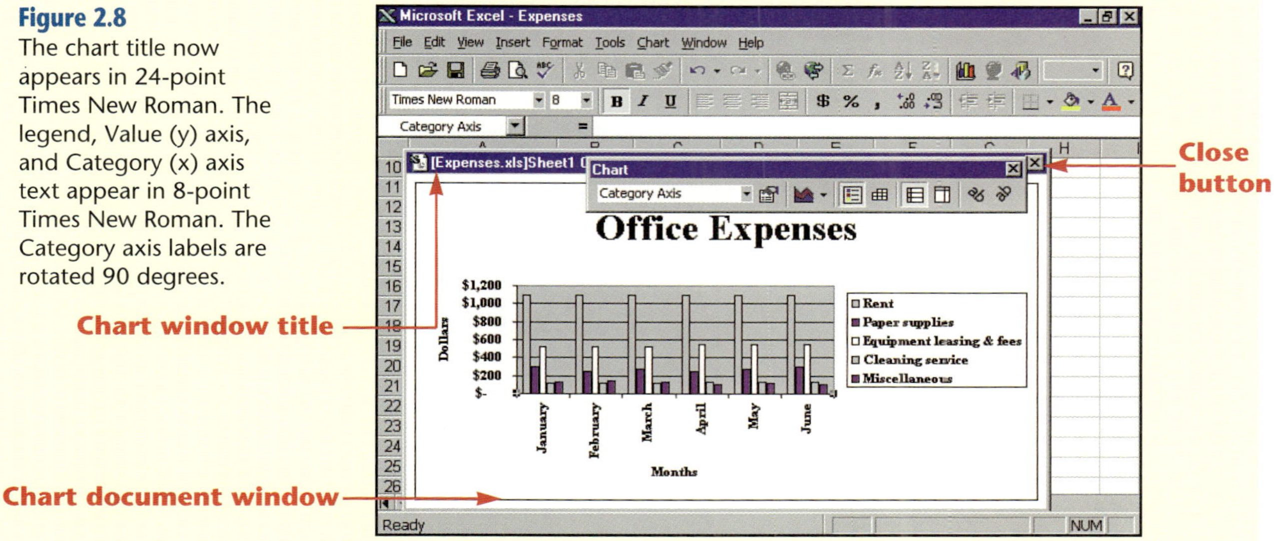

Figure 2.8
The chart title now appears in 24-point Times New Roman. The legend, Value (y) axis, and Category (x) axis text appear in 8-point Times New Roman. The Category axis labels are rotated 90 degrees.

continues

Excel

To Format Text in a Chart (continued)

⑫ **Click the Close button on the chart window.**

The chart window is closed.

⑬ **Save your work and keep the Expenses worksheet open. In Lesson 3, you learn how to change chart types.**

Lesson 3: Changing the Chart Type

After you create a chart, you may decide that you do not like the type of chart you have selected. Because Excel has a wide variety of chart types, you can display information in a way that best conveys its meaning.

Certain chart types are best for certain situations. It's important to select a chart type that can help you display the information in the most dramatic, appropriate, and meaningful manner possible. For example, you can usually spot trends more easily with a line chart, while a pie chart is best for showing parts of a whole.

Now try changing the Expenses chart to a different type of chart.

To Change the Chart Type

① **In the Expenses worksheet, make sure that the chart is selected and the Chart toolbar is displayed.**

Eight selection handles appear on the chart box frame to show that the chart is selected, as shown in Figure 2.9. When you select the chart, the Chart toolbar automatically appears so that the tools associated with charting are available for your use.

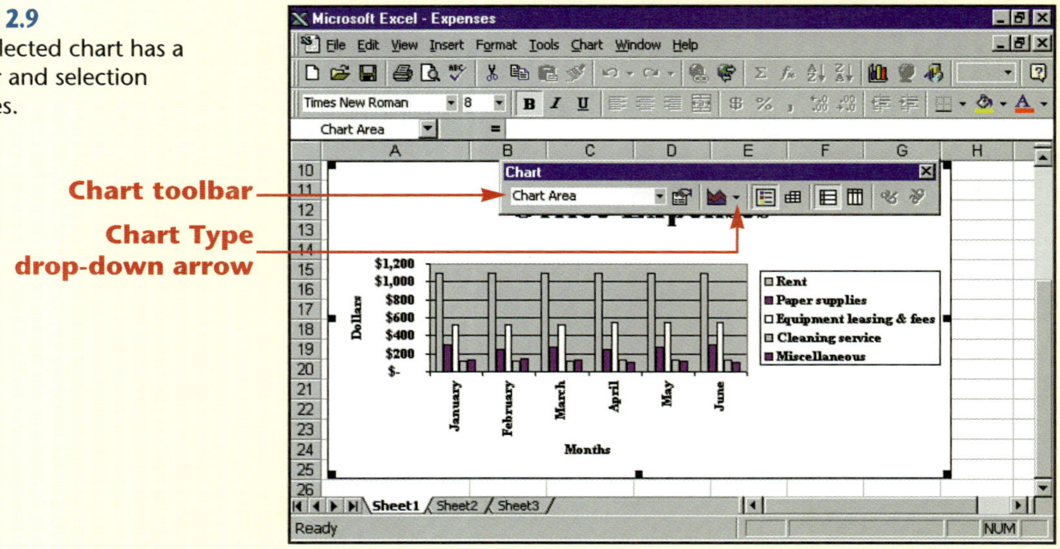

Figure 2.9
The selected chart has a border and selection handles.

2 Click the drop-down arrow next to the Chart Type button on the Chart toolbar.

The various chart types are displayed in a three-column, drop-down list, as shown in Figure 2.10. If you can't see the Chart toolbar on your screen, choose View, Toolbars, and then click the Chart option.

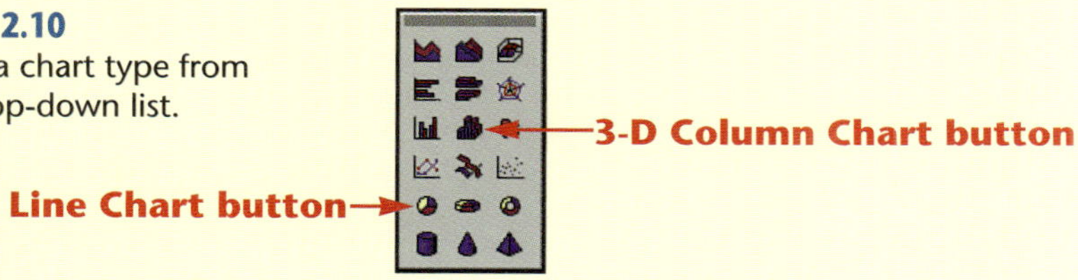

Figure 2.10
Select a chart type from the drop-down list.

3 Click the 3-D Column Chart button (the third button down in the second column).

Excel changes the chart type to the 3-D column format, as shown in Figure 2.11.

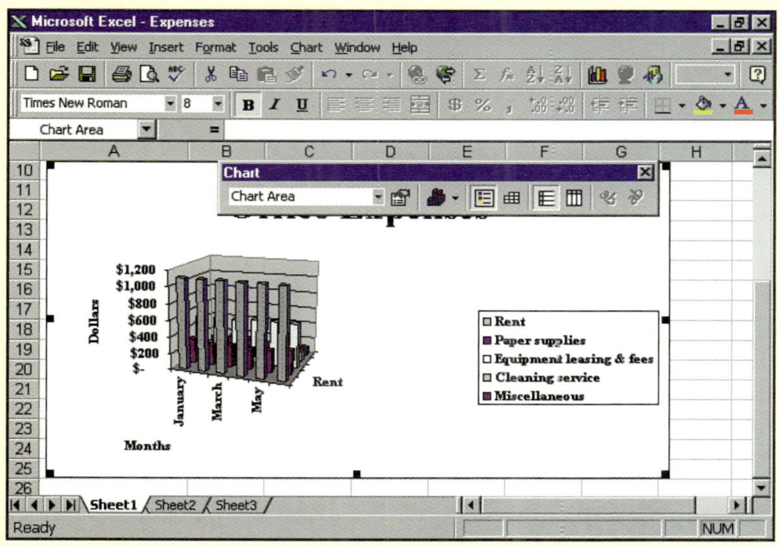

Figure 2.11
The Expenses data appears as a 3-D column chart.

The 3-D column chart does not provide a very good representation of your data. If you want to examine the trends of the source of your income over time, there may be better chart types to use. Consult Table 2.1 to learn more about the different chart types and how they represent your data. Now you select another type of chart that can more clearly illustrate the trend.

4 In the Chart Type drop-down list, click the Line Chart button (the fourth button down in the first column).

The chart type changes to a line chart, as shown in Figure 2.12.

continues

Excel

To Change the Chart Type (continued)

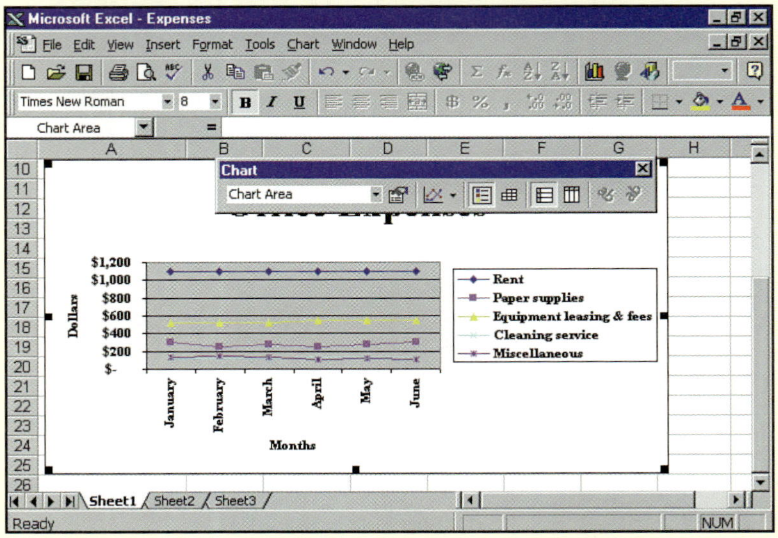

Figure 2.12
In a line chart, you can easily examine trends over time.

5 Save your work and keep the Expenses worksheet open. In Lesson 4, you learn how to enhance your chart's appearance.

If you have problems...

If you aren't sure which chart type to select for a specific job, select one chart type and study the results. Check to see whether the data is accurately represented and conveys the appropriate meaning. Try various chart types until you find the one that best suits your needs.

Table 2.1 describes the various chart types available in Excel.

Table 2.1 Common Chart Types

Chart Type	Description
Area	A line chart that shows the area below the line filled with a color or pattern. Use an area chart to compare several sets of data.
Bar or Column	A chart that represents data by the height of the vertical columns or length of the horizontal bars. Use a bar or column chart to compare one item to another or to compare different items over a period of time.
Line	A chart consisting of a series of data at various points along the axis. The points are connected by a line. Use a line chart to indicate a trend over a period of time.
Pie	A circular chart in which each piece (wedge) shows a data segment and its relationship to the whole. Use a pie chart to sort data and compare parts of the whole.

Chart Type	Description
Doughnut	A circular ring-shaped chart that compares the sizes of pieces in a whole. It is similar to a pie chart but can include multiple data series, appearing in concentric rings.
Radar	A line or area chart enclosed around a central point. Use a radar chart to show the uniformity of data.
XY or Bubble (Scatter)	A chart in which data points are placed along the Value (y) axis and a numeric x-axis, similar to a line chart. Use an XY chart to compare trends over uneven time or measurement intervals (scientific data). Use a Bubble chart to plot two variables against the Category (x) and Value (y) axis, similar to the XY chart, adding a third variable represented by the size of the bubble.
Combination	A chart that combines parts from a line, bar, or area chart so that you can plot data in two forms on the same chart. Use a combination chart to show a correlation between two data series.
Surface	A chart that represents optimum combinations between two sets of data. Patterns and colors are added to indicate sections that are in the same range of values.
Stock	A chart to plot stock prices; the data must be organized in the correct order. It can also be used for scientific data.
3-D (Area, Bar, Line, Pie)	A chart that represents data in the same way as its two-dimensional counterpart. Besides displaying height and width, however, a 3-D chart adds depth to the appearance of the chart.
Cone, Cylinder, Pyramid	A chart that enhances the data markers on 3-D column and bar charts.

Lesson 4: Enhancing a Chart

After you have decided which type of chart best conveys the information in your worksheet, you can enhance the chart's appearance in several ways. The most common enhancements include changing chart colors, adding a grid, and formatting the chart labels.

The easiest way to change any part of a chart is to select the chart, move the mouse pointer over the part you want to change, click the right mouse button, and then choose a command from the shortcut menu.

Now try using this easy method to enhance the Expenses chart.

To Enhance a Chart

1 In the Expenses **worksheet, make sure that the chart is selected.**

With the chart selected, the selection handles are displayed and individual elements of the chart can be edited.

2 Right-click one of the points of the line representing Rent in the chart.

A shortcut menu appears and the Rent line is selected, as shown in Figure 2.13.

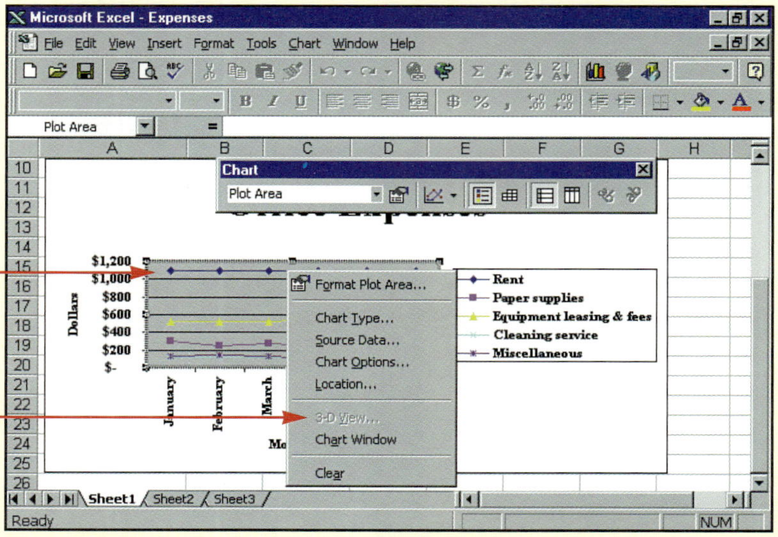

Figure 2.13
Each element of a chart has its own shortcut menu for editing.

3 Choose Chart Type from the shortcut menu.

The Chart Type dialog box appears, as shown in Figure 2.14.

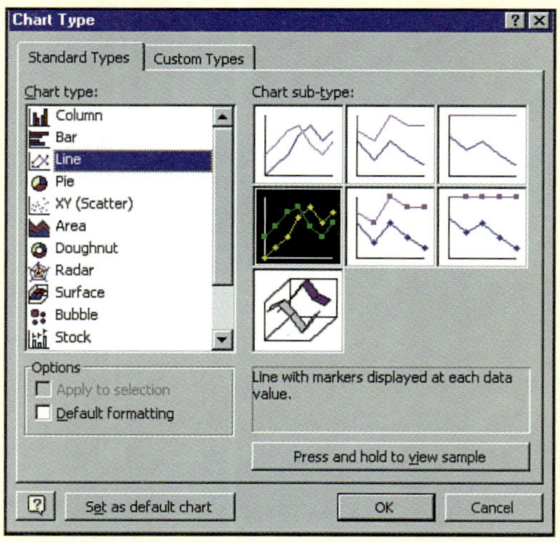

Figure 2.14
The Chart Type dialog box enables you to change the chart type and subtype.

Excel

4 Click Area in the Chart type list and then click the first chart (Area) in the Chart subtype list and click OK.

The chart is now a combination area and line chart, as shown in Figure 2.15. Rent, the element you selected to edit, is represented by the large area from $- to the straight black line at $1100 on the Value (y) axis, while the rest of the chart remains unchanged. Now change the color of the total area.

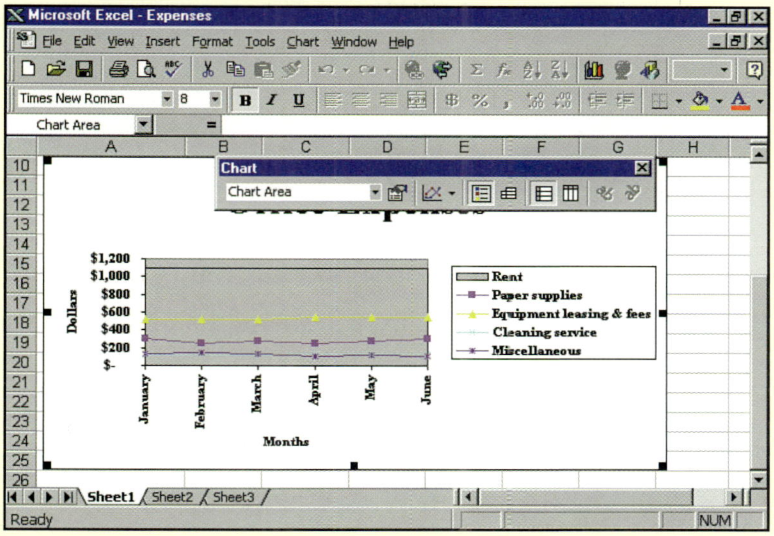

Figure 2.15
This is an example of a combination area and line chart.

5 Right-click the Rent area and choose Format Data Series from the shortcut menu.

The Format Data Series dialog box opens with the Patterns tab selected. In the Area section of the dialog box, a palette of colors is displayed. The current color for the Rent area is shown in the Sample box in the lower-left corner.

6 Select gray, the third color down in the last column.

The new color appears in the Sample box, as shown in Figure 2.16.

7 Click OK.

The dialog box closes and the new color appears in the chart. Now change the number format of the labels on the Value (y) axis to show dollars with two decimal places.

8 Right-click any of the dollar amounts on the Value (y) axis of the chart and choose Format Axis from the shortcut menu.

The Format Axis dialog box appears.

continues

To Enhance a Chart (continued)

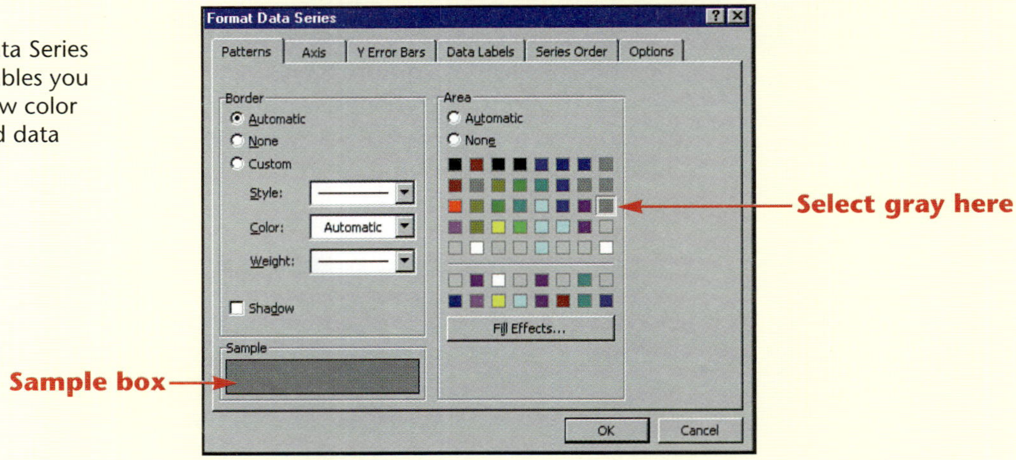

Figure 2.16
The Format Data Series dialog box enables you to choose a new color for the selected data series.

9. **Select the Number tab.**

The Number tab and its options appear with the Custom category selected, as shown in Figure 2.17.

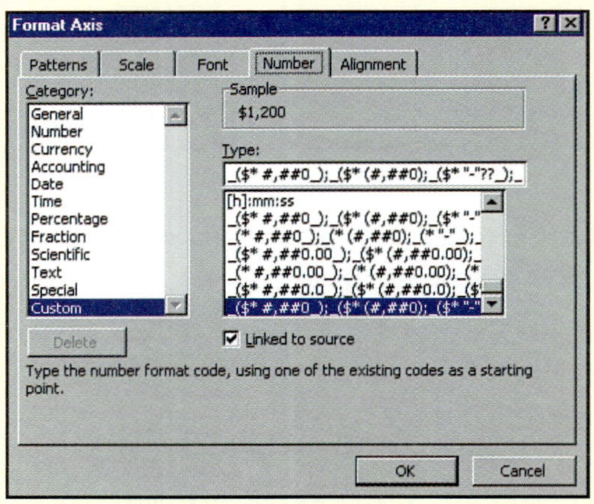

Figure 2.17
On the Number tab of the Format Axis dialog box, you can specify a different number format.

10. **Scroll through the Type list and select the type with a dollar sign and two decimal places, $#,##0.00_);($#,##0.00), and then click OK.**

Excel applies this format, which includes a $ sign, a comma as a thousands separator, and two decimal places, to the dollar values on the Value (y) axis, as shown in Figure 2.18.

11. **Save your work and keep the Expenses workbook open.**

You use it in the next lesson to learn how to print a worksheet that includes a chart.

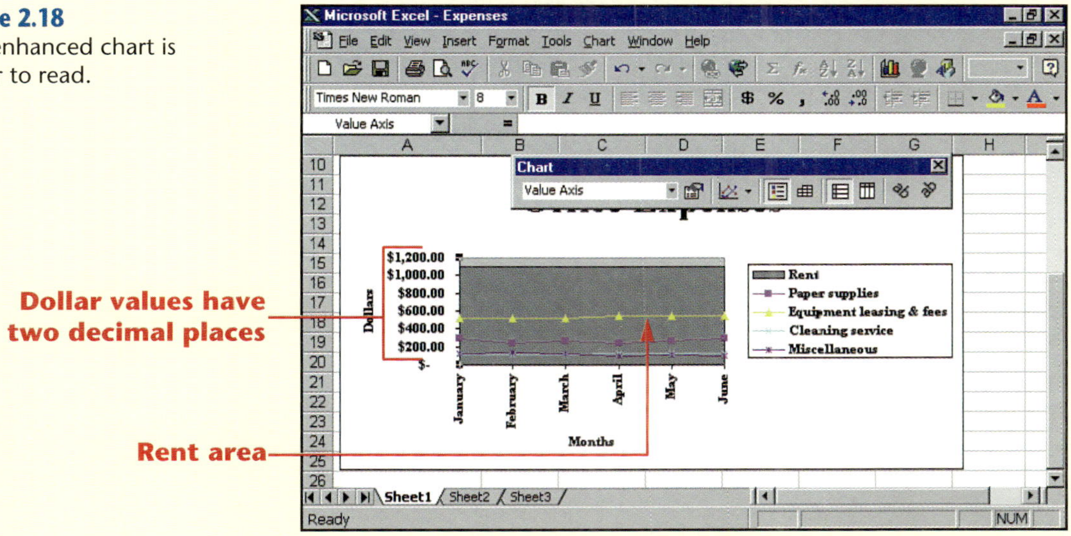

Figure 2.18
The enhanced chart is easier to read.

Inside Stuff

You can modify the format of any element of a chart—the chart title, axis titles, value numbers, axis scale, category axis labels, legend, gridlines, chart area—by right-clicking the element. From the shortcut menu that appears, you select the format command you need to open the specific format dialog box for that element.

A quick way to open the specific format dialog box relating to an element is to double-click the element.

Exam Notes

Pie charts are a little different from charts that have axes. To generate a pie chart, you need only to select a row or column of slice labels from the worksheet and the row or column next to it that contains the values of the slices. Then use the Chart Wizard as you would with any other chart.

Normally, you don't use a legend with a pie chart. Therefore, when you reach the Chart Wizard - Step 3 of 4 - Chart Options dialog box, you should select the Legend tab and remove the check mark from Show legend. To add slice labels to the pie chart, click the Data Labels tab and select Show label or Show label and percent. If you want short lines connecting the label to the appropriate slice on the chart, check Show leader lines.

One other characteristic of pie charts is the capability to explode or cut a slice, which moves a selected slice away from the center of the pie in order to emphasize that slice. Once the pie chart is complete and embedded in your worksheet or displayed on its own sheet, click the center of the pie once to select it (handles appear on the edge of the pie). Click once on the slice you want to explode to select just that slice. Point in the middle of the selected slice and drag it a short distance away from the center of the pie.

If you have a 3-D pie chart, you can also tilt or rotate the pie. Select the pie and choose Chart, 3-D View from the menu. Click the two large up and down arrows to change the tilt of the chart; click the circular arrows to rotate the chart. A sample shows the change in position. Choose OK when you have the position you want.

Lesson 5: Printing a Chart

Unless you want to carry around a laptop computer to show your work onscreen, you need to be able to print your worksheets.

Printing lets you view the worksheets you have created, even when you are away from your computer. A printed copy of a chart combined with the worksheet data makes a very effective presentation. Now try printing the entire `Expenses` workbook file, including the chart.

To Print a Chart

1 In the `Expenses` worksheet, click anywhere outside the chart.

This makes sure that no range in the worksheet is selected, not even the chart. The Chart toolbar is removed from the screen.

2 Choose File, Page Setup.

The Page Setup dialog box appears, as shown in Figure 2.19. Use this dialog box to adjust the page setup before you print your worksheet. This dialog box provides a wide range of options from which you can choose to customize your printed worksheet. For this example, you change the margins, header, and footer for the printed worksheet.

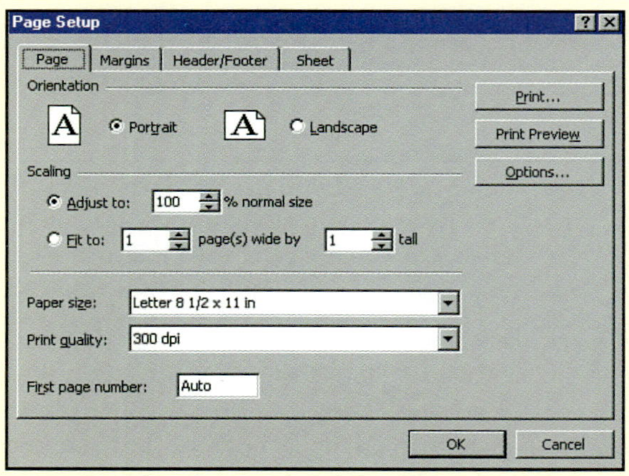

Figure 2.19
The Page Setup dialog box.

3 In the Page Setup dialog box, click the Header/Footer tab.

The Header and Footer options let you specify information to print in the header and footer area of each page. You can choose from predefined headers and footers, or you can create your own.

4 Click the drop-down arrow next to the Header text box, scroll up, and select (none).

This removes the default header text, and nothing will print in the header area.

5 Click the drop-down arrow next to the Footer text box and select Expenses.

This footer prints the current file name in the center of the footer area.

6 Click the Margins tab in the Page Setup dialog box.

This displays the Margins options.

7 In the Top text box, click the up arrow twice.

This changes the top margin from 1 to 1.5.

8 In the Bottom text box, click the down arrow once.

This changes the bottom margin from 1 to 0.75. You have now finished setting up the worksheet page for printing. Now preview the page to make sure it is the way you want it to print.

9 Click the Print Preview button in the Page Setup dialog box.

Excel closes the Page Setup dialog box, makes the changes you requested to the page setup, and displays the Print Preview window, as shown in Figure 2.20. In Print Preview, you can see the worksheet as it will look when you print it. (You can also open the Print Preview window by clicking the Print Preview button on the Standard toolbar when the Page Setup dialog box isn't open.) Everything looks right, so you are ready to print.

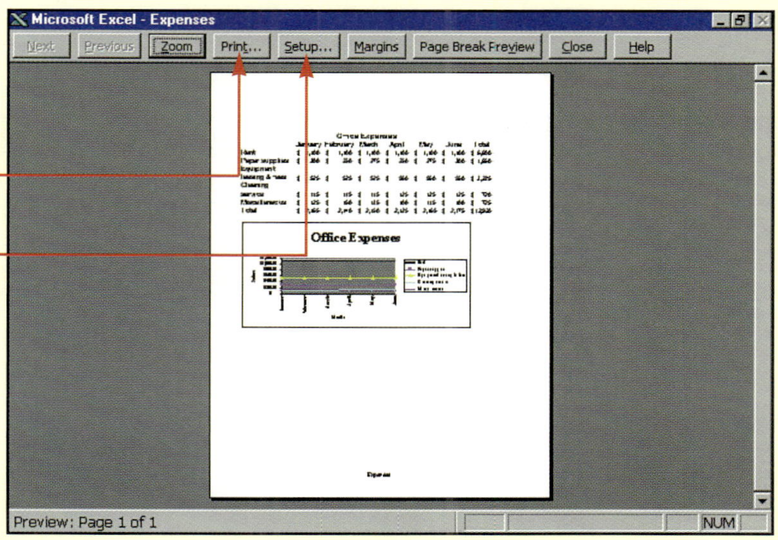

Figure 2.20
Print Preview shows you the page as it will print, including the chart.

continues

To Print a Chart (continued)

10 Click the Print button on the Print Preview toolbar.

The Print Preview window closes and the Print dialog box appears.

11 In the Number of copies text box, change the number of copies to `2` **and then click OK.**

Excel prints two copies of the worksheet, including the chart. When you are done printing, save and close the Expenses workbook. In Lesson 6, you learn how to create a map by using data in a different workbook file.

Inside Stuff

You can print just a chart in Excel without printing the entire worksheet. Select the chart and choose File, Print to open the Print dialog box. Click the Selected Chart option button in the Print What area and click OK.

If you want to leave additional space between the chart and the worksheet data, simply select the chart and drag it down a few rows. Remember to deselect the chart before printing.

Lesson 6: Creating a Data Map

Data maps are useful for charting information that is defined by state, country, or province. Maps are not one of Excel's built-in chart types, but are a separate feature of Excel. Maps can help you visualize your worksheet information geographically. In this lesson, you compare how many company offices are located in different states in the U.S. By creating a map, you can see where most of the offices are located.

Try creating a map now, using the sample worksheet provided.

To Create a Map

1 From the Project-02 folder on the CD, open the file Proj0202 and save it as `SiteMap`**.**

2 Select cell A3. Hold down Shift and press Ctrl+End.

This selects all the data in the worksheet so that the information can be used to create your map.

3 Click the Map button on the Standard toolbar.

The mouse pointer changes to a crosshair, which you can use to specify where in the worksheet Excel should create the map.

4 Click cell A21 and hold down the left mouse button; drag the mouse to cell G35.

When you release the mouse button, Excel begins creating the map in the range A21:G35. This may take a few seconds. Excel looks to see which map the data belongs in, based on the geographical data included in the selected data range. If the data could fit in more than one map (which is the case in this example), the Multiple Maps Available dialog box appears, as shown in Figure 2.21.

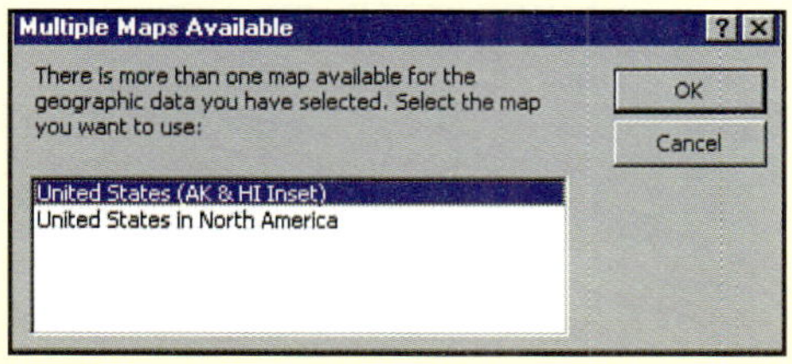

Figure 2.21
The Multiple Maps Available dialog box.

5 Select United States in North America and click OK.

You may have to wait for several seconds while Excel composes the map. The map appears in the selected cells along with the Microsoft Map Control dialog box, as shown in Figure 2.22. The map is inserted into a frame, which you can use to resize and move the map. You can use the Microsoft Map Control dialog box to change some formatting characteristics of the map. Currently, the # of Offices column is displayed in the map. Because the shading values in the map are not easy to discern, try changing the colors of the map now.

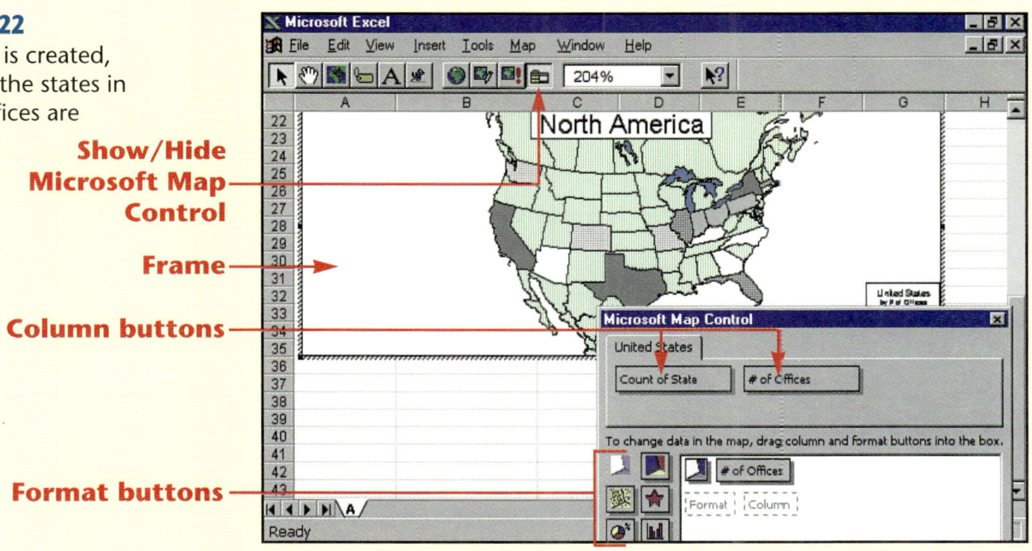

Figure 2.22
The map is created, showing the states in which offices are located.

continues

To Create a Map (continued)

If you have problems...

If the Microsoft Map Control dialog box is covering the map so you cannot see the map, simply drag the dialog box out of the way. You can open and close the dialog box by using the Show/Hide Microsoft Map Control button on the toolbar.

6 In the Microsoft Map Control dialog box, drag the Category Shading button onto the # of Offices button, as shown in Figure 2.23.

This takes the values in the # of Offices column of the worksheet and divides them into categories by color. When you release the mouse button, Excel redraws the map, applying a different color to each state to indicate the number of offices in each state.

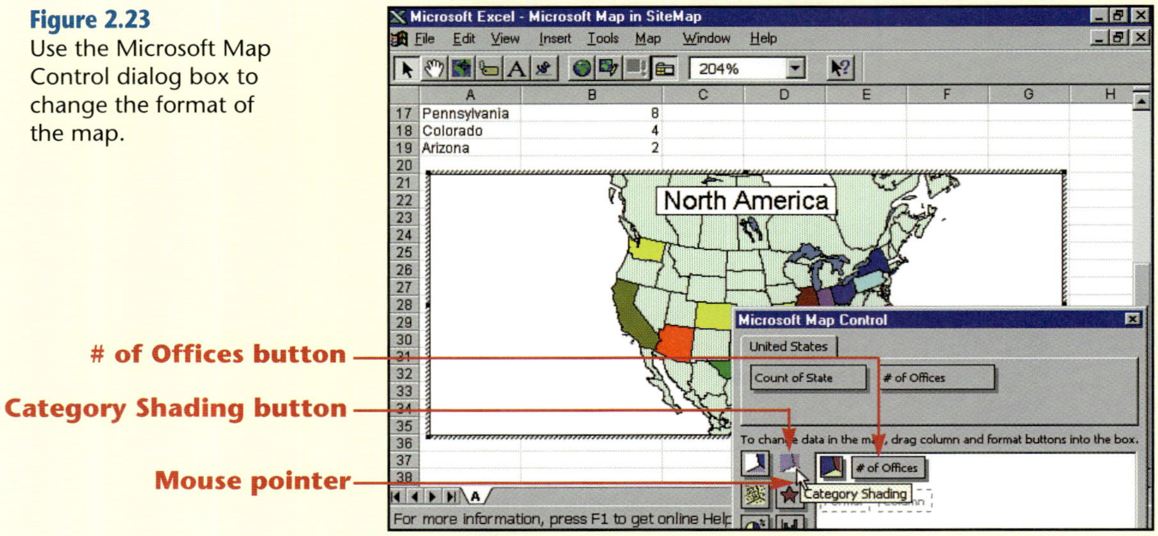

Figure 2.23
Use the Microsoft Map Control dialog box to change the format of the map.

7 Close the Microsoft Map Control dialog box.

The map is complete, as shown in Figure 2.24. The location of offices is now clearly indicated by different colors. The expanded legend is partially hidden in the map frame and is difficult to read.

8 Drag the legend up to display the entire box.

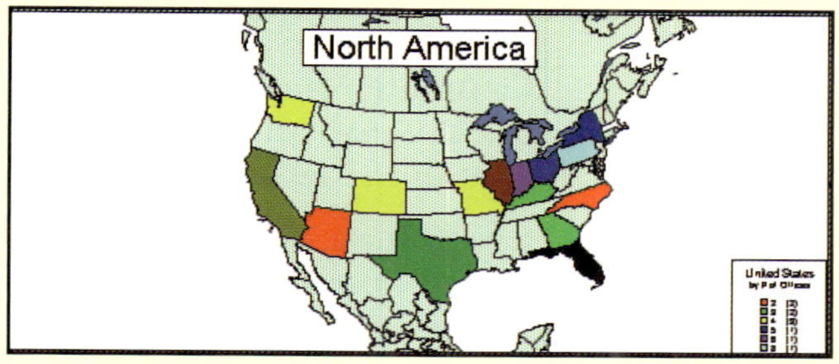

Figure 2.24
The map with an expanded legend.

9 Drag the upper-left corner of the legend box up and to the left (approximately even with row 24); click inside the map to deselect the box.

You can now see the colors and the numbers in the legend to identify which part of the country has the greatest number of offices (the number identifies the number of offices in each state by color; the number in parentheses identifies how many states have that number of offices). You decide to focus your research on the states surrounding Ohio. Try zooming in on the map now.

10 Click the Zoom Percentage of Map drop-down arrow and select 400%.

Excel redraws the map, increasing its magnification. Now change the title of the map.

If you have problems...

If you are unhappy with the view, use the Zoom Percentage of Map button to change the view percentage. You can return to the previous view by opening the View menu and choosing Previous. To view the entire map, choose View, Entire Map.

11 Double-click the map title.

This selects the map's title and positions an insertion point in the text so that you can enter and edit the title text. You can change the text as well as the text attributes, including font, font size, and font style.

12 Change the text to `Office Locations` and press ↵Enter.

This changes the map's title. You can drag it to a new location on the map or resize it so that it doesn't cover any of the target states.

13 Drag the map title to the upper-left corner of the map.

The map title is moved. You can also reposition the map within its frame.

continues

To Create a Map (continued)

14 Click the Grabber button on the Microsoft Map toolbar and then click the map and drag it around in the frame until it is positioned to the left of the legend.

Click anywhere outside the map frame to deselect it. The map is complete, as shown in Figure 2.25. Save your work. If requested by your instructor, print two copies of the worksheet with the map. Then close the workbook.

If you have completed your session on the computer, exit Excel and Windows 95 before turning off your computer. Otherwise, continue with the "Checking Your Skills" and "Applying Your Skills" exercises at the end of this project.

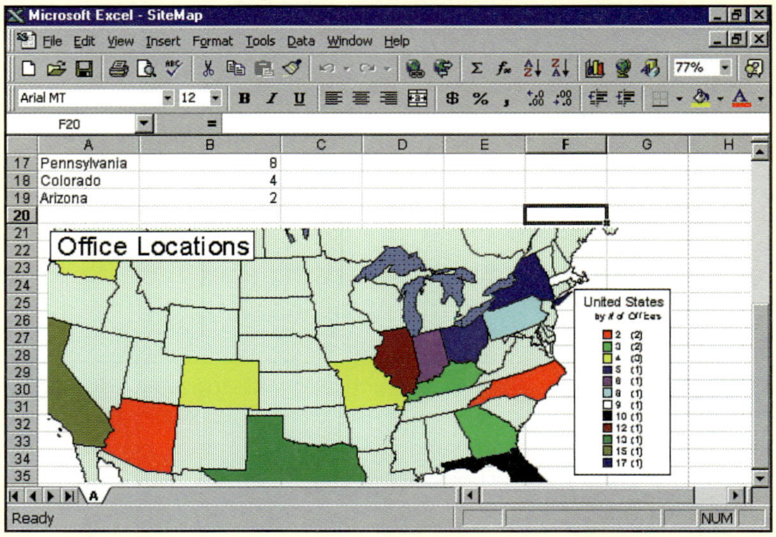

Figure 2.25
The completed map appears below the worksheet data.

Inside Stuff

When creating a map, you need to have two columns of data. The first column contains the name of the region, state, or country. You can use abbreviations—such as WV, TN, NC, and so on—or you can use the state's full name. The second column contains the worksheet information. The data in the second column is represented on the map by colors and/or patterns.

As with the elements in a chart, you can right-click elements in a map to open a shortcut menu. You can use the commands on the shortcut menus to quickly edit or enhance the parts of the map.

To print the worksheet with the map, choose File, Print, select the options you want in the Print dialog box, and then click OK. To print the map without printing the entire worksheet, select the worksheet cells surrounding the map, click the Selection option in the Print dialog box, and then click OK. You can change options such as the header, footer, and margins by using the Page Setup dialog box, just as you do for all worksheets.

Project Summary

To	Do This
Start the Chart Wizard	Select the range to be charted; then click the Chart Wizard button on the Standard toolbar or choose Insert, Chart.
Select a chart	Click the chart.
Format a chart element	Click the chart element and click the right mouse button. From the shortcut menu, choose the Format option.
Change a chart type	Select the chart; then choose a chart type from the Chart Type drop-down list on the Chart toolbar.
Print a chart	Select the chart; then click the Print button on the Standard toolbar.
Create a map	Select the range to be mapped; then click the Map button on the Standard toolbar and click in the worksheet where you want the upper-left corner of the map to appear.

Checking Your Skills

True/False

For each of the following, check *T* or *F* to indicate whether the statement is true or false.

__T __F **1.** A chart can only be placed on the worksheet with the data.

__T __F **2.** Charts and maps are objects on the worksheet.

__T __F **3.** The Category (x) axis provides the scale used to measure the data in the chart.

__T __F **4.** After a chart is created, you can choose another chart type if you are not satisfied with the representation of your data.

__T __F **5.** When creating a map, the first column of data should contain the names of regions, states, or countries.

__T __F **6.** An embedded chart must be viewed in a chart window before the elements can be selected, moved, copied, sized, or formatted.

__T __F **7.** An object has its own frame.

__T __F **8.** Three ways to create a chart from selected data in Excel are by pressing F1, pressing Alt+F1, and using the Chart Wizard.

__T __F **9.** Excel cannot create three-dimensional charts.

__T __F **10.** You should resize a chart before formatting it.

Multiple Choice

Circle the letter of the correct answer for each of the following questions.

1. Which type of chart usually helps you spot trends easily?
   a. Area
   b. Column
   c. Line
   d. Pie
2. Which type of chart is best for showing parts of a whole?
   a. Area
   b. Column
   c. Line
   d. Pie
3. What is the element of a chart that identifies colors or patterns assigned to a data series or chart categories?
   a. Chart area
   b. Chart title
   c. Legend
   d. Value (y) axis
4. What are some common enhancements that are often made to a chart to improve its appearance?
   a. Add a grid
   b. Change colors
   c. Format the chart labels
   d. All of the above
5. How many columns of data are needed in your worksheet to create a map?
   a. One
   b. Two
   c. Three
   d. As many as you want
6. The default chart type is what?
   a. Column
   b. Bar
   c. Pie
   d. Line
7. The mouse pointer changes to which of the following when you drag a chart?
   a. 2-headed arrow
   b. 4-headed arrow
   c. Hand
   d. Pointing finger
8. Three-dimensional charts have a third axis, called what?
   a. x-axis
   b. y-axis
   c. z-axis
   d. d-axis
9. Which of the following is used to identify the data in a chart?
   a. Legend
   b. Gallery
   c. Chart Wizard
   d. None of the above
10. Use which type of chart to show a correlation between two data series?
    a. Column
    b. Combination
    c. Pie
    d. Line

Completion

In the blank provided, write the correct answer for each of the following statements.

1. The ______________ button on the Standard toolbar assists you in creating a chart.
2. Excel creates a chart from a(n) ______________ you specify on the worksheet.
3. Click the ______________ mouse button on a chart or chart element to display a shortcut menu.
4. Select a chart or chart element; then drag a(n) ______________ to resize it.
5. Create a(n) ______________ to chart information that is defined by state, country, or province.
6. A(n)______________ is a range of values in a worksheet.
7. The labels along the bottom of a chart are the ______________labels.
8. The labels along the left side of a chart are the ______________-axis labels.
9. To delete an embedded chart, click it to select it and press ______________.
10. The mouse pointer should be shaped like a(n) ____________ on the worksheet cell where you want the upper-left corner of a map to start.

Matching

In the blank next to each of the following terms or phrases, write the letter of the corresponding term or phrase. (Note that some letters may be used more than once.)

a. Category axis
b. data series
c. embedded
d. handles
e. legend
f. line
g. notes
h. object
i. pie
j. Value axis

_____ 1. A range of values in a worksheet
_____ 2. Identifies data series
_____ 3. Black squares surrounding a chart
_____ 4. Vertical axis of a chart
_____ 5. Horizontal axis of a chart
_____ 6. A chart that appears on the worksheet along with the worksheet data
_____ 7. Brief descriptions of the data in a chart
_____ 8. A chart type in which each segment shows a data segment and its relationship to the whole
_____ 9. A chart type consisting of a series of data at various points along the axis
_____ 10. An item that has its own frame or box

Excel

Applying Your Skills

Practice

The following exercises enable you to practice the skills you have learned in this project. Take a few minutes to work through these exercises now.

Creating a Chart and Map Showing Mail Order Sales

In the past six months, you have tried to expand your business by adding a mail order catalog to send to potential customers in the western United States. Create a chart and a map to show the sales for a mail order catalog business in the first quarter of 1997.

To create a chart and map showing mail order sales, follow these steps:

1. Open the file Proj0203 from the Project-02 folder on the CD and save it as `MOSChart`.
2. Select the data for both columns and create a chart embedded in the worksheet. Think about which type of chart will best show a comparison of the states in the mail order channel. Do not forget to add a title to the chart.
3. Move the chart below the worksheet, starting in cell A20. Increase the size of the chart so that it fills the range A20:G35.
4. Format the chart area, changing the font to a 10-point size.
5. Select the data for both columns and create a map, starting in cell A37 through cell G50 of the worksheet.
6. Experiment with some of the map features to enhance the map. For example, change the colors on the map. Change the zoom percentage to draw attention to the states where the sales are concentrated. Move the legend so that it is displayed inside the map frame.
7. Change the map title to `Mail Order Sales`. Try editing the font and font size in the title text.
8. Save your work. If requested by your instructor, print two copies of the worksheet with the chart and map before closing the file.

Comparing Expenses Using a Chart

Using Proj0204 from the Project-02 folder on the CD, create a pie chart that compares how much you spend on various types of school expenses. Your tuition each semester is determined by the university, but you can try to manage other costs. Use the chart to see how changes in how much you spend on the Books–Additional category affects the makeup of the total amount.

To compare expenses using a chart, follow these steps:

1. Open the file Proj0204 and save it as `Charting Expenses`.
2. Create a pie chart, using the expense data for only the Spring 1997 semester for the following expense headings:

   Books–Main subjects

   Books–Additional

   Supplies–General

   Supplies–Lab

   Lab Fees

   Move the chart below the worksheet data.
3. Now change the chart type so that you can compare how the various types of expenses contribute to your total expenses for the semester. (Tip: Refer to Table 2.1.) Resize the chart and reduce the size of the font for the chart area to make sure that the Category (x) axis displays all the expense labels.
4. What happens to the worksheet and the chart when you decrease the amount in the worksheet for Books–Additional from $85 to $25?
5. What happens to the worksheet and the chart when you drastically increase the amount in the worksheet for Books–Additional to $475?
6. Save your work. If requested by your instructor, print two copies of the worksheet with the increased expense for Books–Additional.

Creating a Map of the Home States of Rollerblading Club Members

In an effort to show prospective club members how diverse the rollerblading club is, you decide to create a map showing the home states of all current members.

To create the map, follow these steps:

1. Open Proj0205 and save it as `Membership Map`.
2. Use the data provided to create a map.
3. Zoom in on the target area.
4. Format the map to clearly show from which states most club members come. For example, make use of the legend, show the states in color, and use titles and text.
5. Save the worksheet. If requested by your instructor, print two copies. Then close the worksheet.

Creating an Embedded Area Chart

In this exercise, you create an area chart for the first quarter sales expenses of Midwestern Enterprises.

To create an embedded area chart, follow these steps:

1. Open Proj0206 from the Project-02 folder on the CD and save it as `Quarterly Expenses`.
2. Create an embedded area chart using the data range of A4:D9.
3. Position the chart below the data area (rows 13 through 24).
4. Use the Chart, Chart Options command to insert a chart title, an x-axis title, and a y-axis title. The chart title is `1st Quarter Expenses`. The x-axis title is Office Expenses, and the y-axis title is in dollars.
5. Adjust the size of the chart so that the category x labels are displayed.
6. If requested by your instructor, print two copies of the worksheet and chart.
7. Save and then close the workbook.

Creating a Line Chart on a Chart Sheet

In this exercise, you have the opportunity to create a chart on a separate chart sheet; then change the chart type and add titles.

To create a line chart on a chart sheet, follow these steps:

1. From the Project-02 folder on the CD, open the Proj0207 file and save it as `Beverages`.
2. Select the data range of A4:D7, then press F11 to create a chart on its own sheet.
3. When the chart sheet appears, right-click to display a chart shortcut menu.
4. Choose the Chart Type command to change the column chart to a line chart.
5. Right-click to display a chart shortcut menu. Then select the Chart Options command to insert a chart title and an x-axis title. The chart title is `1st Quarter Sales`. The x-axis title is `Beverage Sales`.
6. If requested by your instructor, print two copies of the worksheet and chart.
7. Save and then close the workbook.

Challenge

The following challenges enable you to use your problem-solving skills. Take time to work through these exercises now.

Creating an Embedded Pie Chart

To show your employees the sales results for July, you create an embedded pie chart. Open Proj0208 from the Project-02 folder on the CD and save it as `July Sales`. Use the data range A5:B11 to create the chart. Position the chart in rows 14 through 25 below the data area. Insert the chart title `July Sales`. Save and then close the workbook.

Formatting a Chart

Your boss has asked you to format a columnar sales chart that he will be using in a meeting. Open Proj0209 from the Projcet-02 folder on the CD and save it as `Formatted Chart`. Position the chart below the data area (rows 10 through 22). Insert the chart title `Sales`. Label the x-axis as `1997` and the y-axis as `in thousands`. Change the Model B data series to the color yellow. Change the Model C data series to red. Change the chart type to bar. Save and then close the workbook.

Creating a Data Map

Open Proj0210 from the Project-02 folder on the CD and save it as `Company Agents`. Create a map using the State and Agents data columns. Add the map title, `Agents by State`. Apply Category Shading to the Count of State column. Save and close the workbook.

Changing Chart Type

Open Proj0211 from the Project-02 folder on the CD and save it as `Garnet & Gold`. Create a column chart using the data in columns A and B. Move the chart to the range A15:E30. Add a chart title, `Garnet & Gold Industries`. Adjust the size of the chart so that all x-axis labels display. Also, delete the legend by selecting it and pressing Del. Change the chart type to a clustered column with a 3-D visual effect. Save and then close the workbook.

Creating Embedded Charts

Open Proj0212 from the Project-02 folder on the CD and save the workbook with the name `Motor Pool`. Create six embedded column charts, one for each car in the motor pool. Include appropriate chart titles. Save and then close the workbook.

PinPoint Assessment

PinPoint Training

You have completed the project and the associated lessons, as well as the "Checking Your Skills" and "Applying Your Skills" sections. Now use the PinPoint software evaluation mode to assess your comprehension of the specific exam tasks you have just learned. You can also use the PinPoint Trainer Mode and the Show Me tutorials to practice these specific exam tasks.

Project 3

Three

Creating More Complex Charts

Making Formatting Consistent for Better Presentations

In this Project, you learn how to:

Objectives

- Format a Chart with Predefined Formats
- Create a Custom Chart Format
- Add a Trendline to a Chart
- Add a Data Table to a Chart
- Group Charts Together

Why Would I Do This?

One of Excel's greatest strengths is its capacity to create presentations from worksheet data. In your daily work, you might use many different worksheets, some of which might be quite large. As you develop worksheets, you become comfortable with them and can quickly find any data you need. When you must present your data to others, however, you usually cannot just hand them a copy of your worksheets. This is especially true in a meeting or conference. When you must present your data to others, your audience probably wants to see the worksheet data summarized as much as possible, and might prefer to see some of the data condensed in graphical form (charts). Fortunately, Excel provides tools to help you present data in a way that is attractive and easy to understand.

This project helps you build an Excel presentation. Suppose you are part of a team and each team member is responsible for one section of the presentation. Unfortunately, not all the players have the same ideas for how a presentation should look. One player likes the Brush Script font and pie charts. Another player likes Helvetica and bar charts. When the team meets to review the presentation, it does not look professional. You ask each of the players to submit their files to you. With all the files in one workbook, your job is to make the presentation look seamless. To do this, you can apply predefined styles or AutoFormats, as you learned in Project 1, and use predefined chart types for the charts. You enhance the presentation further by adding trendlines and a data table to the charts. Finally, you embed an additional chart on one of your worksheets and group it with the original.

Lesson 1: Formatting a Chart with Predefined Formats

Excel has tools that enable you to automate the formatting of your charts. If you want to use one of Excel's predefined chart formats, you can use the Chart, Chart Type command and select from a variety of chart styles. If you prefer, you can create your own custom formats for your charts to apply them to future charts you create—and even share them with other users.

In this lesson, you use the Chart, Chart Type command to change the chart type and subtype. Then you enhance the appearance of the chart heading and change the colors used for the columns in the chart.

To Format a Chart with Predefined Formats

1. **Open the Proj0301 file from the Project-03 folder on the CD and save it as** `1QA Presentation`**.**

2. **Activate the** `97 vs 96` **worksheet and click the chart to the right of the First Quarter 1997 data to select it.**

   Selection handles appear around the box border.

3 Make sure that the Chart toolbar is displayed.

If you have problems...

If the Chart toolbar does not appear onscreen when you select the chart, right-click anywhere inside the toolbar area; then select Chart from the shortcut menu. The Chart toolbar should appear.

If the toolbar appears on top of the chart, click in the toolbar's title bar and drag it out of the way. Currently, the chart is a bar chart. AQN's president prefers column charts, so you will change the chart to a column chart.

4 With the chart selected, choose Chart, Chart Type; then click the Standard Types tab.

The Chart Type dialog box appears, as shown in Figure 3.1. This dialog box gives you access to all of Excel's predefined chart types. Categories of chart types are separated into two tabs—Standard Types and Custom Types. When you choose a chart type, Excel displays examples of all the subtypes available in that type.

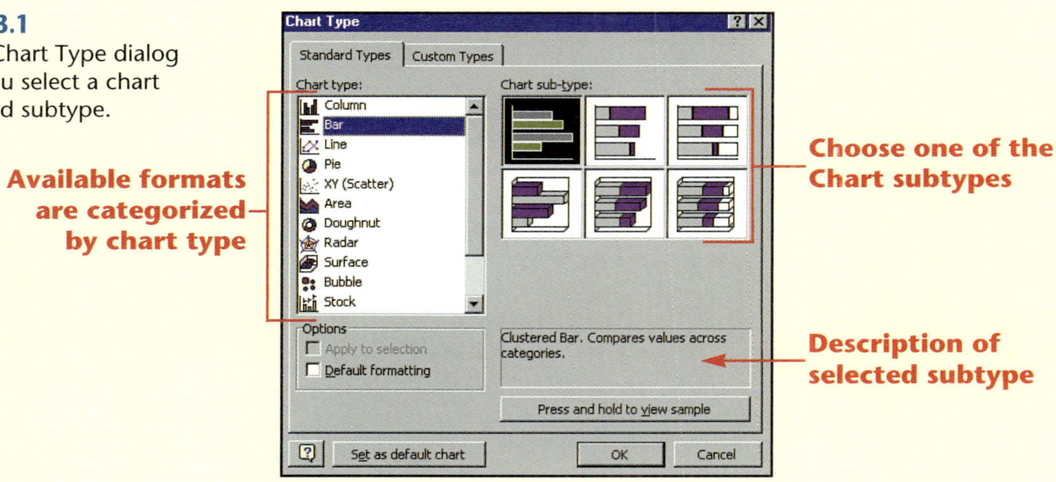

Figure 3.1
In the Chart Type dialog box, you select a chart type and subtype.

5 Choose Column from the Chart type list box.

The Chart subtype area changes to show the different formats available for column charts.

6 Select the first subtype (Clustered Column) and click OK.

Your chart is updated with the new format, as shown in Figure 3.2.

Now refine the chart's formatting. You can start by spicing up the chart title to make it look more attractive.

continues

To Format a Chart with Predefined Formats (continued)

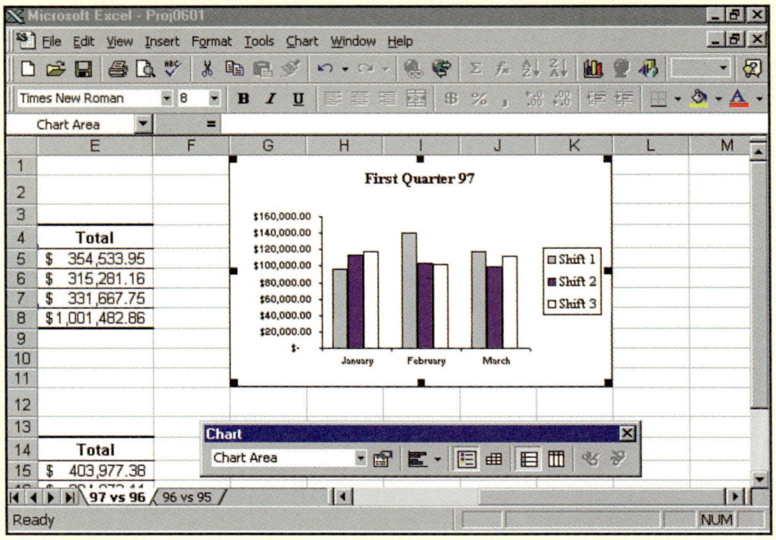

Figure 3.2
The chart type is now changed to clustered column.

7 **With the chart still selected, right-click the chart title** `First Quarter 97`**.**

A shortcut menu appears.

8 **Select Format Chart Title.**

The Format Chart Title dialog box appears, as shown in Figure 3.3.

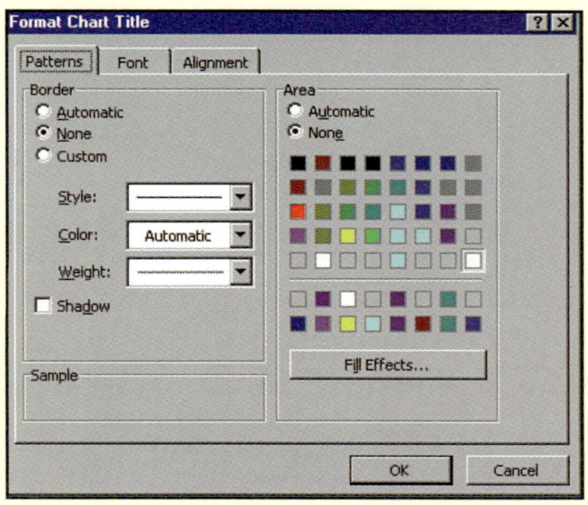

Figure 3.3
Use the Format Chart Title dialog box to enhance the appearance of the chart title.

9 **Make sure that the Patterns tab is selected; then select the Shadow check box in the Border area.**

On the Patterns tab, you can set up a border and background just for the chart title. In the Sample area, you should see an example of a shadow box. This is the type of border selected for the chart title. The shadow box makes the title appear as if it is floating over the chart.

Excel

10 In the color palette of the Area box, choose the light yellow color in the fifth row of colors.

This makes the title area light yellow. Again, this should appear in the Sample box. Now select a new font for the chart's title.

11 Click the Font tab and select the Times New Roman font, bold italic style, 12-point size.

The Font tab is very similar to the Font dialog box that appears when you choose Format, Cells, and click the Font tab. It gives you specific control over the selected text.

The Preview box shows you how the modified font looks on the chart.

12 Click OK.

The chart's title is modified. Now make some enhancements to the actual data in the chart by changing the colors for just Shift 3.

13 Click inside one of the Shift 3 columns within the chart.

A single handle appears on each column, indicating that they have all been selected. Any changes you make apply to all the selected columns.

14 Right-click one of the selected columns.

The shortcut menu appears.

15 Choose Format Data Series.

The Format Data Series dialog box opens, as shown in Figure 3.4.

Figure 3.4
You change the format of the columns you have selected in the Format Data Series dialog box.

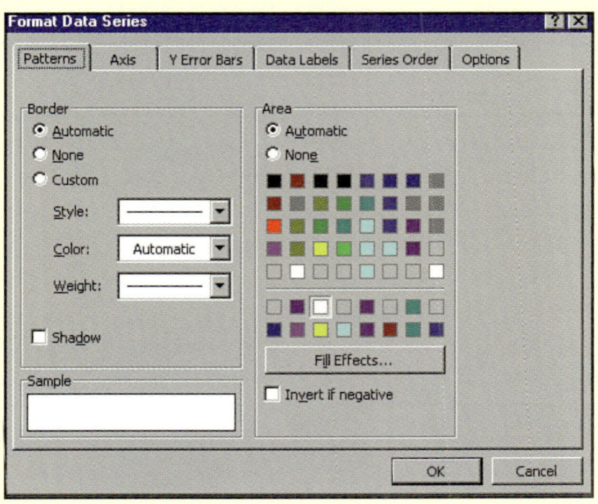

16 Click the Patterns tab.

This tab lets you change the appearance of the columns themselves.

continues

To Format a Chart with Predefined Formats (continued)

17 In the color palette of the Area box, click the fifth button in the third row of colors.

18 Click OK and then click outside the chart to deselect the chart.

The formatting changes for the chart are complete, as shown in Figure 3.5.

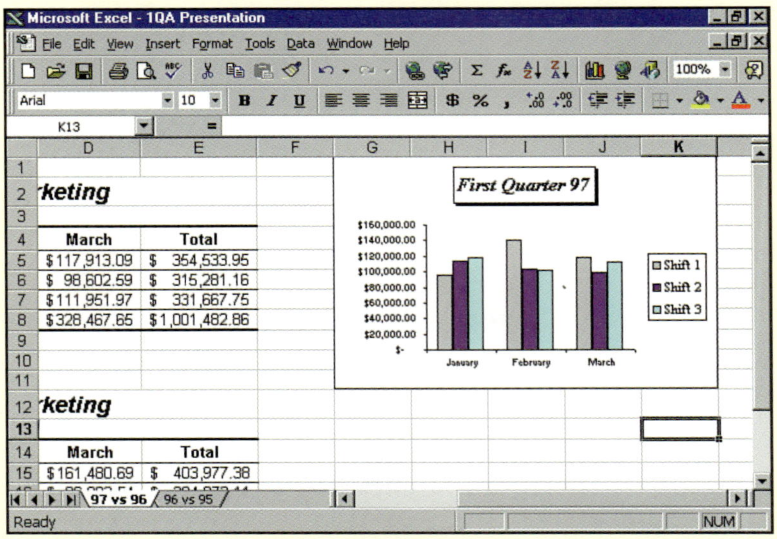

Figure 3.5
You now have changed the color of the Shift 3 data series of the chart.

With the formatting done, you can make a custom format and apply the same attributes to all your charts.

19 Save the workbook and keep it open for the next lesson.

Inside Stuff

In the previous version of Excel, you had to double-click an embedded chart to activate it before you could select and edit the chart elements. Now, just a single click on a chart or its elements is needed to select. (If a border shows a single-line box with handles, the box is selected.) Right-click any chart element to display a shortcut menu for formatting. To view an embedded chart in its own window, select the chart and then choose View, Chart Window. Even if the chart is partially hidden on your screen, it will appear full-size in the chart window, and you can edit while in this view.

Lesson 2: Creating a Custom Chart Format

In this lesson, you work with several charts that were created by different people and formatted differently. Your goal is to find a chart format you like and then apply that format to all the charts in the workbook to make them match. In the preceding lesson, you learned how to use Excel's predefined formats to change the first chart. This lesson shows you how to modify that chart to look exactly the way you want it for the presentation. Finally, you create a custom format from the chart, which you can apply to the other charts.

To Create a Custom Chart Format

1. **Make sure that the file 1QA Presentation is still open with the `97 vs 96` worksheet displayed.**

2. **Select the chart; then choose Chart, Chart Type.**

   The Chart Type dialog box appears.

3. **Click the Custom Types tab and select User-defined in the Select from area.**

   The Custom Types tab of the Chart Type dialog box opens with the active chart displayed in the Sample box, as shown in Figure 3.6. The User-defined option displays custom chart types that you defined and enables you to add or delete new custom formats. The Built-in option displays Excel's built-in custom chart formats. You are going to create a user-defined custom chart type based on the selected chart.

Figure 3.6
Use the User-Defined option on the Custom Types tab of the Chart Type dialog box to set up the active chart as a custom chart type.

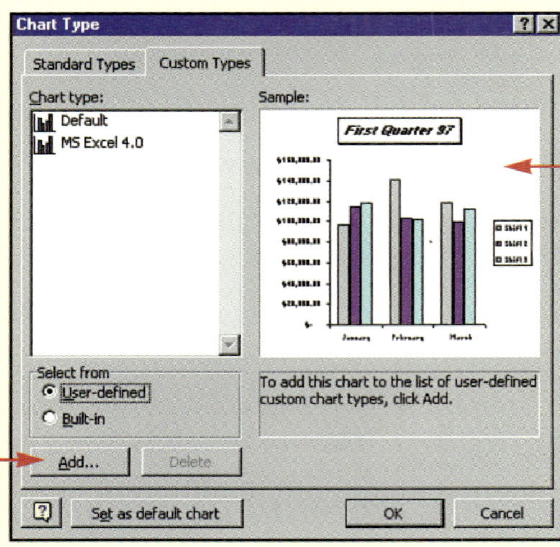

View the active chart here

Click this button to add your active chart as a custom chart type

4. **Choose Add.**

   The Add Custom Chart Type dialog box appears, as shown in Figure 3.7. In this dialog box, you assign a name and description to your custom chart.

5. **In the Name text box, type `Sales 1Q`; then press Tab to move the insertion point to the Description text box.**

   You have named the new chart format `Sales 1Q`.

continues

Excel

To Create a Custom Chart Format (continued)

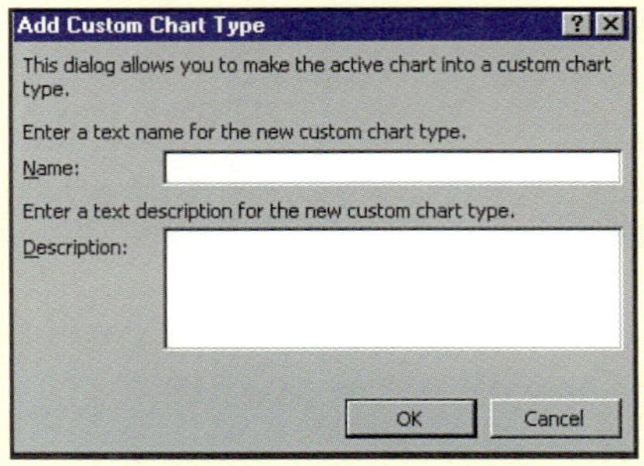

Figure 3.7
Use the Add Custom Chart Type dialog box to enter a name and description for the new custom chart.

6 In the Description text box, type `Column Chart for Sales` **then click OK.**

The Add Custom Chart Type dialog box closes. The new chart type named Sales 1Q appears in the Chart Type list box on the Custom Types tab. Also, the Sample box displays the active chart.

If you have problems...

If an alert box appears with the message `Replace existing user-defined format?`, you can click OK to clear it. The user-defined format was previously created on your computer, and you replace it.

7 Click OK.

The Chart Type dialog box closes. Your new custom chart type is now available for use on other charts.

8 Activate the `96 vs 95` **worksheet.**

Now apply the new format to this worksheet's charts, so all the charts look consistent.

9 Click the chart to the right of the 96 sales data.

The creator of this chart got fancy by using a 3D column chart. While these charts look slick, data can get hidden behind columns. In this chart, some of the Shift 2 and Shift 3 data cannot be seen.

10 With the chart selected, choose Chart, Chart Type.

The Chart Type dialog box appears.

11 On the Custom Types tab, select the User-defined option.

The dialog box displays all the available user-defined chart types. In the Chart type list, you should see your custom type named `Sales 1Q`.

12 Select Sales 1Q and click OK.

The chart type changes to the formatting from Sales 1Q. Unfortunately, the text of the chart title also changes.

13 **Select the chart title by clicking it.**

A border and handles appear around the title.

14 **Place the insertion point after the `7` in `97`, press Backspace to delete the `7`, and type `6`.**

This changes the title from First Quarter 97 to `First Quarter 96`.

15 **Click the chart to the right of the 95 sales data. Choose Chart, Chart Type, click the Custom Types tab, select User-defined, choose Sales 1Q, and click OK.**

16 **Edit the chart title to read `First Quarter 95`.**

Now all the charts are formatted consistently throughout your workbook.

17 **Save the workbook and keep it open for the next lesson.**

Lesson 3: Adding a Trendline to a Chart

In some charts, it is helpful to emphasize how a specific data series is performing. For example, if you want to point out how one shift is performing, you can add a *trendline* to that shift's data series, which clearly shows the shift's performance relative to the other shifts.

Trendline
A line added to a bar, column, area, line, or XY scatter chart to show the overall performance of one data series on the chart.

You can add a trendline to bar, column, area, line, or XY scatter charts. You cannot add a trendline to pie, doughnut, 3D, or radar charts. You add a trendline to a specific data series, not the whole chart. If you remove the series from the chart, you also remove the trendline. If you change the chart type to one that is incompatible with trendlines, the chart's trendline is lost.

You can choose from several types of trendlines. The type of trend you want to show determines the type of trendline you choose. If you are showing the change in sales for a shift, you can use a linear trendline. If you want to show an exponential change in a value, you should use the exponential trendline.

Suppose you want to show how Shift 2 has been performing in relation to the other shifts, and to specifically point out that Shift 2 sales have steadily declined throughout the quarter. This lesson shows you how to add a simple linear trendline to the Shift 2 data series.

To Add a Trendline to a Chart

1. **Activate the** 97 vs 96 **worksheet in the 1QA Presentation file.**
2. **Select the chart to the right of the First Quarter 97 data.**
3. **Click any column in the Shift 2 data series.**

   The Shift 2 series is selected.
4. **Choose Chart, Add Trendline.**

   The Add Trendline dialog box appears, as shown in Figure 3.8.

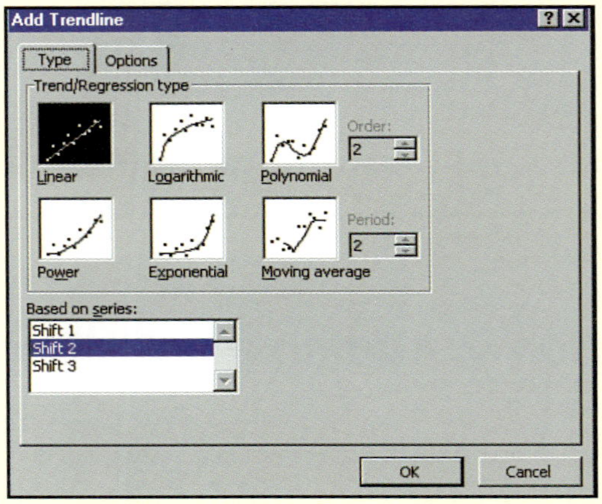

Figure 3.8
Use the Add Trendline dialog box to add a trendline to your chart.

5. **Click the Type tab.**

   This tab shows the various types of trendlines available.
6. **Select Linear and click OK.**

   The dialog box closes and a linear trendline is added to the Shift 2 data series.

   Now place the legend at the bottom of the chart so that the entire plot area can be viewed.
7. **Right-click the legend and choose Format Legend from the shortcut menu.**

   The Format Legend dialog box is displayed.
8. **Click the Placement tab, select Bottom from the Type area, and click OK.**

   The legend is moved to the bottom of the chart and the plot area can be viewed more easily, as shown in Figure 3.9.
9. **Save the workbook and keep it open for the next lesson.**

Figure 3.9
A trendline for Shift 2 has been added to the chart.

The linear trendline

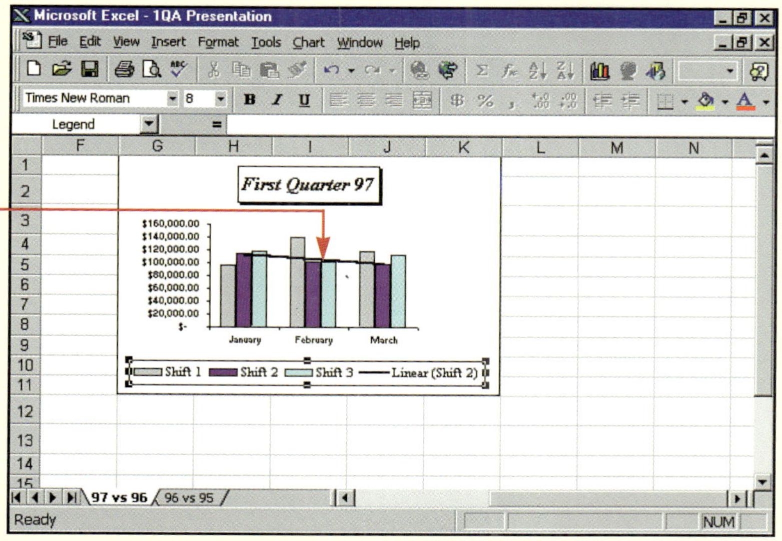

Lesson 4: Adding a Data Table to a Chart

Data table
A table that is aligned to the Category (x) axis of a chart and that shows the numeric data from the source worksheet.

In Project 2, you learned that you can print an embedded chart without its source worksheet. If you would like to show the numeric data from the source worksheet on your chart, you can create a *data table*. The table is placed on the Category (x) axis of the chart, replacing the tick-mark labels. Data tables can be added to area, bar, column, and line charts.

In this lesson, you delete the legend in your chart and create a data table to present the numeric details of each shift's performance from its source worksheet.

To Add a Data Table to a Chart

1. **Activate the** 97 vs 96 **worksheet in the 1QA Presentation file.**
2. **Select the chart to the right of the First Quarter 97 data.**
3. **Click the Legend button on the Chart toolbar.**

The legend is removed from the chart.

4. **Click the Data Table button on the Chart toolbar.**

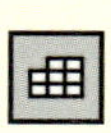

The data table is added in a grid to the chart, aligned with the Category (x) axis, as shown in Figure 3.10.

continues

Excel

To Add a Data Table to a Chart (continued)

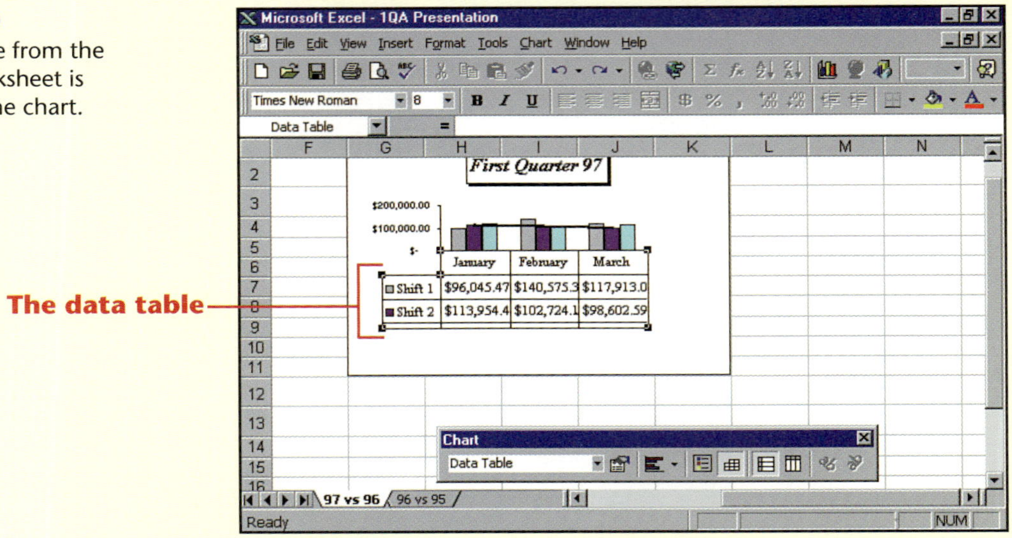

Figure 3.10
A data table from the source worksheet is added to the chart.

5 With the chart selected, click the Print Preview button on the Standard toolbar.

The chart is previewed without the source worksheet. The included data table presents the numeric data from the chart. Even though the entire data table is not visible in the worksheet, it appears when previewed and printed.

6 Close the Preview window.

The First Quarter 97 chart is complete.

7 Save the workbook and keep it open for the next lesson.

Lesson 5: Grouping Charts Together

After you have formatted your charts and have them looking just the way you want, you might want to group them together. With your charts grouped, their spacing and arrangements will not change. Grouping the objects makes multiple items behave as one object. This makes them easier to move and size.

In this lesson, you group the 96 and 95 First Quarter charts together. If you need to move the charts around in the worksheet, they move in unison.

To Group Charts Together

1 Activate the `96 vs 95` worksheet in the 1QA Presentation file.

2 Click the `First Quarter 96` chart; then hold down Shift and click the `First Quarter 95` chart.

Both charts now have handles around them.

3 With both charts selected, right-click the chart area in either of the charts.

4 Choose Grouping, Group from the shortcut menu.

Excel now recognizes the two charts as one object. There are now only 8 handles rather than 16.

5 With the chart group still selected, place your mouse pointer over the chart area of the group and drag the left side of the charts to the middle of column G.

Because the charts have been grouped together, they move as a single object. Now you can further improve the worksheet's appearance by turning off the gridlines.

6 Choose Tools, Options.

The Options dialog box appears.

7 Click the View tab, if necessary, to bring it to the front of the dialog box.

8 In the Window options area, deselect the Gridlines check box; then click OK.

Your worksheet gridlines have been turned off. Now view the completed worksheet.

9 Click the Print Preview button on the Standard toolbar.

Print Preview shows the completed worksheet with its charts, as shown in Figure 3.11.

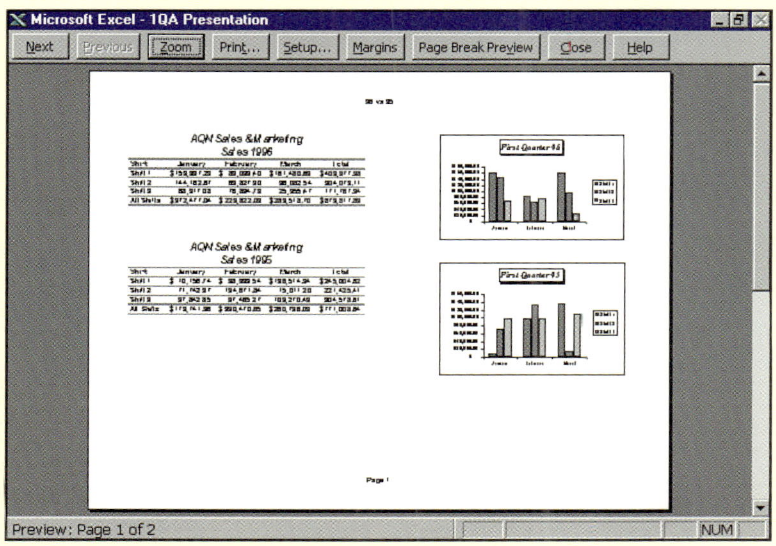

Figure 3.11
The 96 vs 95 worksheet now shows the completed tables and charts.

continues

To Group Charts Together (continued)

10 Click the Close button.

The Print Preview window closes. Save the workbook. If requested by your instructor, print two copies; then close the workbook. If you have completed your session on the computer, exit Excel and Windows 95 before turning off your computer. Otherwise, continue with the "Checking Your Skills" and "Applying Your Skills" sections.

Inside Stuff

You may need to work with a chart individually after it has been grouped. To ungroup a chart, right-click any chart box and choose Grouping, Ungroup from the shortcut menu.

Project Summary

To	Do This
Select a predefined chart format	Select the chart and choose Chart, Chart Type. Choose a Chart type from the list box; then choose the Chart subtype. Click OK.
Modify elements of a chart	Right-click the element to be changed and choose the appropriate command from the shortcut menu.
Create a custom chart	Activate the chart that will be used as the format model. Choose Chart, Chart Type, and click the Custom Types tab. In the Select From area, select User-defined. Click the Add button; the Add Custom Chart Type dialog box appears. Type a new name in the Name text box; then click OK.
Add a trendline to a chart	Click any column in the data series to which you want to add a trendline. Choose Chart, Add Trendline. Choose the type of trendline desired; then click OK.
Add a data table to a chart	Select the chart; then click the Data Table button on the Chart toolbar.
Group charts together	Activate the worksheet containing the charts to be grouped. Click one of the charts; then hold down Shift and click the other charts. Right-click the chart area and choose Grouping, Group from the shortcut menu.

Checking Your Skills

True/False

For each of the following statements, check *T* or *F* to indicate whether the statement is true or false.

__T __F 1. To create a custom chart type from your current chart, you choose Chart, Chart Type, click the Custom Types tab, select User-defined, and then click Add.

__T __F 2. After a chart is created, you cannot change your mind and select a different chart type and subtype.

__T __F 3. To format a chart element, right-click it; then choose the appropriate command from the shortcut menu shown.

__T __F 4. When you delete a data series with a trendline, the trendline is also deleted.

__T __F 5. A data table can be moved around to other locations on the chart.

__T __F 6. Trendlines are always linear.

__T __F 7. You can add a trendline to a bar or pie chart.

__T __F 8. Doughnut is one of the standard chart types.

__T __F 9. You must draw the trendline on the chart.

__T __F 10. You can add data tables to line, bar, and pie charts.

Multiple Choice

Circle the letter of the correct answer for each of the following.

1. What chart element would you add to emphasize how a specific data series is performing in relation to the other data series?

   a. Chart title

   b. Data table

   c. Legend

   d. Trendline

2. What types of trendlines are available?

   a. Exponential

   b. Linear

   c. Both a and b

   d. Neither a nor b

3. What command would be used to choose from a list of predefined Excel chart formats?

   a. Chart, Chart Type

   b. Chart, Chart Options

   c. Format, AutoFormat

   d. Format, Sheet

4. What chart element displays the data from a source worksheet on the Category (x) axis?

   a. Chart title

   b. Data table

   c. Legend

   d. Trendline

5. Which elements can be added to and removed from the chart by using the Chart toolbar?
   a. Chart title
   b. Data table
   c. Legend
   d. Both b and c
6. Which command do you use when you want to size all the charts in a worksheet so they maintain the same spacing and arrangement?
   a. Format, Charts
   b. Tools, Options
   c. Grouping, Group
   d. None of the above
7. To see the chart toolbar, which command do you use?
   a. Chart, Toolbars
   b. View, Toolbars, Chart
   c. None, just click the chart
   d. Tools, Options.
8. What types of predefined chart types are available in Excel?
   a. Standard
   b. Built-in
   c. User-defined
   d. All of the above
9. Chart subtypes are only available for which of the following chart types?
   a. Standard
   b. User-defined
   c. Built-in
   d. Custom
10. When you add a custom chart type, what information do you supply in the Add Custom Chart Type dialog box?
    a. Name, chart type, chart subtype
    b. Name, data series, chart type
    c. Chart title, chart type, data series
    d. Name, description

Completion

In the blank provided, write the correct answer for each of the following statements.

1. To view an embedded chart in its own window, select the chart and then choose _______________.
2. Add a(n) _______________ to your chart to emphasize how a specific data series is performing.
3. You can _______________ charts together so that they will behave as one object.
4. To apply the same format you created as a custom chart type, you choose Chart, Chart Type, click the Custom Types tab, and click _______________ under Select from.
5. To select more than one chart, in order to group them, click the first chart; then _______________ the subsequent charts.

6. To choose a variation of the standard chart type you picked, select a ______________.

7. If you want to add a shadow box to your chart title, right-click the chart title and choose ______________ and then select Shadow on the Patterns tab.

8. To format a chart element, right-click it and choose a formatting command from the shortcut menu, double-click the chart element, or click the ______________ button on the Chart toolbar and select the element before clicking the Format Objects button.

9. In addition to bars and columns, you can create charts that use cones, pyramids, and ______________.

10. To add a data table to an existing chart, select the chart and choose Chart, ______________, click the Data Table tab, and select Show data table. Or, simply click the Data Table button on the Chart toolbar.

Matching

In the blank next to each of the following terms or phrases, write the letter of the corresponding term or phrase. (Note that some letters may be used more than once.)

a. Group
b. trendline
c. data table
d. User-defined custom chart
e. View, Chart Window
f. Standard
g. Tools, Options
h. exponential
i. Placement
j. Built-in

_____ 1. A custom chart type you create
_____ 2. A custom chart type you didn't create
_____ 3. Chart subtypes are displayed for this type of predefined chart
_____ 4. Do this to make more than one chart act as one object
_____ 5. Use this command to turn off worksheet gridlines
_____ 6. To emphasize how a data series is doing in relation to the other data series in the chart, use this
_____ 7. To view an embedded chart in its own window, select the chart and choose this command
_____ 8. Click this tab in the Format Legend dialog box to determine the location of the legend
_____ 9. Shows numeric data from the source worksheet on the chart
_____ 10. If you want to show an exponential change in a value, use this type of trendline

Applying Your Skills

Practice

The following exercises enable you to practice the skills that you have learned in this project. Take a few minutes to work through these exercises now.

Grouping Charts for Sizing and Moving

When you have several charts on a worksheet, it's difficult to change the size of each one and make sure that the size is the same for each one. It's also hard to keep the charts evenly spaced if you move them one at a time. Grouping solves this problem.

To group charts, follow these steps:

1. Open the file Proj0302 from the Project-03 folder on the CD and save it as `Quarterly Metal`.
2. Click the tab marked `Qtrly Summaries`. There are four charts on this worksheet, each one representing a different quarter.
3. Group the charts and size them so each chart is about the same width as the worksheet data for the quarter it represents.
4. Move the charts down the worksheet until the top of the charts starts at row 25.
5. Ungroup the charts.
6. Save the workbook and keep it open for the next exercise. If requested by the instructor, print two copies of the worksheet.

Creating Custom Charts

The owners of the business have decided that they would like to have customized charts to go with their quarterly summaries. You will set these up in the next exercise.

To create custom charts, follow these steps:

1. Click the tab marked `Qtrly Charts`. One of the charts has been set up already. This one is a model for the rest.
2. Make the chart for the First Quarter, 1996 into the model for the custom chart format. Add this chart as a user-defined, custom chart named `Qchart`.
3. Use the Qchart format to finish the other charts. (Hint: Remember to change the chart titles.)
4. Save the workbook and keep it open for the next exercise. If requested by your instructor, print two copies of the worksheet.

Checking Trends

It is hard to tell just how well the company is doing from the charts seen so far. What you need is a trendline.

To create a trendline, follow these steps:

1. Click the tab marked `Trends`.
2. Add a Linear trendline to the chart titled `P&L, 1996` so that the company owners can see how they are doing.
3. For a nice surprise, add a trendline to the chart for zinc.
4. Save the workbook and keep it open for the next exercise.

Adding a Data Table

Suppose you would like to see the data from the source worksheet on the Category (x) axis of the chart. You also might want to print the chart separate from the worksheet and reference the exact numbers for each quarter on the chart.

To add a data table, follow these steps:

1. Make sure that the `Trends` worksheet is active.
2. Select the `P&L, 1996 Tin` chart and add a data table.
3. Preview the chart.
4. To make it easier to move this group of charts around, group them together.
5. Now move the charts so that they are positioned starting in column A.
6. Several of the charts need to be resized to display the labels on the Category axis. They can be resized as a group. Increase the size of the group of charts so that the labels are displayed on the Category axis of all the charts.
7. Preview the worksheet. Change the page setup to landscape orientation. Make sure that the entire worksheet can be printed on one page. Close the Preview window.
8. If requested by your instructor, print two copies of the worksheet. Save the workbook and then close it.

Challenge

The following challenges enable you to use your problem-solving skills. Take time to work through these exercises now.

Formatting a Chart

Open the Proj0303 file from the Project-03 folder on the CD and save it as `Profits`. Activate the 1st Quarter worksheet. Select the chart in row 8. Add `1st Quarter Profits` as the chart title, `Store Locations` as the Category axis title, and `Thousands` as the Value axis title. Change the alignment of the Value axis title to 90 degrees. Change the size of the chart so you can see the elements clearly. If necessary, adjust the size of the text for the Value and Category axis labels.

Creating a Custom Chart Format

Select the chart. Add a User-defined custom chart type based on the selected chart. Call it `Profits`. Apply the Profits custom format to the column charts on the 2nd Quarter, 3rd Quarter, and 4th Quarter worksheets. Change the chart titles for each chart to reflect the quarter it represents.

Adding a Trendline

Activate the 1st Quarter worksheet and select the chart. Add a linear trendline that represents the Philadelphia data series. Change the placement of the legend so it appears along the bottom of the chart.

Adding a Data Table

Activate the 2nd Quarter worksheet and select the chart. Add a data table to the chart and remove the legend.

Grouping Charts

Activate the 4th Quarter worksheet. Select both the column and the pie chart on the worksheet. Group them and size them to make them about two columns wider.

PinPoint Assessment

PinPoint Training

You have completed the project and the associated lessons, as well as the "Checking Your Skills" and "Applying Your Skills" sections. Now use the PinPoint software evaluation mode to assess your comprehension of the specific exam tasks you have just learned. You can also use the PinPoint Trainer Mode and the Show Me tutorials to practice these specific exam tasks.

Project 4
Four

Managing Multiple Worksheets and Workbooks

Organizing Sales Figures and Sharing Information Across Workbooks

In this Project, you learn how to:

Objectives	Required Activities
➤ Edit Multiple Worksheets Simultaneously	
➤ Build and Organize a Multiple-Sheet Workbook	
➤ Move and Copy Worksheets Between Workbooks	
➤ Link Cell Data Across Workbooks	Link Workbooks
➤ Annotate a Worksheet with Comments	Cell Tips
➤ Annotate a Worksheet with Text Boxes	
➤ Preview and Print Workbooks	Preview Workbooks; Print Workbooks
➤ Manage Multiple Workbooks	Use Multiple Workbooks

Excel

Why Would I Do This?

Workbook
An Excel file that contains multiple worksheets. Sometimes called a 3D workbook because it isn't flat, a workbook allows you to see more than one set of data in the same—giving more than one dimension to your data.

Worksheet
One page (or sheet) of your work in an Excel workbook.

In Excel, a file is called a *workbook*. A workbook can contain several worksheets, chart sheets, or macro sheets. You can have just one or as many as 255 different sheets in a workbook. By default, a workbook contains only 3 *worksheets*—you can add as many as 252 new sheets, for a total of 255. Keep in mind, though, that the number of open applications, the contents of the worksheets, and the amount of random access memory in your computer may limit the size of a workbook. When you open a workbook file, its worksheets are immediately accessible. Excel's workbook structure lets you move easily among the different worksheets, move worksheets around, and name each worksheet to make it more identifiable. With all these tools at your disposal, you can easily manage a workbook of any size. You can even add comments to help other users understand the workbook.

In this project, you learn how to activate and edit more than one worksheet at a time, maneuver through multiple worksheets in a workbook, copy or move a worksheet from one workbook to another, and link cell data across workbooks. You also learn how to document your worksheet by adding comments and text boxes.

Lesson 1: Editing Multiple Worksheets Simultaneously

Just as you can select multiple cells in Excel, you can select and work with more than one worksheet at a time. This is very helpful if you need to enter the same data and formatting (for a row of headers, for example) in several worksheets. After you select multiple worksheets, you can type the data in any one of the selected worksheets. As you type, Excel enters the data in the other selected worksheets for you. This enables you to input data and format multiple worksheets at the same time.

You also can use this method to edit data that resides in the same cell in multiple worksheets. When you change the data (or formula, macro, and so on) in one of the worksheets, the edit takes effect in the other sheets too.

This lesson shows you how to select several worksheets and enter data in all of them at the same time.

To Edit Multiple Worksheets Simultaneously

1. **Open the file Proj0401 from the Project-04 folder on the CD and save it as `Sales`.**

   This workbook contains the worksheets you will use for most of this project. Notice that the first worksheet is already named (`First Quarter 97`). You work with some of the other, unnamed worksheets in this lesson.

2 Click the `Sheet3` tab.

Sheet3 is now the active sheet. Select some other sheets now, to make several sheets active.

3 Press and hold down ⇧Shift and click the `Sheet5` tab.

The tabs for `Sheet3`, `Sheet4`, and `Sheet5` are now highlighted and active, as shown in Figure 4.1.

Figure 4.1
Three sheets are active in the workbook.

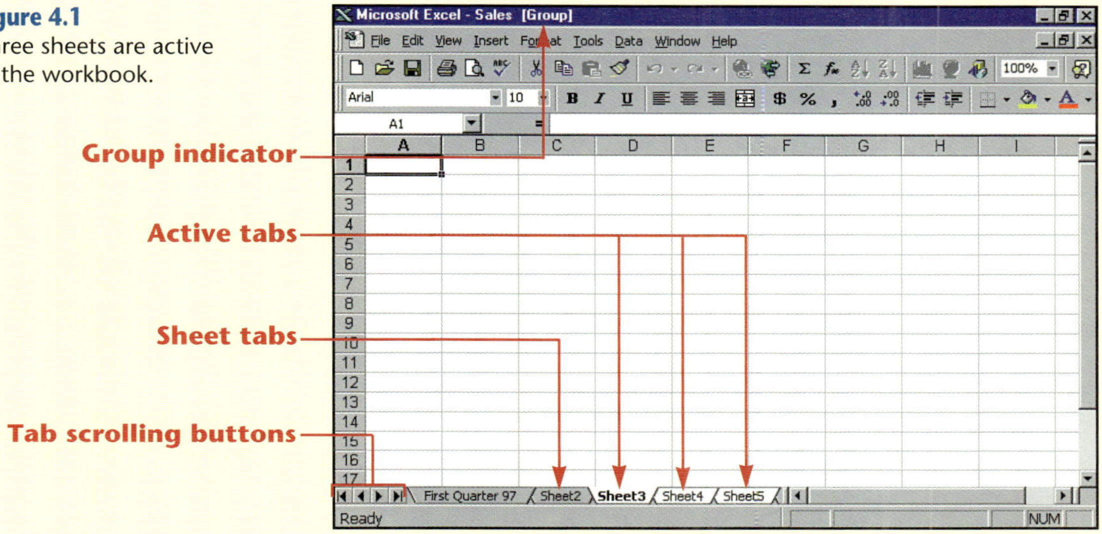

4 On Sheet3 (which should be the topmost active worksheet), select cell A2.

5 Type `1997 Sales Figures` and press ↵Enter.

6 Select cell A2 again and click the Bold button on the Formatting toolbar to make the text bold. Adjust the column width to best fit the data.

7 In cells A4, A5, A6, and A7, enter the following sales figures, respectively: `3200`, `2500`, `4000`, and `3700`.

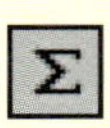

8 Select cell A8 and click the AutoSum button on the Standard toolbar to sum the data in the range A4:A7.

9 Click the Enter button on the formula bar.

The result of the SUM formula appears in cell A8, as shown in Figure 4.2.

continues

To Edit Multiple Worksheets Simultaneously (continued)

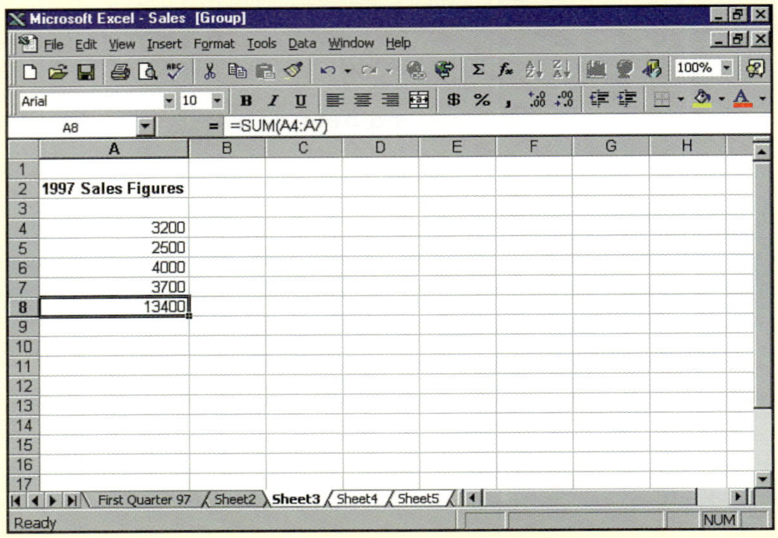

Figure 4.2
The worksheet now includes sales figures and a SUM formula.

⑩ **Select the range A4:A8; then click the Currency Style button on the Formatting toolbar to apply the currency format to the selected values.**

⑪ **Click the** `Sheet4` **tab.**

Sheet4 is displayed. The text, values, and formula in Column A look exactly like the data you typed and formatted in Sheet3.

⑫ **Select** `Sheet5` **and look at the data in Column A.**

The text and formatting appear exactly the same there, too.

⑬ **Click the** `Sheet2` **tab.**

When you select a worksheet that is not part of the group of active worksheets, Excel deactivates the grouping. Sheet2 now becomes the only active sheet.

Now you will add another sales figure to the worksheet.

⑭ **Click the** `Sheet3` **tab. Then press and hold down** Shift **and click the** `Sheet5` **tab to select a group of worksheets.**

⑮ **Select cell A3, type** `2800`**, and press** Enter**. Apply the currency style to cell A3.**

⑯ **Edit the formula in cell A8 to include the value in cell A3, as shown in Figure 4.3.**

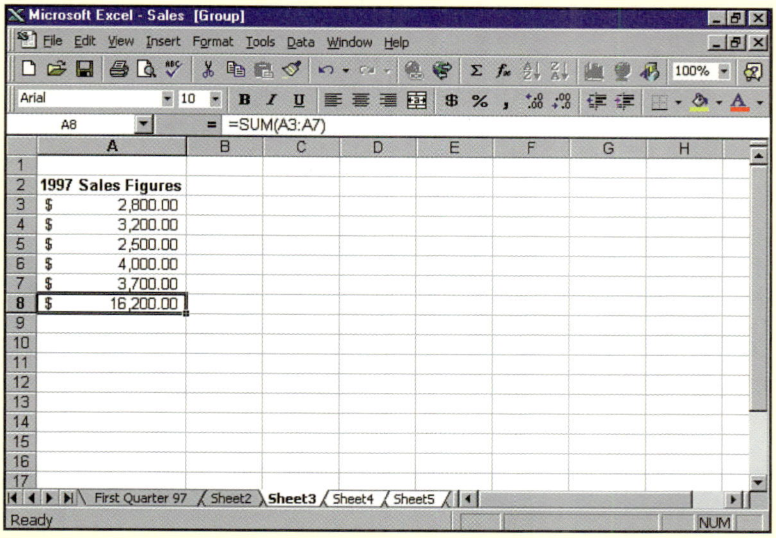

Figure 4.3
The adjusted formula result appears in cell A8.

⑰ **Look at the data in Sheet4 and Sheet5.**

The changes you made are also updated in the other sheets in the group.

⑱ **Save the file and keep it open for the next lesson.**

Inside Stuff

Notice that when you switch to any of the three selected worksheets, the other two remain active. That is because the three worksheets are temporarily considered a "group" by Excel, keeping them all active until you select a worksheet that is not in the group.

Selecting multiple worksheets is as simple as a mouse click. If the worksheets are adjacent to one another, click the first worksheet's tab, press and hold down Shift, and click the last worksheet's tab. Excel highlights all the tabs between the first one and the last one. The word [Group] is displayed in the title bar of the workbook window. This is how you activated multiple worksheets in Lesson 1.

If the sheets are not adjacent, you can select them by clicking the first sheet's tab, pressing and holding down Ctrl, and clicking the other tabs.

Lesson 2: Building and Organizing a Multiple-Sheet Workbook

When you create a workbook, you might know what kind of data it contains, but you might not know how to organize it. For example, suppose you are building a workbook that contains monthly sales information. Perhaps you put each month's data in its own sheet and then summarize the data in a separate sheet. But do you want the summary sheet at the beginning of the workbook or at the end? People have different opinions about this sort of thing. A busy executive might want the summary on top so it is the first thing you see without having to look for it. A business manager, however, might want the details on top.

Fortunately, you can easily rearrange your worksheets if their order is not just right. You can also insert new sheets, delete sheets, and copy sheets in a workbook.

This lesson shows you how to perform all these worksheet manipulations, so you can keep your workbook organized in any manner you like.

To Build and Organize a Multiple-Sheet Workbook

1 Start by deleting a sheet from the `Sales` workbook. Click the `Sheet2` tab.

To delete a sheet from a workbook, you first must activate the sheet.

2 Choose Edit, Delete Sheet.

Excel asks for confirmation to continue, as shown in Figure 4.4.

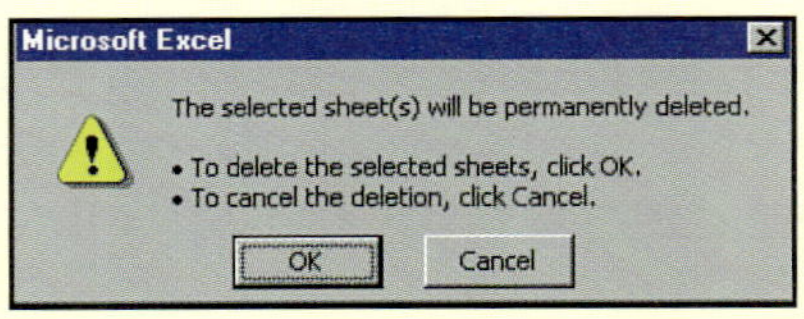

Figure 4.4
This alert box appears when you try to delete an entire worksheet.

3 Click OK to confirm the deletion.

Sheet2 is now deleted, and Sheet3 follows the First Quarter 97 sheet. Sheet2 is gone permanently from this workbook; note that the other sheets do not renumber themselves.

If you have problems...

When deleting a worksheet in Excel, make sure you choose Edit, Delete Sheet. If you choose Edit, Delete by mistake, the Delete dialog box appears, which prompts you to delete one or more rows or columns in the active sheet. The Delete Sheet option deletes the entire worksheet. If you prefer, you can right-click the sheet tab to display the worksheet shortcut menu, and then choose Delete to permanently delete the selected worksheet.

After you delete the worksheet, you can't undo the deletion. You can immediately close the workbook without saving it, and then reopen the workbook as it was before you deleted the sheet. However, you also risk losing other data you might not have saved.

4 Now it is time to start renaming some of the worksheets and making sure they are in the right order. Double-click the `Sheet3` tab.

The sheet name is highlighted, as shown in Figure 4.5.

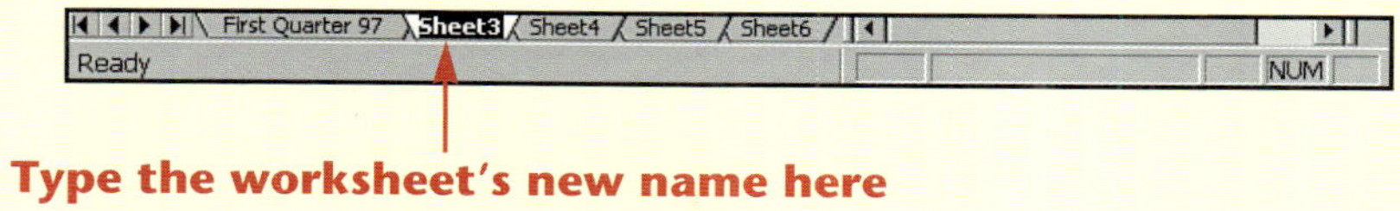

Figure 4.5
With the sheet name highlighted, you can type a different name.

5 With the sheet name highlighted, type `January Sales` and press Enter.

Sheet3 is now named `January Sales`.

Note: To edit a sheet name, double-click the sheet tab to highlight the name. Then click anywhere in the name to position the insertion point, make your corrections, and press the Enter key.

6 Rename Sheet4 and Sheet5 as `February Sales` and `March Sales`, respectively.

Now copy the March Sales sheet to help you create a new sheet for the month of April.

7 While `March Sales` is the active sheet, press Ctrl and click the sheet's tab. Do not release the mouse button.

Your mouse pointer changes to look like a small sheet with a plus sign on it.

8 Drag the pointer until it appears immediately to the right of the March Sales sheet tab, as shown in Figure 4.6.

The pointer displays a small triangle that shows where the sheet is being copied.

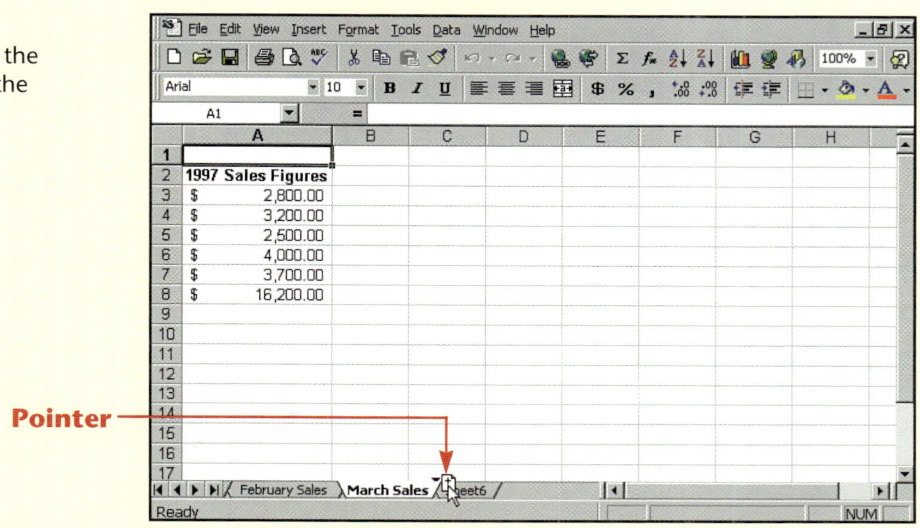

Figure 4.6
Drag the pointer to the desired location of the copied sheet.

continues

To Build and Organize a Multiple-Sheet Workbook (continued)

9 Release the mouse button; then release Ctrl.

The March Sales sheet is copied to the new location, as shown in Figure 4.7. Excel has named the copied sheet `March Sales (2)`.

Figure 4.7
The copy of the worksheet now appears beside the worksheet you copied it from.

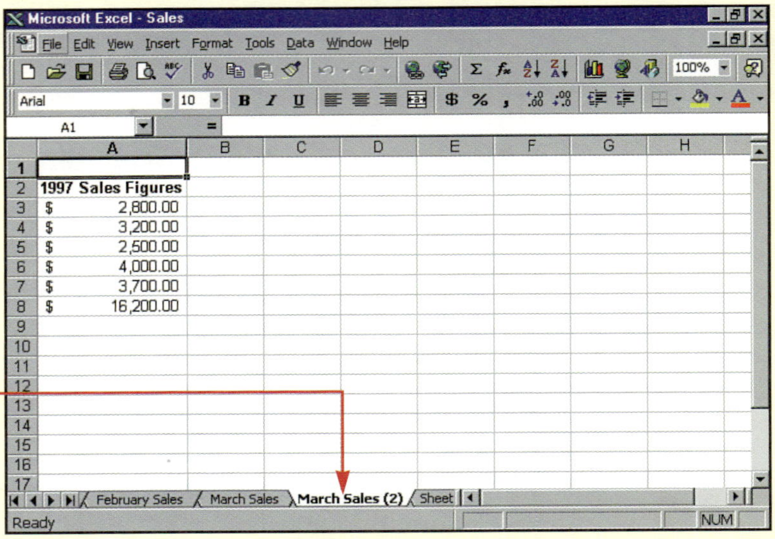

The copied sheet has a new name

10 Double-click the `March Sales (2)` tab, rename it `April Sales`, and press ↵Enter.

Move the First Quarter 97 sheet to follow the March Sales sheet.

11 Click the tab for `First Quarter 97`.

If you have problems...

If the First Quarter 97 tab is not visible onscreen, click the first of the four tab scrolling buttons that appear to the left of the worksheet tabs. This moves you to the first worksheet tab, which, in this example, is the First Quarter 97 tab. Then click the First Quarter 97 tab to make it active.

This activates the First Quarter 97 worksheet. Now move the First Quarter 97 worksheet to a different position in the workbook.

12 Place the mouse pointer on the `First Quarter 97` tab, hold down the left mouse button, and drag the tab to the right. Drop the tab in front of the `April Sales` tab.

The worksheets are rearranged, as shown in Figure 4.8.

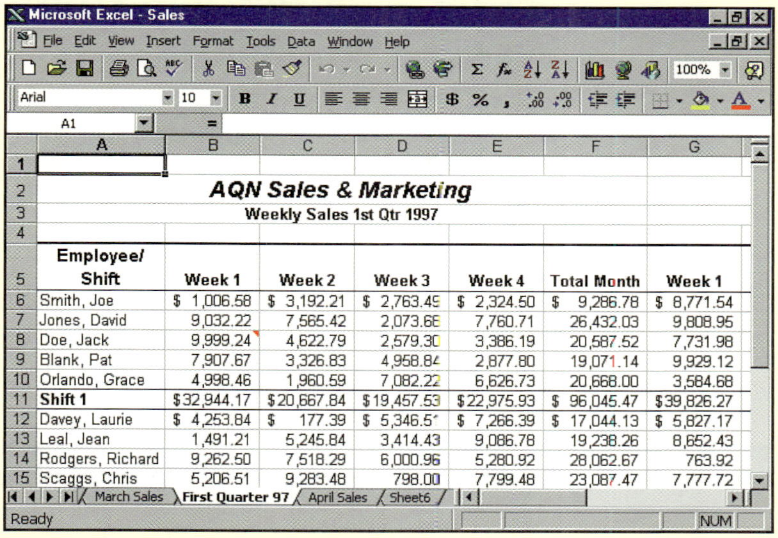

Figure 4.8
The First Quarter 97 sheet now follows the March Sales worksheet.

Now you need to add a new sheet at the beginning of the workbook to summarize sales data for the entire year.

13 **Select the `January Sales` sheet tab. With the January Sales sheet selected, choose Insert, Worksheet.**

You can also right-click the sheet tab to display the shortcut menu; then choose Insert, Worksheet, and click OK. A new sheet with a newly numbered sheet tab, named `Sheet1`, is inserted before the January Sales sheet. Note that the newly inserted sheet might not have the number you would expect it to have. Instead of naming it Sheet7 (using the next number in the current series), Excel starts a new series with Sheet1.

14 **Double-click the new sheet tab, name it `Total Sales 97`, and press ↵Enter.**

15 **Save the workbook, but do not close it.**

Inside Stuff

Note that if you have a group of worksheets selected in a workbook, the Edit, Delete Sheet command will delete all selected sheets—not just the active sheet. Make sure you carefully select only the sheet you want to delete before you choose this command. This is especially important because you cannot undo the Delete Sheet command after you choose it. Of course, you can close the workbook without saving it—this restores the deleted sheet—but you would lose any other changes you made to the workbook since you last saved the file.

Lesson 3: Moving and Copying Worksheets between Workbooks

In Lesson 2, you learned how to move and copy worksheets in the same workbook. But what if you have a worksheet in one workbook and need to have the same information in another workbook? One option is to copy the worksheet from the first workbook to the second. Similarly, one workbook might contain a worksheet that belongs in a completely different workbook (this often happens to users who build multiple related workbooks). You can move that worksheet from the first workbook to the second. In this lesson, you learn how to copy and move worksheets from one workbook to another.

To Move and Copy Worksheets between Workbooks

1. **From the Project-04 folder on the CD, open the file Proj0402 and save it as `Consultant`.**

   Both the `Sales` and `Consultant` workbooks should be open on your computer; `Consultant` is the active workbook.

2. **Activate the `March 97` worksheet.**

3. **Choose Edit, Move or Copy Sheet.**

   If you prefer, right-click the sheet tab and choose Move or Copy from the worksheet shortcut menu. The Move or Copy dialog box opens, as shown in Figure 4.9.

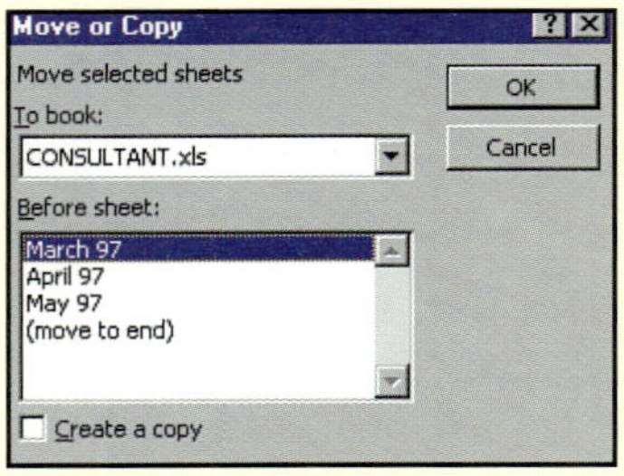

Figure 4.9
The Move or Copy dialog box enables you to move or copy worksheets between different workbooks.

4. **In the To Book list box, click the drop-down arrow.**

   The drop-down list contains the names of the open files and offers to make a new workbook.

5. **Select `Sales.xls`.**

   The Before Sheet list box changes to reflect the worksheets that are contained in `Sales.xls`.

6. **In the Before Sheet list box, choose First Quarter 97.**

   This places a copy of the March 97 worksheet in the `Sales` workbook to the left of the First Quarter 97 sheet.

7. Select the Create a Copy check box, as shown in Figure 14.10.

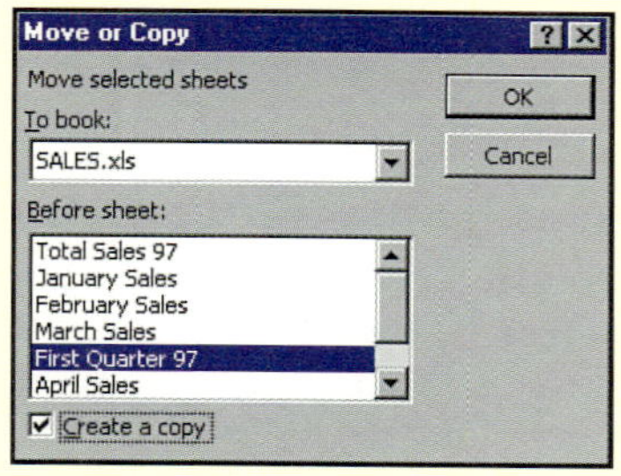

Figure 4.10
The Move or Copy dialog box should now appear as shown.

8. Click OK.

A copy of the March 97 worksheet is now in the Sales workbook. `Sales` becomes the active workbook and appears onscreen. All original formatting in the March 97 worksheet has been retained.

The `Consultant` workbook is still open; it is just hidden behind the `Sales` workbook. Return the `Consultant` workbook to the screen.

9. Choose Window from the menu bar and select the Consultant workbook from the menu.

The `Consultant` workbook is back onscreen. Notice that it still contains the March 97, April 97, and May 97 worksheets. You have simply copied the March 97 worksheet to the Sales workbook.

Now remove a worksheet from `Consultant` and place it in `Sales`. This process is called moving, and differs from copying.

10. Right-click the April 97 sheet tab.

11. Choose Move or Copy from the worksheet shortcut menu.

The Move or Copy dialog box opens.

12. In the To Book text box, click the drop-down arrow.

13. Select `Sales.xls` from the list.

The Before Sheet list box changes to reflect the worksheets listed in `Sales.xls`.

14. In the Before Sheet list box, scroll down and select Sheet6.

This moves the April 97 worksheet to the `Sales.xls` workbook and places it to the left of Sheet6, following the April Sales worksheet.

15. If necessary, deselect the Create a Copy check box (make sure there is no check mark in the box).

continues

To Move and Copy Worksheets between Workbooks (continued)

16 Click OK.

April 97 moves from the `Consultant` workbook to the `Sales` workbook. `Sales` becomes the active workbook and appears onscreen.

17 Choose Window and select Consultant to bring that workbook back to the screen. Notice that the April 97 worksheet no longer exists in it.

18 Save the `Consultant` workbook and close it. Save `Sales` and keep it open for the next lesson.

Excel

Inside Stuff

You can move or copy multiple sheets at one time. Simply group the sheets as you did in Lesson 1. Then, choose Edit, Move or Copy sheet.

Lesson 4: Linking Cell Data Across Workbooks

Do you ever keep track of or accumulate data, such as monthly expenses, in one worksheet and then reuse or recap the data in another worksheet or workbook? If you create a **link** to the data instead of just copying it, you can bring the data from a **source** worksheet directly onto a **target** worksheet. You can also update the target worksheet when changes occur to the linked data in the source worksheet.

In this lesson, you learn how to write a formula in a recap workbook to create a link to data already existing in your `Sales` workbook.

The structure of a formula created in a target worksheet to link cell data in the source worksheet is shown in the following line. The exclamation point (!) separates the workbook name and sheet name from the cell reference.

```
='Path\[WorkbookName]SheetName'!CellRef
```

The following table describes each of the formula's elements:

Table 4.1

Element	Description
Path	(Optional) The disk drive that contains the source workbook
Workbook Name	(Optional) The name of the source workbook, if linking across workbooks
SheetName	(Optional) The name of the source worksheet, if linking across worksheets
CellRef	The cell to be linked

Jargon Watch

Linking data is used to share information in a current worksheet or across worksheets or workbooks. You can link or connect to a cell, a range of cells, a named formula or constant, and one or more sheets. The **source** or original worksheet or workbook contains the data to be linked, while the **target** worksheet or workbook receives the data. The linked data in the target worksheet or workbook is updated when changes are made to the linked data in the source workbook. When the target file is accessed with the source file open, the linked data is updated automatically. If the source file is not open, you are prompted to update the links.

To Link Cell Data Across Workbooks

1. **Open the file Proj0403 from the Project-04 folder on the CD and save it as `Budget`.**

   Both `Sales` and `Budget` should be open on your computer; `Budget` is the active workbook with one worksheet named `1st Quarter`. This worksheet is used to compare Projected and Actual Budget figures for the first quarter of 1997.

2. **Select cell C8.**

   Now write the formula in this cell to link the January total sales data from the `Sales` workbook. Although this linking formula can be typed in, the pointing method for selecting cells is easier and is usually more accurate—eliminating incorrectly typed cell addresses.

3. **Type `=` (the equal sign).**

   The equal sign starts the formula.

4. **Choose Window and select Sales from the menu.**

   The `Sales` workbook is back onscreen. (Since you are linking to a cell in `Sales`, you switch to that workbook, and then select the cell to be linked.)

5. **Activate the First Quarter 97 worksheet. Scroll down the worksheet and click cell F24.**

   A moving border surrounds the cell that represents the total sales for all shifts for the month of January. The formula bar contains the formula being written, as shown in Figure 4.11.

6. **Click the Enter button on the formula bar.**

   The Budget workbook is back onscreen with the linking formula entered into cell C8. The data received from cell F24 of the First Quarter 97 worksheet in the Sales workbook, `$327,551.21`, is displayed in the cell. Now create a second link to the Sales workbook.

7. **Click cell E8 and type `=` (the equal sign).**

8. **Choose Window and select Sales from the menu.**

continues

To Link Cell Data Across Workbooks (continued)

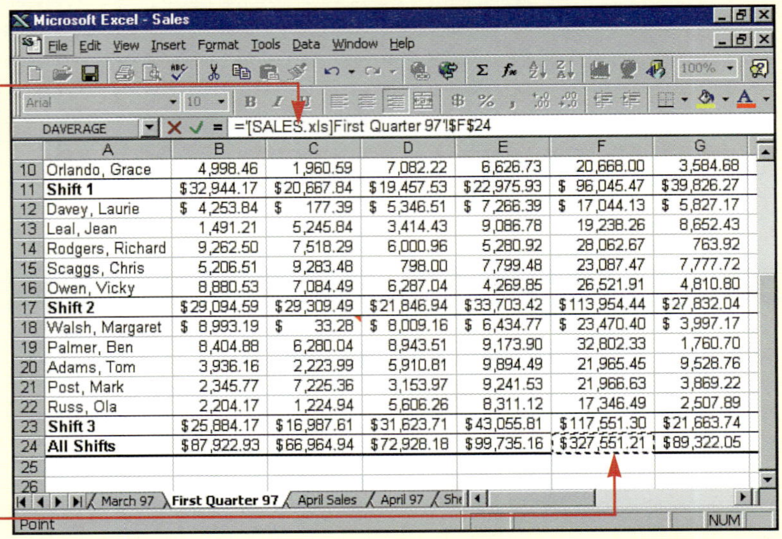

Figure 4.11
The linking formula is displayed in the Formula Bar.

9 **Click cell K24 on the First Quarter 97 worksheet; then click the Enter button on the formula bar.**

The second linking formula is complete and the data successfully received. Now complete the link for March.

10 **Click cell G8 and type = (equal symbol).**

11 **Choose Window and select Sales from the menu.**

12 **Click cell P24 on the First Quarter 97 worksheet; then click the Enter button on the formula bar.**

The three linking formulas are complete, as shown in Figure 4.12.

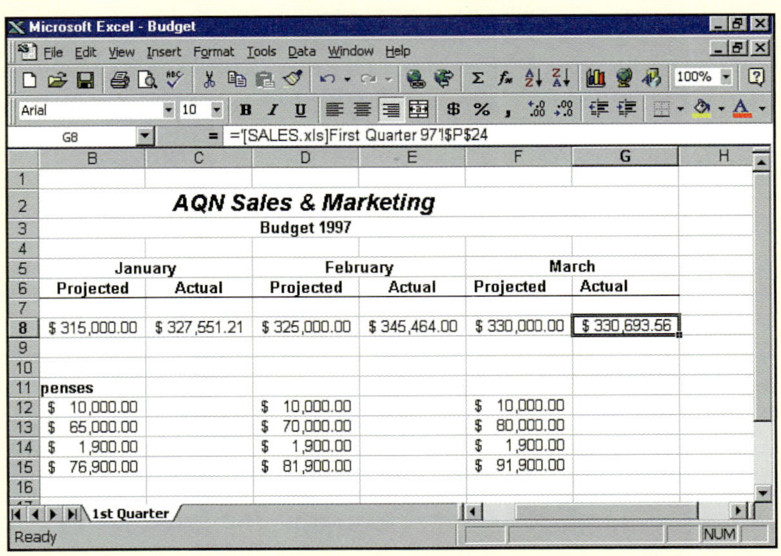

Figure 4.12
The `Budget` workbook contains three formulas linking data from the `Sales` workbook, in cells C8, E8, and G8.

13 **Save the `Budget` and `Sales` workbooks and close them.**

Inside Stuff

When exiting Microsoft Excel with multiple workbooks open, you can close and save them at one time instead of being prompted to save each individual file. With multiple workbooks open, choose File, Exit. You are prompted to save the open files with a Yes button to save files individually or the Yes to All button to save all open files in one step.

Lesson 5: Annotating a Worksheet with Comments

Sometimes, don't you want to stand behind the person reading your worksheets so you can answer questions and explain things? Unfortunately, that is not always possible (and besides, it can be time-consuming). However, you can annotate your worksheets, adding comments that the reader can open to see more information about a cell's contents. A comment can be a description of what a formula does, an explanation of why you put data in a certain spot, an explanation of why certain things might look out-of-line, or anything you think might need further explanation.

Comment
An explanatory note added to the worksheet, sometimes called a "cell tip." A comment is normally hidden from view.

One of the easiest and most efficient ways to document your worksheet is with the comments feature. A *comment* is a note that is directly related to a cell. If a comment has been assigned to a cell, Excel places a red triangle in the upper-right corner of the cell.

In this lesson, you learn how to add comments to a worksheet and how to read a comment that already exists in a worksheet. You also learn how to edit and delete comments.

To Annotate a Worksheet with Comments

1. **Open the** `Sales` **workbook, activate the** `First Quarter 97` **worksheet, and select cell D15.**

2. **Choose Insert, Comment.**

   If you prefer, right-click a cell to display the shortcut menu; then choose Insert Comment. A text box is displayed, noting the name of the individual writing the comment, as shown in Figure 4.13.

3. **In the text box, type** `Chris was on vacation 4 days this week`**.**

4. **Click cell C14 (or any other cell on the worksheet) to close the comment box.**

   The comment text box is hidden. Notice that a red triangle (indicating a comment) appears in the upper-right corner of the cell.

continues

To Annotate a Worksheet with Comments (continued)

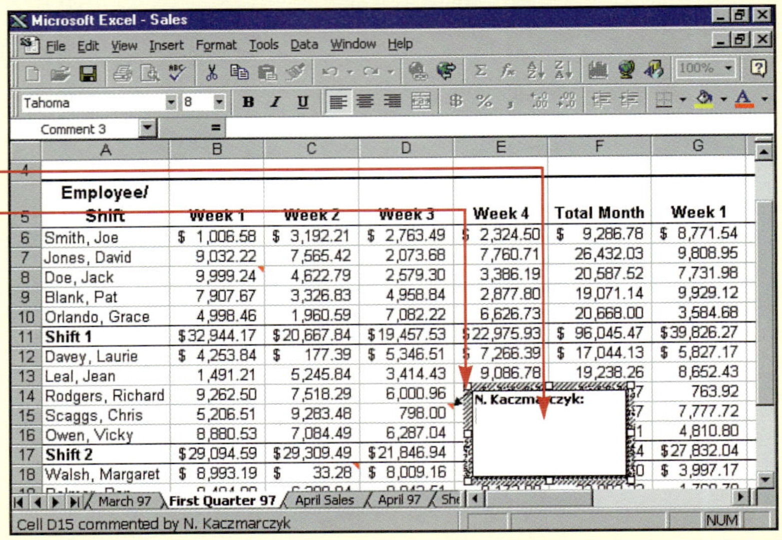

Figure 4.13
The Comments text box is used to attach a comment to a worksheet cell.

If you have problems...

If a comment indicator does not appear in the cell, you might need to turn on the indicators. You turn on comment indicators by choosing Tools, Options. In the Options dialog box, click the View tab. In the Comments section of the View tab, select Comment Indicator Only. Click OK.

If the comment doesn't go away when you click another cell, you should follow the above directions to view only the comment indicator.

5 Place the cross-shaped mouse pointer over cell D15 and pause briefly.

The comment appears to the right of the pointer, as shown in Figure 4.14.

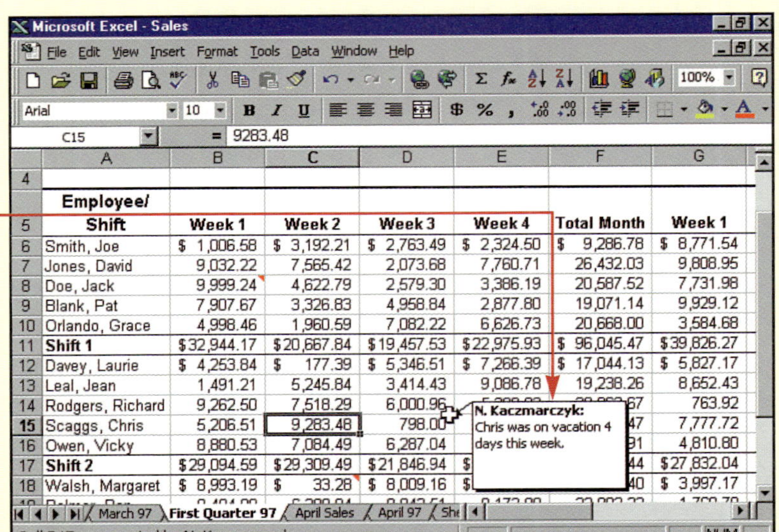

Figure 4.14
To display comment text, just place the mouse pointer over any cell with a comment indicator.

6. **Select cell C18.**

This cell already has a comment attached, stating that Ms. Walsh was on medical leave. Your boss has seen this worksheet and has asked you to change the note from medical leave to time off. Edit the comment to reflect the new information.

7. **Choose Insert, Edit Comment.**

The comment text box opens.

8. **Edit the text (as you would any cell) in the text box. Highlight the text `was on Medical` and type `had time off` in place of it. The comment attached to cell C18 has now been changed, as shown in Figure 4.15.**

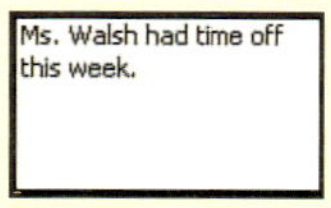

Figure 4.15
The text box displays the modified comment.

9. **Click cell C14 (or any other cell on the worksheet) to close the comment box.**

The comment is hidden from view.

Sometimes comments are no longer relevant to the cell and need to be deleted.

10. **Select cell B8 and read that cell's comment.**

The comment states that this was Jack's highest production ever. When the worksheet was started and the comment was added, this was true; but by the end of the third month, Jack had increased his production. You need to delete the first month's comment.

11. **Choose Edit, Clear, Comments.**

The comment in cell B8 is now deleted; however, you can use the Undo feature if you made a mistake in deleting the comment.

12. **Save the `Sales` workbook and keep it open for the next lesson.**

Inside Stuff

You can select all the cells with comments by choosing Edit, Go To and clicking the Special button. Select Comments and click OK. Use the Tab and Enter keys to move between the selected cells.

You can also print a worksheet's comments. To print comments at the end of the sheet, choose File, Page Setup. When the Page Setup dialog box appears, choose the Sheet tab and click the drop-down arrow next to Comments. Select the At End of Sheet option and click OK. Print your worksheet as normal, and your comments appear at the end of the printout.

To print worksheet comments as displayed on the sheet, you must first display the comments on the worksheet. Right-click a comment cell and choose Show Comment from the shortcut menu. Choose File, Page Setup, and click the Sheet tab. From the Comments drop-down list, choose As Displayed on Sheet; then click OK. Print your worksheet as normal, and your comments appear as displayed on the worksheet.

You can also keep the comments displayed on the worksheet. Choose Tools, Options; then choose Comment & Indicator from the Comments section of the View tab and click OK. If one comment text box overlaps another when displayed, you can move it. Point to a border of the comment text box (the mouse displays a four-headed arrow); then click and drag the text box to a new position.

Lesson 6: Annotating a Worksheet with Text Boxes

Text box
A visible explanatory note added to the worksheet.

In Lesson 5, you documented a worksheet by using comments. Another method for adding notes to cells is with a text box. *Text boxes* are areas of text that sit on top of the worksheet and are very visible. You can create a text box to annotate onscreen presentations or incorporate them in workbooks that you are sharing with other users on a network.

In this lesson, you learn how to add text boxes to your worksheet and how to format them so they attract attention.

Jack Doe has had some successes lately. In week one of the first month of data, he had sales of nearly $10,000. This sales week was noted with a comment. When a salesperson at your company reaches the $10,000 sales mark, he or she gets corporate recognition as well as a bonus. The fourth week of the third month, Jack sold over $10,000. You want to make a note of this so it is visible to all.

Excel

To Annotate a Worksheet with Text Boxes

1 The `First Quarter 97` worksheet of the `Sales` workbook should be open. On the Standard toolbar, click the Drawing button.

This opens and displays the Drawing toolbar. The toolbar may be docked at the bottom of the window or floating on the worksheet window.

2 On the Drawing toolbar, click the Text Box button.

When positioned on the worksheet, your mouse pointer turns into a crosshair, waiting for you to draw the box where the data will go. You can use this tool to draw a box for your text anywhere on the worksheet.

3 Place the mouse pointer in the upper-left corner of cell P2, click the left mouse button, and drag the mouse to the lower-right corner of cell R4. Release the mouse button.

You just created a text box. The insertion point is flashing inside the text box, waiting for text to be typed.

4 In the text box, type `Over $10,000 in Sales in one week`.

Handles
Small squares surrounding a selected object, shape, or graphic. By dragging any one of the handles, you change the size and shape of the selected item.

5 Select cell N1 (or any other cell outside the text box).

This deselects the text box.

6 Click the text box once.

The text box appears with eight squares—called *handles*—around it. The handles show that the object is selected, as shown in Figure 4.16.

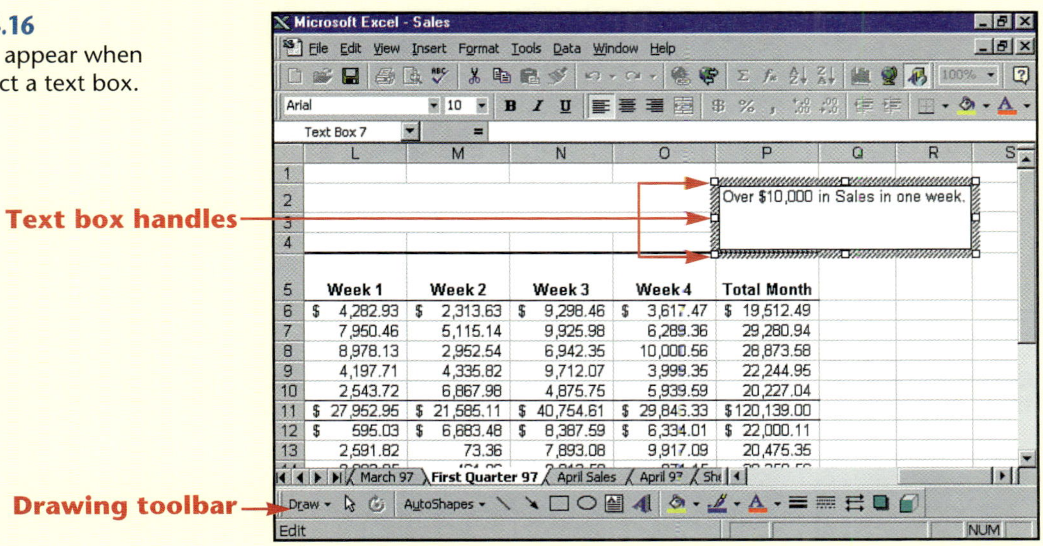

Figure 4.16
Handles appear when you select a text box.

continues

To Annotate a Worksheet with Text Boxes (continued)

The insertion point is flashing in the box, waiting for you to edit the text. You can edit this text the same way as an Excel cell.

7 Place the insertion point between the words `Sales` and `in`. Press ↵Enter.

This allows you to create the next line without waiting for word wrap.

8 Select cell N1 (or any other cell outside the text box).

Selecting a cell on the worksheet deselects the text box.

This text box contains some good news (which is rare for many worksheets), but it is not going to get much attention with its current appearance. Reformat the text box and its text to make it stand out a little more.

9 Select the text box again; then place the mouse pointer on a border of the box and right-click.

This opens the shortcut menu.

10 Select Format Text Box from the shortcut menu.

The Format Text Box dialog box opens, as shown in Figure 4.17. You can use this dialog box to control all your text box attributes.

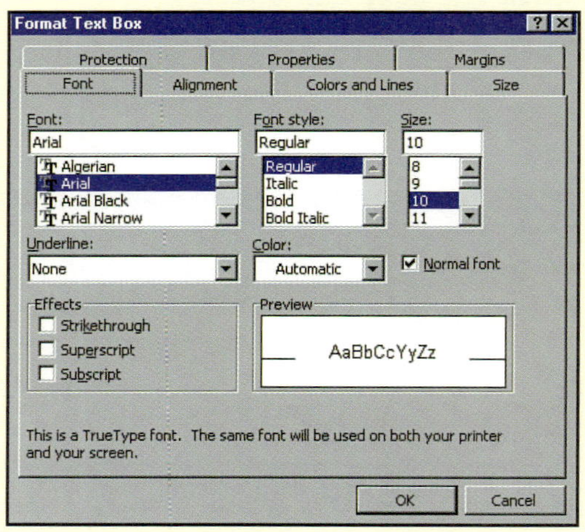

Figure 4.17
The Format Text Box dialog box enables you to enhance the look of your text box.

If you have problems...

Make sure your dialog box looks like the one in Figure 4.17. If it does not, you cannot do all the formatting called for in this lesson. To get the proper Format Text Box dialog box, select a cell outside of the text box; then click the text box once to select it. Place your mouse pointer on a border of the text box (the pointer becomes a four-headed arrow) and click the right mouse button; then choose Format Text Box from the shortcut menu. A different dialog box opens if you right-click the text box in the center.

⑪ **Select the Colors and Lines tab.**

The Colors and Lines tab opens. You use these settings to format the text box itself. (You format the text in a couple of steps.)

⑫ **In the Fill area, click the Color drop-down arrow and choose the Light Yellow color box.**

This fills the text box with the light yellow color, which makes it stand out on the worksheet.

That takes care of the text box itself. Now format the text inside the box.

⑬ **In the Format Text Box dialog box, select the Font tab.**

The Font tab opens, as shown in Figure 4.17, giving you all the text formatting options available when you choose Format, Cells from the menu, and click the Font tab.

⑭ **In the Font list box, select Bookman Old Style. (If that font isn't available, ask your instructor for an appropriate substitution.)**

⑮ **In the Size list box, select 12.**

In the lower-right corner of the dialog box, the Preview box shows you how the font will appear.

Next, change the font alignment.

⑯ **Select the Alignment tab.**

The Alignment tab opens, so you can align the text in the box (see Figure 4.18).

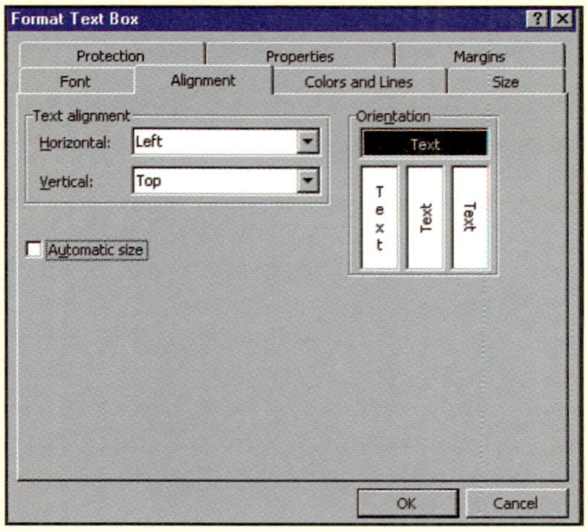

Figure 4.18
Use the Alignment tab of the Format Text Box dialog box to align the text in the text box.

continues

To Annotate a Worksheet with Text Boxes (continued)

17. **In the Text Alignment section, choose Center from the Horizontal drop-down list.**

    This centers the text horizontally in the text box.

18. **Choose Center from the Vertical drop-down list.**

    This centers the text vertically in the text box.

19. **Select the Automatic Size check box.**

    This resizes the text box automatically if you add or delete text. It also resizes the box to better fit the current text.

20. **Click OK. Then click cell N1 (or any other cell in the worksheet) to deselect the text box.**

    The completed text box is displayed. Now add an arrow from the text box to cell O8.

21. **On the Drawing toolbar, select the Arrow button.**

    The pointer changes to a crosshair when the mouse is positioned on the worksheet.

22. **Place the center of the crosshair at the bottom center of the text box. Click and drag down and to the left (to the right center of cell O8), and release the mouse button.**

    An arrow appears, pointing from the text box to cell O8. There should be two handles on the arrow—one at its head and one at the tail end. You can drag the handles to move or resize the arrow.

23. **Select cell N1 (or any other cell in the worksheet) to deselect the arrow.**

    Your worksheet should look like Figure 4.19.

24. **Right-click the Drawing toolbar, then click Drawing to remove the check mark and close the toolbar.**

25. **Save the file but leave it open for the next lesson.**

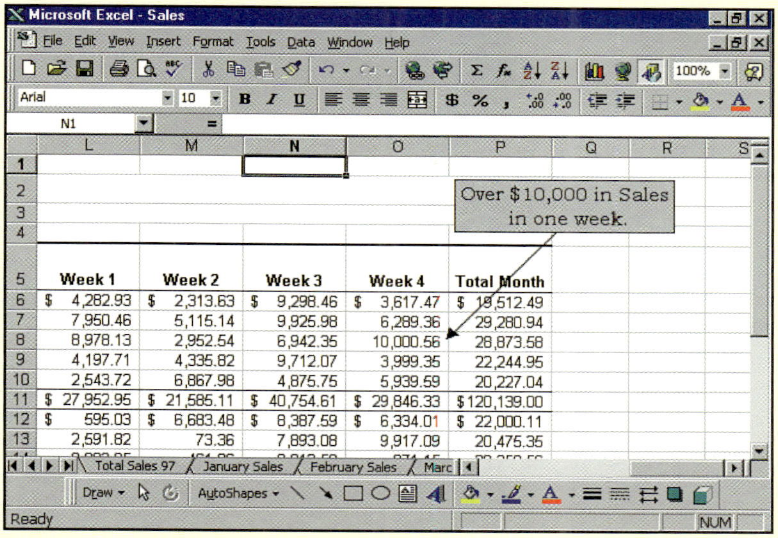

Figure 4.19
The completed text box and arrow.

Inside Stuff

You can manually resize a text box by selecting the text box and placing the mouse pointer over one of the handles. The pointer turns into a double-headed sizing arrow. You resize the box by clicking and dragging the handles, but only in the direction the arrows are pointing. Drag toward the center of the text box to shrink it; drag away from the center to enlarge it.

To get the text box to align itself with the gridlines, press and hold down Alt when you draw or resize the box. You will not see the lines being drawn until you move the mouse more than halfway over the cell; it then moves all the way to the next gridline.

If you select Center in the Vertical drop-down list (on the Alignment tab of the Format Text Box dialog box), make sure you did not press ↵Enter at the end of your text. If you did, Excel includes the new line in the text to be centered and your data might look a little off-center. Go back and edit to delete the extra ↵Enter at the end, and all will center properly.

Lesson 7: Previewing and Printing Workbooks

Printing a workbook doesn't differ that much from printing a single worksheet, except that you can print more than one worksheet at a time. With headers and footers, you can unify the print job and number all the pages consecutively. It is important, however, to control your page breaks so each printed page shows a significant portion of the workbook.

In this lesson, you add headers and footers to the Sales workbook, insert page breaks, and print the Sales workbook.

To Preview and Print a Workbook

1 In the `Sales` **workbook, select the** `Total Sales 97` **tab.**

This worksheet is blank, as is the Sheet6 worksheet. When you print your workbook, you don't want to print these two worksheets. To designate the worksheets you want to print, select them before printing.

2 Click the `January Sales` **worksheet tab. Hold down Ctrl, and then click the** `February Sales`**,** `March Sales`**,** `March 97`**,** `First Quarter 97`**,** `April Sales`**, and** `April 97` **tabs.**

This selects all the worksheets that have data.

3 Choose File, Print.

The Print dialog box appears (see Figure 4.20).

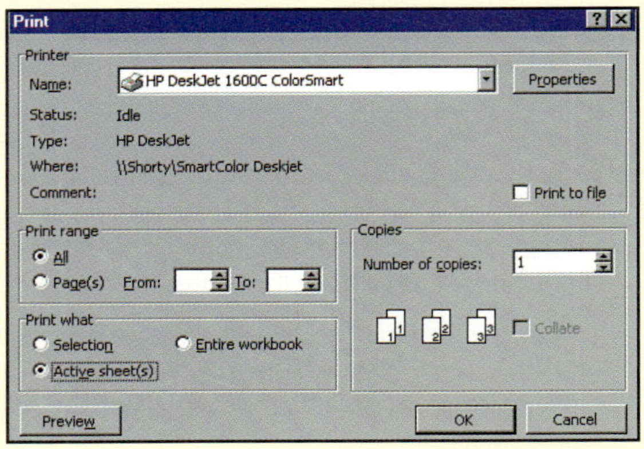

Figure 4.20
Choose to print just the active worksheets or the entire workbook.

4 In the Print what area, select Active sheet(s).

The Active sheet(s) option prints only the worksheets you have selected. To print all the sheets in the workbook, select Entire workbook. Each sheet in the workbook starts on a new page. If you define a print area for a worksheet, Excel prints only the print area for that worksheet.

5 To see how your workbook will print, click the Preview button.

The Print Preview window opens (see Figure 4.21). The mouse pointer looks like a magnifying glass; click on any area of the displayed page to zoom in on the contents. Click again to return to the full-page view. Press PgDn to see the rest of the pages in the workbook.

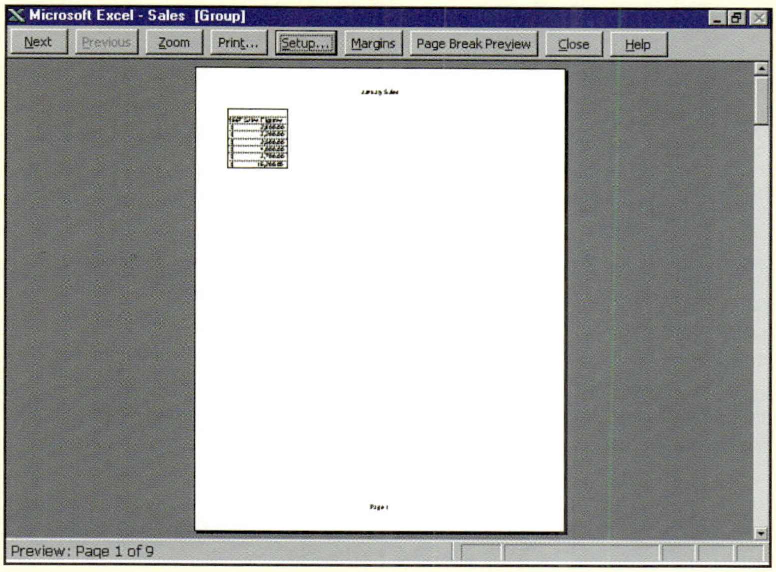

Figure 4.21
The Print Preview window enables you to see how all your worksheets will print.

Notice, as you look at the worksheets, that the default header and footer have been applied and that at least one worksheet is spread over three pages. Your next step is to set up the pages the way you want them printed.

6 Click the Setup button.

The Page Setup dialog box appears (see Figure 4.22).

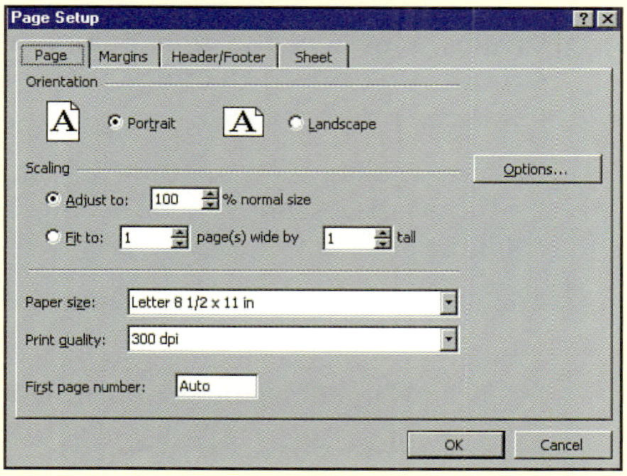

Figure 4.22
Set your page orientation, margins, headers, and footers in the Page Setup dialog box.

7 Click the Page tab and select Landscape under Orientation.

8 Click the Margins tab and change the Left and Right margins to 0.5 inch.

continues

To Preview and Print a Workbook (continued)

9 Click the Header/Footer tab. Click the Custom Header button. Delete any text in any of the text boxes. Click in the Left section box and then click the Filename button (see Figure 4.23). Click in the Right section and then click the Worksheet button. Choose OK.

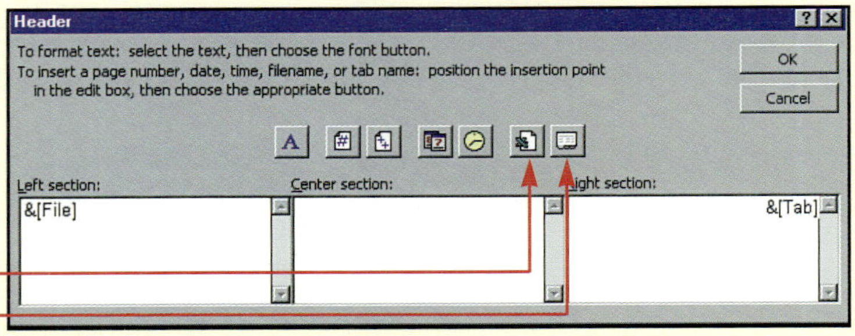

Figure 4.23
The Header dialog box enables you to create a custom header by entering text to appear on the left, center, or right of the header.

The header has `Sales` on the left side of the page and the name of the worksheet on the right side of the page.

10 From the Footer drop-down list, select Page 1 of ?. Choose OK.

As you look through the workbook pages in Print Preview, notice that the header and footer you chose don't appear on all the pages. Some of the worksheets in your workbook may already have a page setup, especially the ones you brought in from another workbook. In that case, you must go to each page and make individual settings.

11 Display page 5 of the workbook in Print Preview. Click Setup. On the Page tab of the Page Setup dialog box, select Landscape. Choose OK.

In Print Preview, you see that the First Quarter 97 worksheet now fits on two pages, but you may want the page to break at a different column.

12 Click the Page Break Preview button.

An alert box appears telling you that you can adjust the page breaks by clicking and dragging them with your mouse.

13 Choose OK to close the dialog box.

Your worksheet appears with the page breaks displayed as dashed lines (see Figure 4.24). To move a single page break, make sure you have selected only the worksheet that the page break is on and then point at the page break until you see a double-headed arrow. Drag the page break line to a new location.

Figure 4.24
In the Page Break Preview view, you see the page breaks as dashed lines.

Page break

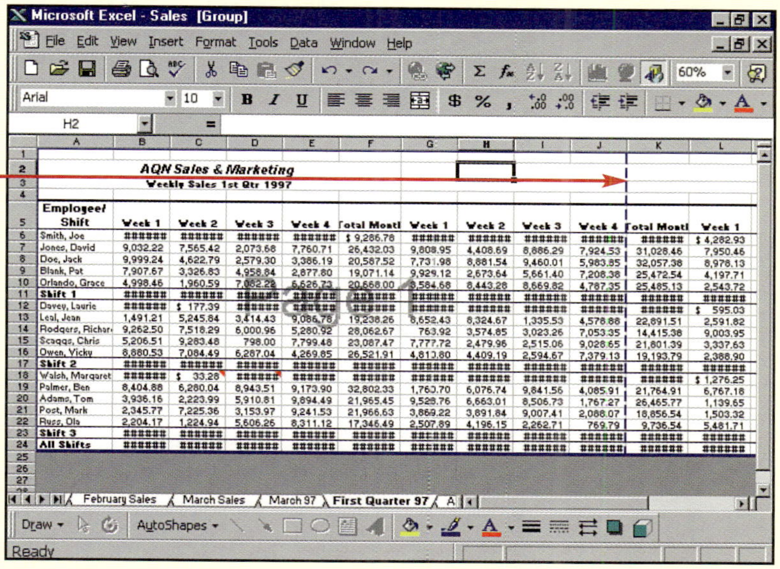

⑭ **Move the page break between Columns J and K and drag it to the right side of Column F.**

Your adjustment makes the page break after the Total Month figures. To make another logical page adjustment, add a page break after Column K.

If you have problems...

You may not be able to move the page break while you have all the worksheets selected. Click on one of the inactive worksheet tabs and then click back on the First Quarter 97 tab. Then move the page break.

⑮ **Click L1. Choose Insert, Page Break.**

When you add a page break, select a cell to the right and below where you want the break to appear (if you get it wrong, you can undo the step). Page breaks you insert appear as solid lines. Automatic page breaks set by Excel are dashed lines.

Inside Stuff

A quick way to insert a page break is to right-click the cell to the right and below where you want the break to appear and choose Insert Page Break.

To delete a page break, drag it off the screen or right-click a cell next to the break and choose Remove Page Break from the shortcut menu.

To return the page breaks to their previous settings, right-click a cell next to one of the breaks and choose Reset All Page Breaks from the shortcut menu.

⑯ **Choose View, Normal to turn off the Page Break Preview view.**

⑰ **Choose File, Print from the menu. Select Entire workbook and choose OK.**

⑱ **Save the `Sales` workbook and close it.**

Lesson 8: Managing Multiple Workbooks

There are several ways to work with multiple workbooks. Excel allows you to open more than one workbook file at a time. To work in a workbook other than the one you have open, do one of the following:

- If the other workbook is open, switch between the open workbooks by choosing Window from the menu and selecting the name of the other workbook.
- If the other workbook is not open, choose File, Open from the menu or click the Open button on the Standard toolbar. Select the file from the dialog box and click Open.
- A recently used file might be listed at the bottom of the file menu, in which case you choose File from the menu and then select the file name.
- A workbook referenced in a link can be opened from the Links dialog box, as you learn in this lesson.

To Work with Multiple Workbooks

1 Open the `Budget` **workbook you worked with earlier in this project.**

In Lesson 4, you learned to link cell data between workbooks. When you open a workbook that has links to other workbooks, Excel asks if you want to update your workbook to include the changes to the referenced workbooks (see Figure 4.25).

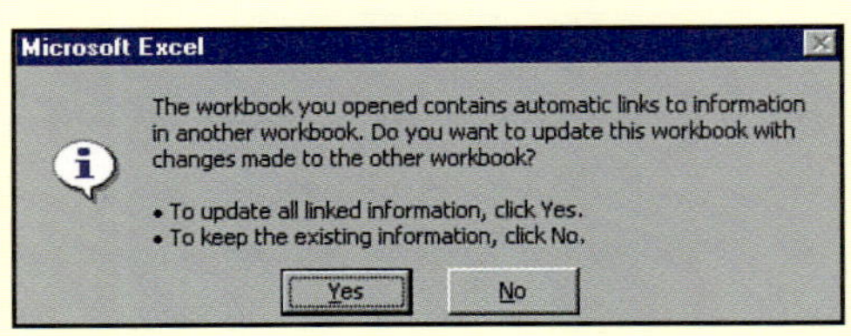

Figure 4.25
When you open a workbook that contains links, Excel asks if you want to update the links.

2 Click Yes to update all the linked information.

To open or switch to the workbook referenced in a link, you need to open the Links dialog box.

3 Choose Edit, Links from the menu.

The Links dialog box opens (see Figure 4.26).

4 Select the `Sales` **workbook from the Source file list. Click the Open Source button.**

The `Sales` workbook opens.

Figure 4.26
The Links dialog box listed all workbooks that are referenced in linking formulas in the current workbook.

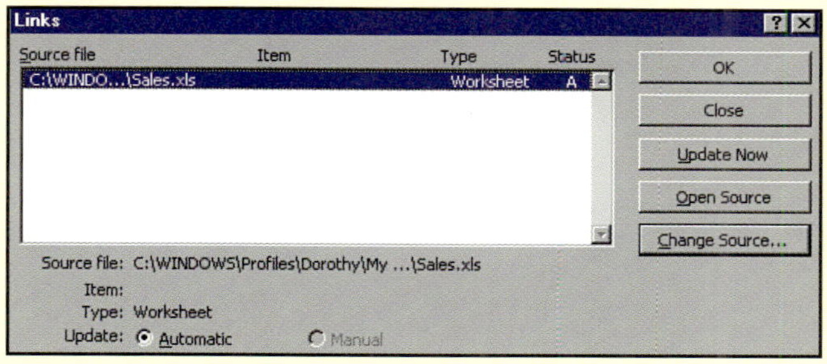

Inside Stuff

If you have moved a source workbook to another folder or drive or you renamed the file, the workbook containing the formula that references that source file will not be able to update the links.

Choose Edit, Links. From the Source file list, select the name of the file for which you need to update the reference. Click the Change Source button. When the Change Links dialog box appears, select the drive, folder, and name of the workbook you want to reference. Choose OK.

5. **Choose Window from the menu and select the `Budget` worksheet.**

   You switch to another open workbook by using the Window menu.

6. **Save and close both workbooks.**

   If you have completed your session on the computer, exit Excel and Windows 95 before turning off your computer. Otherwise, continue with the "Checking Your Skills" and "Applying Your Skills" sections.

Project Summary

To	Do This
Create a group of worksheets that are adjacent to one another	Click the first sheet tab in the group to select it. Hold down Shift and click the last sheet tab to be included in the group.
Create a group of worksheets that are not adjacent to one another	Click the first sheet tab in the group to select it. Hold down Ctrl and click each sheet tab to be included in the group
Delete a worksheet	Select the sheet tab(s) for the sheets you want to delete. Choose Edit, Delete Sheet and click OK.
Rename a worksheet	Double-click the sheet tab you want to rename. Type the new name.
Create a copy of a worksheet in the current workbook	Point to the sheet tab. Hold down Ctrl and drag the sheet tab right or left. Release Ctrl and then the mouse button to create the copy.

continues

To	Do This
Move a worksheet	Point to the sheet tab and drag the tab right or left to a new position; then release the mouse button.
Copy a worksheet to another workbook	Activate the worksheet you want to copy. Choose Edit, Move or Copy Sheet. Choose a current or new workbook from the To Book list. Choose a worksheet from the Before Sheet list. Select the Create a Copy check box and click OK.
Move a worksheet to another workbook	Activate the worksheet you want to move. Choose Edit, Move or Copy Sheet. Choose a current or new workbook from the To Book list. Choose a worksheet from the Before Sheet list. Deselect the Create a Copy check box and click OK.
Create a data link between workbook cells	Open the source and target workbooks. Select the cell in the target workbook to receive the data. Type = (the equal sign). Choose Window and select the source workbook. Click the cell containing the data to be linked. Click the Enter button on the formula bar.
Create a cell comment	Select the cell and choose Insert, Comment. Type the comment and click another cell on the worksheet.
Edit a cell comment	Select the cell and choose Insert, Edit Comment. Correct the comment and click another cell on the worksheet.
Create a text box	On the Drawing toolbar, click the Text Box button. Position the mouse on the worksheet, click the left mouse button, and drag down and across to create the box.
Format a text box	Click the text box to select it. Click the right mouse button on a box border and choose Format Text Box from the shortcut menu. Make selections from the Font, Alignment, and Color and Lines tabs.
Add an arrow object	On the Drawing toolbar, click the Arrow button. Click the worksheet at the position to begin the arrow and drag in the direction the arrow will point. Release the mouse button.
Print a workbook	Choose File, Print. Select Entire workbook (or Active sheet(s) if you selected several worksheets in the workbook). Choose OK.
Preview a workbook	Choose File, Print. Select Entire workbook (or Active sheet(s) if you selected several worksheets in the workbook). Click the Preview button.

To	Do This
Switch to another open workbook	Choose Window and select the name of the workbook.
Open a workbook referenced in the link	Choose Edit, Links. Select the file from the Source file list and click Open Source.
Update link references	Choose Edit, Links. Select the file from the Source file list and click Change Source. Select the new file and choose OK.

Checking Your Skills

True/False

For each of the following statements, check *T* or *F* to indicate whether the statement is true or false.

__T __F **1.** Worksheets can be grouped only if they are adjacent to one another.

__T __F **2.** When a worksheet is copied using Edit, Move or Copy Sheet, the formatting is retained.

__T __F **3.** Once worksheets are created, they cannot be moved to another location in the workbook.

__T __F **4.** Since comments are hidden on the worksheet, they cannot be printed.

__T __F **5.** Worksheet cells can be linked between either worksheets or workbooks.

__T __F **6.** By default, a new workbook has three worksheets.

__T __F **7.** You can enter data in only one worksheet at a time.

__T __F **8.** You can only print one worksheet at a time.

__T __F **9.** If you delete a worksheet, Undo can get it back.

__T __F **10.** A text box disappears when you click on another cell.

Multiple Choice

Circle the letter of the correct answer for each of the following.

1. Which key is used with the mouse to drag a sheet tab and create a copy of it?

a. Shift

b. Ctrl

c. Tab

d. Enter

2. Which command is used to delete a worksheet?

a. Edit, Clear, All

b. Edit, Delete

c. Edit, Delete Sheet

d. Insert, Worksheet

3. To view a hidden comment in a cell,
   a. Select the cell
   b. Point to the cell and pause the mouse
   c. Choose View, Comment
   d. Print the worksheet
4. When a text box is selected, what are the eight squares that are displayed called?
   a. Squares
   b. Markers
   c. Arrows
   d. Handles
5. When linking data cells across workbooks, the workbook containing the original data is called the
   a. Destination
   b. Target
   c. Source
   d. Main
6. When you want to create a group of worksheets that are adjacent to each other, which key do you press when you select the worksheets?
   a. Enter
   b. Shift
   c. Ctrl
   d. Backspace
7. Which key do you press when you want to select worksheets that aren't adjacent to each other?
   a. Enter
   b. Shift
   c. Ctrl
   d. Backspace
8. Which command do you use to move a worksheet to another workbook?
   a. Edit, Cut
   b. Edit, Copy
   c. Edit, Move or Copy Sheet
   d. None of the above
9. When printing all the sheets of a workbook, which option do you choose from the Print dialog box?
   a. All
   b. Pages
   c. Selection
   d. Entire workbook
10. When drawing a text box, what key do you press to have the text box align itself with the worksheet gridlines?
    a. Shift
    b. Ctrl
    c. Alt
    d. Enter

Completion

In the blank provided, write the correct answer for each of the following statements.

1. When you insert a new worksheet in a workbook, the worksheet is placed _______________ the active sheet.

2. To select a group of worksheets that are adjacent, click the first sheet tab in the group; then hold down the ______________ key while clicking the last worksheet in the group.

3. To rename a worksheet, ______________ the sheet tab and type the new name.

4. To delete a comment, select the cell; then choose ________________ from the Edit menu.

5. When an arrow is created, ______________ handles appear for resizing.

6. To switch to another open workbook, choose ______________ and then select the name of the workbook.

7. When you have moved a source file referenced in a formula, you must ______________ the links.

8. To create a formula that draws data from another workbook, type ______________ and then switch to the other workbook and select the cell you want to reference. Then click the Enter button on the formula bar.

9. When you want to change the appearance of a text box, right-click the box and choose ______________ from the shortcut menu.

10. To have the text appear in the middle of a text box, change the horizontal alignment to center and the ______________ to center.

Matching

In the blank next to each of the following terms or phrases, write the letter of the corresponding term or phrase. (Note that some letters may be used more than once.)

- **a.** [Group]
- **b.** Tab scrolling buttons
- **c.** Create a copy
- **d.** Double-click
- **e.** Edit, Move or Copy Sheet
- **f.** Target worksheet
- **g.** Three
- **h.** Page break
- **i.** Text box
- **j.** Comment

_______ 1. Default number of worksheets in a workbook

_______ 2. When you have a large number of worksheets, use these to see more sheets at the bottom of the screen

_______ 3. Command to move a worksheet to another workbook

_______ 4. When you select more than one worksheet, this appears on the title bar

_______ 5. Be sure to check this option if you only want to copy a worksheet

_______ 6. Do this to a worksheet tab to rename it

_______ 7. The worksheet that receives linked data

_______ 8. Cell tip is another name for this

_______ 9. A visible explanatory note added to the worksheet

_______ 10. Drag this to change what parts of a worksheet appear on a page

Applying Your Skills

Practice

The following exercises enable you to practice the skills you have learned in this project. Take a few minutes to work through these exercises now.

Building and Printing a Multiple-Sheet Workbook

Put together a workbook that tracks the expenses of employees who travel. Some techniques you can use to build this application include copying a master Expense Report form so that each employee has his or her own sheet, moving the worksheets around, and adding new worksheets.

To create and print an entire workbook, follow these steps:

1. Open Proj0404 from the Project-04 folder on the CD and save it as `Expense Reports July 14 1997`.
2. Change the name of Sheet1 to `Master`.
3. Copy the Master sheet to three new sheets, inserted in front of Sheet2.
4. Assign each of the new sheets to an employee in the department. Change the name of Master(2) to `Natalie`, Master(3) to `Grover`, and Master(4) to `Pat`.
5. Change the order of the sheets in the workbook so that the employee names appear alphabetically and the Master sheet is the last of the four sheets.
6. Insert a new, blank sheet between Pat and the Master and name it `Weekly Summary`.
7. Select the `Grover`, `Natalie`, and `Pat` worksheets. View the worksheets in Print Preview.
8. Add a header to appear on each sheet that includes the name of the file, the date, and the worksheet name.
9. Print the selected sheets.
10. Save the workbook and close it.

Editing Multiple Worksheets

A company has set up a standard workbook to use for cash flow analysis on various projects. The company is acquired by another firm, and the new firm has allocated a fixed amount of headquarters overhead to be charged against each of the projects. The cash flow analysis worksheets must be changed, effective with the third quarter.

To edit multiple worksheets, follow these steps:

1. Open Proj0405 from the Project-04 folder on the CD and save it as `Project Cash Flow Analysis`.
2. After the row titled Bad Debt Provision, insert a new row into the Master CFA sheet and all four project sheets; title the row `Headquarters Allocation`.
3. Add a charge of $10,000.00 in the third and fourth quarters on all four project sheets, but not on the Master CFA sheet.
4. The Gifts project had some cash flow problems in the third quarter. On the `Gifts` worksheet, enter a comment in cell D15: `Find out why ads weren't cut`.
5. On the same worksheet, put the following note in a red text box located in columns F and G, between rows 17 and 20: `This needs to be controlled!` Draw an arrow from the box to cell D19.
6. Save the workbook and close it.

Moving and Copying Worksheets between Workbooks

A company maintains Automobile Expense Logs as Excel sheets in workbooks. All sheets for autos assigned to a district are kept in one book. The company is growing, and has just created a new district for Fort Worth. The District Manager is being promoted out of the Dallas office. Set up a new workbook for vehicles to be assigned to the Fort Worth district, and move the Expense Log for the District Manager's car to the new workbook.

To move and copy worksheets between workbooks, follow these steps:

1. Open the file Proj0406 from the Project-04 folder on the CD and save it as `Dallas Auto Logs`.
2. Copy the Master sheet to a new workbook. Name the new workbook `Fort Worth Auto Logs`.
3. Move the auto log for Sue Marshall, the new District Manager, to the Fort Worth Auto Logs workbook before the Master sheet.
4. Change the tab on Sue's log in the Fort Worth Auto Logs workbook to reflect her new status as District Manager (DM).
5. Move the Master log in the Fort Worth Auto Logs workbook, positioning it in front of the Sue Marshall (DM) sheet.
6. Save both Auto Logs and keep them open.

Linking Data Cells Across Workbooks

Sue Marshall, the new District Manager, wants to create a recap workbook to keep track of mileage on all the company vehicles. The Dallas Auto Logs and Fort Worth Auto Logs workbooks accumulate expenses on a daily basis. The cells from these workbooks that contain mileage information totals can be linked to the Corporate Vehicle Mileage Report. When mileage data is added to the source auto log workbooks, the target vehicle mileage workbook is updated.

To link data cells across workbooks, follow these steps:

1. Make sure the `Fort Worth Auto Logs` and `Dallas Auto Logs` workbooks are open. Make the `Fort Worth Auto Logs` workbook the active workbook.
2. Open the file Proj0407 from the Project-04 folder on the CD and save it as `Company Vehicles`.
3. Select cell C5 in the Company Vehicles workbook. Create a formula to link the cell in the Mike Jones (DM) worksheet of the Dallas Auto Logs workbook that totals the miles for April in Column C.
4. Select cell C6 in the Company Vehicles workbook. Create a formula to link the cell in the Pool Car worksheet of the Dallas Auto Logs workbook that totals the miles for April in Column C.
5. Select cell C8 in the Company Vehicles workbook. Create a formula to link the cell in the Sue Marshall (DM) worksheet of the Fort Worth Auto Logs workbook that totals the miles for April in Column C.
6. Make the Fort Worth Auto Logs workbook the active workbook. Select the Sue Marshall (DM) worksheet. Fill in the following data in cells A9, B9, C9, D9, E9 and F9, respectively: `4/5/97`, `Waco`, `170.6`, `$5.10`, `$0.00`, `$0.00`.
7. Make the Company Vehicles workbook the active workbook. Select cell C8. The data is updated from the source workbook (Fort Worth Auto Logs).
8. Save and close the three open workbooks.

Using Multiple Workbooks

When you have a workbook that contains links to other workbooks, you can open the linked workbooks from your current workbook.

To use multiple workbooks, follow these steps:

1. Open the `Company Vehicles` workbook. If asked, choose to update all linked information.
2. Open the source files of the linked information (Dallas Auto Logs and Fort Worth Auto Logs).

3. Switch to the `Dallas Auto Logs` workbook and make `Mike Jones (DM)` the active worksheet. Fill in the following data in cells A9, B9, C9, D9, E9, and F9, respectively: `4/6/97`, `Abilene`, `257.8`, `$7.35`, `$0.00`, `$0.00`.

4. Switch to the `Company Vehicles` workbook. Note that cell C5 has been updated from the source workbook.

5. Exit Excel and save the three open workbooks in one step.

Challenge

The following challenges enable you to use your problem-solving skills. Take time to work through these exercises now.

Edit Multiple Worksheets Simultaneously

From the Project-04 folder on the CD, open Proj0408 and save it as `1998 Sales`. Select all the worksheets in the workbook. On the 1st Quarter worksheet, click G4 and type `1997`. Type `20000` in G5, `21505` in G6, `22543` in G7, and `19876` in G8. Click G4 and then make it centered and boldface. Apply the Currency Style to G5, but eliminate the decimal places. Apply the Comma Style to G6 through G8, but eliminate the decimal places. Click on the `4th Quarter` worksheet tab to deselect the group. Save the file.

Organizing the Workbook

Rearrange the worksheets in the 1998 Sales workbook so that the 4th Quarter worksheet appears first, followed by the 3rd Quarter, 2nd Quarter, and then 1st Quarter. Save the file.

Copying Worksheets Between Workbooks

Open a new workbook and save it as `Final Quarter`. Copy the 4th Quarter worksheet from 1998 Sales to the new workbook, placing it before Sheet 1. Then delete the remaining worksheets from that workbook file. Save the Final Quarter workbook. Switch to the 1998 Sales workbook.

Linking Cell Data Between Workbooks

In the `1998 Sales` workbook, click F5. Type `=`, click cell E5, type `+`, switch to the `1st Quarter` worksheet, and then click F5. Click the Enter button on the formula bar. Copy that formula down to F6 through F8. Switch to the 3rd Quarter worksheet. To calculate the YTD figure for Philadelphia, add the Total figure for the current quarter (E5) to the YTD of the previous quarter (F5 on the 2nd Quarter sheet). After you create that formula, copy to the other cities for that quarter. Then repeat the procedure to get the figures for the YTD of the 4th Quarter.

Switch to the Final Quarter workbook. Click F5. Create a formula that brings in the YTD figure from the 4th Quarter worksheet of the 1998 Sales workbook. You won't be able to copy the formula to F6 through F8, so you'll have to create separate formulas for each city. Save and close the Final Quarter workbook.

Annotating a Workbook

In the 3rd Quarter worksheet of the 1998 Sales workbook, create a text box in F10 through G12. Enter the text `Sales have exceeded totals for last year!` Make the text bold and center it in the box both vertically and horizontally. Make the fill color of the box yellow.

In the 4th Quarter worksheet, click G8 and enter the following as a comment: `This was the startup year for this store`. Save the file. Print the entire workbook. Then close the workbook.

PinPoint Assessment

PinPoint Training

You have completed the project and the associated lessons, as well as the "Checking Your Skills" and "Applying Your Skills" sections. Now use the PinPoint software evaluation mode to assess your comprehension of the specific exam tasks you have just learned. You can also use the PinPoint Trainer Mode and the Show Me tutorials to practice these specific exam tasks.

Project 5

Five

Personalizing the Excel Workspace

Working with Workspace Settings

In this Project, you learn how to:

Objectives

- ➤ Change Excel's Default Settings
- ➤ View and Move Toolbars
- ➤ Customize a Toolbar
- ➤ Create a New Toolbar
- ➤ Add Menus to Toolbars and Buttons to Menus
- ➤ Zoom In and Out on a Worksheet
- ➤ Split and Freeze Window Panes
- ➤ Arrange Multiple Windows
- ➤ Use Summary Information

Excel

Why Would I Do This?

You are already familiar with the richness of Excel's working environment. The array of tools is amazing, but can also be confusing. You might also find that Excel's *default* tools and settings do not meet your day-to-day needs, or that you spend a lot of time opening menus to reach the same tools.

Default
The setup a program such as Excel uses unless you specify a different setting.

If that is the case, you need to optimize your workspace so that the information and tools you most commonly need are always readily available. In this project, you learn how to customize Excel so it best suits your personal work habits and preferences. You learn how to customize toolbars so you can remove the tools you do not use and add the ones you do. You become acquainted with Excel's window controls so you can arrange multiple windows and split your window into panes to show different views of your worksheet. You also learn how to attach summary information to your files to make your workbooks easier to categorize.

Lesson 1: Changing Excel's Default Settings

Many companies or departments set standards for their documents. These standards might dictate what fonts you should use or where your data should be stored. The president of AQN, a fictional company, has decided to implement some company-wide standards. To make correspondence look uniform from all departments, he has decided that all documents (including spreadsheets) will be formatted in 11-point Times New Roman. The president also has asked the staff to set up standard directories on all machines so anyone can go to any machine and find needed data.

In the meantime, you have set some of your own standards. When you open a new workbook, for example, you feel that a new workbook should have five worksheets instead of just three (even though some of your coworkers feel that three worksheets are sufficient for their needs). Excel provides tools that let you control all these settings; this lesson shows you how to use them.

To Change Excel's Default Settings

1. **Make sure that Excel is running and a new, blank workbook is open.**

2. **Choose Tools, Options. Click the General tab to bring it to the front of the dialog box.**

   The Options dialog box appears, as shown in Figure 5.1.

Figure 5.1
The General tab of the Options dialog box enables you to change settings such as the number of sheets in a workbook and the default font.

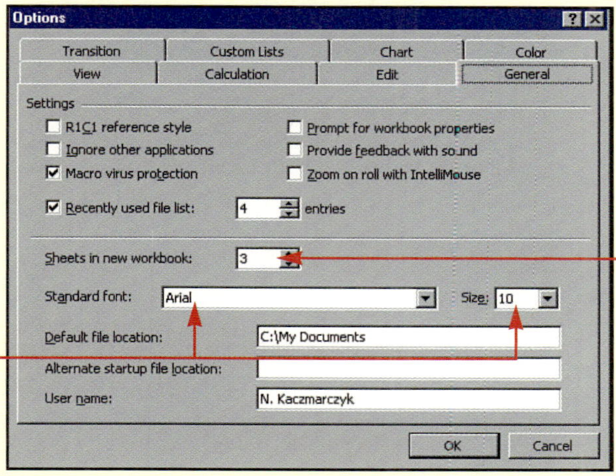

Start by increasing the number of worksheets Excel provides when you open a new workbook. Three worksheets are not enough for you, so increase the number to five.

3 In the Sheets in new workbook box, click the up arrow until the number 5 appears in the box.

Now when you open a new workbook, it will contain five worksheets. (If you need more than five worksheets in an individual workbook, you can use the Insert, Worksheet command. If you prefer, you can right-click the sheet tab, choose Insert from the shortcut menu, and then double-click the Worksheet icon in the General tab of the Insert dialog box.)

Now change the default font for your worksheets. By default, Excel uses 10-point Arial. (You might find, however, that your machine has a different default font.)

4 In the Standard font list box, click the down arrow.

A drop-down list appears, listing all the fonts available on your system.

5 Scroll through the list until you find Times New Roman and select it.

Times New Roman replaces Arial in the list box and becomes the new default font. Now make sure that the new font is set to the correct size.

6 In the Size list box, set the font size to 11 points (if it is not set that way already).

7 Click OK.

A warning box indicates that your changes to the standard font will not take effect until you exit Excel and open it again, as shown in Figure 5.2.

continues

To Change Excel's Default Settings (continued)

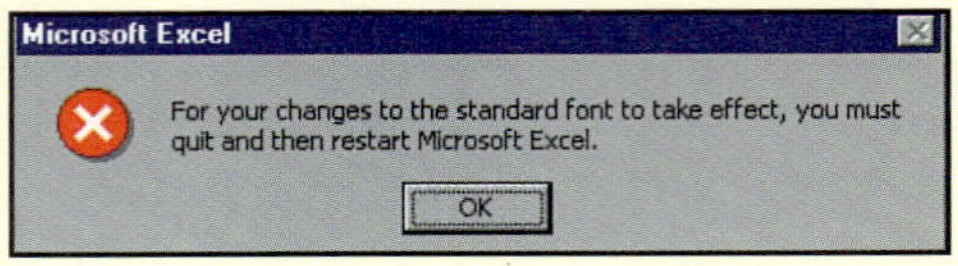

Figure 5.2
If you change the default font, a warning box appears.

8. **Click OK.**

   The warning box closes.

9. **If the Office Assistant appears with a Help message, read the tip regarding font changes for the current workbook only and click Close.**

10. **Exit Excel.**

11. **Open Excel again.**

    Your changes have now taken effect. Workbooks you used and saved prior to changing the default settings are not affected by these changes, however.

    Keep Excel and the blank workbook open for the next lesson.

Lesson 2: Viewing and Moving Toolbars

Docking a toolbar
Moving the toolbar so that it is attached to an edge of the program window.

Floating toolbar
When a toolbar is not attached to an edge of the program window, it appears to float on top of the worksheet and can be resized.

If you worked with Excel in the past, you probably noticed that a toolbar opens or closes when you take certain actions. For example, when you use the Chart Wizard to create a chart, the Chart toolbar opens. When you deselect the chart, the toolbar closes. This automatic opening and closing of toolbars makes things convenient, but what if you need a toolbar that is not open at the current time? You can easily open and close toolbars by using the shortcut menu or the View, Toolbars command. When a toolbar appears onscreen, you can move it to any edge of the screen (this is called *docking* the toolbar). You also can make the toolbar *float* on top of the worksheet. In this lesson, you learn how to display and move toolbars.

To View and Move Toolbars

1. **With a blank workbook open after completing Lesson 1, right-click anywhere within a displayed toolbar.**

   The shortcut menu appears, as shown in Figure 5.3. Notice that Standard and Formatting have check marks next to them. The check marks indicate that those toolbars are selected and currently appear onscreen.

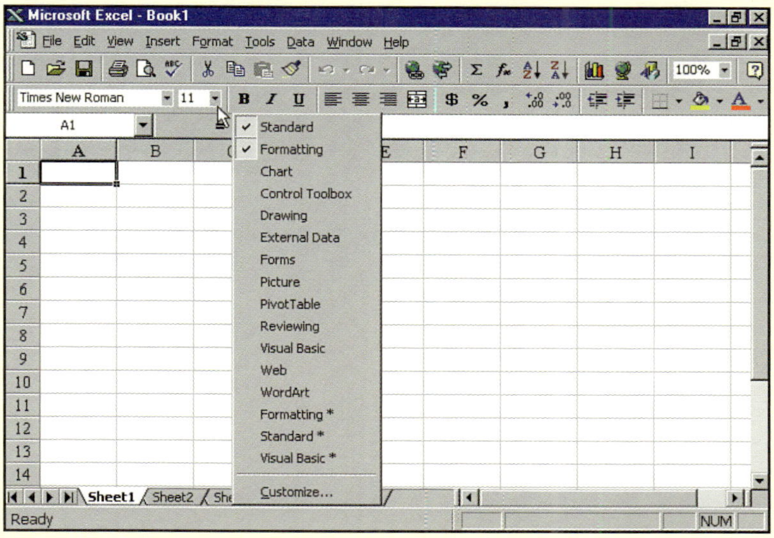

Figure 5.3
The shortcut menu appears when you right-click any toolbar onscreen.

2 Click Formatting in the shortcut menu to remove its check mark.

The shortcut menu disappears and the Formatting toolbar closes.

3 Choose View, Toolbars.

The menu appears. Notice that the Formatting toolbar is not selected. This is because you turned it off from the shortcut menu in the previous step. Now turn the Formatting toolbar back on so it is displayed onscreen.

4 Click the word Formatting in the toolbar list to display the toolbar.

The menu disappears from the screen, and the Formatting toolbar again becomes visible.

Next, you want to move the Formatting toolbar so that it floats in the middle of the screen.

5 Click the move handle at the left edge of the Formatting toolbar. Hold down the mouse button and drag the toolbar to the worksheet area.

6 Release the mouse button.

Your toolbar may appear as two rows of icons if it was previously resized. You can also double-click the move handle to float the toolbar. The Formatting toolbar now appears on top of the worksheet, as shown in Figure 5.4.

continues

To View and Move Toolbars (continued)

Figure 5.4
The Formatting toolbar is now a floating toolbar.

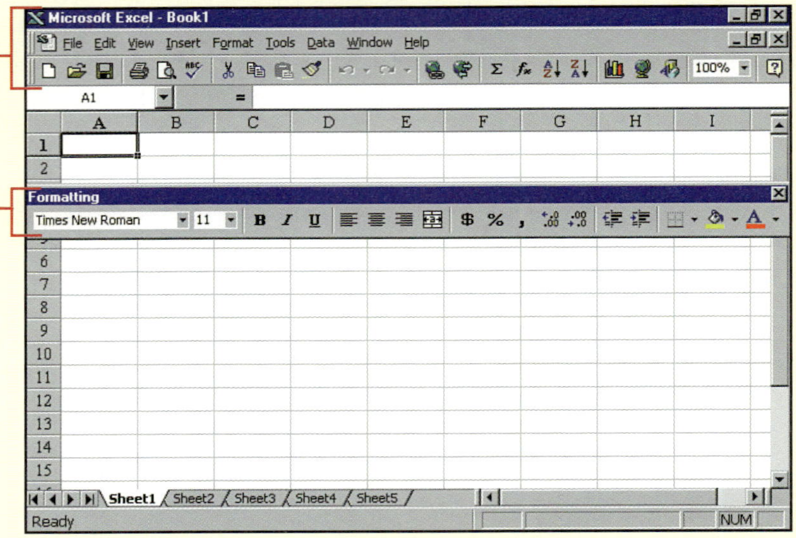

You can drag the title bar of a floating toolbar to move the toolbar around the screen or "dock" the toolbar at an edge of the screen. You can also drag any toolbar border to resize a floating toolbar.

7 Drag the title bar of the floating Formatting toolbar down to the bottom of the worksheet below the sheet tabs and release the mouse button.

The Formatting toolbar is docked at the bottom of the screen, as shown in Figure 5.5.

Figure 5.5
You can move toolbars to display them at any edge of the screen.

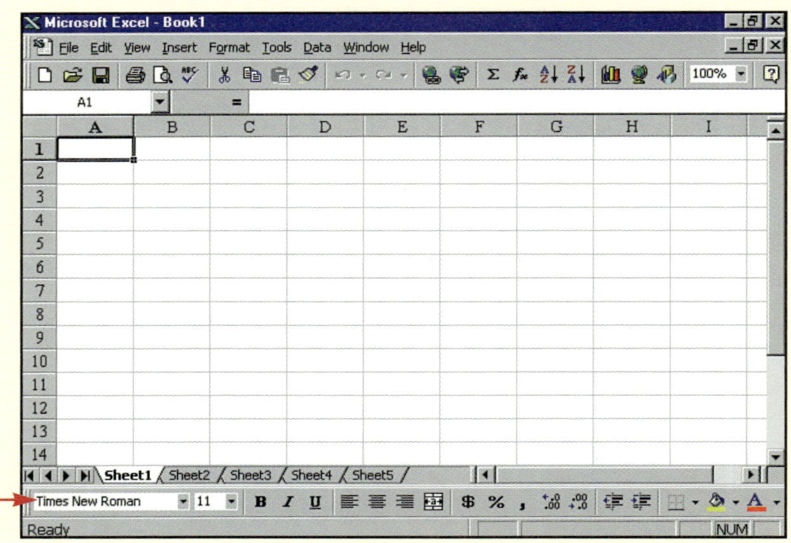

If you have problems...

If the toolbar does not dock into position, make sure that the toolbar border changes from a thick line to a thin, dotted line as you are dragging it and before you release the mouse button at any edge of the window.

Now move the Formatting toolbar back to its original position near the top of the screen, just below the Standard toolbar.

8. **Click the move handle of the Formatting toolbar (next to the Font box). Hold down the mouse button and drag the toolbar to the top of the screen below the Standard toolbar.**

9. **Release the mouse button.**

   The Formatting toolbar drops into place, in its original position.

   Keep the blank workbook open for the next lesson.

Inside Stuff

To float a toolbar on top of the worksheet, double-click its move handle. To return a floating toolbar to its previous docked position, double-click its title bar.

Lesson 3: Customizing a Toolbar

Now that you know how to turn toolbars on and off and move them, take a look at ways to customize them. You can customize Excel's toolbars by adding, removing, or repositioning toolbar buttons. In this lesson, you add a toolbar button to an existing toolbar, move the button to a different location, and remove it from the toolbar.

To Customize a Toolbar

1. **Right-click anywhere within a displayed toolbar.**

   The shortcut menu appears.

2. **Click Customize in the shortcut menu.**

   The Customize dialog box appears, as shown in Figure 5.6. There are three tabs in this dialog box. You can show and hide toolbars from the Toolbars tab and add command buttons to toolbars from the Commands tab. The Options tab lets you control button size, show ScreenTips, or include menu animations to change the way your menus are displayed when you choose a command. Changes made on the Options tab are reflected in all Office applications.

continues

To Customize a Toolbar (continued)

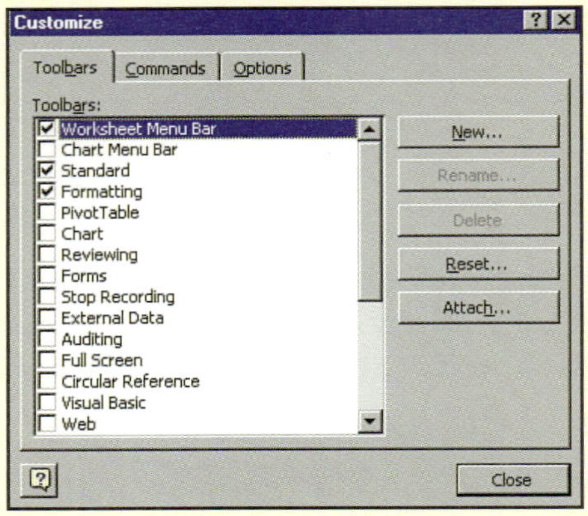

Figure 5.6
With the Customize dialog box, you can show and hide toolbars, add buttons to toolbars, and change toolbar options.

3 Click the Commands tab.

Excel groups buttons by functional categories, as shown in Figure 5.7. For example, the buttons that help you manage files are grouped in the File category, buttons that help you draw are in the Drawing category, and so on. When you click a category in the Categories list box, the buttons for that category appear in the Commands area. When you click a button in the Commands area, the Description button becomes available. When you click the Description button, a description of the command appears in the Description area.

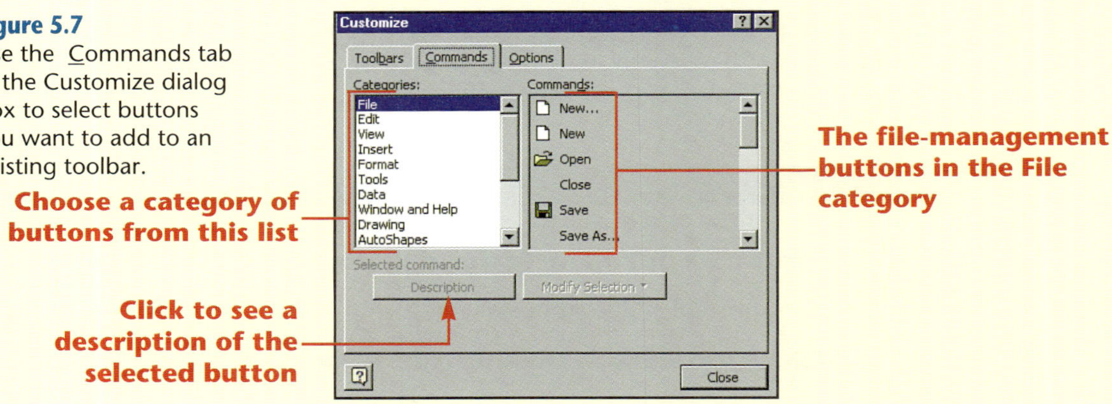

Figure 5.7
Use the Commands tab in the Customize dialog box to select buttons you want to add to an existing toolbar.

Because you modified the default settings earlier to display only five worksheets in each new workbook, you want to be able to add a new worksheet quickly, if needed. You can add a button to the Standard toolbar that adds a new worksheet to the current workbook when you click the button.

4 Select Insert from the Categories list.

5 Select the Worksheet button from the Commands list and click the Description button.

As you can see by the description at the bottom of the dialog box shown in Figure 5.8, this is the button you want to use. You decide that you want to place the Insert Worksheet button just to the right of the New button in the Standard toolbar.

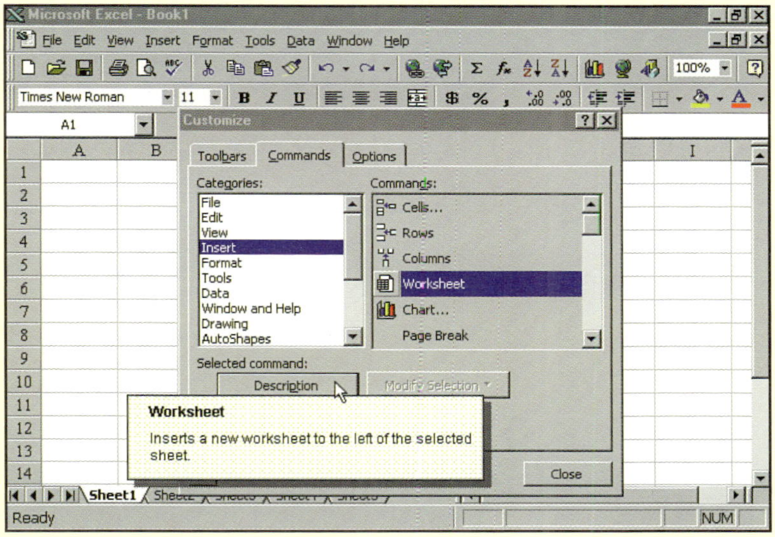

Figure 5.8
When you click the Description button, a description of the selected command button appears on the screen.

6 Click the Worksheet button in the Commands list. Hold down the mouse button and drag the Worksheet button to the desired position on the Standard toolbar. The mouse pointer changes to an arrow with a rectangle and an X, as shown in Figure 5.9.

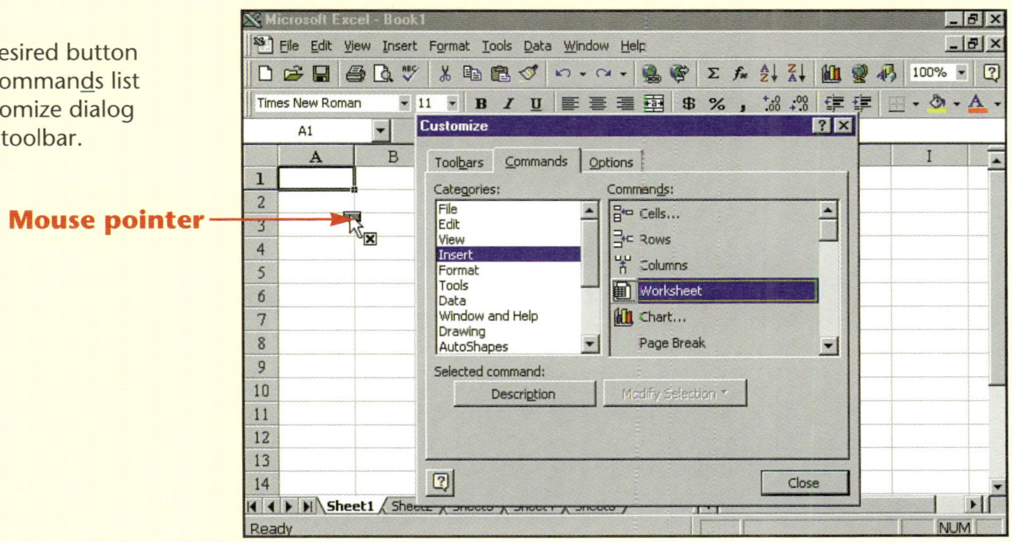

Figure 5.9
Drag the desired button from the Commands list in the Customize dialog box to the toolbar.

continues

To Customize a Toolbar (continued)

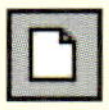

7 Release the mouse pointer when the rectangular pointer appears to the right of the New button. A thick vertical line appears as your mouse pointer comes over the toolbar. This marks the spot where the button is displayed when you release the mouse button.

The Insert Worksheet button now appears in the Standard toolbar, as shown in Figure 5.10.

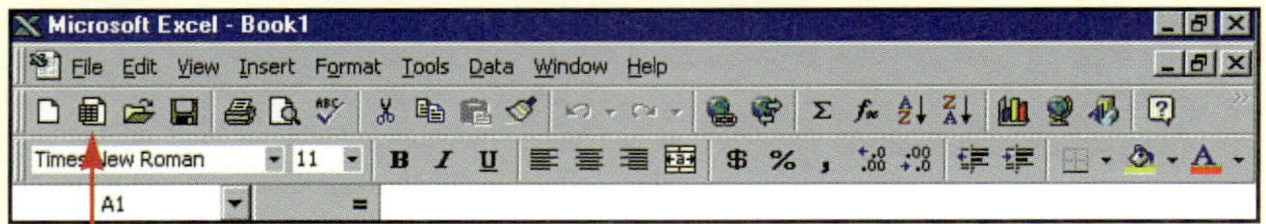

Figure 5.10 You can now use the Insert Worksheet button that you added to the Standard toolbar.

8 Click the Close button to close the Customize dialog box.

Now check to see whether the new button works as you expected.

9 Click the Insert Worksheet button you added to the Standard toolbar.

A new sheet named Sheet6 appears onscreen to the left of Sheet1.

Now move the Insert Worksheet button to a different location on the Standard toolbar.

10 Right-click inside a toolbar and choose Customize from the shortcut menu. Click the Commands tab if it is not already displayed.

While the Customize dialog box is displayed, you can move any of the buttons on the onscreen toolbars to a new location.

11 Click and drag the Insert Worksheet button so that it appears just after the Save button. Release the mouse button.

The Insert Worksheet button appears in the new location beside the Save button. You probably do not need the Insert Worksheet button after all, so now you remove it.

12 With the Customize dialog box still displayed, drag the Insert Worksheet button off the Standard toolbar (into the worksheet area of the screen).

The remaining buttons on the Standard toolbar adjust to fill the space formerly occupied by the Insert Worksheet button.

13 Click the Close button to close the Customize dialog box.

Keep the blank workbook open for the next lesson.

Inside Stuff

If you have made several changes to an existing toolbar, you can easily reset the toolbar to its original configuration. Right-click inside a toolbar and choose Customize. In the Customize dialog box, click the Toolbars tab. From the Toolbars list, select the toolbar you want to restore. Click the Reset button. An alert message appears to confirm that you want to reset the changes made to the toolbar. Click OK to close the alert message and reset the toolbar; click Close to close the Customize dialog box.

The Formatting and Drawing toolbars contain several buttons (Borders, Font Color, AutoShapes, Fill Color, and Line Color) with drop-down lists called "palettes." You can "tear off" these palettes from the toolbars and float them on the worksheet. Follow these steps: Click the arrow next to the button to display the palette, click the palette's title bar, and drag the palette onto the worksheet. (The floating palette cannot be reshaped.) The options on the palette are readily accessible while you do your formatting. Close the palette by clicking the Close button in the upper-right corner.

Lesson 4: Creating a New Toolbar

You just learned how to customize an existing toolbar. You also can create your own toolbars. In this lesson, you create a new toolbar that contains a set of buttons that you use frequently. By adding these favorite buttons to a new toolbar, you can ensure that they are always available onscreen when you need them.

To Create a New Toolbar

1. **With the blank workbook still open, choose View, Toolbars.**

   The Toolbars menu opens.

2. **Choose Customize and make sure that the Toolbars tab is at the front of the dialog box.**

   The New button on the Toolbars tab enables you to create a new toolbar.

3. **Click the New button.**

   The New Toolbar dialog box appears with the Toolbar Name text box highlighted.

4. **Type `My Toolbar`.**

   As you type the new text, it overwrites the existing text. By typing this new name (which is different from any of the existing toolbar names), you are telling Excel that you want to create a new toolbar using this name.

continues

To Create a New Toolbar (continued)

5 Choose OK.

My Toolbar is added to the Toolbars list. The new toolbar is selected and appears onscreen in the dialog box, as shown in Figure 5.11. Now you need to customize the toolbar, adding your choice of command buttons. As buttons are added, the toolbar increases in size.

If you have problems...

If you do not see the new toolbar on your screen, it might be displayed on the worksheet under the Customize dialog box. Drag the dialog box out of the way to see the new toolbar.

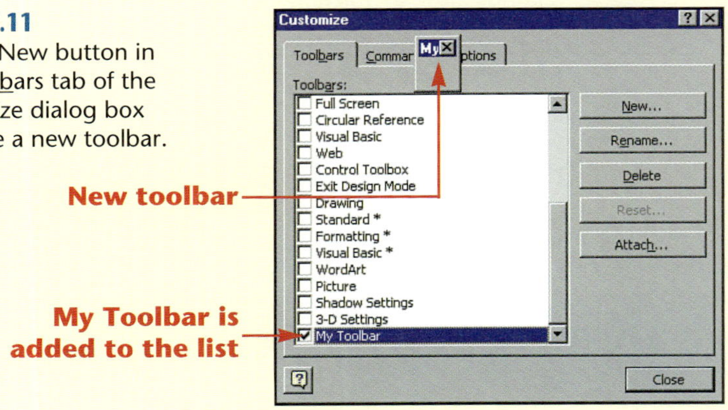

Figure 5.11
Use the New button in the Toolbars tab of the Customize dialog box to create a new toolbar.

6 Drag the new toolbar to cell A3 of the worksheet.

7 Click the Commands tab; make sure that File is the selected category.

From the Categories list, you can now choose the category and then the buttons to add to your new toolbar.

8 In the Commands area, scroll through the list and click the Set Print Area button.

If you click the Description button, you see a description of the button that is selected in the Commands area.

The Set Print Area button is handy because it lets you specify a certain part of your worksheet for printing. Suppose you work with a number of large worksheets but usually need to print only certain parts of the worksheets. If you use this button a lot, it would be helpful to have it on a toolbar. Add it to the new toolbar now.

9 Click and drag the Set Print Area button to your new toolbar.

The empty toolbar expands to hold the button, as shown in Figure 5.12. Notice that a copy of the button remains in the Customize dialog box. You can add it to as many toolbars as you want.

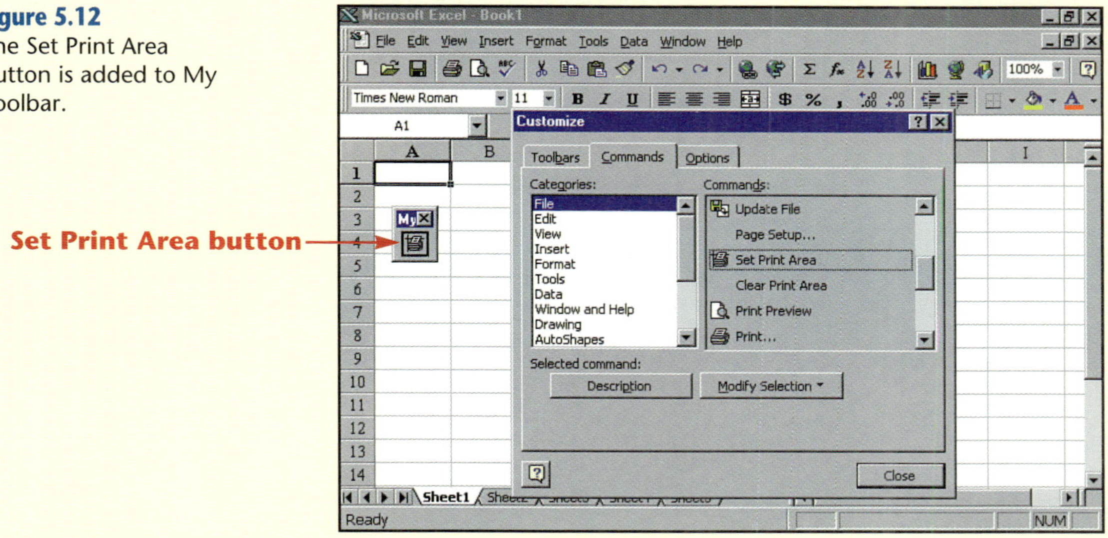

Figure 5.12
The Set Print Area button is added to My Toolbar.

Now add more buttons to your new toolbar.

⑩ **In the Categories list box, select Insert.**

Suppose you spend a lot of time inserting columns in your worksheets. There is a button in this category that can do this chore instantly.

⑪ **Drag the Columns button to your new toolbar.**

The toolbar expands to hold the new button.

⑫ **In the Categories list box, select Window and Help.**

This category contains a variety of buttons that lets you control your windows and access Help. Suppose you like to set up your worksheet windows in panes; you can add a button to help you control those panes. You learn about freezing worksheet panes in Lesson 7.

⑬ **Drag the Freeze Panes button from the Commands list to your new toolbar.**

You now have a new toolbar with three buttons. Notice, however, that your buttons are bunched together. In Excel's default toolbars, buttons are divided into categories and the categories are separated by separator bars. On the Formatting toolbar, the Bold, Italic, and Underline buttons are grouped together because they perform related functions, but a separator divides them from the alignment buttons, which perform different functions. Separate your new buttons so that they are grouped by function, too.

continues

To Create a New Toolbar (continued)

14 On your new toolbar, drag the Freeze Panes button a little to the right, but not off the toolbar (or you will have to go back and insert it again).

A separator bar appears between the Columns button and the Freeze Panes button.

15 On your new toolbar, drag the Columns button a little to the right, but not over the Freeze Panes button.

A separator bar appears between the Set Print Area button and the Columns button, as shown in Figure 5.13.

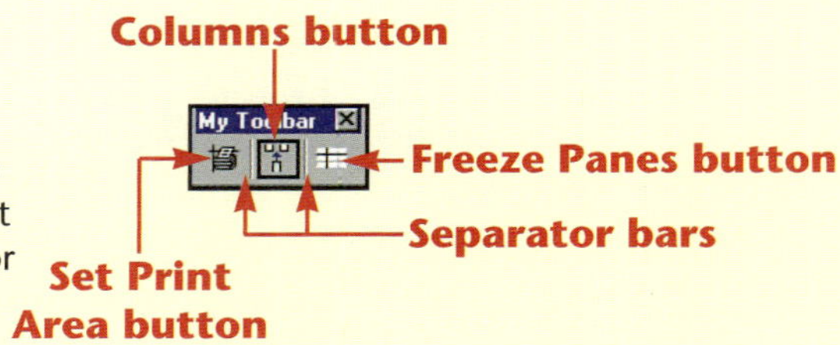

Figure 5.13
Your new toolbar now includes three different buttons, with separator bars between button groups.

16 Click the Close button in the Customize dialog box.

The dialog box closes and your new toolbar remains onscreen, ready for use.

To remove the new toolbar from the screen, click the Close button (the X) on the right side of the new toolbar's title bar. You can redisplay the toolbar later by choosing View, Toolbars, Customize, and then selecting My Toolbar from the Toolbars list.

Now delete this toolbar so that it is no longer available for use.

17 Choose View, Toolbars, Customize, and click the Toolbars tab; then choose My Toolbar from the bottom of the Toolbars list.

The Delete button now becomes available for use.

18 Click Delete.

A warning box appears, prompting you to confirm that you want to delete the toolbar.

19 Choose OK; then click Close on the Customize dialog box.

The Customize dialog box closes.

Keep the workbook open for the next lesson.

Lesson 5: Adding Menus to Toolbars and Buttons to Menus

Not only can you modify existing toolbars or create new toolbars as you did in Lessons 3 and 4, but Excel also gives you the capacity to customize menus. You can add toolbar buttons to the menus or add menus to toolbars because a menu is considered another type of toolbar.

In this lesson, you add a menu to a toolbar to save you time as you work.

To Add Menus to Toolbars and Buttons to Menus

1. **Choose View, Toolbars, Customize. Make sure that the Toolbars tab is at the front of the dialog box.**

   The Customize dialog box appears with the list of available toolbars.

2. **Select the Chart toolbar to display it and click the Commands tab.**

   Now you can choose Built-in Menus from the Categories list and indicate the command you want to add to the Chart toolbar.

3. **Scroll through the Categories list and click Built-in Menus.**

   You decide to add the Picture menu to the Chart toolbar so that you can quickly add a picture to your charts.

4. **Scroll through the Commands list to find Picture. Drag the Picture command to the end of the Chart toolbar.**

   The Chart toolbar is modified to include the Picture menu. Now you can quickly access these commands when you want to add them to your chart.

5. **Click the Picture menu on the Chart toolbar.**

   The Picture menu appears onscreen, as shown in Figure 5.14.

Figure 5.14
The Chart toolbar now displays the Picture menu.

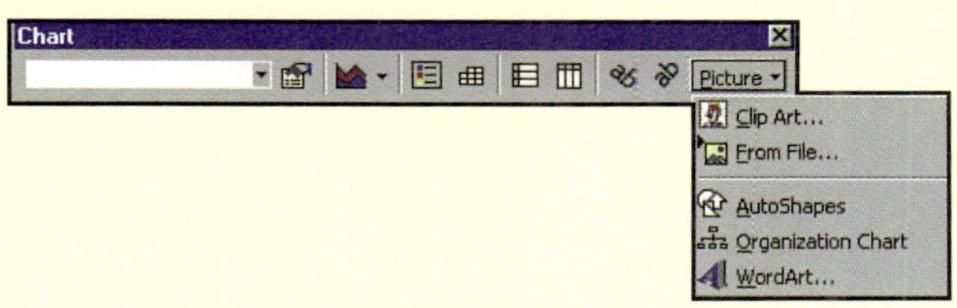

6. **Click the Picture menu again.**

   The menu is closed. Now remove the menu from the toolbar. The Customize dialog box must be open.

7. **Drag the Picture menu to the worksheet area.**

   The Picture menu is removed from the Chart toolbar.

continues

Excel

To Add Menus to Toolbars and Buttons to Menus (continued)

8 Close the Chart toolbar and then click Close on the Customize dialog box.

Now you decide to add a command button to the existing File menu. The menu must be in view before it can be modified.

9 Right-click a toolbar and choose Customize from the shortcut menu.

The Customize dialog box appears.

10 Click the Commands tab and make sure that the File category is highlighted.

Now you need to display the menu that you want to modify.

11 Choose File from the menu bar.

If the File menu appears on top of the Customize dialog box, drag the dialog box to the right to view it. The File menu and the Customize dialog box are displayed, as shown in Figure 5.15.

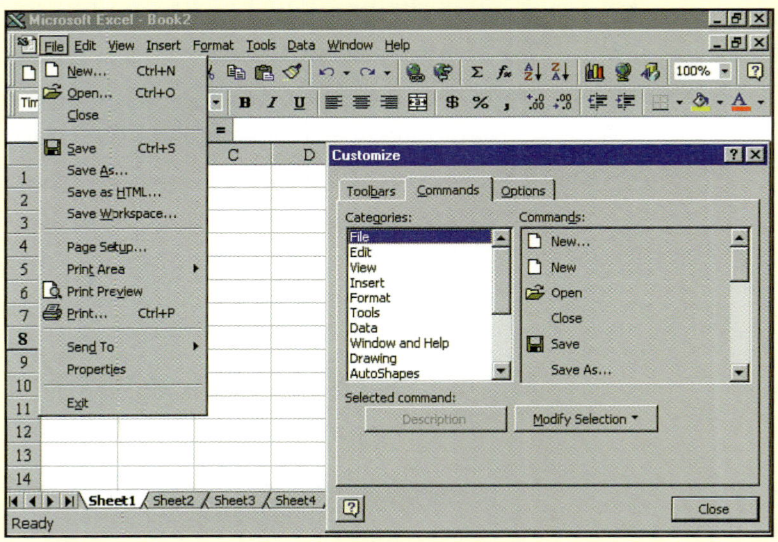

Figure 5.15
Display the menu to be modified and the Customize dialog box in order to drag a command to the menu.

12 From the Commands list, drag the Update File button to the File menu and place it below the Save Workspace command.

You have modified the File menu and added a new command, as shown in Figure 5.16. You can use the Update File command to update changes made by other users to a shared workbook. Shared workbooks are covered in Project 14.

Figure 5.16
The Update File command has been added to the File menu.

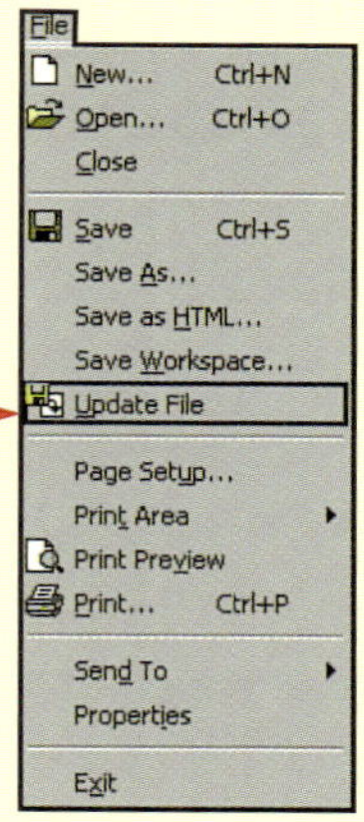

Now remove the new command from the File menu. The Customize dialog box must be open to modify menus.

13. **Drag the Update File command from the menu to the worksheet area.**

The Update File command is removed from the File menu.

14. **Close the Customize dialog box.**

The File menu and the Customize dialog box are removed from the screen. Now return the default settings that you changed in Lesson 1 to their original settings.

15. **Choose Tools, Options, and click the General tab. Change the Sheets in New Workbook option to 3, change the Standard font to Arial, and change the Size to 10. Choose OK twice.**

Exit Excel. It is not necessary to save the changes to the current workbook. Now restart Excel to accept the new settings.

Lesson 6: Zooming In and Out on a Worksheet

The default Excel worksheet contains 65,536 rows and 256 columns. Depending on the size and type of computer monitor you have, you see about 14 to 26 rows and 9 to 12 columns in the Excel window. The number of columns and rows displayed also depends on whether your Excel and worksheet windows are maximized, how many toolbars you have displayed, and the position and size of your Windows taskbar. Even if you use only a small portion of a worksheet, you can easily fill more cells than can fit on your screen at one time.

When you are working on a large worksheet, you might want to view more of the worksheet than is showing onscreen. Fortunately, Excel provides **zoom** controls that let you view more or less of your worksheet, without changing any of your actual display settings. You can **zoom out** to see more of the worksheet, or you can **zoom in** to see less of it. This lesson shows you how to command a better view of your worksheet.

To Zoom In and Out on a Worksheet

1 Open the file Proj0501 from the Project-05 folder on the CD and save it as `1996 Sales`.

2 Activate the 1996 worksheet by clicking its tab.

This is a relatively large worksheet with 13 columns and 18 rows of data. Notice, too, that some of the columns have been expanded so that they are wider than their default width, making fewer of them fit onscreen at one time.

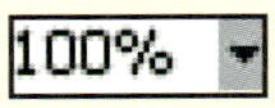

3 Click the drop-down arrow next to the Zoom Control button on the Standard toolbar.

The Zoom Control button lets you quickly change the zoom setting, or magnification level, at which you view a worksheet. By default, the zoom is set at 100 percent, which is a normal view. The zoom level in the 1996 Sales workbook is 100 percent.

When you click the arrow button, a list appears displaying the standard zoom percentages. Now zoom out on the worksheet to get a bird's-eye view of it.

4 Choose 75%.

The worksheet is now condensed to 75 percent of its default size to show more on the screen, as shown in Figure 5.17.

Next, zoom in on the worksheet to focus on a smaller area.

5 Click the Zoom Control button and select 200% from the drop-down list.

The magnification level is now increased to 200 percent, as shown in Figure 5.18.

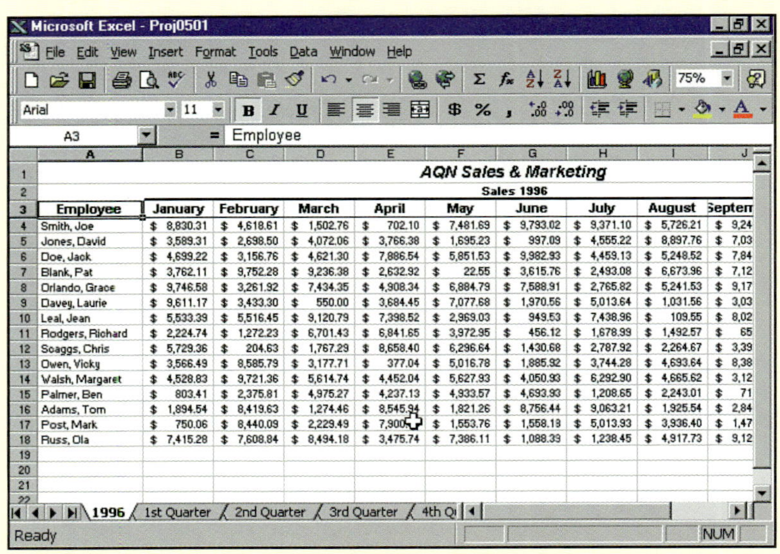

Figure 5.17
You can see more of the worksheet at 75 percent zoom level.

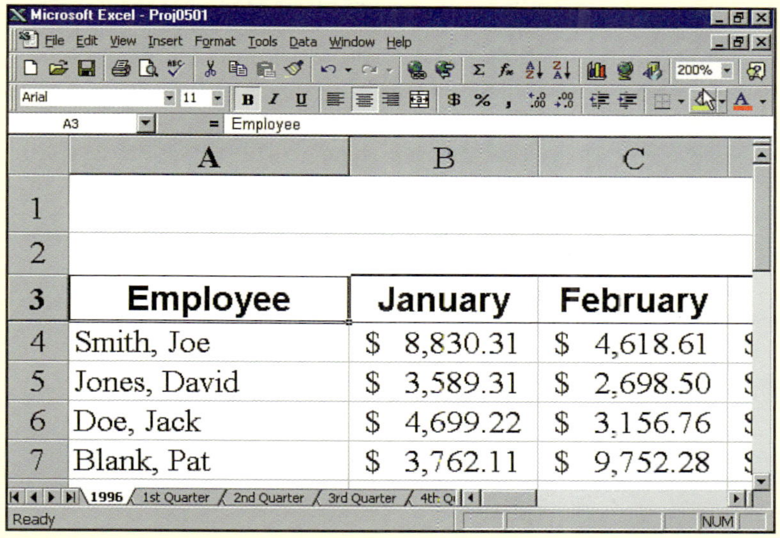

Figure 5.18
You see less of the worksheet at 200 percent zoom level.

Now return to the normal zoom level.

6. **Click the Zoom Control button and select 100% from the drop-down list.**

Your view of the worksheet returns to normal.

Keep the worksheet open for the next lesson.

Jargon Watch

Some people get confused about the concept of **zooming** with a computer. But zooming works the same in Excel as it does with a camera, a telescope, or a microscope. (Excel just gives you some cooler options.) When you **zoom in** on a worksheet, you increase the magnification level—say, from 100 to 150 percent. It is like moving closer to the worksheet; the cells become larger and easier to see, but you see fewer of them because each one takes up more space on the screen.

Conversely, when you **zoom out** on a worksheet, you decrease the magnification level—say, from 100 percent to 75 percent. This is like moving away from the worksheet; the cells become smaller and you can fit more of them on the screen.

You should practice using different zoom levels to find the one that works best for you. Remember, though, that zooming has disadvantages. Zoom in too much, and you will not see enough of the worksheet to be useful. If you zoom out too much, you might not be able to read any of the data.

Inside Stuff

In addition to the standard zoom settings that appear in the Zoom Control list, you can also enter a custom zoom setting. Click the Zoom Control button on the Standard toolbar and enter any number between 10 and 400. Then press ↵Enter. The worksheet is displayed at the zoom setting you specified.

There are times when you just want to see specific cells onscreen. You can use the Zoom Control button to view any section of data. First, highlight the data you want to view. Then choose Selection from the Zoom Control drop-down list. Excel fits your selection to the screen.

Lesson 7: Splitting and Freezing Window Panes

Split
Splitting an active window divides it into two panes (sections) horizontally or vertically, or four panes if split both horizontally and vertically.

Freeze
Freeze window panes to keep column or row titles in view as you scroll through a worksheet.

When you are working with large worksheets (such as those in the 1996 Sales workbook), you often have column headings and row headings. When you scroll through the worksheet, however, the headings disappear. When you get deep in the worksheet, it can be impossible to tell what data goes with which heading.

As you see in this lesson, Excel allows you to *split* your window into panes and then *freeze* some of the panes so they are always visible onscreen. This enables you to keep your row and column headings onscreen all the time, even as you scroll through many rows and columns of data.

To Split and Freeze Window Panes

1. **With the `1996 Sales` workbook open and the 1996 worksheet active, select cell J18.**

   With cell J18 selected, you cannot tell who the salesperson is. You might not be able to see the month, either.

2. **Press Ctrl+Home to jump to cell A1.**

   Notice that Column A contains headings for your rows (the names of the sales personnel) and that rows 1 through 3 contain the column headings.

   You need these headings to remain visible all the time; that way, when you scroll to cell J18 (or further down), you can always see what month and salesperson the data applies to. One way to do this is by splitting the document window into panes.

3. **Select cell B4.**

   This cell is the first cell of data. Everything above and to the left of this cell is a heading and should stay put.

4. **Choose Window, Split.**

   This command divides the window into *panes* by inserting a horizontal split above and a vertical split to the left of the current cell. Your screen is now divided into four parts, as shown in Figure 5.19.

Pane
A division in a window that has its own scroll bars so you can view a portion of the worksheet separately from the sections displayed in other panes.

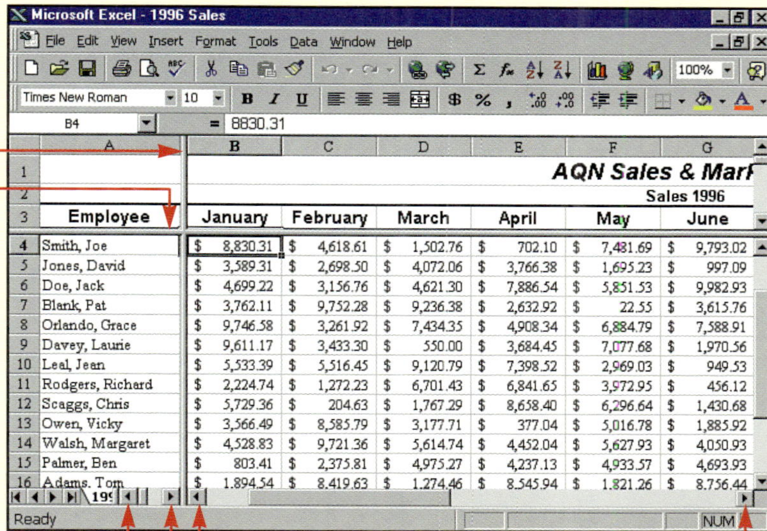

Figure 5.19
The screen appears with horizontal and vertical splits at cell B4.

You now can scroll in any of the four sections. By scrolling in the lower-right section, your headings remain in place, but the data changes.

5. **Choose Window, Remove Split.**

   This step removes the splits from your worksheet; the view returns to normal.

6. **Make sure that A1 is still in the upper-left corner of your screen by pressing Ctrl+Home.**

   Now try splitting the screen so the headings appear in one pane and all the data appears in another.

7. **Select cell B4.**

   Again, this is where you want the window to be divided—between the headings and the data.

8. **Choose Window, Freeze Panes.**

   Your window is now divided into panes, but without the additional scroll bars, as shown in Figure 5.20. The headings are frozen in place.

continues

To Split and Freeze Window Panes (continued)

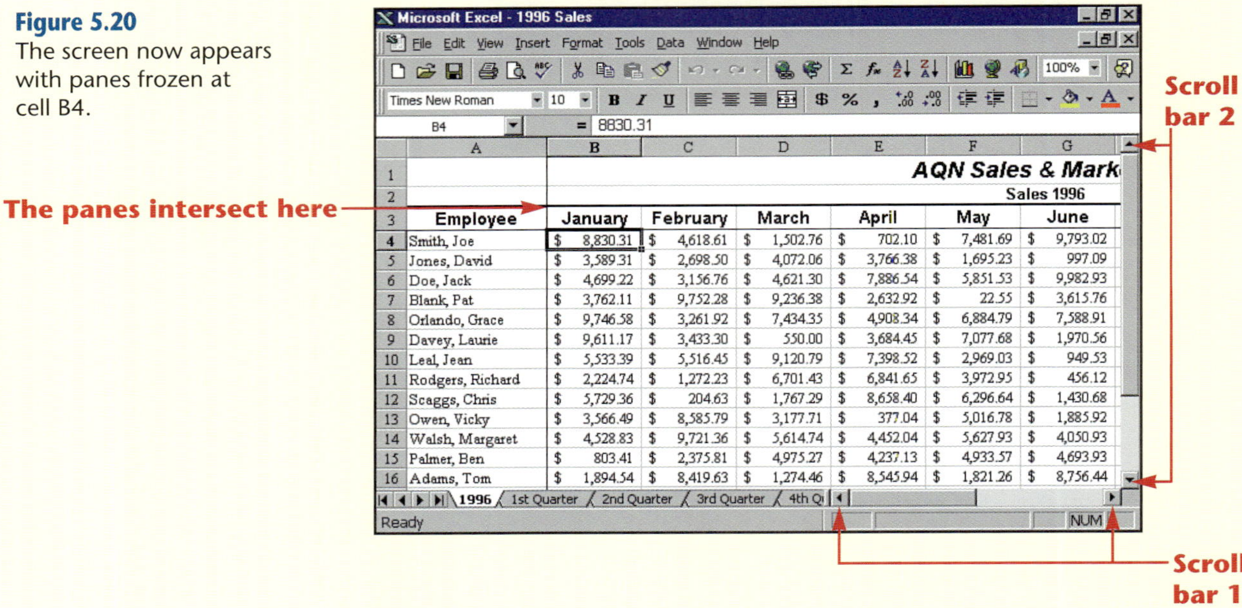

Figure 5.20
The screen now appears with panes frozen at cell B4.

9 Select cell J18.

Even though you moved far down and to the right, the headings remain onscreen with the data. You can still see that cell J18 applies to Ola Russ and that it reflects sales for September. When you scroll horizontally, the row headings remain on the screen. When you scroll vertically, the column headings remain on the screen. Even though column A and rows 1, 2, and 3 are frozen, you can still activate any cell in this area for editing.

10 Use the scroll bars to practice scrolling around. Notice how the headings behave as you scroll.

11 Choose Window, Unfreeze Panes.

This step unfreezes the panes on your worksheet, and you return to a normal view.

Keep this workbook open for the next lesson.

Inside Stuff

If you are using a Super VGA monitor set at 800x600 or 1024x768 resolution, you may not have as much difficulty viewing the salesperson names or month names in this example. However, if you are using a larger worksheet than the one discussed in this lesson, you would still benefit by learning how to split and freeze window panes.

Use the Window, Split command when you want to line up two sections of a large worksheet that cannot be viewed on the same screen (for example, monthly data and totals). When you enter data or make changes to the monthly data in one pane, you can immediately see the totals update in the other pane.

Excel

After you split the worksheet window, you can drag the horizontal split line and the vertical split line to different locations. To drag both lines at the same time, position the mouse pointer on the intersection of the lines and drag to the new position.

Note also that you see four different scroll bars onscreen when you use the Window, Split command. Try navigating the windows by using different scroll bars. Depending on which scroll bars you use, you might end up with duplicate data in different panes, which can be confusing. Double-click a split line to remove it. A better method for this worksheet example is to freeze panes rather than split the window.

When you choose Window, Freeze Panes, only the current worksheet displays the panes. If you switch to another worksheet in that workbook, notice that it does not contain frozen panes. Even if you preselect multiple worksheets in a workbook and then choose Window, Freeze Panes, only the topmost worksheet displays the panes. Therefore, you must set panes one worksheet at a time.

Lesson 8: Arranging Multiple Windows

Earlier in this project, you learned how to zoom to see the data you needed on your worksheet. You also learned how to divide your document window into panes and freeze them to keep data handy. But what if you need to see more than one worksheet at a time? Like all Windows-based applications, Excel lets you open and arrange several windows at a time on your screen. You can have one workbook displayed in several windows, or you can have several workbooks in separate windows. To see all the title bars for your open windows, you can **cascade** them. If you'd rather split up the available screen area between the open windows, you can **tile** the windows.

The 1996 Sales workbook contains the total 1996 sales data on one worksheet and sales figures for each quarter in four other worksheets. Suppose your sales manager wants to see the four quarterly summaries onscreen at the same time to compare them. In this lesson, you create three additional windows and arrange them so they are all visible.

Jargon Watch

Of course, the more windows you have open, the harder it is to see your data. But Excel lets you arrange windows in different ways to get the best possible view. You can arrange windows so that they are **cascaded**; that is, inactive windows remain mostly hidden behind the active window—only their title bars show. The disadvantage of cascading your windows is that while multiple windows are open, the data for only one window is actually visible.

You also can arrange windows so that they are **tiled**, like ceramic tiles in a bathroom. Each window gets the same amount of space on the screen if an even number of windows is open. If an uneven number of windows is open, one or more windows will be larger than the rest. The more tiled windows you have onscreen, the less room there is for each window. The disadvantage of tiled windows is that, while all the open windows are visible, you can see only a small part of the individual worksheets.

To Arrange Multiple Windows

1 **With the** `1996 Sales` **workbook open, activate the** `1st Quarter` **worksheet.**

2 **Choose Window, New Window.**

3 **Repeat step 2 two additional times.**

You have opened three additional windows. Each window contains the 1996 Sales workbook with the 1st Quarter worksheet active. However, you still see only one window on your screen. Your title bar should show the document's name as `1996 Sales:4`. The `4` indicates that there are four windows open, each one containing this workbook.

4 **Open the Window menu.**

The bottom of the menu shows that four windows are open.

5 **From the Window menu, choose** `1996 Sales:2`**.**

This step opens the second window; again, it contains the 1st Quarter worksheet. You create a different view in this window.

6 **Activate the** `2nd Quarter` **worksheet by clicking its tab.**

The 2nd Quarter sheet appears in the 1996 Sales:2 window.

7 **Open the Window menu and choose** `1996 Sales:3`**.**

The third window opens.

8 **Activate the** `3rd Quarter` **worksheet.**

The 3rd Quarter sheet appears in the 1996 Sales:3 window.

9 **Open the Window menu and choose** `1996 Sales:4`**.**

The fourth window opens.

10 **Activate the** `4th Quarter` **worksheet.**

The 4th Quarter sheet appears in the 1996 Sales:4 window.

11 **If another open window appears in the Window menu, activate it and close it.**

12 **Choose Window, Arrange.**

The Arrange Windows dialog box appears, as shown in Figure 5.21.

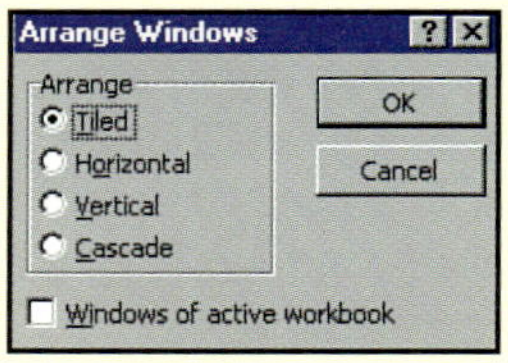

Figure 5.21
You can use the Arrange Windows dialog box to tile or cascade multiple windows onscreen.

13 In the Arrange area of the dialog box, choose Tiled, if it is not already selected.

This option divides the screen into four equal sections. Each section contains one of the four open worksheets. Windows 95 arranges and tiles the windows; however, they do not necessarily appear tiled in the order you prefer. To change the order, you can click the preferred sheet tab in each window.

14 Choose OK.

The Arrange Windows dialog box closes, and your windows are now arranged as four tiles on the screen, as shown in Figure 5.22.

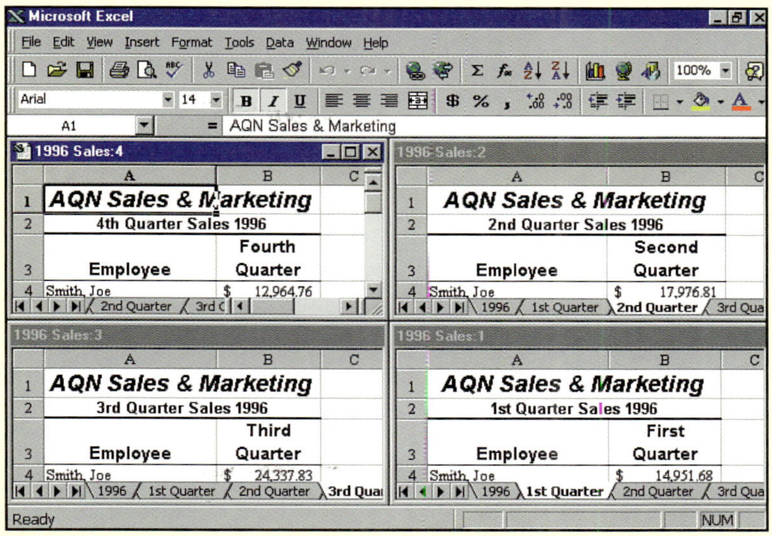

Figure 5.22
Your screen now appears with four tiled views.

Now close some of the windows and display just one active window.

15 Activate the `1996 Sales:4` window and click the Close button (the X) in the upper-right corner of the window.

The window closes. Notice the gap it leaves; Excel does not automatically rearrange the remaining windows to fill the empty screen space.

16 To fill in the gap using the three displayed windows, choose Window, Arrange again. Click the Tiled option and choose OK.

17 Activate the `1996 Sales:3` window and click the Close button.

18 Activate the `1996 Sales:2` window and click the Close button.

Now you need to maximize the 1996 Sales window.

continues

To Arrange Multiple Windows (continued)

19 **Click the Maximize button on the `1996 Sales3` window.**

The remaining window now fills the screen; only one copy of 1996 Sales remains open and maximized. Keep the worksheet open for the next lesson.

Inside Stuff

If you have multiple workbooks open but want to arrange only the windows of the current workbook, select the Windows of Active Workbook check box in the Arrange Windows dialog box before you click OK. If you have only one workbook open, it is not necessary to select this option. The Horizontal option in the Arrange Windows dialog box displays the open worksheets in horizontal bars across the screen; the Vertical option displays all open worksheets in vertical panels. Experiment with each of these options until you get the results you want.

Lesson 9: Using Summary Information

By now you probably have created many documents with Excel. If you are like most computer users, filenames sometimes give you problems. You might have named some of your documents in a hurry, so their names might not be perfectly descriptive. Some very different files might have similar names. Perhaps you just cannot remember what you named some of your files.

Fortunately, Excel lets you attach file summary information to your files. This capability lets you assign additional information to a file so that you can easily distinguish it from other files or identify it without opening it first.

To Use Summary Information

1 **With the `1996 Sales` workbook open, choose File, Properties.**

The Properties dialog box appears, as shown in Figure 5.23.

2 **Click the Summary tab to bring it to the top if it is not already there.**

3 **In the Title text box, type `1996 Sales`.**

You can use up to 255 characters (including blank spaces) to fill in the fields in this dialog box. When you finish typing and are ready to move to the next box, press Tab—do not press Enter. Pressing Enter closes the dialog box.

Figure 5.23
The Properties dialog box enables you to enter general information about the current workbook.

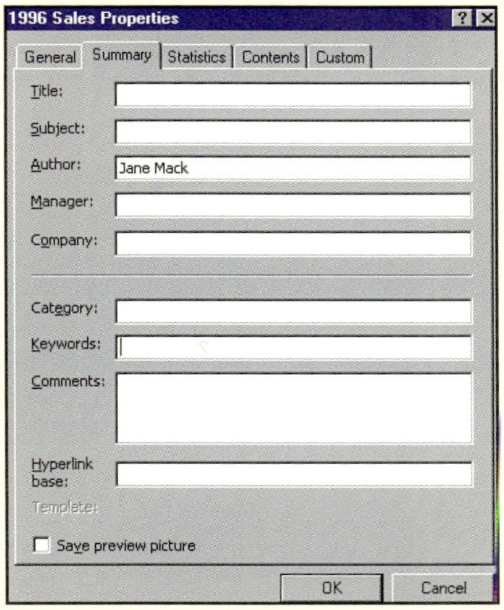

If you have problems...

If you press Enter instead of Tab and the dialog box closes, choose File, Properties to restore the dialog box.

4. **In the Subject text box, type** `Individual Sales` **and press** Tab.
5. **In the Author text box, type your name (unless it already appears there) and press** Tab.
6. **In the Manager text box, type** `Greg Macuck` **and press** Tab.
7. **In the Company text box, type** `AQN Sales and Marketing` **and press** Tab.
8. **In the Category text box, type** `Sales` **and press** Tab.
9. **In the Keywords text box, type** `Quarter, 1996, Sales` **and choose OK.**

   The dialog box closes. You are now able to search by any of these properties to find a file, including the keywords typed into the Keywords text box.

10. **Save your work and close the workbook.**

    Filling in the Properties dialog box might seem like a hassle, but taking a few moments now can save time later. The Properties dialog box can help you keep your workbooks organized and can save time if your coworkers also use it.

    Suppose a coworker was sent out of town on unexpected business and you need one of his files to finish your project. If your coworker filled in the Properties dialog box for that file, you can look up the files with the same category, thus relieving you of having to look at every file.

continues

To Use Summary Information (continued)

11 Click the Open button on the Standard toolbar.

The Open dialog box appears, displaying the list of Excel files from the folder you have been using.

12 Click the Advanced button.

The Advanced Find dialog box appears, as shown in Figure 5.24.

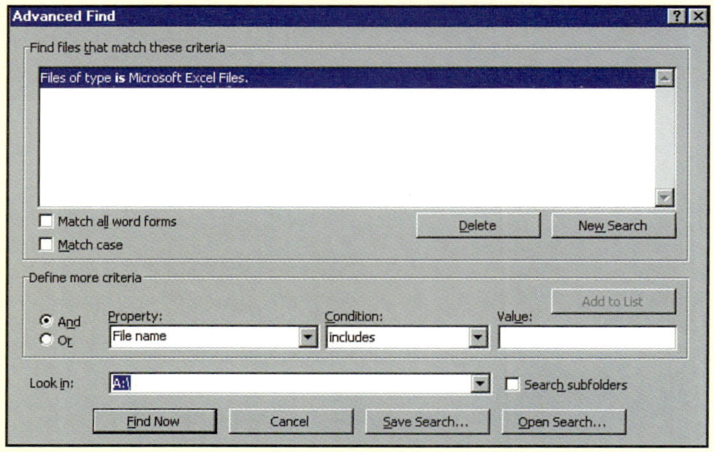

Figure 5.24
Use the Advanced Find dialog box to find specific files you are looking for.

This dialog box lets you do advanced file searches on your system, using a variety of properties. You do not need to know the file name to find it, but you do need to know something about the file to narrow your search.

13 In the Define more criteria area, click the Property arrow button.

A list of properties appears. You can search for files that have any of these properties assigned to them.

14 Choose Author.

Leave the Condition box as it is.

15 Click the Value text box and type your name.

Type your name just as you did previously in this lesson.

16 Click the Look In arrow button and choose 3½ Floppy: from the list, if it is not already displayed.

If your files have been saved to a different drive, choose the drive you are using rather than A:.

17 Select the Search subfolders check box.

This option tells the computer to check all the folders on the drive you specified.

18 Click the Add to List button.

The criteria you defined now appear in the list box at the top of the Advanced Find dialog box.

19 Click the Find Now button.

The computer searches for all the files on your computer with your name as the Author in the Properties dialog box. The Open dialog box appears again and lists all the files that meet the criteria, as shown in Figure 5.25.

Figure 5.25
The Open dialog box displays the results of the Advanced Find.

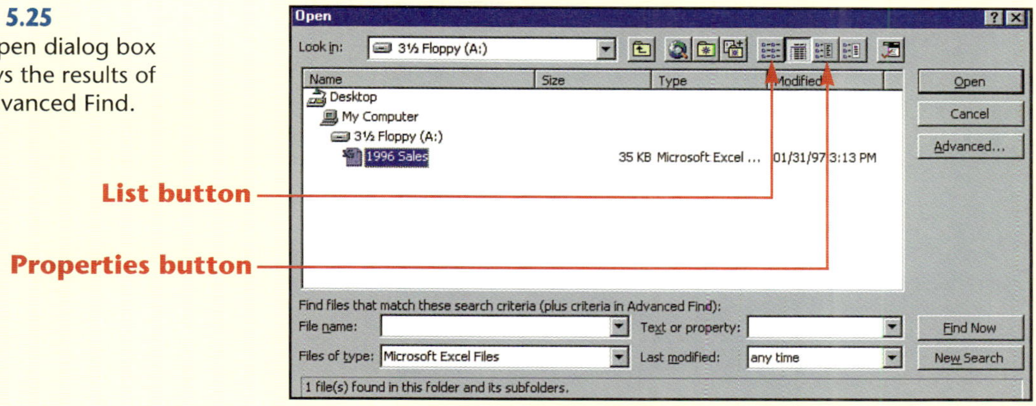

20 Select the 1996 Sales file by clicking its name once.

Check the properties of this file to see if it is the one you need.

21 Click the Properties button.

This shows the file properties you filled in earlier in this lesson.

22 Click the List button to return to list view and click the Open button.

This step opens the 1996 Sales workbook.

Close the workbook without saving it. If you have completed your session on the computer, exit Excel and Windows 95 before turning off your computer. Otherwise, continue with the "Checking Your Skills" and "Applying Your Skills" sections.

Inside Stuff

When you type your file summary information, be consistent from file to file. For example, if you use your name in the Author field, type your name the same way every time. Otherwise your searches might fail, and you might have to conduct multiple searches for variations of your name.

The same is true with other fields in the Properties dialog box. For example, if your company's name is AQN Sales & Marketing, be sure to use the ampersand (&) symbol consistently instead of using the word *and*.

When trying to find a file, you may not know the exact spelling of a word or words to match. To find text that has some characters in common, you can use a *wildcard character*. Type a question mark (?) to replace a single character in the same position as the question mark. Type an asterisk (*) to replace any number of characters in the same position as the question mark. For example, if you are not sure how to spell the author's first name, you could type J* in the Value text box of the Advanced Find dialog box to find files with an author whose first name starts with the letter J.

Project Summary

To	Do This
Change the number of worksheets that Excel includes in a new workbook	Choose Tools, Options and click the General tab. Change Sheets in New Workbook to the desired number. Click OK to close the Options dialog box.
Change the default font for worksheets	Choose Tools, Options and click the General tab. Change Standard Font and Size to the desired specifications. Click OK to close the Options dialog box, exit Excel, and open Excel again to put the changes into effect.
View a toolbar not currently displayed	Right-click any toolbar that is displayed or choose View, Toolbars; then select the toolbar to display from the menu.
Remove a toolbar that is currently displayed	Right-click any toolbar that is displayed or choose View, Toolbars; then click the name of the toolbar to be removed. This removes the check mark next to the name of the toolbar on the menu.
Reposition a toolbar onscreen	To move a docked toolbar, click the move handle; then hold down the left mouse button and drag the toolbar to the desired position. Release the mouse button. To move a floating toolbar, drag the title bar of the toolbar to the desired position.

To	Do This
Add a button to a toolbar	Right-click the toolbar and choose Customize from the shortcut menu. From the Commands tab, select the category and then the command. Drag the command to the toolbar where desired. Close the Customize dialog box.
Move a button on a toolbar	Open the Customize dialog box and drag the button where desired. Close the Customize dialog box.
Remove a button from a toolbar	Open the Customize dialog box, drag the button off the toolbar and onto the worksheet area of the screen, and then release the mouse button. Close the Customize dialog box.
Restore a toolbar to its original configuration	Right-click the toolbar, choose Customize, and then click the Toolbars tab. Select the toolbar you want to reset; then click Reset and click Close.
Create a new toolbar	Choose View, Toolbars, Customize. Click New on the Toolbars tab. Name the toolbar and click OK. Then click the Commands tab, choose the category, and drag the buttons you want to add to the toolbar from the Commands list. Close the Customize dialog box.
Add a menu to a toolbar	Choose View, Toolbars, Customize. On the Toobars tab, select the toolbar. Click the Commands tab. Choose Built-in Menus from the Categories list. Drag the menu from the Commands list to the toolbar. Close the Customize dialog box.
Add a button to a menu	Choose View, Toolbars, Customize. Click the Commands tab; then choose the category and command. Open the menu to be modified; then drag the command button to the menu. Close the Customize dialog box.
Remove a command	Open the Customize dialog box and drag the command off the menu and onto the worksheet area of the screen. Then release the mouse button. Close the Customize dialog box.
Delete a custom toolbar	Choose View, Toolbars, Customize. On the Toolbars tab, select the toolbar to remove. Click Delete. Click OK on the warning dialog box and click Close to close the Customize dialog box.

continues

To	Do This
Zoom in or out of a worksheet	Click the arrow button next to the Zoom Control button and select the desired zoom level. Or type the desired zoom level in the Zoom Control box. Smaller numbers mean smaller character size but more visible area.
Enlarge a specific part of a worksheet	Select the area to enlarge; then click the arrow button next to the Zoom Control button, and click Selection.
Keep headings visible on a large spreadsheet by splitting the window	Select the upper-left cell of the data area, leaving headings visible. Then choose Window, Split.
Remove the split in a window	Choose Window, Remove Split.
Keep headings visible on a large spreadsheet by freezing panes	Select the upper-left cell of the data area, leaving the headings visible. Choose Window, Freeze Panes.
Unfreeze frozen panes in a window	Choose Window, Unfreeze Panes.
View one or more worksheets in more than one window	Choose Window, New Window as many times as required to accommodate your work with a single workbook. If you need to work with individual files, simply open them. Then select Window, Arrange and choose the layout required.
Close worksheets in a multiple-window display	Click the Close button(s) for the window(s) to be closed. Then select Window, Arrange again and select the option you want.
Attach or edit file summary information to find files	Choose File, Properties and click the Summary tab of the Properties dialog box.
Use summary information	Click the Open button on the Standard toolbar; to find the files, click the Advanced button. Use the Advanced Find dialog box to form and execute your search.

Checking Your Skills

True/False

For each of the following statements, check *T* or *F* to indicate whether the statement is true or false.

__T __F 1. If you change Excel's default number of sheets in a new workbook, you must exit and then restart Excel before the change will be effective.

__T __F 2. Commands can be added to or removed from Excel's menus.

__T __F 3. To access the Toolbars shortcut menu, click any toolbar that is displayed or choose View, Toolbars.

__T __F 4. A floating toolbar can be docked at any edge of the worksheet window by dragging the title bar.

__T __F 5. If you want to return a toolbar to its original configuration, you can reset it with the Customize dialog box.

__T __F 6. To set the default font for your workbooks, choose Format, Font from the menu.

__T __F 7. You double-click the title bar of a floating toolbar to dock it.

__T __F 8. To get a close up view of your worksheet, you need to zoom out.

__T __F 9. After you split the window, you can only edit the lower-right pane.

__T __F 10. The Window, Freeze Pane command only affects the current worksheet.

Multiple Choice

Circle the letter of the correct answer for each of the following questions.

1. What menu and command would you use to change Excel's default settings?
   a. Edit, Replace
   b. Tools, Customize
   c. Tools, Options
   d. None of the above

2. How can you change a toolbar from docked to floating on the worksheet?
   a. Point to the move handle and drag the toolbar to the worksheet area
   b. Double-click the move handle
   c. Right-click the toolbar
   d. Both a and b

3. Which toolbar button is used to magnify the view of a worksheet?
   a. Drawing
   b. Print Preview
   c. Zoom Control
   d. None of the above

4. What command would you use to keep headings visible on a large worksheet?
   a. Window, Arrange
   b. Window, Freeze Panes
   c. Window, Split
   d. Both b and c

5. What is the first command you must choose before you can view two or more worksheets in more than one window?
   a. Window, New Window
   b. Window, Arrange
   c. Window, Split
   d. Window, Freeze Panes

6. Which of the following defaults can't be changed from the General tab of the Options dialog box?
   a. Sheets in a new workbook
   b. Standard font
   c. Standard font size
   d. Column width

7. What do you call a toolbar that is not attached to an edge of the program window?
   a. Detached
   b. Undocked
   c. Floating
   d. Separate

8. Which command do you use when you want to add a new button to a toolbar?
   a. Tools, Options
   b. View, Toolbars, Customize
   c. Insert, New Button
   d. Edit, Toolbars

9. How do you remove the customization from a toolbar?
   a. Right-click the added button(s) and press Del
   b. Drag the added button(s) off the toolbar
   c. Choose View, Toolbars, Customize, select name of the toolbar, and click Reset.
   d. None of the above.

10. Which command do you choose to edit the summary information for a workbook file?
   a. File, Properties
   b. Edit, Summary
   c. Tools, Options
   d. Format, Summary

Completion

In the blank provided, write the correct answer for each of the following statements.

1. In order to remove a button from a toolbar or delete a toolbar, the ______________ dialog box must be open.
2. The fastest way to close a floating toolbar is to click its ______________ button.
3. The ______________ button in the Open dialog box will assist you in finding a file.
4. Use the ______________ option in the Window, Arrange command to divide the screen into equal sections, depending on the number of open windows.
5. Click the ______________ command on the File menu to assign additional information to a file and distinguish it from other files.

Excel

6. In the Customize dialog box, click the ______________ tab to choose a function for a new toolbar button.

7. To make it easier to find files, assign keywords to each file in the ______________ dialog box.

8. When you have two workbooks open and want to see them both on the screen, side by side, choose ______________.

9. To display windows side by side so you can see parts of each window, you ______________ them.

10. When you want to continue seeing the row or column headings as you scroll down a worksheet, you can ______________ the window into panes.

Matching

In the blank next to each of the following terms or phrases, write the letter of the corresponding term or phrase. (Note that some letters may be used more than once.)

a. Zoom
b. View, Toolbars, Customize
c. Tools, Options
d. File, Properties
e. Reset
f. Freeze panes
g. Floating toolbar
h. Split
i. Built-in menus
j. Docking

_______ 1. Command to change standard font and font size

_______ 2. Attaching a toolbar to the side of the program window

_______ 3. Command to use to add new buttons

_______ 4. A toolbar that isn't docked

_______ 5. Click this button in the Customize toolbar to remove customization from a selected toolbar

_______ 6. Select this category in the Customize dialog box to add a menu to a toolbar

_______ 7. Click this to change the magnification of the worksheet

_______ 8. To separate a worksheet into separate panes, each with separate scroll bars

_______ 9. Dividing a worksheet into panes without separate scroll bars

_______ 10. Command to use when you want to enter summary information about the workbook

Applying Your Skills

Practice

The following exercises enable you to practice the skills you have learned in this project. Take a few minutes to work through these exercises now.

Setting Up a New Workbook and Custom Toolbar

You change the standard workbook to support a quarterly accounting system in this project. You also add a custom toolbar that gives you the extra tools you need to work with on a regular basis.

To set up a new workbook and custom toolbar, follow these steps:

1. Start Excel and change the default workbook size to four worksheets. Also change the standard font size to 12 points.
2. When you have restarted Excel, open a new four-sheet workbook and save it as `Quarterly Record`.
3. Create a new toolbar called `Handy Bar`. From the Window and Help category, place the Freeze Panes button on the new toolbar. From the View category, place the Zoom In and Zoom Out buttons on the new toolbar. From the File category, place the buttons for New (worksheet), Set Print Area, and Open on the new toolbar.
4. Arrange the buttons on the Handy Bar toolbar so that Zoom In and Zoom Out are together in their own group at the right end of the bar. Place the Open, New, and Set Print Area buttons in their own group on the left end of the bar. Place the Freeze Panes button in the middle in its own group.
5. Now add the Format menu from the Built-In Menus category to the Handy Bar toolbar. Place the menu at the right end of the toolbar.
6. Close the Handy Bar toolbar, but leave the Quarterly Record workbook open.

Using Zoom and Freeze

Use Excel's built-in functions and the tools on your new Handy Bar toolbar to work with a file from an earlier exercise.

To use zoom and freeze, follow these steps:

1. From the Project-05 folder on the CD, open the Proj0502 file. Save it as `Project Cash Flow Analysis` and store in the My Documents folder on your hard drive (or to a location specified by your instructor). Close the file.
2. Display the Handy Bar toolbar again and use the Open button to locate Project Cash Flow Analysis. Use the Advanced button to assist you in finding the file.

3. Open `project Cash Flow Analysis` and go to the `Beauty Supplies` tab.
4. Use the Freeze Panes button on the Handy Bar toolbar to freeze the panes so that you can scroll around the worksheet and still keep the headings in sight.
5. Unfreeze the window, using the same tool.
6. Use the Zoom In tool on the Handy Bar toolbar to take a closer look (200%) at the cost of sales in the Beauty Supplies project for the first quarter.
7. Use the Handy Bar toolbar to insert a new worksheet into the workbook, following the `Accessories` tab.
8. Go back to the `Beauty Supplies` tab and zoom back out.
9. Close `Project Cash Flow Analysis`. You do not need to save the changes.

Using Multiple Windows

Being able to open multiple windows is a real bonus when you need to look at more than one worksheet and more than one workbook at a time. In this project, you open several files created in previous projects.

To use multiple windows, follow these steps:

1. From the Project-05 folder on the CD, open the file Proj0503. Save it as `Store Markup` and close it.
2. From the Project-05 folder on the CD, open the file Proj0504. Save it as `Outbound Sales` and close it.
3. From the Project-05 folder on the CD, open the file Proj0505. Save it as `Receivables` and close it.
4. `Quarterly Record` still is open on your desktop (if not, open it), with the Handy Bar toolbar still available from an earlier exercise.
5. Use the Open button on the Handy Bar toolbar to open the `Store Markup`, `Outbound Sales`, and `Receivables` workbooks. The Advanced button assists you in finding these files.
6. Tile these three document windows and cascade them.
7. With the document windows cascaded, use the Window menu to select the window that is in the upper-left position. Use the Freeze Panes button on the Handy Bar toolbar in the different windows.
8. Delete the Handy Bar toolbar.
9. Return Excel's default settings to 3 sheets in a workbook and 10-point font size.

10. Exit Excel, closing the files that were open—without saving any changes that you made to them. The Handy Bar toolbar is deleted, even though you close these files without saving any changes.

Challenge

The following challenges enable you to use your problem-solving skills. Take time to work through these exercises now.

Setting Defaults

Change Excel's default settings so each new workbook has 12 worksheets, the standard font is Times New Roman, and the font size is 12. Exit and restart Excel so the defaults can take effect. Start a new workbook and save it as `Year End`.

Creating Custom Toolbars

Create a new toolbar and name it `Important`. From the Edit category, add the Clear Contents button. From the View category, choose Zoom In and Zoom Out. From the Format category, add the Cells button. From the Window and Help category, add Split, Arrange, and Freeze Panes.

Viewing Large Worksheets

From the Project-05 folder on the CD, open Proj0506 and save it as `1997 Expenses`. Zoom out to see the entire worksheet. Split the window so you can see the column headings and the first three columns on the left. Zoom in to 100%. Remove the split. Freeze the panes at the same location.

Using Multiple Windows

Tile the two open workbooks—1997 Expenses and Year End. Close the Year End workbook. Delete the Important toolbar and return Excel's default settings to 3 worksheets, Arial, and 10 points. Save the 1997 Expenses workbook and exit Excel.

PinPoint Assessment

PinPoint Training

You have completed the project and the associated lessons, as well as the "Checking Your Skills" and "Applying Your Skills" sections. Now use the PinPoint software evaluation mode to assess your comprehension of the specific exam tasks you have just learned. You can also use the PinPoint Trainer Mode and the Show Me tutorials to practice these specific exam tasks.

Project Six 6

Using Excel with Other Programs

Integrating Applications

In this Project, you learn how to:

Objectives	Required Activities
➤ Switch among Applications	
➤ Copy Data between Applications	Export to Other Applications
➤ Link Data between Applications	Export to Other Applications
➤ Work with Embedded Data	Export to Other Applications
➤ Save Files in Other Formats	Export to Other Applications
➤ Import Data from Other Applications	Import from Other Applications

Why Would I Do This?

While at your desk, you probably do several things in rapid succession: work on a paper, talk on the phone, punch numbers into your calculator, and so on. Similarly, when you work on your computer, you may work for a few minutes on a document in a word processor, take a moment to update a worksheet, then look up a phone number in an electronic phone book.

Multitasking
The execution of more than one program at a time on a computer system.

One of the advantages of using software that runs under Windows 95 is that you have the capability to exchange data among various applications. In Windows 95, you can have more than one application running at once—called *multitasking*—so you can switch among applications as you need to work on different tasks. You can display several applications' documents at the same time, if necessary, and exchange data among those documents.

Integration
Using two or more software applications together to create a single document.

In addition, with Excel 97, you can easily open and work with documents that were created in different applications, such as Lotus 1-2-3. You can also save documents in different file formats so that people using other applications can open and work with worksheets created with Excel. This feature of Windows software is called *integration*, and it makes working with the computer easier and more intuitive.

Lesson 1: Switching among Applications

You can use the taskbar to switch among open applications and to start additional programs. The number of applications that you can have open at one time is largely determined by the amount of available memory in your computer.

To Switch among Applications

1. **In Excel, open the Project-06 folder on the CD and double-click on the file Proj0601. Save the file as `Office Expenses`.**

   The worksheet lists typical office expenses for the months of January through June.

2. **Click the Start button on the taskbar and then choose Programs.**

3. **Click Microsoft Word on the submenu.**

   Microsoft Word opens, as shown in Figure 6.1; Excel remains open and moves to the background. Notice that a button for Microsoft Word has been added to the taskbar. Microsoft Word is often used in conjunction with Excel.

Figure 6.1
In this project, you integrate word processing documents with spreadsheet documents.

Microsoft Word button

Microsoft Excel button

Start button

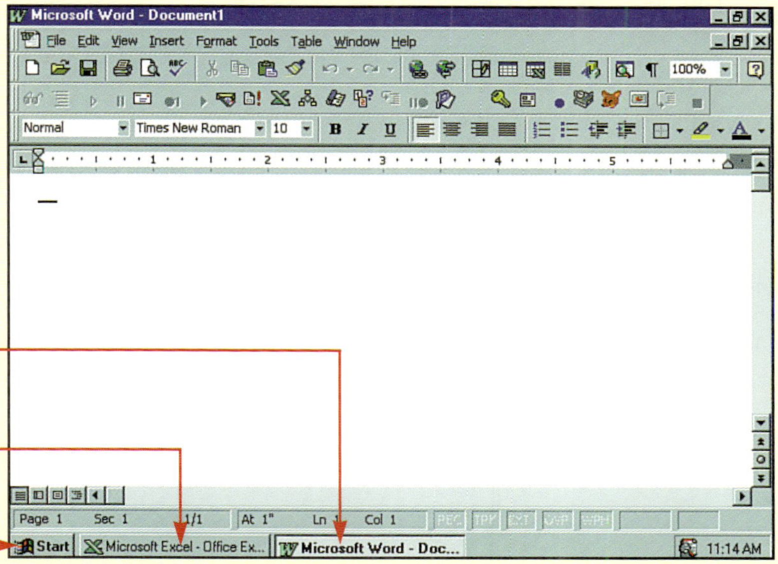

If you have problems...

Microsoft Word was chosen for this example because it is a popular word processing program that is widely available. If you cannot find Microsoft Word listed in the Programs submenu or if you have a different version of Microsoft Word installed, check with your instructor for information about what to do in this project. Your instructor might have you use a different word processing application to complete the lessons in this project.

Don't worry if you have never used Word or any other word processing software before. The instructions in this project tell you exactly what to do. Remember, just about everything you do with Excel and Word in this project can be done using other Windows 95 applications. However, if you are using a different word processing application, the steps you use to complete the lessons may be slightly different.

4. **In Word, open the Project-06 folder on the CD and then double-click the file Proj0602. Save the file as `Memo`.**

You use the `Memo` document with the Excel Office Expenses document throughout this project (see Figure 6.2).

5. **Click the Microsoft Excel button on the taskbar.**

This switches you back to Excel. Word remains open, running in the background. Keep all these documents and applications open. In Lesson 2, you learn how to copy data from one application to another.

continues

To Switch among Applications (continued)

Figure 6.2
Memo is a Microsoft Word document.

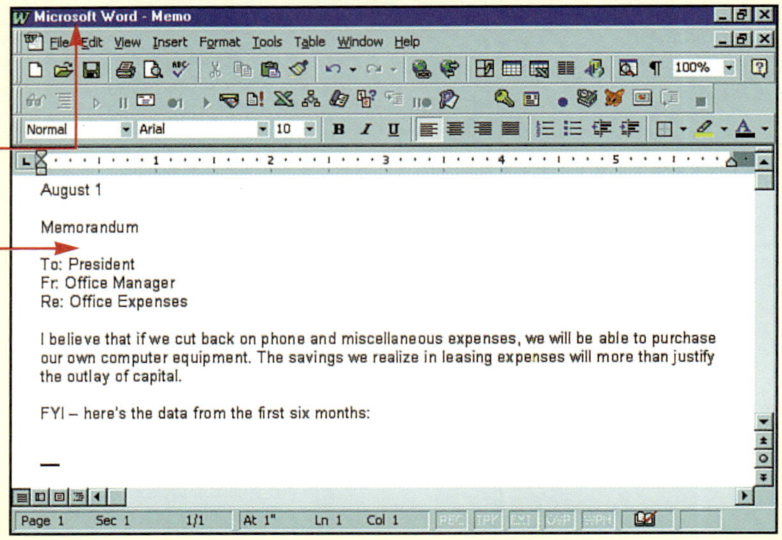

Inside Stuff

Another quick way to switch among open applications is to press and hold down Alt as you press Tab. Each time you press Tab, the name of the next open application appears. When you see the name of the application you want to use, release both keys.

If you are distracted by an open application that is visible on the desktop behind the active application, maximize the active application to fill the desktop. If you want to switch to the application in the background, use the taskbar or press Alt+Tab.

If you are using a suite of applications, such as Microsoft Office, you can use the shortcut bar included with the suite to switch among programs. The shortcut bar usually appears in the title bar of the active applications, and it displays one button for each application in the suite. Click the application button to open or to switch to a different application.

Microsoft Office is a collection of several Microsoft applications sold in one package, which usually includes Excel, Word, PowerPoint (a presentation graphics software package), and Access (a database program). Microsoft Office also includes special features, such as the shortcut bar designed to make integration with other Microsoft applications easier.

If you have problems...

If you find that your system is slow or locking up, you may have unintentionally launched a program twice instead of simply switching to it. (You can launch a program again from the Programs menu, even if it is already running.) To avoid this problem, just check the taskbar before opening a new program to make sure that the program is not already running. If two buttons for the same program appear, right-click one of them and choose Close from the shortcut menu.

Lesson 2: Copying Data between Applications

It's easy to copy information from one application to another, and it saves you from having to re-enter data. For example, suppose that you want to include data from a worksheet in a letter to your company's president. You can perform this task easily by using the Windows Clipboard and task-switching capabilities.

To Copy Data between Applications

1 In Excel, select cells A6:H9 in the `Office Expenses` worksheet.

This is the data you want to copy to the memo document.

2 Click the Copy button on the Standard toolbar, or press Ctrl+C.

The data is copied to the Windows Clipboard. You can use the menu commands or the toolbar buttons to copy, cut, and paste data among applications. In short, you can use the Clipboard to copy or move data from one Windows application to another, just as you can copy or move data within a single document.

3 Click the Microsoft Word button on the taskbar.

The `Memo` file that you opened earlier in this project should now be on your screen.

4 Press Ctrl+End to move the insertion point to the blank line at the end of the memo.

This is where you want to insert the data you just copied from Excel.

5 Click the Paste button on the Standard toolbar, or press Ctrl+V.

The data is pasted from the Clipboard into the letter at the insertion point's location (see Figure 6.3). The data is inserted in Word as a table and retains most of the formatting from Excel. The table is in no way connected to the original data in Excel. If you know how to use Word, you can edit and format the data using the Table menu features. The changes have no effect on the worksheet data in Excel. Likewise, if you edit the Excel worksheet, the changes do not affect the table in Word.

To prepare for the next lesson in this project, undo the paste action now to remove the Excel data from the Word document.

continues

To Copy Data between Applications (continued)

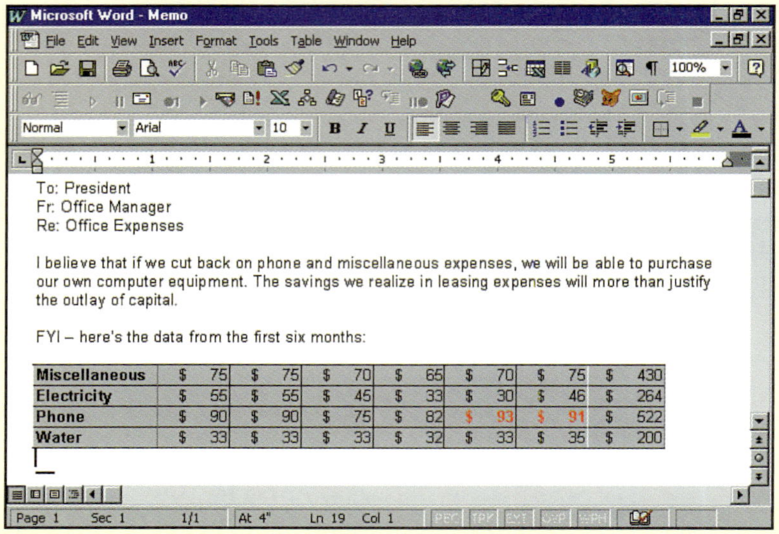

Figure 6.3
Selected data from the Excel worksheet now appears in the Word document.

6 In the `Memo` document, click the Undo button, or press Ctrl+Z.

Word reverses the paste action, and the Excel data is removed from the `Memo` document.

7 Save your work, and keep all the current files and applications open. In the next lesson, you learn how to link data between Excel and Word.

Inside Stuff

To move data from one application to another, use the Cut command or its toolbar button rather than the Copy command. If you are concerned about losing data, you can use the Copy command and then after you paste the data in the new location, return and delete it from the original location. You can also display both documents onscreen at the same time, then select and drag the data you want to move from one worksheet to the other.

Lesson 3: Linking Data between Applications

The next level of sophistication in using Excel with other applications is to **link** data from Excel to a document in another program. For example, you can link a range of cells from the expense worksheet to the memo in Word. Then, if you change any values in the worksheet, the information in the Word document is updated automatically. Keep in mind, however, that you cannot edit the linked data in the Word document. (Look for the Jargon Watch at the end of this lesson for more information about the terminology of sharing information between applications.)

You can link Excel data to many applications, including Word; presentation programs, such as PowerPoint; and database programs, such as Access. You can even link Excel data to programs that are not part of the Microsoft Office suite, as long as they support linking.

Another benefit of linking Excel data to other applications is that you can double-click the Excel data in the other document to quickly switch to the Excel worksheet where you originally created the data. Also, unlike the copy you made of the chart in the previous lesson, linking the chart updates the chart in the Word document when you change the data in the Excel worksheet.

You create a link so that you don't have to remember to update the same information in two places: the original worksheet and its representation in the letter.

To Link Data between Applications

1 Click the Excel button on the taskbar to switch to Excel and then select cells A1 through H11 in the `Office Expenses` worksheet.

This time, you want to link all of the worksheet data to your letter.

2 Click the Copy button.

This copies the selected range to the Windows Clipboard.

3 Click the Microsoft Word button on the taskbar to switch to Word.

Word is once again onscreen with `Memo` open.

4 Press Ctrl+End to move the insertion point to the blank line at the end of the document.

This is where you want to insert the linked data from Excel.

5 Choose Edit, Paste Special.

The Paste Special dialog box appears, as shown in Figure 6.4.

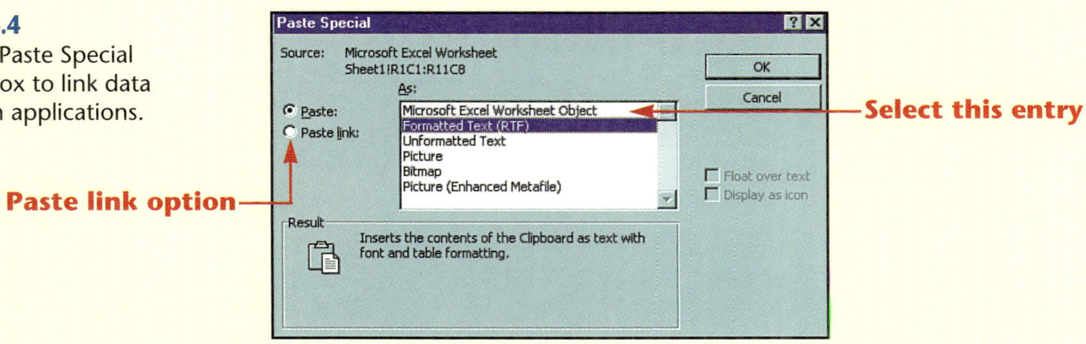

Figure 6.4
Use the Paste Special dialog box to link data between applications.

continues

To Link Data between Applications (continued)

6 Click the Paste link option button.

This tells Word that you want to link the Excel data to the Word document.

7 Select Microsoft Excel Worksheet Object from the As data type list.

This tells Word that you want to paste the data as an actual Excel worksheet that will be updated any time changes are made in the `Office Expenses` worksheet. Notice that a description of the results of your selections appears in the Result area of the dialog box.

8 Choose OK.

The Excel data is pasted into the memo as an actual Excel worksheet object, as shown in Figure 6.5. Notice that Word changes the display view on the screen so that it can show the object in the document. The white boxes around the edges of the worksheet are called *selection handles*. You can drag a handle to change the size of the worksheet in the document.

Selection Handles
Small boxes that appear around an object to indicate that the object is selected. By dragging the handles toward or away from the center of the object, you can change the size and shape of the object.

Now try changing a cell in the Excel worksheet to see how the linked data changes automatically.

Figure 6.5
Linked data from Excel is pasted into the Word document.

Selection handles

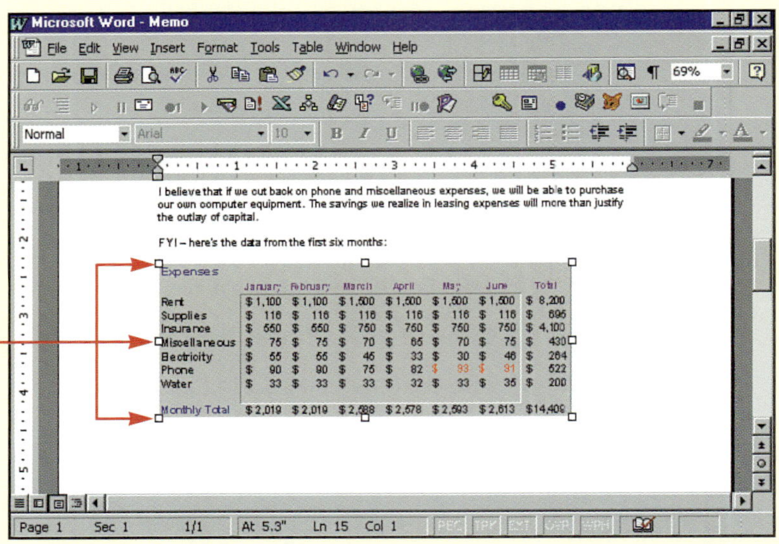

9 Double-click anywhere within the Excel data in the Word document.

This switches back to Excel with the `Office Expenses` worksheet open. If necessary, maximize the worksheet.

Excel

10 Change cell F8 in the worksheet to `$80.00`.

This shows a decrease in the amount spent on phone expenses in May. Make sure that you press Tab or Enter to update the change to the cell. Notice that Excel automatically updates the conditional formatting, as well as the totals that depend on the data in cell F8.

11 Click the Microsoft Word button on the taskbar.

Word appears, displaying the `Memo` document. Notice that the linked worksheet has been automatically updated to reflect the changes made in Excel, as shown in Figure 6.6. The May phone expenses, the totals, and the conditional formatting have all changed.

Figure 6.6
The values changed in Excel are updated automatically in the linked data in Word.

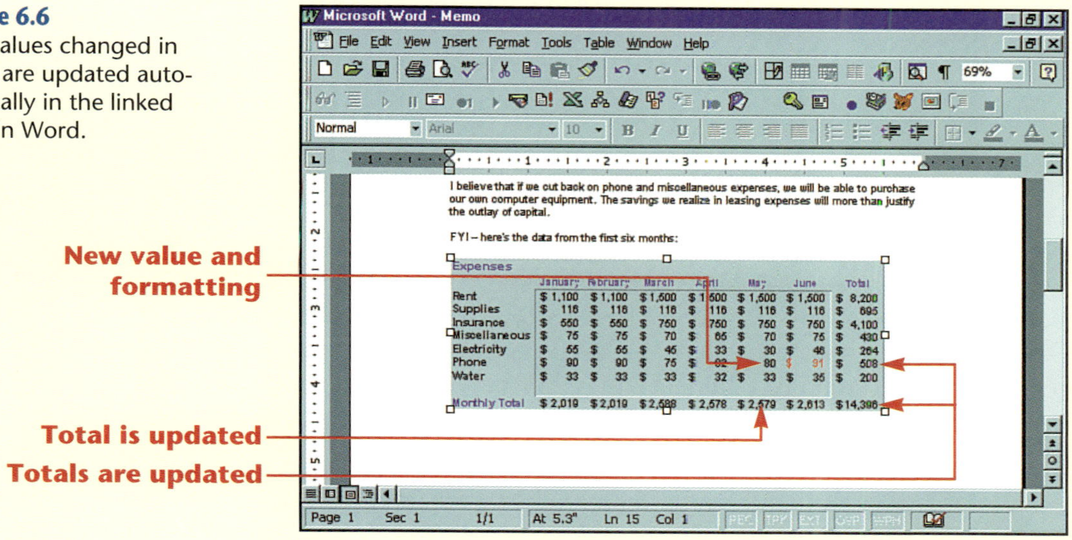

Save your work in the Word document, `Memo`, and in the Excel worksheet, `Office Expenses`.

12 Keep all the current files and applications open for the next lesson. In Lesson 4, you work directly with the Excel object embedded in Word.

If you have problems...

If the data does not update in Word, you may have only pasted instead of pasting a link. Go back to Excel and copy the spreadsheet again, then switch to Word and make sure you choose Edit, Paste Special.

Also, if you change the location of either the source or the target document, the link between the two is broken. (See the following Jargon Watch for definitions of these terms.) For example, if you move the target document to a different folder or disk and then change the data in the source, Excel cannot automatically update the link. You must repeat the link procedure. If you plan to change the location of either document, you should consider simply copying the data from one to the other or embedding the data, as described in Lesson 4.

Jargon Watch

These days, **integration** is a hot buzz word in computing. For example, the Microsoft Office **suite** of applications is referred to as integrated because they share many features and standard commands and because it is easy to integrate data from one program into another.

The common Windows platform enables many Windows applications to easily share data. This feature goes by the catchy names **OLE**, which stands for **object linking and embedding**, and **DDE**, which stands for **dynamic data exchange**.

DDE uses **linking** to set up communication between two files so that when you update the **source** file, the **target** file in the link is automatically updated. Office Expenses is the source file in Lesson 3, while `Memo` is the target file.

OLE uses **embedding** to create an **object** in the client file. You use embedding in Lesson 4 to make changes in an Excel object that resides in Word. With embedding, the object is not linked in any way to the source file; you can edit the worksheet data using Excel functions, but the changes do not affect the original data.

Lesson 4: Working with Embedded Data

In Lesson 3, you linked an Excel worksheet object into the Word document `Memo`. This is useful for keeping both the source and target documents current. However, there may be times when you want to keep the two separate—perhaps to experiment with the effects of possible changes in data or when you may not have access to the source file once the target file has been created. In cases such as these, you can embed the Excel worksheet object into the Word document instead of linking it.

Embedding the data enables you to edit the worksheet in the Word document without switching back to Excel. For example, if you want to take a quick look at the effect of decreased leasing costs on your expenses, double-click the embedded Excel worksheet object and make changes directly to the worksheet—without ever leaving the memo you are writing. The original source file, `Office Expenses`, is not affected by the change.

To Work with Embedded Data

1. **In the Word file `Memo`, click the Excel data and press Del.**

   This selects the data, then deletes it, severing the link between the two applications. Now try embedding an Excel worksheet object into the Word document.

2. **Click the Microsoft Excel button on the taskbar.**

   This switches you back to the `Office Expenses` worksheet.

3 Select cells A1 through H11 and click the Copy button on the Standard toolbar.

This copies the data you want to embed in the Word document onto the Windows Clipboard.

4 Click the Microsoft Word button on the taskbar.

This switches you back to Word.

5 Press Ctrl+End to position the insertion point on the blank line at the end of the memo, then open the Edit menu and choose Paste Special.

The Paste Special dialog box opens.

6 Choose Microsoft Excel Worksheet Object in the As list box, then choose OK.

Excel embeds the worksheet object at the insertion-point location. Do not choose the Paste Link option button in the Paste Special dialog box. To embed the object, leave the Paste option button selected. Now try editing the worksheet.

7 Double-click the Excel worksheet object in the Word document.

The worksheet appears in its own Excel window within Word, as shown in Figure 6.7. Although the title bar tells you that you are still in Word, notice that the menu bar and toolbars have changed to include Excel commands and options. The formula bar even appears in your Word window now. Next, see what effect removing miscellaneous costs would have on your worksheet.

Figure 6.7
You can use Excel functions to edit embedded worksheet data in Word.

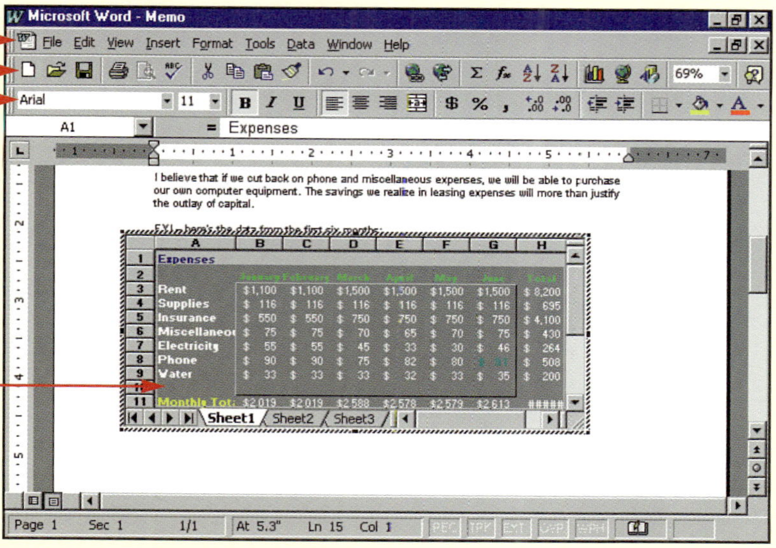

continues

To Work with Embedded Data (continued)

8 In the worksheet window, click the row header for row 6 in the worksheet frame and choose Edit, Delete.

This selects and then removes row 6 from the embedded worksheet. Notice that the total cells change automatically to reflect that miscellaneous expenses are no longer included.

9 Click anywhere in the Word document outside the worksheet window.

This closes the Excel worksheet, and Word returns to its normal state. Notice that the change you made in the data appears in the Word worksheet object, as shown in Figure 6.8. Save the Word document, then switch back to see how the changes affected the original worksheet document.

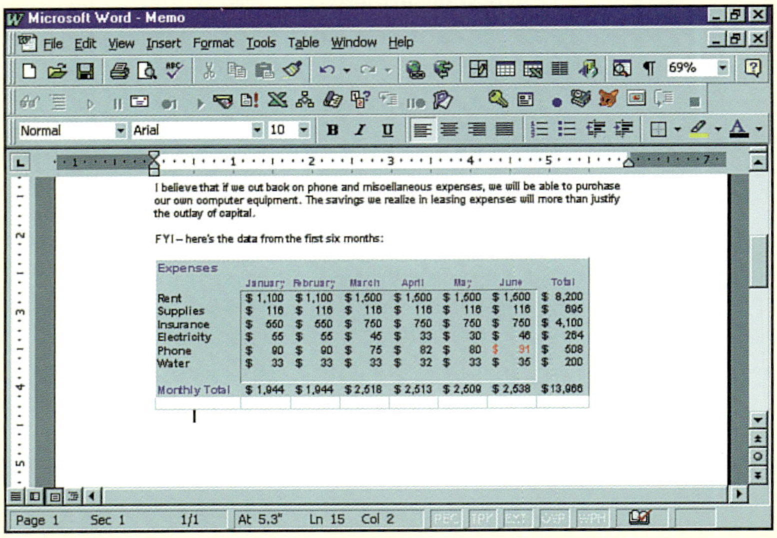

Figure 6.8
The changes appear in the embedded worksheet, but not in the original Excel file.

10 In Word, choose File, Close and click Yes to save the changes to the Word document `Memo`**. Close Word.**

When Word closes, Excel remains open on your screen. In Excel, you can see that no changes have been made to the original data.

11 Save your Excel work. In the next lesson, you learn how to share data across different applications.

Lesson 5: Saving Files in Other Formats

Sometimes you may need to open files that have been created in a different application. Likewise, you may want to be able to open an Excel file using a different application. For example, you may use Excel at work but have Lotus 1-2-3 at home, or a coworker or client may use a different application.

Excel 97 is able to open and save files in a wide variety of file formats. When you open a file created in a different file format, Excel simply converts the data to the Excel format, so you can easily use all Excel commands and options. When you save the file, you have the option of saving it in its original format or in Excel 97 format. When you save a file in a different file format, Excel converts the file so that you can open it and edit it in the other application. In this lesson, you save the `Office Expenses` workbook file in a different file format.

To Share Data across Different Applications

1. **In the `Office Expenses` worksheet, choose File, Save As.**

   The Save As dialog box is displayed. The default file type is Microsoft Excel Workbook. However, you want to save the file so that you can open it with Lotus 1-2-3.

2. **Click the Save as type drop-down arrow.**

   A list of file formats that you can use to save the file opens, as shown in Figure 6.9.

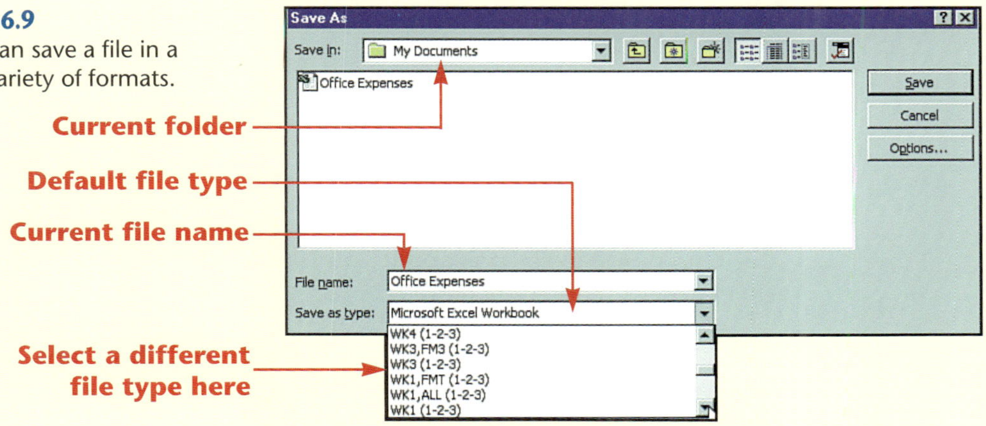

Figure 6.9
Excel can save a file in a wide variety of formats.

3. **Scroll down the list and choose `WK4 (1-2-3)`.**

   This tells Excel you want to save the file in Lotus 1-2-3 Release 4 format.

continues

To Share Data across Different Applications (continued)

4 In the File name text box, type Expenses123**.**

This changes the filename to make it easier to identify which file is the Excel file and which is the Lotus 1-2-3 file. If necessary, select the folder or disk where you want to save the file from the Save in drop-down list.

5 Choose Save.

Excel saves the file in 1-2-3 format and keeps it open on the screen, as shown in Figure 6.10. The Excel Office Expenses worksheet is saved in its original format and closed. All of the data in the Expenses123 file appears as it did in the Excel format file. You won't see any changes until you close the file and reopen it.

Figure 6.10
When saving a workbook as a different file type, you may lose some of the formatting that you applied in Excel.

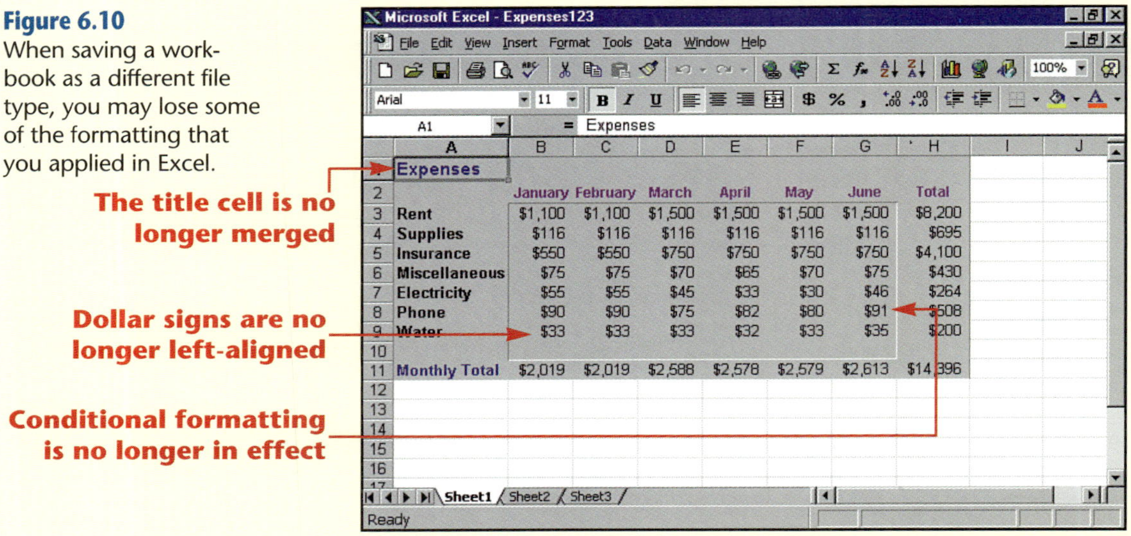

6 Choose File, Close.

The first time you close a file saved in a different file format, Excel displays a message box asking if you want to convert the file back to Excel format before you close it.

7 Choose No.

Excel saves the file in 1-2-3 Release 4 format and closes it. Now, try opening a file saved in a different file format.

8 In Excel, choose File, Open.

The Open dialog box is displayed. Notice that only Excel files are listed.

9 From the Files of type drop down list, choose Lotus 1-2-3 Files.

This tells Excel to list files saved in the Lotus 1-2-3 format. In the Open dialog box, you see the Expenses123 filename (see Figure 6.11).

Figure 6.11
You can use Excel to open files saved in other file formats.

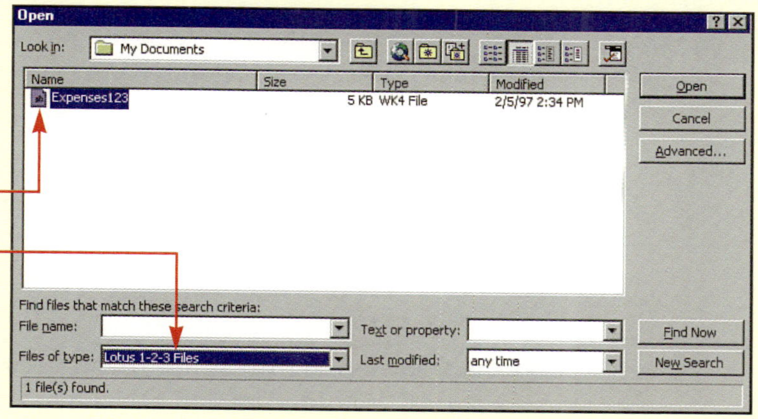

10. **Select the** Expenses123 **file name, then choose Open.**

    Excel opens the file. Some of the formatting you had in the Excel file is changed to conform to the 1-2-3 standard. For example, notice that the dollar signs are no longer left-aligned in the cells formatted as currency. Also, notice that the conditional formatting is no longer in effect and that merged cells are split.

11. **Close the** Expenses123 **file but do not exit Excel.**

Inside Stuff

With Excel 97, you can save data in the HTML format, which is used to store files on the Word Wide Web. To save data in HTML format, choose File, Save as HTML to start the Internet Assistant Wizard, then follow the instructions that the wizard displays on your screen.

In the Open dialog box, you can display all files stored in the current folder—regardless of file type—by choosing All Files from the Files of type drop down list.

Lesson 6: Importing Data from Other Applications

The same methods you use to copy, link, or embed worksheet data into another application can also be applied to bringing data from other applications into Excel. For example, you can import a piece of text or a table from a word processing application or a chart from a presentation application such as PowerPoint. By importing this information, you save yourself time that you would have used to create the same item in Excel.

To Import Data from Other Applications

1 Click the New button on the Standard toolbar.

Into this new workbook, you import information from a Word report that you need as the beginning of your first worksheet.

2 Click the Start button on the taskbar and choose Programs, Microsoft Word from the menu.

Microsoft Word appears with a new document, but Microsoft Excel is still open.

3 Click the Open button on the Standard toolbar. From the Project-06 folder on the CD, select `Proj0603` and click Open.

This document is an explanation of the Internet and intranets. As part of a presentation to the Board, you want to show your company's current use of the Internet and explain the advantages of using an intranet. You need to include some of the text from this document in your worksheet, as well as a graph and a table from another Word document.

4 Press Ctrl+End.

This moves your insertion point to the end of the document.

5 Select the third paragraph from the end of the document.

The paragraph, which begins with `The Internet is a public network`, explains the difference between the Internet and an intranet.

6 Click the Copy button on the Standard toolbar.

A copy of the paragraph is now stored in the Clipboard. Now you want to put it into your worksheet.

7 Click the Microsoft Excel button on the taskbar.

The blank worksheet should now appear on your screen.

8 Click A3 and then the Paste button on the Standard toolbar.

There is more text than easily fits into a single cell. You need to merge some cells to contain the text and then format the text.

9 Select the range A3:C12. Choose Format, Cells from the menu.

The Format Cells dialog box appears (see Figure 6.12).

10 Click the Alignment tab and then select both Wrap text and Merge cells in the Text control area. Choose OK.

The selected cells have been merged into a larger text area in which the text wraps. To make it more attractive, apply bold and italic attributes to the text.

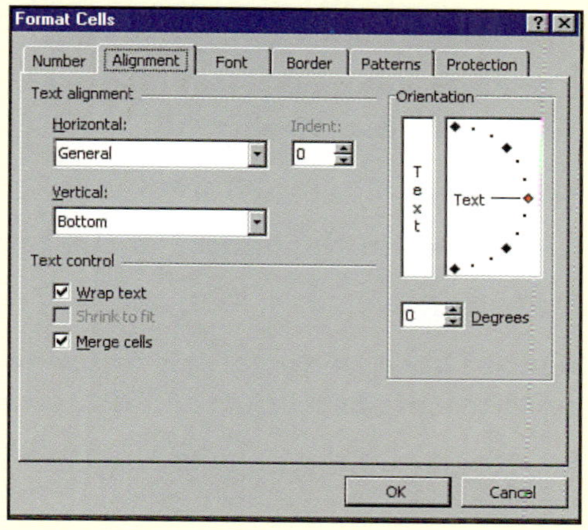

Figure 6.12
To display the imported text so it can be read, merge a group of cells and wrap the text within that area.

⑪ **Click Bold and then Italic on the Formatting toolbar.**

Now you need to import a table that appears in the Word report. However, you want that table to update every time data is added or changed in Word.

⑫ **Click the Microsoft Word button on the taskbar. Scroll up to find Table 1.1 and select the entire table.**

If you're not familiar with Word, select the table by clicking once in the table and choosing Table, Select Table from the menu.

⑬ **Click the Copy button on the Standard toolbar.**

⑭ **Click the Microsoft Excel button on the taskbar and then D4 in the worksheet.**

⑮ **Choose Edit, Paste Special.**

The Paste Special dialog box appears (see Figure 6.13).

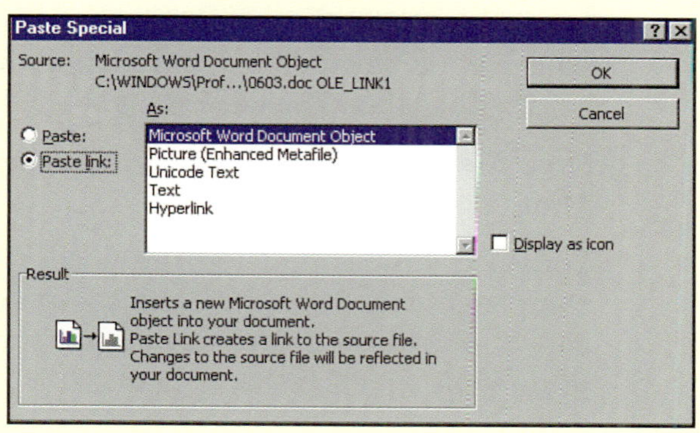

Figure 6.13
Make sure you select Paste link so your worksheet automatically updates when the Word table changes.

continues

To Import Data from Other Applications (continued)

16. **Click Paste link and select Microsoft Word document Object from the As list. Choose OK.**

    The table appears in your worksheet.

17. **Double-click in the middle of the table.**

    This switches you back to the table in the Word document.

18. **Change the** `Stock Quotations` **figure for** `Executives` **to** `30`**. Click the Microsoft Excel button on the taskbar.**

    The change automatically appears in Excel, even though you didn't save the Word document first.

    Now you decide you don't really need the table linked to the Word document—instead, make changes in Excel.

19. **Click the table once to select it and press Del.**

20. **Click the Microsoft Word button on the taskbar.**

21. **Select the table and copy it to the Clipboard.**

22. **Click the Microsoft Excel button on the taskbar and then D4 on the worksheet.**

23. **Choose Edit, Paste Special.**

    The Paste Special dialog box appears. This time, you want to embed the table in your worksheet.

24. **Click Paste and then choose Microsoft Word Document Object from the As list. Choose OK.**

25. **Double-click on the table.**

    Now when you double-click the table, you don't switch to the Microsoft Word document. Instead, a frame appears around the table and Word toolbars and commands display on the screen for editing the table. The table is embedded in the worksheet.

26. **Save the worksheet file as** `Import`**. Close the file and exit Excel. Then exit Microsoft Word.**

    You have now completed the lessons in this project. If you have completed your session on the computer, exit all open applications and Windows 95 before turning off the computer. Otherwise, continue with the "Checking Your Skills" and "Applying Your Skills" sections.

Project Summary

To	Do This
Switch applications	On the Windows 95 taskbar, click the button for the application you want to make active, or press Alt+Tab.
Copy data between applications	Select the data to copy and click the Copy button on the Standard toolbar. Change to the target document, position the insertion point, and click the Paste button on the Standard toolbar.
Move data between applications	Select the data to move and click the Cut button on the Standard toolbar. Change to the target document, position the insertion point, and click the Paste button on the Standard toolbar.
Link data between applications	Select the data to link and click the Copy button on the Standard toolbar. Change to the target document, position the insertion point, and choose Edit, Paste Special. Click the Paste link option button, select the object type, and choose OK.
Edit linked data	Double-click the data to open the source document. Make changes, then close the source document.
Embed data	Select the data to embed and click the Copy button on the Standard toolbar. Change to the target document, position the insertion point, and choose Edit, Paste Special. Select the object type, and choose OK.
Edit embedded data	Double-click the data to open an editing window. Edit the document, then close the editing window.
Save a file in a different format	Choose File, Save As. Select the file format from the Save as type drop-down list, then choose Save.
Open a file in a different format	Choose File, Open. Select the file type from the Files of type drop-down list, select the file you want to open, then choose Open.

Checking Your Skills

True/False

For each of the following, check *T* or *F* to indicate whether the statement is true or false.

__T __F 1. You cannot use the keyboard shortcuts for copying, cutting, and pasting when you are integrating applications.

__T __F 2. Use the Edit, Paste Special command to link or embed data between applications.

__T __F 3. If two documents are visible on your screen, you can drag data from one document to another.

__T __F 4. Excel 97 is capable of opening and saving files in different formats, such as Lotus 1-2-3.

__T __F 5. If you use the Copy and Paste commands to copy data from a worksheet to a word processing file, the data will be automatically updated when you make changes to one of the files.

__T __F 6. You can use the Windows taskbar to switch among programs, but not to open them.

__T __F 7. If your system slows down, it could be because you have two copies of the same program open.

__T __F 8. You cannot link data between programs that are not part of the Microsoft Office suite.

__T __F 9. The number of applications you can have open at one time is largely determined by the size of your computer's memory.

__T __F 10. Excel cannot open a file created by another application if the file format doesn't appear on the Files of type list in the Open dialog box.

Multiple Choice

Circle the letter of the correct answer for each of the following questions.

1. Which of the following can be passed over a link between applications?

   a. Numbers

   b. Charts

   c. Ranges of cells

   d. All the above

2. One application opens within the other application when you do what between two applications?

   a. Copy

   b. Link

   c. Move

   d. Embed

3. Embedding and linking are part of a Windows feature called what?
   a. OLE
   b. LEO
   c. ELO
   d. LLE
4. You can make a change in the source, and the destination automatically updates when you do what?
   a. Link
   b. Embed
   c. Copy
   d. Paste
5. What occurs when you double-click a linked object?
   a. The object is deleted from the document.
   b. You are switched back to the originating program.
   c. An error message displays.
   d. You can edit the document in the target file.
6. Which of the following is an easy way to switch among open applications?
   a. Press Ctrl+Del.
   b. Press Alt+Ctrl.
   c. Click the application's button on the Windows 95 taskbar.
   d. Click the application's Start box.
7. The changes you make in the target document do not affect the source file when you do what to the data?
   a. Link
   b. Embed
   c. Copy
   d. Paste
8. Which of the following formats is used to store Excel files on the World Wide Web?
   a. WWW
   b. WK4
   c. HTML
   d. XLS
9. To embed data into a file, you use which dialog box to paste it into the target document?
   a. Paste Special
   b. Paste Object
   c. Embed Object
   d. Embed Data
10. To paste a link into a document, you choose which option button in the Paste Special dialog box?
    a. Paste
    b. Link
    c. Link document
    d. Paste link

Completion

In the blanks provided, write the correct answer for each of the following statements.

1. When pasting data into another program, the data appears at the _______________ point.
2. The _______________ application is the one in which the original object was created.

3. To switch to an application in the background, use the taskbar or press ______________+______________.

4. To move data from one application to another, use the ______________ command.

5. If you change the location of the source or target document, the link between the two is ______________.

6. A link is a(n) ______________-way connection.

7. If your system slows when embedding, you may want to consider sharing your data by ______________ instead.

8. The taskbar displays buttons for all ______________ applications.

9. You can use the ______________ to copy or move data from one application to another.

10. When saving a file in a different format, you choose the format from the ______________ drop-down list in the Save As dialog box.

Matching

In the blank next to each of the following terms or phrases, write the letter of the corresponding term or phrase. (Note that some letters may be used more than once.)

a. taskbar
b. Paste
c. Paste Special
d. object
e. selection handles
f. multitasking
g. target file
h. integration
i. dynamic data exchange (DDE)
j. source file

_______ 1. White boxes around the edges of a worksheet object

_______ 2. The file in which linked data originates

_______ 3. The file in which linked data is pasted

_______ 4. Executing more than one program at a time

_______ 5. Using two or more software applications together to create a single document

_______ 6. Embedding is used to create this in a file

_______ 7. Uses linking to set up communication between two files

_______ 8. Used to switch among open applications and to start additional programs

_______ 9. Use this command to paste information from the Clipboard to another application

_______ 10. Use this command to paste a link or embed data into a document

Applying Your Skills

Practice

The following exercises enable you to practice the skills you have learned in this project. Take a few minutes to work through these exercises now.

Switching among Applications

In this project, you learned how easy it is to open additional applications and to switch among these applications. In this exercise, you practice switching among applications.

To switch among applications, follow these steps:

1. In Excel, open the file Proj0603 from the Project-06 folder on the CD and save it as `Profit Loss 4`.
2. Start the Word application by using the Start button on the taskbar. If Word is not on your computer, ask your instructor which application to use.
3. Open one more application located in the Accessories submenu. You choose which of these applications to open. Notice that a button for each of these applications displays on the taskbar.
4. Click the Microsoft Excel button to switch to this application.
5. Click the Microsoft Word button to switch to this application.
6. Hold down the Alt key and press Tab until the name of the Accessories application that you opened appears on the screen. Release both keys to access this application.
7. Close the Accessories application and Microsoft Word. Leave Excel open for the following exercise.

Copying Excel Data to a Letter

A friend of yours is thinking about relocating to a new state and has asked you where your company has offices so she can contact them about employment opportunities. You agree to provide a list of the states where your company has offices. Because you already have a list of sites stored in an Excel worksheet, you simply copy the data into a word processing document to send to her.

To copy Excel data to a letter, follow these steps:

1. In Excel, open the file Proj0604 from the Project-06 folder on the CD and save it as `Relocate`.
2. In Word, open the file Proj0605 from the Project-06 folder on the CD and save it as `Site Letter`.
3. Copy the entire list of offices and locations in the worksheet to the Clipboard.
4. Move to the end of `Site Letter` in Word, then paste the worksheet data.

5. Save and close the letter.
6. Save and close the workbook.

Importing Data from Another Application into Excel

The company president sends you a file of a memo with the names of four new contacts who he thinks might be interested in your product. You want to add the names to the phone list that you already created in Excel. Instead of retyping the names and phone numbers, copy the data from the word processing document into Excel.

To import data from another application into Excel, follow these steps:

1. Open the file Proj0606 from the Project-06 folder on the CD in Excel and save it as `Contacts`.
2. Open the file Proj0607 from the Project-06 folder on the CD in Word,and save it as `New Names`.
3. Select the table in the Word document and copy it to the Windows Clipboard.
4. Switch to Excel and paste the data from the Clipboard to the end of the list.
5. Save and close the worksheet.
6. Save and close the Word document.

Linking Excel Data to a Presentation Document

Heading into your second year in business, you want to make a presentation to potential investors that will convince them to provide capital so you can open a second coffee shop. To do this effectively, you need to create a report in Word that includes narrative, as well as a worksheet showing strong sales for the current year. Link data from an Excel worksheet to the presentation document in Word, then make some last-minute changes in the Excel worksheet that will be updated in the linked chart.

To link Excel data to a presentation document, follow these steps:

1. In Excel, open the file Proj0608 from the Project-06 folder on the CD and save it as `Coffee Sales`.
2. In Word, open the file Proj0609 from the Project-06 folder on the CD and save it as `Presentation`.
3. In the Coffee Sales worksheet, select the entire worksheet (cells A1:E12) and copy it to the Clipboard.
4. Switch to Word and link the chart to the end of the `Presentation` document.
5. Switch back to the worksheet and make the following changes: in the January Mocha sales, change the value to `$300`; in the February Espresso sales, change the value to `$250`. Save the worksheet.

6. Switch back to the Word document to view the changes in the chart. Save and close the Presentation document.
7. Save and close the workbook.

Opening a File from Another Application

The New England regional sales manager has submitted sales figures on a disk in Lotus 1-2-3 file format. You want to be able to compare the figures with other regional figures that you have already entered into Excel and then give the comparison back to the sales manager for review. Open the 1-2-3 file, copy the data into the Excel worksheet, then save the Excel worksheet as a new 1-2-3 file.

To open a file from another application, follow these steps:

1. Open the file Proj0610 from the Project-06 folder on the CD in Excel and save it as `Sales Comparison`.
2. Open the Lotus 1-2-3 file Proj0611 from the Project-06 folder on the CD in Excel and save it in 1-2-3 format as `NE Sales123`.
3. Copy the sales data from the `NE Sales123` file into cells D2 through E12 in the `Sales Comparison` Excel workbook file.
4. Adjust the column width so you can read the data, then save the Excel file.
5. Save the `Sales Comparison` file in 1-2-3 file format with the name `Comparison123`.
6. Close all the files.

Embedding an Object in a Worksheet

You have been preparing an Excel application that will be used by everyone in your office. Before you open that application to all the users, you want to prepare a presentation to acquaint them with the application. You have an outline in Word of the application process, and you want to include that outline in your worksheet. However, you also want to be able to change that document without changing the original. You need to embed the document in your Excel worksheet.

To embed an object in a worksheet, follow these steps:

1. Start a new worksheet in Excel.
2. The Word document that contains the outline is `Proj0612` from the Project-06 folder on the CD. Click A1 and insert the outline there as an object.
3. Double-click the embedded object. After `Collect current forms and completed documents` press ↵Enter and type `Collect sketches of additional documents that may be needed`.
4. Click outside the embedded object.
5. Save the worksheet as `Application Presentation` and close it.
6. Start Microsoft Word and open Proj0612. Note that the change you made in Excel doesn't appear in the document.

7. Close the document and exit Word.
8. Exit Excel.

Challenge

The following challenges enable you to use your problem-solving skills. Take time to work through these exercises now.

Copying Data from One Application to Another

Your boss has asked you to create a document containing data from an Excel worksheet. To save having to reenter the information, you decide to copy the data from one application to another. From the Project-06 folder on the CD, open the Word file Proj0613 and save it as `Quarterly Update`. In the `Profit Loss 4` Excel worksheet (created in the previous exercise), copy the data in cells A4:D13 to the Clipboard. Switch back to the Word document and paste the data at the end of the Word document. Save the Word file and keep both Word and Excel open for the next exercise.

Linking Data

Now that you have copied the data, you realize that you could have linked the data. Then, if you had made changes to the data in the original application, the target document would automatically be changed.

Switch to the Word document, `Quarterly Update`. Select the information that you copied in the previous exercise and then delete it. Switch back to the Excel document, `Profit Loss 4`. Copy the cells A4:D13 to the Clipboard and switch back to the Word document. Use the Paste Special dialog box to link the Excel worksheet object. In the Excel worksheet, change the April sales number in cell B5 to `4,700`. Switch back to Word to see the change in the Quarterly Update document. Save `Quarterly Update` and leave it open for the following exercise. Switch to Excel and save the `Profit Loss 4` workbook. Leave it open for the following exercise.

Embedding Data

Because you now want to make some changes in the Word document but don't want to affect the original Excel worksheet, you decide to embed the data instead of linking it.

Switch to the Word `Quarterly Update` document and delete the data you linked from the Excel worksheet. Switch back to Excel. Copy the data in cells A4:D13 and use the Paste Special dialog box to embed the data at the end of the Word document. Double-click the Excel worksheet object in the Word document to display the worksheet in its own Excel window within Word. Change the number in cell B5 to `4,500`. Save the Word document before closing it. Switch to Excel. Notice that the value in cell B5 has not changed. Save the Excel workbook and leave it open for the following exercise. Reader should exit Word here.

Sharing Data across Applications

One of your coworkers needs to access some data in one of your Excel worksheets. The only problem is that he doesn't have Excel on his system; only Lotus 1-2-3. You decide to save the Excel file as a Lotus 1-2-3 file so that he can access the information.

In the `Profit Loss 4` workbook, choose File, Save As to display the Save As dialog box. In the Save as type drop-down list, select WK3 (1-2-3). Choose Save to save the file with the same name, but in the different format. Choose File, Close. Excel displays a message box asking if you want to convert the file back to Excel format. Choose No. The file is saved in the 1-2-3 format. Choose File, Open. Because only Excel files display in the dialog box, click the Files of type drop-down list. Choose Lotus 1-2-3 files. Select the Profit Loss 4 file, then choose Open. The file is opened in the Lotus 1-2-3 format. Close the `Profit Loss 4` file.

Opening Files Created in a Different Application

Your checking account file was originally saved in Lotus 1-2-3 format. Now you have upgraded to the latest version of Excel, and you want to be able to use this file without having to reenter any information. You open the 1-2-3 file, then save it as an Excel file.

From the Project-06 folder on the CD, open Proj0614.wk4. (Hint: You need to display Lotus 1-2-3 files to locate this file.) Save the file as `Checking Account 8` in Microsoft Excel 97 & 5.0/95 Workbook format. Close the file and reopen the Checking Account 8 file, which is now in Excel format. When you have finished, close the `Checking Account 8` file.

PinPoint Assessment

PinPoint Training

You have completed the project and the associated lessons, as well as the "Checking Your Skills" and "Applying Your Skills" sections. Now use the PinPoint software evaluation mode to assess your comprehension of the specific exam tasks you have just learned. You can also use the PinPoint Trainer Mode and the Show Me tutorials to practice these specific exam tasks.

Project 7
Seven

Automating Tasks With Macros

Performing Repetitive Tasks Automatically

In this Project, you learn how to:

Objectives	Required Activities
➤ Prepare to Record a Macro	Create and Record Macros
➤ Record a Macro	Create and Record Macros
➤ Play a Macro	Run Macros
➤ Record a Macro to the Personal Macro Workbook	
➤ Play a Macro from the Personal Macro Workbook	
➤ Unhide and Edit the Personal Macro Workbook	Edit Macros
➤ Create a Macro Button in a Workbook	
➤ Add a Macro Button to a Toolbar	

Excel

Why Would I Do This?

Macro
A series of commands and operations that are recorded and played back whenever you need to perform the task for which the macro was designed.

A *macro* is a series of Excel commands that performs a specific action. You can do just about anything with a macro that you can do directly on the worksheet; for example, you can open new worksheets, select and print worksheets, and create charts. Excel provides a macro feature to automate repetitive tasks and enhance productivity. If you turn on the macro recorder and give a macro a name, Excel saves your keystrokes and commands as you type. Just play back the macro whenever you want to execute the same keystrokes. For example, perhaps your company name is lengthy. Save it as a macro and play it back each time you need to type the company name in a worksheet.

In this project, you record and play back simple macros that save time by automating the keystrokes (or mouse clicks) used in your work.

Lesson 1: Preparing to Record a Macro

Before recording a macro, you need to name it and decide where to store it. Although you can run any macro from the Tools, Macro command, you also can assign it to shortcut keys or a toolbar button.

A Current Projects worksheet contains a list of your current departmental projects. When a project is completed, the completion date is entered into the worksheet and the project is transferred to the Completed Projects worksheet. In this lesson, you prepare to record a macro, named `Completed`, that is stored and used in the current workbook. This macro automates a repetitive task, making you more productive.

When you run a macro, Excel performs the tasks recorded under that name. In this example, the macro copies completed projects from one worksheet to another and then deletes the completed project from the original worksheet.

To Prepare to Record a Macro

1. **Open the Proj0701 file from the Project-07 folder on the CD and save it as `Project List`.**

   This workbook contains two worksheets labeled `Current Projects` and `Completed Projects`.

2. **Type `4/8/98` in cell F4 of the Current Projects worksheet and press ↵Enter.**

   The project listed in row 4 has been completed.

3. **Select row 4 by clicking the row heading.**

   The row you want to transfer is selected prior to recording the macro because it may change, depending on which project was completed.

4 Choose Tools, Macro, Record New Macro.

The Record New Macro dialog box is displayed, as shown in Figure 7.1. You name the macro before you record it. If you don't name it, the macro is given the default name of `Macro1`.

Figure 7.1
In the Record Macro dialog box, you enter a name and set other options for the procedure you are about to record.

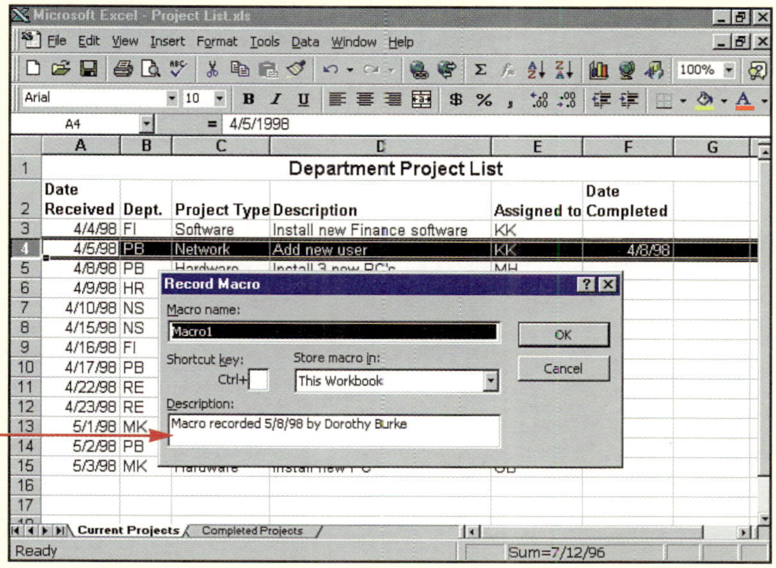

Default description shows date and author

5 With the Macro Name text box highlighted, type `Completed`.

The macro name is displayed in the Macro Name text box.

Inside Stuff

If you choose, you can assign a shortcut key combination to the macro. The macro name can be an upper- or lowercase letter. After the macro is recorded, you run it by pressing Ctrl and the shortcut key you specified. If you name the macro using an uppercase letter, you run the macro by pressing Ctrl and Shift and the shortcut key.

6 In the Store Macro In text box, make sure `This Workbook` is displayed. If it isn't, click the drop-down arrow and choose from the list.

The macro is stored in the current workbook because it is used only with this Project List worksheet.

The Description text box is available so you can add an optional description; otherwise, the current date and author's name is entered as the default.

The completed Record Macro dialog box is displayed in Figure 7.2.

continues

To Prepare to Record a Macro (continued)

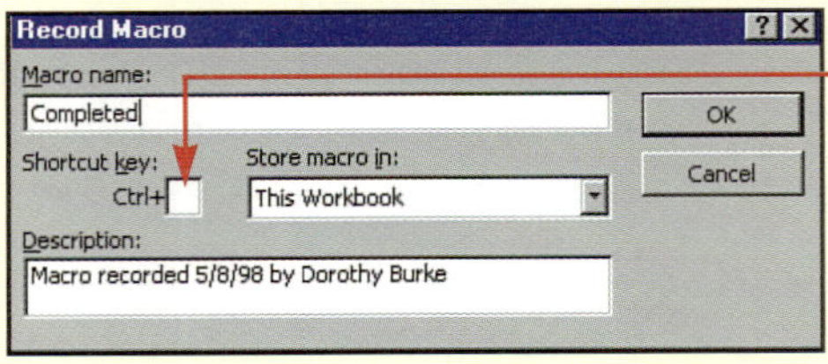

Figure 7.2
The name of the macro is Completed, and it is stored in This Workbook.

7 Click OK.

The macro recorder is now on. The message `Recording` is displayed in the status bar at the bottom of the Excel worksheet window, and a Stop Recording toolbar is displayed onscreen, as shown in Figure 7.3.

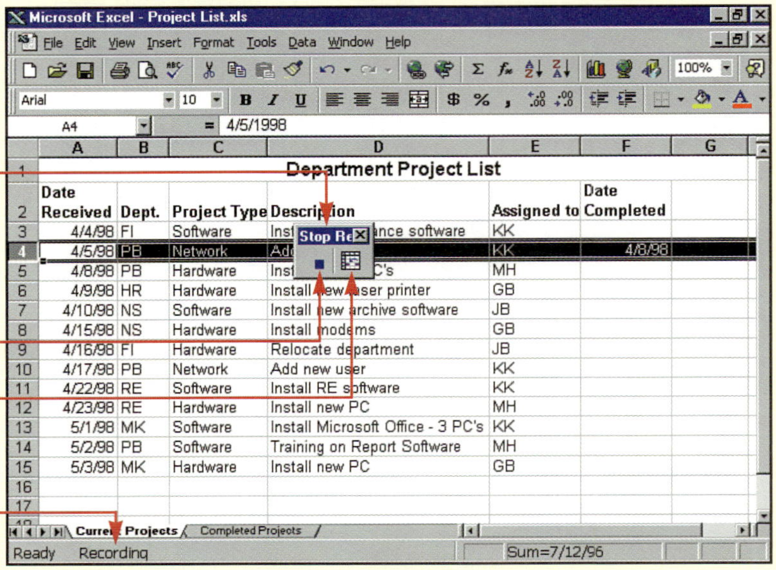

Figure 7.3
You use the Stop Recording toolbar when you finish recording the macro.

If you have problems...

If the Stop Recording button doesn't appear onscreen as shown in Figure 7.3, it may be docked below the Formatting toolbar.

You are almost ready to record your macro.

8 Click the Relative Reference button on the Stop Record toolbar.

By default, a macro procedure is written with *absolute references* to cells (a macro performs the instruction on the same cells on which you originally recorded the macro). If you want the macro to play back anywhere on a worksheet, make sure that you click the Relative Reference button on the Stop Recording toolbar before you start recording the macro.

Absolute references
The exact cell addresses you used when recording the macro. When playing back the macro, its operations will involve only those cell addresses.

You are now ready to record your macro. Keep this worksheet open for the next lesson, where you record a macro.

If you have problems...

If you do not see the `Recording` message or if other problems arise and you want to start over, click the Stop Recording button or choose Tools, Macro, Stop Recording. This action stops the current recording, and you can start again.

Lesson 2: Recording a Macro

Now that the macro has a name and storage location, you can proceed with recording. After you start the macro recorder, all typing and mouse clicks are saved until you stop the recorder.

In this lesson, you record the procedure. The completed project row was selected before starting the macro recorder. Now record the steps that you want the macro to perform. First, you copy a completed project from the Current Projects worksheet to the Clipboard. Next, you paste it into the Completed Projects worksheet. Then you delete the completed project from the Current Projects worksheet.

To Record a Macro

1. **Before you begin recording, make sure that you are in the** `Current Projects` **worksheet of the** `Project List` **workbook, with row 4 selected.**

2. **Make sure that the status bar shows** `Recording`**.**

   This status bar message indicates that Excel is recording all your actions in the worksheet as a macro.

3. **Click the Copy button on the Standard toolbar.**

   This copies the data in row 4 to the Clipboard. A marquee surrounds row 4.

4. **Click the** `Completed Projects` **sheet tab.**

   The active sheet is the `Completed Projects` worksheet.

5. **Press Ctrl+Home.**

   Cell A1 is the active cell.

continues

To Record a Macro (continued)

6 Press End and then press ↓ twice.

With these keystrokes, check to ensure that the active cell is the first blank cell below the data (in case the position of the active cell was changed between transfers of data). The active cell now is A5, the first cell in the blank row below the data.

7 Click the Paste button on the Standard toolbar.

The data from row 4 of the Current Projects worksheet is pasted into row 5 of the Completed Projects worksheet.

8 Press ↓ and then click the `Current Projects` sheet tab.

This step removes the selection, makes the first blank cell in the next row the active cell, and returns the screen to the Current Projects worksheet to delete the row that was just copied. Note that row 4 is still selected.

9 Choose Edit, Delete.

Because the project was completed and transferred to the Completed Projects worksheet, row 4 is deleted from the Current Projects worksheet to update it.

10 Click elsewhere on the worksheet to deselect the row. Click the Stop Recording button.

The highlight is removed from row 4, and the macro recorder is stopped. The macro is stored in a module of the *Visual Basic Editor*. If it is the first macro stored in the workbook, it's in Module1. Each macro is stored in a different module, and the modules are attached to the workbook.

Save the changes to the worksheet and keep it open for the next lesson, where you play back the macro you just recorded.

Visual Basic Editor
Visual Basic is a programming language used to create graphical interfaces. Macros are recorded in Visual Basic, and you edit them in a program called the Visual Basic Editor.

Inside Stuff

You can use the Visual Basic toolbar instead of menu commands to record macros. To display the toolbar, choose View, Toolbars, Visual Basic.

It is important to plan your macro before recording. You can see from the preceding exercise that several steps are involved in accomplishing the task. Take the time to walk through and jot down the steps that you want to record. It is much easier to record the keystrokes after they have been tested.

Lesson 3: Playing a Macro

After a macro is recorded, you can replay it whenever you need it. To run the macro, choose the Tools, Macro, Macros command or use the shortcut keys you assigned.

In this lesson, you play back the Completed macro from the Tools menu to update your Department Project List. Completed projects are copied from the Current Projects worksheet to the Completed Projects worksheet and then deleted from the Current Projects worksheet.

To Play a Macro

1 In the `Project List` workbook, type `8/12/98` in cell F4 of the `Current Projects` worksheet and press ↵Enter.

In this step, you update the Department Project List. The project in row 4 was completed on 8/12/98.

2 Click the row 4 heading.

Now copy the data in row 4 to the Completed Projects worksheet, and then delete it. After you select the row to copy, you can use the Completed macro to perform the keystrokes.

3 Choose Tools, Macro, Macros.

The Macro dialog box is displayed (see Figure 7.4).

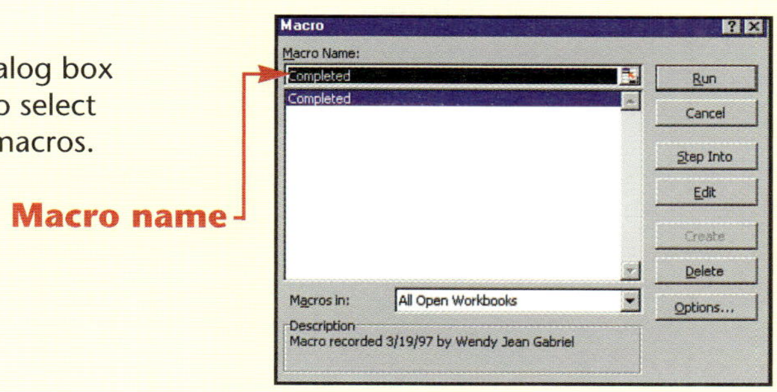

Figure 7.4
The Macro dialog box enables you to select and execute macros.

4 Click Completed from the Macro name list and click Run.

The Completed macro goes through the designated instructions and returns to the Current Projects worksheet.

5 Click the `Completed Projects` sheet tab.

The last project on this worksheet shows a Date Completed of 8/12/98. Your macro performed the instructions to copy the project to the Completed Projects worksheet, as shown in Figure 7.5. The macro then deleted the project from the Current Projects worksheet.

continues

Excel

To Play a Macro (continued)

6 Save your work. Print two copies of the workbook, if requested by your instructor; then close the workbook.

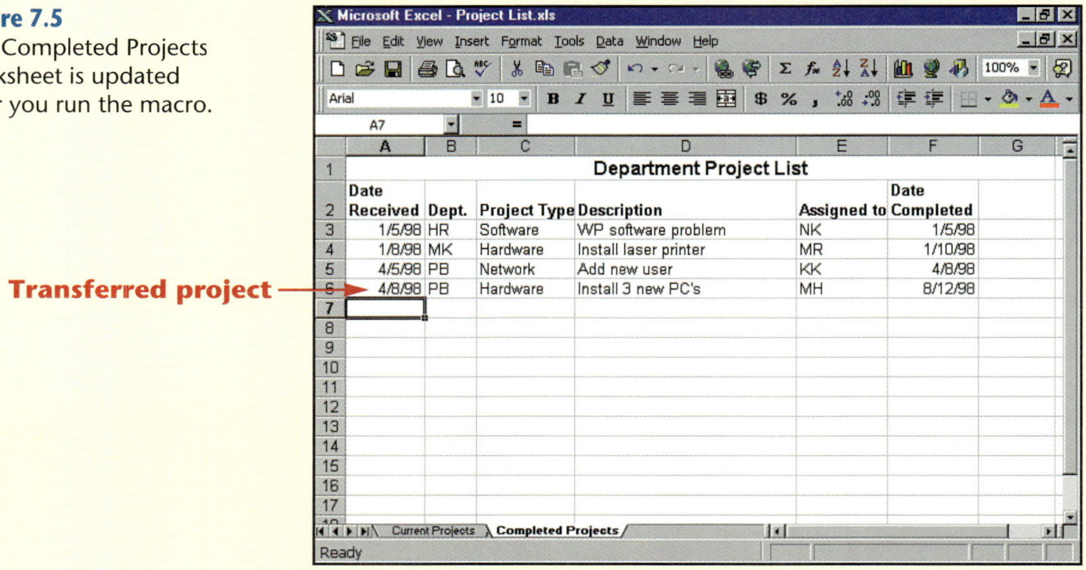

Figure 7.5
The Completed Projects worksheet is updated after you run the macro.

Inside Stuff

The macro that you recorded in Lesson 2 is saved in a sheet named Module1. With each new macro recorded, another consecutively numbered module sheet is added. To go behind the scenes and view the most recently recorded macro, choose Tools, Macro, Macros. Click Completed from the list of macro names and click Edit. The macro is displayed onscreen, as shown in Figure 7.6. The macro keystrokes are displayed in color, with the words Sub and End Sub in blue, comments (like when the macro was recorded and by whom) in green, and everything else in black. When you finish examining the macro, close the window by choosing File, Close, and Return to Microsoft Excel. To examine other recorded macros, choose Tools, Macro, Macros. When the Macro dialog box is displayed, click the name of the macro you want to view from the Macro Name list and click Edit.

If you have problems...

If your display does not look like Figure 7.6, double-click the Projects folder in the Project Explorer window. This opens the Projects folder. Double-click Module1, which appears directly underneath the Projects folder.

Figure 7.6
The Macro Recorder places the commands in a module and are viewed through the Visual Basic Editor.

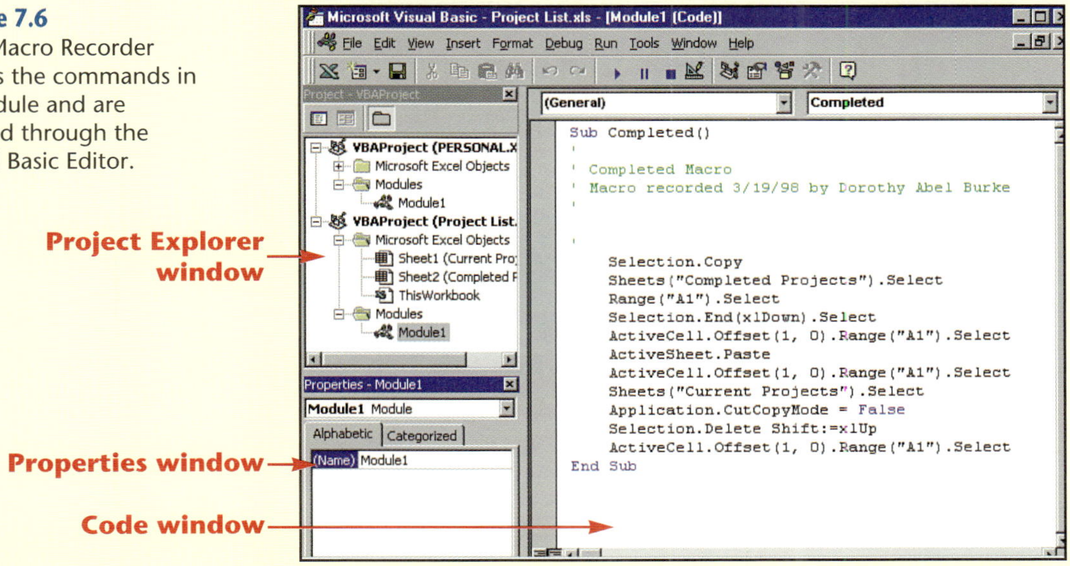

Inside Stuff

The Macro dialog box provides several additional capabilities. To delete a macro that was stored to a workbook, choose Tools, Macro, Macros; click the name of the macro in the list and then click Delete.

To run the recorded macro step-by-step, choose Step Into. With this feature, you can watch and analyze the macro keystrokes one step at a time within the Visual Basic Window. For programmers, this is a useful tool.

If you decide to assign a keyboard shortcut after you create a macro, or if you need to change the keyboard shortcut, choose Options from the Macro dialog box and change or add a shortcut and macro description.

Lesson 4: Recording a Macro to the Personal Macro Workbook

In Lesson 2, you recorded a macro to use with only a specific workbook, so it was saved in a module sheet in the current workbook. Now, you need to record a macro to use in any workbook. You record the macro to the Personal Macro Workbook so that it is available at any time. Each macro procedure saved to the Personal Macro Workbook is stored in its own module sheet. The module sheet displays the name and description of the macro procedure it contains. The Personal Macro Workbook is always available, but it is hidden so that you don't have to view it each time you start the Excel program.

In this lesson, you record a macro that inserts a page number footer in a worksheet. Because you want this macro to be available with any workbook, you store it in the Personal Macro Workbook.

To Record a Macro to the Personal Macro Workbook

1 Open a new workbook.

You use a new workbook for this lesson. (You could record the macro in any worksheet and still save it to the Personal Macro Workbook.) As you record this macro, it is saved to the Personal Macro Workbook so that it can be replayed in any workbook.

2 Choose Tools, Macro, Record New Macro.

The Record Macro dialog box is displayed.

3 With the Macro name text box highlighted, type `Footer` and press Tab.

4 Type the letter `f` (in lowercase) in the Shortcut Key text box and press Tab.

If you have problems...

Excel warns you if the keyboard shortcut name has already been assigned to another macro. You can decide if you want to replace the existing name or assign a shortcut that has not previously been used.

5 Click the arrow beside the Store macro in box and choose Personal Macro Workbook from the drop-down list. Press Tab.

6 Type `Page Number Footer` in the Description text box.

The completed dialog box is shown in Figure 7.7.

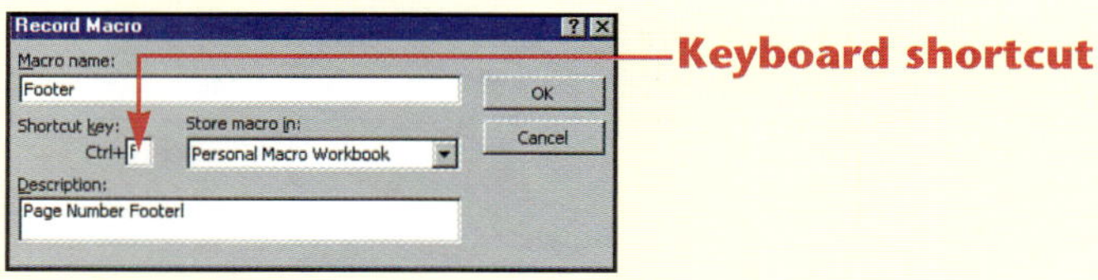

Figure 7.7
The Footer macro is stored as a keyboard shortcut in the Personal workbook.

7 Click OK.

The Macro Recorder turns on. The Stop Recording toolbar now displays, floating on the worksheet or docked below the Formatting toolbar, and the word `Recording` appears in the status bar. You are almost ready to start recording the macro.

8 Verify that the Relative Reference button on the Stop Recording toolbar is pressed. (If you completed Lesson 1, the Relative Reference button should still be pressed. If not, click this button.)

You are now ready to record the macro.

9 Choose File, Page Setup and click the Header/Footer tab.

The Header/Footer tab of the Page Setup dialog box is displayed, as shown in Figure 7.8.

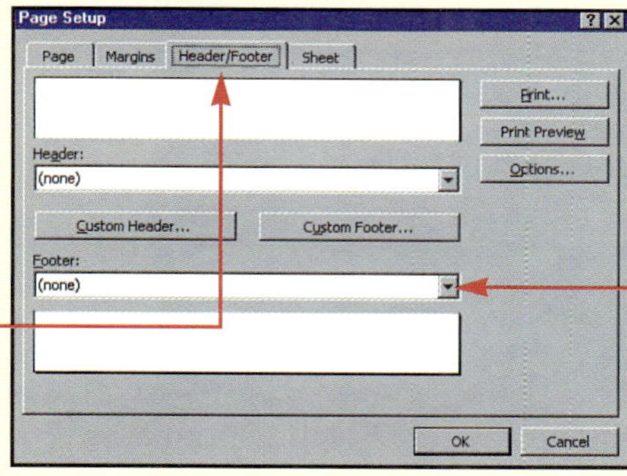

Figure 7.8
You add page numbers in the Header/Footer tab of the Page Setup dialog box.

10. **Click the Footer drop-down arrow.**
11. **Click Page 1 and click OK.**
12. **Click the Stop Recording button.**

You have finished recording the macro and stopped the recorder.

Close the current workbook without saving the changes. The macro is available because it was saved to the Personal Macro Workbook. In the next lesson, you test the Footer macro.

Lesson 5: Playing a Macro from the Personal Macro Workbook

In the previous lesson, you created a macro to insert a page number in a footer, then you saved it to the Personal Macro Workbook to make it available to use with any workbook. When the macro is assigned to shortcut keys, the shortcut keys can be used within any workbook.

In this lesson, you test the Footer macro by playing it back in another workbook.

To Play a Macro from the Personal Macro Workbook

1. **Open the** `Project List` **workbook and click the** `Current Projects` **worksheet.**

You use the `Project List` workbook to test your Footer macro.

If you have problems...

When you open a workbook that has macros in it, you may see a dialog box that alerts you that some macros contain viruses that may be harmful to your computer. Because your workbook contains macros, this gives you some choices about your next step. If the workbook is from a trusted source and you're not worried about viruses, click Enable Macros. To prevent any macros from running, click Disable Macros. Click Do Not Open to avoid the

continues

To Play a Macro from the Personal Macro Workbook (continued)

problem altogether by not opening the file. Click Tell Me More to learn more about macro viruses. Deselect "Always ask before opening workbooks with macros" if you do not want the warning dialog box to appear whenever you open a workbook with macros.

2. **Click the Print Preview button.**

   The Print Preview screen displays the `Current Projects` worksheet. You may have to Zoom in to read the worksheet.

3. **Click the Close button.**

   You have now viewed the current worksheet without a page number at the bottom. Run the Footer macro to add a footer to the worksheet.

4. **Press and hold down the Ctrl key and type the letter `f` (in lowercase).**

   The macro is played back into the open workbook.

If you have problems...

If you receive the error message, `Ambiguous name detected`, when trying to run the macro, the software detected more than one copy of the macro in the Personal Macro Workbook. You can remove the unwanted macro by deleting its module sheet. Follow the steps in Lesson 6 to unhide the Personal Macro Workbook, delete the unwanted module sheet, resave the file, and then hide the Personal Macro Workbook.

5. **Click the Print Preview button.**

   The Print Preview screen shows that a page number has been added to the footer in the worksheet. If you play this macro when you create a new workbook, a page number displays in the footer of the worksheet.

6. **Click the Close button.**

7. **Save the changes to the file and keep it open for the next lesson.**

Lesson 6: Unhiding and Editing the Personal Macro Workbook

The Personal Macro Workbook is always open in Excel, but you usually don't see it because it is hidden. You can always unhide the Personal Macro Workbook and view the Visual Basic code that it contains. You can edit a macro's module sheet or even delete a module sheet if you no longer need the macro.

In this lesson, you unhide the Personal Macro Workbook to view the module sheet, edit the sheet to change the footer default, and then hide it again.

To Unhide and Edit the Personal Macro Workbook

1 With the `Project List` **workbook open, choose Window, Unhide.**

The Unhide dialog box displays, as shown in Figure 7.9.

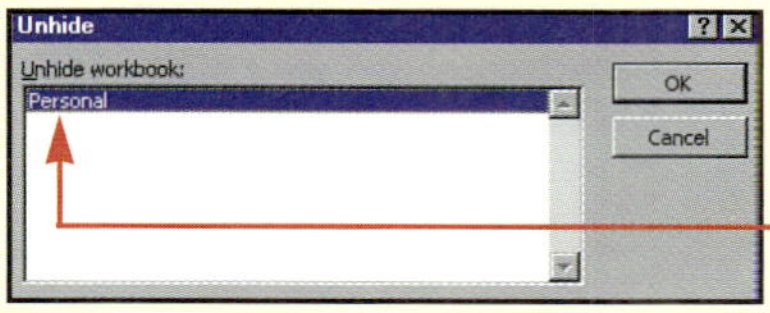

Figure 7.9
The Windows command reveals the Personal Macro Workbook Unhide dialog box.

2 Click Personal from the list and click OK.

The Personal workbook displays as a blank worksheet. Now that the window has been displayed, you can proceed with the next step to edit the Personal workbook. Note that each macro that was written is saved to its own module sheet. If other macros were already saved to the Personal Macro Workbook, you see more than just a Module1 sheet.

3 Choose Tools, Macro, Macros.

The Macro dialog box is displayed (see Figure 7.10).

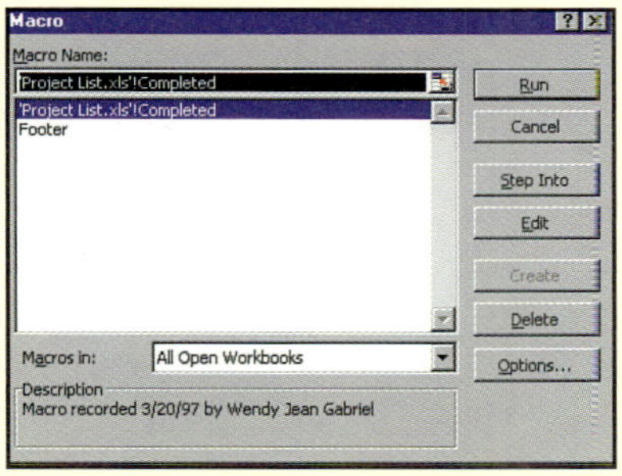

Figure 7.10
The Macro dialog box lists the macro names stored in the Project List worksheet and the Personal Workbook.

4 Click Footer from the list and click Edit.

The Microsoft Visual Basic window is displayed (see Figure 7.11). Note the Module1 sheet window. Each macro that was written is saved to its own module sheet. If other macros were already saved to the Personal Macro Workbook, you would see more than just a Module1 sheet.

5 In the Module1 sheet window, scroll through the procedure code and find the line `.LeftFooter = ""`**.**

Edit this line to add your name to the footer.

Notice that the `CenterFooter` option displayed just below this line includes the Footer text that was specified in Lesson 4.

continues

To Unhide and Edit the Personal Macro Workbook (continued)

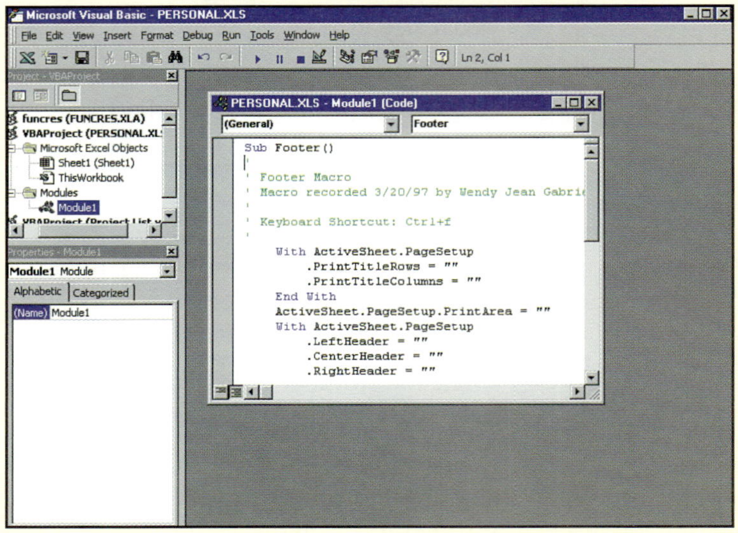

Figure 7.11
The Microsoft Visual Basic window displays the programming code for the macro stored in the Personal Workbook.

6 **Click between the "" (double quotation marks) symbols and type** `Prepared by`**. Type a colon (**`:`**) followed by your initials, as shown in Figure 7.12.**

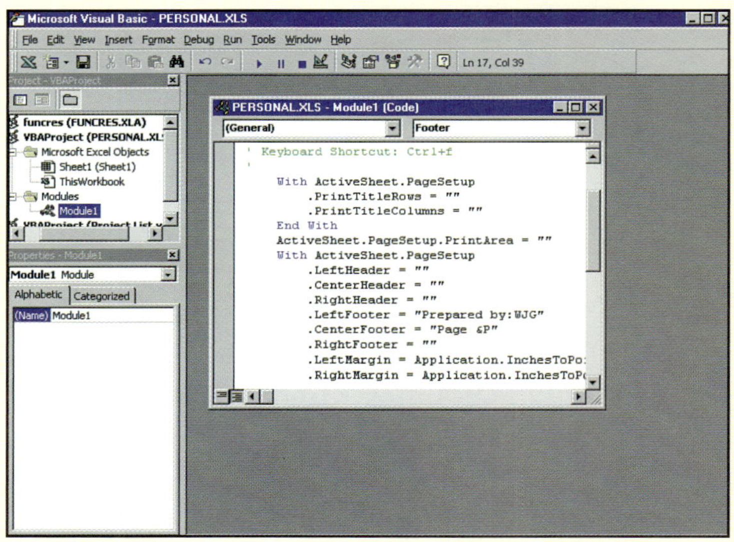

Figure 7.12
The new macro after you complete step 6.

7 **Choose File, Save PERSONAL.XLS.**

The macro is edited and saved. Now you can close the Visual Basic Editor.

8 **Choose File, Close and Return to Microsoft Excel.**

Now you can hide the Personal workbook.

9 Choose Window, Hide.

You did not close the Personal workbook; you just hid the window. Now test the change in the Project List workbook that should still be open.

If you have problems...

If you close the Personal workbook instead of hiding it, the Footer macro and any other macros stored in the Personal workbook become unavailable in the current session. To activate the personal workbook, exit Excel. PERSONAL.XLS automatically opens each time you start Excel and is usually hidden. If the workbook opens when you start Excel, simply choose Window, Hide.

10 Press Ctrl+F.

The Footer macro is played back in this workbook. Now preview the worksheet to view the footer change.

11 Click the Print Preview button and scroll down to view the footer. You may have to zoom in to read the footer.

The Print Preview screen displays the new footer that contains your name and the page number.

12 Click the Close button.

The Preview screen is closed.

13 Save the changes to the worksheet, and keep the workbook open for the next lesson, where you create a macro button.

Lesson 7: Creating a Macro Button in a Workbook

In Lesson 4, you assigned a macro to a shortcut key, which can be useful for frequent, repetitive tasks. Just press the shortcut key combination to play the macro. Besides using the shortcut key method, Excel provides two other ways to gain fast access to your macros. First, you can assign a macro to a button control within a workbook as a reminder to you or others who use the worksheet that a macro is available. Second, just as toolbars give you quick access to many Excel commands, you can assign a macro to a toolbar button to speed up your work.

You created a macro in the Project List workbook to transfer completed projects to the Completed Projects worksheet. This macro is used in only this workbook. In this lesson, you create a macro button on a worksheet and assign the Completed macro to it.

To Create a Macro Button in a Workbook

1 Click cell G2 in the `Current Projects` worksheet of the `Project List` workbook.

Cell G2 is where you want to place the macro button.

2 Choose View, Toolbars and click Forms from the submenu.

The Forms toolbar displays.

3 Click the Button tool on the Forms toolbar.

With the Button tool, you draw the button to which you assign the macro. The Button tool is pushed in and the mouse pointer changes to a small, thin cross. You are ready to draw the button.

4 Click cell G2 and drag the mouse to create a rectangle the full size of the cell. Release the mouse button.

A button is created in cell G2 that contains the text `Button 1`. The Assign Macro dialog box displays with a list of macros, as shown in Figure 7.13.

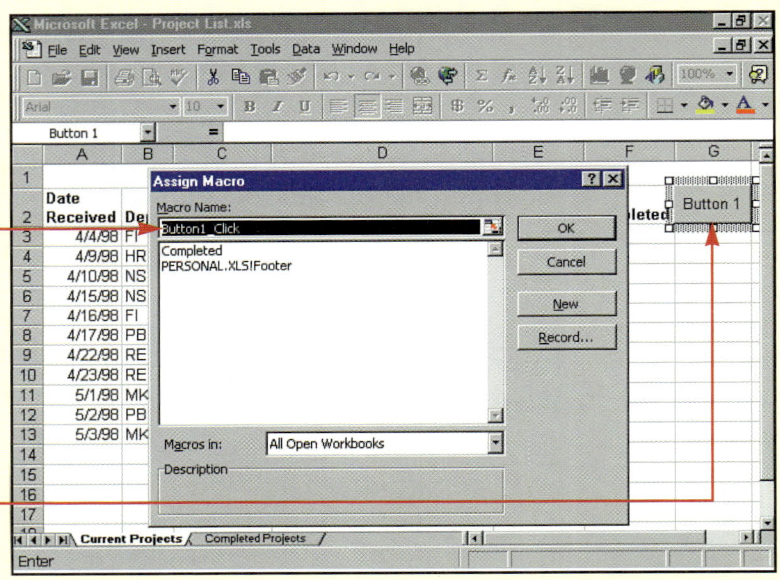

Figure 7.13
Use the Assign Macro dialog box to assign a macro to the button on screen.

5 Click the `Completed` macro name from the Macro Name list and click OK.

The macro is assigned to the button. Handles appear around the button.

6 With the button still selected, click inside the button. Delete the words `Button 1` and type the word `Completed`.

If you have problems...

If the button is too small and doesn't display the entire word `Completed`, you can resize the button. If the button is not selected (surrounded by handles), point the mouse pointer on the button and press Ctrl while you left-click. Then drag the handles to resize the box. (You cannot select a button by just left-clicking—this action runs the macro attached to the button.)

7. **Close the Forms toolbar.**

   The Forms toolbar is removed from the screen. Now you can test the macro by using the Completed button.

8. **Click cell F7. Type** `4/13/98` **and press** ↵Enter**. Click the row 7 heading.**

   The project in row 7 was completed on 4/13/98. You selected it, and now the macro transfers it to the Completed Projects worksheet.

9. **Click the Completed button.**

   The macro transfers the project to the Completed Projects worksheet and deletes it from the Current Projects worksheet.

10. **Save the changes to the workbook. If requested by your instructor, print two copies; then close the workbook.**

If you have problems...

For the macro to execute properly, you must select the row heading before you click the Completed button or run the macro from the Tools, Macro, Macros command.

Inside Stuff

To remove a macro button from a worksheet, point the mouse to the button and right-click. From the shortcut menu, choose Cut.

To change the font, font style, and size of a macro button, point the mouse to the button and right-click. From the shortcut menu, choose Format Control and click the Font tab.

To move the macro button to another location on the worksheet, press Ctrl and click to select the button. Drag the border of the button and place the button wherever you like on the worksheet.

Lesson 8: Adding a Macro Button to a Toolbar

In Lesson 7, you assigned a macro to a control in the Project List workbook. You also can assign a macro to a button on a toolbar for fast access. There are 42 buttons available.

In this lesson, you create a Smiley Face button to represent the macro button for the Header/Footer macro and assign it to the Formatting toolbar.

To Add a Macro Button to a Toolbar

1 Click the New button on the Standard toolbar.

Make sure that a new workbook is open onscreen.

2 Choose View, Toolbars and choose Customize from the submenu.

The Customize dialog box is displayed, as shown in Figure 7.14.

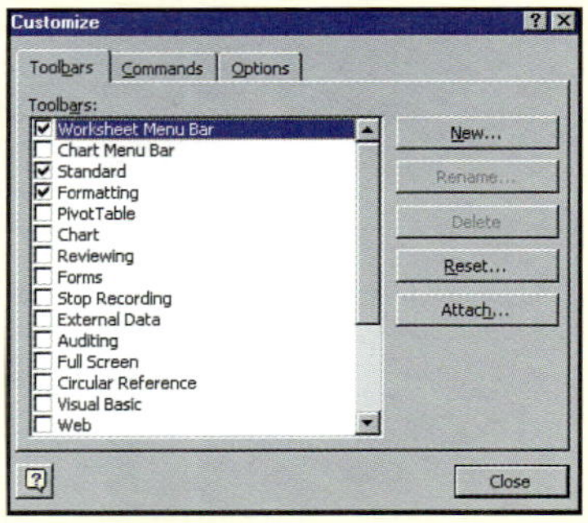

Figure 7.14
The Toolbars tab in the Customize dialog box lists all the toolbars.

3 Click the Commands tab from the Customize window; then scroll down the Categories list and click Macros.

The Commands tab lists all the Excel commands by category (see Figure 7.15).

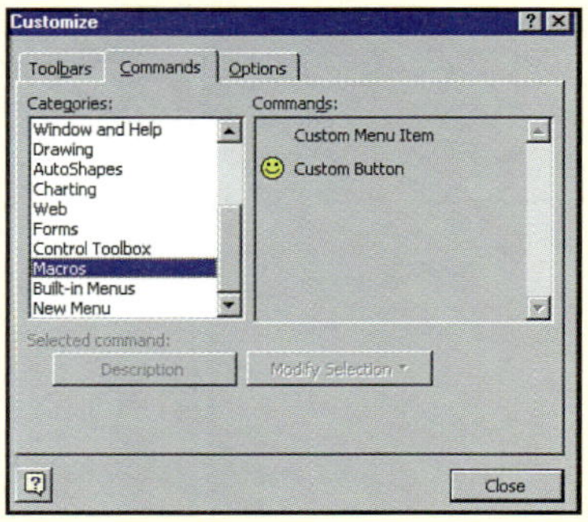

Figure 7.15
The Commands tab lists the categories on the left and the available commands on the right.

4 Drag the Custom button, Smiley Face, into position to the left of the Bold button on the Formatting toolbar. Release the mouse button.

The Smiley Face button appears to the left of the Bold button, as shown in Figure 7.16.

Now assign a macro name to the Smiley Face button.

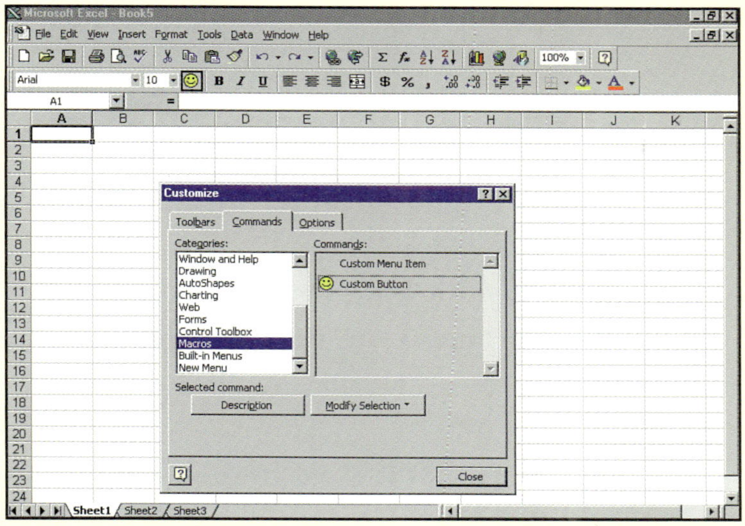

Figure 7.16 The Smiley Face button now appears in the Formatting toolbar between the bold and point size icons.

5 Right-click the Smiley Face button on the Formatting toolbar (with the Customize dialog box still onscreen) and choose Assign Macro from the shortcut menu.

The Assign Macro dialog box is displayed (see Figure 7.17).

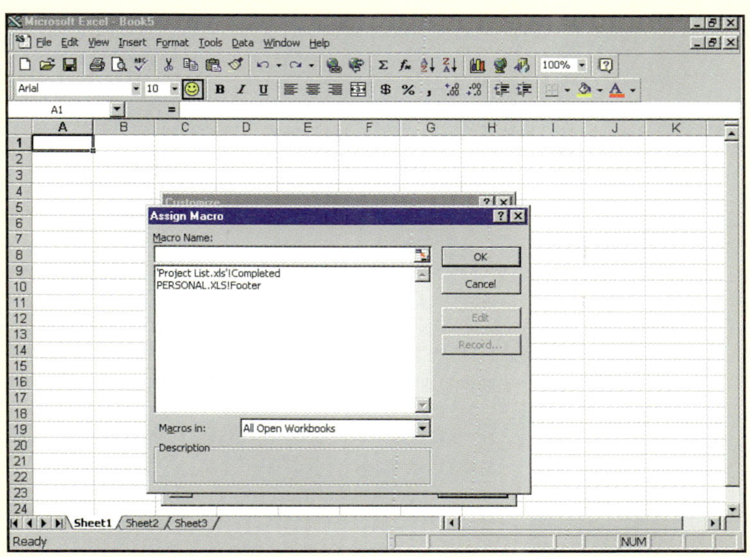

Figure 7.17 You use the Assign Macro dialog box to assign a macro name to the Smiley Face button.

continues

To Add a Macro Button to a Toolbar (continued)

6 Click `PERSONAL.XLS!Footer` **from the Macro Name list and then OK.**

7 Close the Customize dialog box.

The Footer macro is assigned to the toolbar button. Now test the macro button from the toolbar.

8 In cell A1 of the new worksheet, type your first name and press ↵Enter.

Something needs to be in a cell before you can preview it.

9 Choose File, Print Preview.

The Print Preview window appears without a footer on the page.

10 Click Close.

11 Click the Smiley Face button on the Standard Toolbar.

12 Choose File, Print Preview.

This time, when you preview the page, the Preview window appears with the footer.

Now remove the macro button from the toolbar.

If you have problems...

You don't have to use the Smiley Face button when adding a macro button to a toolbar. You can use any of Excel's 42 built-in buttons to customize your macro. Make sure the Customize dialog box is open after assigning a macro to a toolbar button. Right-click the mouse on the toolbar button you want to change. Choose Change Button Image and select one from the list of buttons from the submenu.

You can further customize a macro button and draw a face that you feel represents your macro. First, make sure that the Customize dialog box is open after assigning a macro to a toolbar button. Next, click the right-hand mouse button on the toolbar button you want to customize. Choose Edit Button Image from the shortcut menu to access the Button Editor. Finally, you can erase all or portions of the picture by clicking a color from the color group, then clicking the picture grid to draw.

13 Choose View, Toolbars and click Customize from the submenu.

14 Click the Commands tab from the Customize window; scroll down the list and click Macros from the Categories list.

15 Drag the button off the toolbar. Close the Customize dialog box.

16 If your instructor asks you to complete the "Checking Your Skills" and "Applying Your Skills" sections, please do the exercises now. After completing these sections, return to this lesson and complete steps 17 through 21.

17. **Choose Window, Unhide; then choose Personal and click OK.**

    The Personal Macro Workbook is displayed.

    Delete all the macro sheets you created.

18. **Choose Tools, Macro, Macros.**

    The Macro dialog box is displayed, listing all the saved macros.

19. **Delete each macro separately by selecting the macro name and using the Delete button in the Macro dialog box until all the macros are deleted. If a request for confirmation appears, click Yes.**

    All the macros are permanently deleted.

20. **Choose Window, Hide.**

    The Personal Macro Workbook is now hidden.

21. **Choose File, Exit and then Yes when Excel prompts you to save the changes you made to the Personal Macro workbook.**

    Your changes to the Personal Macro Workbook are saved, and you can exit Excel.

Inside Stuff

Macro recording is a feature available in many current software packages. As you know, the Excel macro recorder helps you create simple macros to automate repetitive tasks. There are limitations, however, to the macro recorder. To perform more extensive tasks with looping structures, conditional branches, built-in functions and dialog boxes, and custom dialog boxes, you need to add programming code to the recorded macro.

The programming language used by Excel 97 is the Visual Basic for Applications language (VBA). The Excel Help utility provides information on VBA statements and functions to assist you in editing a recorded macro procedure or creating your procedure. Que and Sams publish technical reference books that describe Visual Basic programming techniques. (For further information try *Special Edition Using Microsoft Excel 97, Bestseller Edition*, Bruce Hallberg; and *Special Edition Using Visual Basic for Applications*, Paul Sanna, both by Que Corporation.) These books are available where computer books are sold. You also can check the Help utility, under Visual Basic code, for more information.

Excel

Project Summary

To	Do This
Create a new macro	Choose Tools, Macro, Record New Macro.
Create a new macro that can be played back in any cell on any worksheet	Choose Tools, Macro, Record New Macro. Complete the Record Macro dialog box and click OK. Click Relative Reference from the toolbar.
Assign a macro to a shortcut key	Choose Tools, Macro, Record New Macro. In the Shortcut Key text box, type the shortcut key combination, and click OK.
Assign the macro to a button in a worksheet	Display the Forms Toolbar. Click the Button tool and draw a rectangle. Select a macro from the Macro Name list and click OK. Click inside the button while it's selected. Delete the button name and type the macro name in the button.
Assign a macro to a toolbar button	Choose View, Toolbars, Customize. Click the Commands tab and select the Macros category. Drag a Custom button onto a toolbar. Right-click the button and choose Assign Macro. Click the name of the macro you want to assign to the button and click Close.
Remove a macro button from a worksheet	Point the mouse to the button and right-click. Click Cut.
Remove a macro button from a toolbar	Choose View, Toolbars, Customize. Click the Command tab and click Macros. Drag the button off the toolbar and release the mouse button. Click Close.
Store a macro in a current Workbook	Choose Tools, Macro, Record New Macro. Click Store macro in arrow and click This Workbook. Click OK.
Store a macro in the Personal Macro Workbook	Choose Tools, Macro, Record New Macro. Click Store macro in arrow and click Personal Macro Workbook. Click OK.
Play back a shortcut key macro	Press the shortcut keys.
Play back a macro assigned to a toolbar	Click the button on the toolbar.

Checking Your Skills

True/False

For each of the following, check *T* or *F* to indicate whether the statement is true or false.

__T __F 1. You must know Visual Basic programming to record a simple macro that speeds up repetitive tasks.

__T __F 2. If a macro is stored in the Personal Macro Workbook, it can be replayed in any workbook.

__T __F 3. The Personal Macro Workbook opens when the Excel program starts, but it is hidden.

__T __F 4. You can replay a macro only in the same cell in which it was written.

__T __F 5. Besides assigning a macro to a keyboard shortcut, you can also assign a macro to a toolbar button.

__T __F 6. A macro performs the same steps as you recorded.

__T __F 7. You can't change a macro once you've recorded it.

__T __F 8. All macro keyboard shortcuts start with pressing the Alt key.

__T __F 9. Excel automatically assigns a name to a macro but you can change it.

__T __F 10. You can use the buttons on the Visual Basic toolbar to help create macros.

Multiple Choice

Circle the letter of the correct answer for each of the following.

1. A macro can be assigned to
   a. a toolbar.
   b. a shortcut key.
   c. a button.
   d. All of the above

2. If you want to play back a macro across workbooks, store it in
   a. the workbook in which it was created.
   b. a new workbook.
   c. the Personal Macro Workbook.
   d. Either (a) or (b)

3. To create a macro button in the current worksheet, use the _______ toolbar.
   a. Visual Basic
   b. Formatting
   c. Forms
   d. Drawing

4. By default, a macro is written by using
   a. relative cell references.
   b. absolute cell references.
   c. both (a) and (b).
   d. None of the above

5. If you no longer need a macro, you
   a. cannot delete it.
   b. can only delete it from the Windows Explorer.
   c. can delete it from the Macro dialog box.
   d. can delete it by first unhiding the window and choosing delete from the edit menu.
6. Which command do you use to create a macro?
   a. Tools, Macro, Macro
   b. Insert, Macro
   c. Tools, Macro, Record New Macro
   d. Tools, Macro, Create Macro
7. What command do you choose to make the Personal Macro Workbook visible?
   a. View, Personal Macro Workbook
   b. File, Open Personal Macro Workbook
   c. Tools, Macro, View Personal Macro Workbook
   d. Window, Unhide
8. When you click the Edit button in the Macro dialog box, what opens?
   a. A new workbook
   b. Macro Editor
   c. Visual Basic Editor
   d. Personal Macro Workbook
9. When does the Assign Macro dialog box automatically appear?
   a. When you add a button to a toolbar.
   b. When you draw a button on the worksheet.
   c. When you click the Stop Recording button.
   d. None of the above
10. How do you play a macro?
   a. Press the shortcut keys.
   b. Click the toolbar button.
   c. Choose Tools, Macro, Macro. Select the macro and click Run.
   d. All of the above

Completion

In the blank provided, write the correct answer for each of the following statements.

1. A(n) _______________ is a procedure that is written in Visual Basic programming code to automate repetitive tasks.
2. Visual Basic procedures are stored in a(n) _______________ sheet, either in the current workbook or in the Personal Macro Workbook.
3. If you want to record a macro that plays back in any cell of your worksheet, choose _______________ from the Stop Recording toolbar.

4. To add a macro button to a toolbar, use the Toolbars Customize commands from the ______________ menu.

5. As you are recording your macro, the word Recording is displayed at the bottom in the ______________ ______________.

6. Enter a letter in the ______________ box in the Record Macro dialog box to be able to run the macro by pressing keys.

7. To be able to play a macro in any workbook, choose ______________ from the Store macro in drop-down list in the Record Macro dialog box.

8. You must open the ______________ to make changes to a macro.

9. Click the ______________ button in the Macro dialog box to run a macro one step at a time so you can analyze problems.

10. Choose ______________ from the menu when you want to assign a macro to a toolbar.

Matching

In the blank next to each of the following terms or phrases, write the letter of the corresponding term or phrase. (Note that some letters may be used more than once.)

_______ 1. A series of commands or operations you record to play back when doing the same task

_______ 2. The key combination you press to start a macro

_______ 3. Stores macros for use in any workbook

_______ 4. To play back a macro from anywhere in a workbook, click this button

_______ 5. Where the Visual Basic Editor stores your macro

_______ 6. Command to make the Personal Macro Workbook visible

_______ 7. Toolbar needed to add buttons on worksheets

_______ 8. Toolbar that appears when you start recording a macro

_______ 9. Command used to create a macro

_______ 10. Press this key to drag a macro button to a new location on a worksheet

a. Module

b. Shortcut keys

c. Ctrl

d. Forms

e. Personal Macro Workbook

f. Tools, Macro, Record New Macro

g. Macro

h. Window, Unhide

i. Stop Recording

j. Relative Reference

Applying Your Skills

Practice

The following exercises enable you to practice the skills that you learned in this project. Take a few minutes to work through these exercises now.

Recording a Macro

You record a simple macro that types your company name and address. The macro is assigned to a shortcut key.

To record the macro, follow these steps:

1. Open a new workbook file.

   The macro is recorded in the current workbook.

2. Choose Tools, Macro, Record New Macro.
3. Name the macro `Company`. The macro is stored in This Workbook only. Click OK.
4. Click the Relative Reference button.
5. Click cell A1.

   Type the following address, press ↓ or ↵Enter at the end of each line, as indicated.

   `Cabtel Cable TV Corporation` ↓

   `5151 Reed Road` ↓

   `Columbus, OH 43221` ↵Enter

6. Select cells A1:A3 and click the Bold button on the Standard toolbar.
7. Click cell A4.
8. Click the Stop Recording button.

The macro is recorded and assigned the name `Company`. Keep the workbook open for the following exercise.

Playing Back the Macro

Because this macro was written by using relative references, the macro can be played back in any cell in the workbook. Test the macro.

To play back the macro, follow these steps:

1. Click cell A10.
2. Choose Tools, Macro, Macros.
3. Click `Company` and click Run.
4. Save the workbook with the file name `Macro1 test`.
5. Close the workbook.

Recording a Macro in the Personal Macro Workbook

Your company uses the TODAY function regularly in its use of Excel. Here, you create a macro that uses this function and stores it in the Personal Macro Workbook so that it can be used at any time across workbooks.

To record the macro, follow these steps:

1. Open a new workbook. Click cell A1.
2. Choose Tools, Macro, Record New Macro.
3. Name the macro `TODAY`.
4. Assign the macro to a shortcut key (Ctrl+T) and store the macro in the Personal Macro Workbook; then click OK.
5. Click the Relative Reference button to deselect it.
6. Type `=TODAY()` in cell A1 and press ↵Enter. Click the Stop Recording button.
7. Close the workbook without saving the changes.

Testing the Macro

The TODAY macro was written with an absolute cell reference stored in the Personal Macro Workbook and assigned to a shortcut key. Even when the current workbook is closed, the macro is still accessible from any workbook.

To test the macro, follow these steps:

1. Open a new workbook.
2. Press Ctrl+T.
3. Save the workbook with the new file name `Macro2 test`.
4. Close the workbook.

Editing the Module Sheet

Because your company address has changed, the macro you wrote with your company name and address needs to be modified. You edit the Module1 sheet in the Macro1 test workbook.

To edit the module sheet, follow these steps:

1. Open the Macro1 test workbook and choose Tools, Macro, Macros.
2. Click `Company` from the name list and click Edit.
3. Scroll through the procedure until you find the text `5151 Reed Road`. Replace this with `10 South Reeves Drive`.
4. Make sure that quotes still surround the street address.
5. Save the changes and exit the Visual Basic window.

6. Click the Sheet2 tab and then cell F1.
7. Execute the macro.
8. Save the changes to the worksheet and keep it open for the following exercise.

Adding a Button to the Workbook

You want to create a button in this worksheet to automatically play back your company name and address.

To create the button, follow these steps:

1. Make sure that `Sheet1` of the `Macro1 test` workbook is displayed.
2. Display the Forms toolbar.
3. Create a button in cell range B15:B16 by using the Button tool on the Forms toolbar.
4. Assign the company macro to the button.
5. Delete the `Button1` text and type `Company` in the button.
6. Close the Forms toolbar.
7. Click cell F6; then click the `Company` macro button.

   The company name and address is entered, starting in cell F6.
8. Right-click the button.
9. Choose Format Control and click the Properties tab.
10. Make sure that a check mark appears in the Print object check box and click OK.
11. Save the changes to the worksheet and then close the workbook.

Adding a Button to the Toolbar

You previously created a macro that plays back the TODAY function. Because you use this macro frequently, you decide to add it to the Formatting toolbar.

To create the button, follow these steps:

1. Open a new workbook.
2. Choose View, Toolbars, Customize.
3. Choose the Commands tab.
4. Choose the Macros category.
5. Drag the Smiley Face to the Formatting toolbar.
6. Right-click the Smiley Face button in the toolbar.

7. Assign the `PERSONAL.XLS!today` macro to it; then close the dialog box.
8. Test the macro by clicking the Smiley Face button.
9. Remove the Smiley Face button from the toolbar by using the Customize dialog box.
10. Close the workbook without saving it.

Challenge

The following challenges enable you to use your problem-solving skills. Take time to work through these exercises now.

Recording a Macro to the Personal Macro Workbook

Open a new workbook and save it as `Test`. Make sure A1 is the active cell. Record a new macro called `Months` that will automatically enter the months of the year across a row of a worksheet. Store the macro in your Personal Macro Workbook. Assign it a shortcut key.

Click the Relative Reference button on the Stop Recording toolbar. Type `January` in cell A1. Press ↵Enter. Press ↑ to make A1 active. Drag the fill handle for A1 across the row to L1 (the ScreenTip displays `December`), and then release the mouse button. Press F and then → to move to the cell next to December. Type `Total` and press ↵Enter. Stop recording.

Click C7 and run the macro to test it.

Editing a Macro

Make the Personal Macro Workbook visible. Edit the `Months` macro. Change `Total` to `YTD`. Exit the Visual Basic Editor. Switch to the Test workbook. Test your macro to see if your change registers.

Recording a Macro

Open Proj0702 from the Project-07 folder on the CD and save the file as `Employees`. This list of employees always needs updating. Every time an employee leaves, the name has to be removed from the Current worksheet and transferred to the Termination sheet. Then the blank row on the Current worksheet has to be deleted. Record a new macro to perform this operation. Name the macro `Termination` and give it a shortcut key. Store it in the current workbook. Remember to plan your steps first.

Playing a Macro

Use your new macro to remove Susan Richards from the current list and add her to the list of terminations. Save your workbook but leave it open.

Adding a Macro Button to a Worksheet

Switch to the Employees workbook. Click H2. Add a button there. Assign the Terminate macro to the button, and change the button name to `Terminate`. You may have to resize the button after you enter the text. To test your new button, terminate Olivia Sylvan.

Please return to Lesson 8 to complete steps 17 through 21 before exiting Excel.

PinPoint Assessment

PinPoint Training

You have completed the project and the associated lessons, as well as the "Checking Your Skills" and "Applying Your Skills" sections. Now use the PinPoint software evaluation mode to assess your comprehension of the specific exam tasks you have just learned. You can also use the PinPoint Trainer Mode and the Show Me tutorials to practice these specific exam tasks.

Project 8

Eight

Managing Data

Creating an Address Database

In this Project, you learn how to:

Objectives	Required Activities
➤ Name a List	
➤ Add Records	
➤ Sort Records	Sort Data, Perform Multi-Level Sorts
➤ Find and Delete Records	Query From a List, Query Databases
➤ Extract Records Using AutoFilter	Extract Data, Use Filters

Why Would I Do This?

The purpose of creating a database (called a list in Excel) is to organize information and view selected parts of the information. A good example of a database is a phone book, which organizes information by city and then by name. To see only a portion of the phone book, you turn pages and scan columns of names arranged alphabetically. To see only part of a list in Excel, you use commands.

Computer databases provide you with a powerful way to organize and search for information. In this project, you learn to use a sample database of names, company names, addresses, and telephone numbers. A simple Excel list, such as the one in this project, can make staying in contact with business associates easy.

Lesson 1: Naming a List

A **list** in Excel is a special kind of worksheet in which column headings are **fields**, and each row of worksheet data is a **record**. To continue with the phone book example, last name is one field, first name is another field, address is yet another field, and so on. A record consists of the set of information for one person: the person's first name, last name, address, and telephone number. (See the Jargon Watch that follows this lesson for more information about the database terminology used in this lesson.)

Each workbook file can contain more than one list, just as it can contain more than one worksheet; or you can create one workbook for each list. Each list can be on a separate worksheet or in separate ranges in a single worksheet.

Before you start to create a list, give some thought to the structure you want. Think about what you want to do with the information in the list; planning can keep you from having to move and insert columns later.

Follow these rules when creating a list in Excel:

- The field names (column headings) must be in a single row.
- A field name can contain letters, numbers, and spaces, but it should not start with a number.
- The field names must be unique.
- Don't leave a blank row between the row of field names and the first data record. Use cell borders to separate labels from data, or specify a different font, alignment, format, shading, or capitalization to distinguish the labels.
- A list should not contain blank columns; it's best not to have blank rows, either. However, you should have at least one blank row between the end of the list and other data on the worksheet.

- Don't put extra spaces at the beginning of a cell because this affects sorting and searching.
- Don't place any critical data to the left or right of the list, so it isn't hidden when you filter your list.
- Every record must have the same fields, but you don't have to enter data into all the fields for every record. If the information is not available, you can leave some of the cells in a record empty.

Now that you know a little about how lists are created, try opening a worksheet file that already contains information suitable for a list, then naming the list in the file. As a list grows, referring to the collection of data by name is much easier than trying to remember the first and last cells of the list.

To Name a List

1 Open the file Proj0801 from the Project-08 folder on the CD and save it as `Address Book`.

This is a sample database of business associates that you use throughout this project (see Figure 8.1). Notice that no empty rows or columns are within the worksheet. The column headings in row 1, such as First Name and Last Name, are the field names for the list.

Figure 8.1
In Excel, a list of names and addresses can be used as an address database.

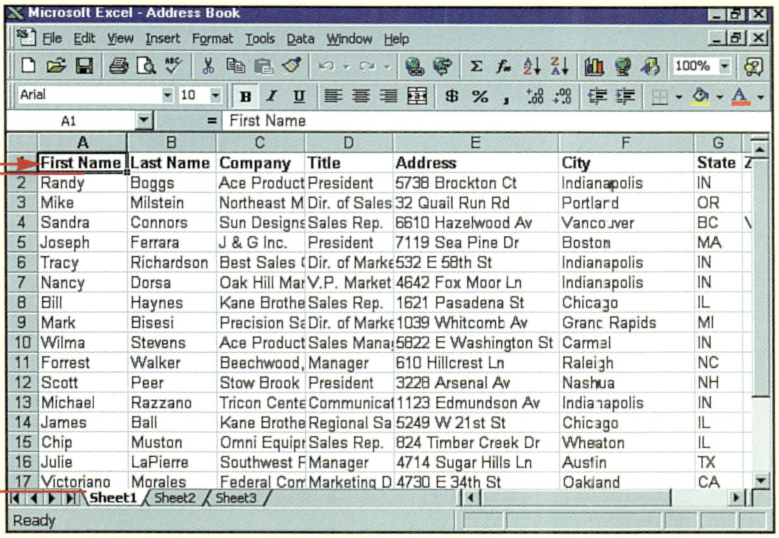

2 Select the entire list, including the field names (cells A1:I21).

Naming a list is similar to naming any range of cells. You must first select the range you want to name—in this case, the entire list.

continues

To Name a List (continued)

3 Choose Insert, Name from the menu, then choose Define from the submenu that appears.

The Define Name dialog box appears, as shown in Figure 8.2. By default, Excel lists the data from the active cell in the Names in workbook text box.

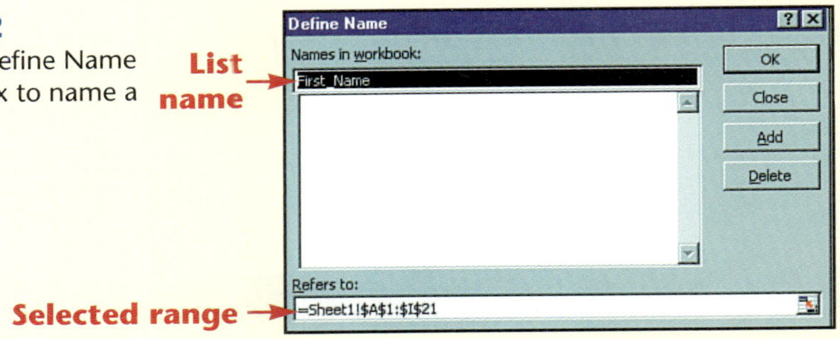

Figure 8.2
Use the Define Name dialog box to name a list.

4 In the Names in workbook text box, type `Address` and choose OK.

You have now named the database list so that you can easily refer to it in your work. You can deselect the list, then save the Address Book file and keep it open to use in the next lesson.

Jargon Watch

You may already know that the term **database** can also refer to a separate type of application software for personal computers. Applications such as Access, Paradox, and dBASE are powerful database programs used by all types of organizations and businesses. Many databases used in business and scientific research are so large and complex that they must run on mainframe computers.

In general terms, however, you can think of a database as an organized collection of related information—whether the information takes the form of a phone book, a recipe card file, or a disk file in a computer program.

Many database programs use what's called a **table** to organize the information contained in a database file. In Excel, this concept is referred to as a **list**, which is simply a worksheet of columns and rows.

Each collection of related information in a database is called a **record**. For example, in your `Address Book` database from Lesson 1, each name and its accompanying address, city, state, zip code, and phone number is considered a record. A single database list can contain thousands of records; the only real limitation is the amount of memory of the computer holding the information.

Each record in a database contains several parts, or **fields**. For example, in the `Address Book` database, the first name is a field, the last name is a field, the address is a field, the city is a field, and so on. Each field must have a designated field name so that it is easy to identify when used in the program. A field name can consist of up to 255 characters, but as a rule, you should keep field names brief and descriptive of the field's contents.

Lesson 2: Adding Records

Data form
A dialog box that displays only one row of your list—in other words, one record. Column headings appear as field labels. You can enter data or work with existing data using a data form.

After the initial database list is created, you may decide to add records to the list. You can simply type the new data into the rows at the end of the list, or you can use Excel's data form feature to add a number of records all at once.

A *data form* is a dialog box that shows all the fields in one data record. The data form presents an organized view of the data and makes data entry easier and more accurate. The data form is especially useful with much larger databases than the sample Address Book database used in this project.

Try adding records to the Address Book database now.

To Add Records

1 In the `Address Book` worksheet, select any cell in the list and then choose Data, Form from the menu.

A data form dialog box opens, displaying the contents of the first record in the Address list, as shown in Figure 8.3. The field names correspond to the column headings in the list. Notice that in the upper-right corner of the data form, Excel displays the record number and the total number of records in the list.

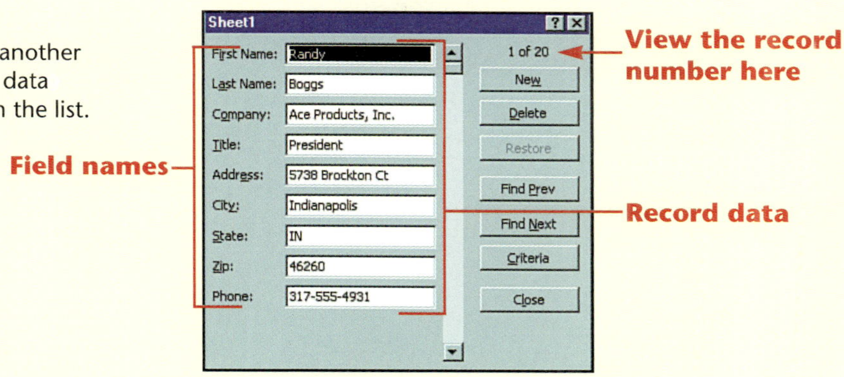

Figure 8.3
A data form is another way to display data from records in the list.

2 Click the New button in the data form dialog box.

A new, blank form appears. You enter data for new records in the blank form.

3 Type `Mohammed` in the First Name field text box, then press Tab.

This enters the data into the First Name field of a new data record. Pressing Tab moves the insertion point to the next field text box.

4 Type `Khalili` in the Last Name field text box, then press Tab.

This enters the data into the Last Name field of the data record.

continues

To Add Records (continued)

If you have problems...

If you press ↵Enter or ↓ instead of Tab, Excel adds the new record to the list and displays a new, blank data form. If you had not completed filling out the data form, click the Find Prev button in the data form dialog box to display it. You can press Tab to move forward through the data fields or ⇧Shift+Tab to move backward. Alternatively, click in the field you want to edit. If you make a mistake when typing in a field, simply use the ←Backspace or Del key to delete the error, then type the data correctly.

5 Continue entering the record using the following data:

Company: `Gadgets, Inc.`

Title: `Sales Manager`

Address: `526 Lynn St.`

City: `Ithaca`

State: `NY`

Zip: `14850`

Phone: `607-555-3421`

Don't forget to press Tab to move from one field to the next. When you are done, the record should look similar to the one in Figure 8.4.

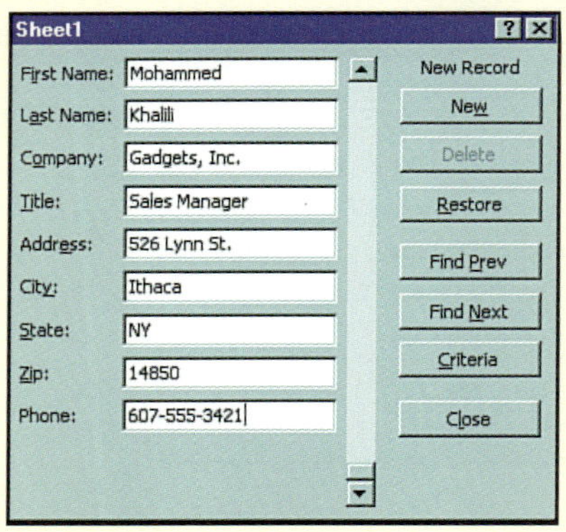

Figure 8.4
A new record is entered in the data form.

6 Press ↵Enter after typing all the field information.

This enters the new data record into the list and displays a new blank form, which you can use to continue adding records. You can also click the New button in the data form dialog box. Now add three more records to Address Book.

7 Enter the following record data:

`Natalie, Burnett, Style Systems, V.P. Marketing, 21 Magnolia St, Battle Creek, MI, 49017, 616-555-2394`

`Wendell, Feldman, Baker Computing, Dir. Sales, 270 West Limestone St, Orem, UT, 84057, 801-555-3002`

`Eve, Shaw, Baker Computing, Sales Rep., 1170 North 17th St, Orem, UT, 84057, 801-555-8202`

Remember to press Tab to move from field to field, and press Enter to display a new, blank data form.

8 Click the Close button in the data form dialog box.

This clears the dialog box from the screen and displays the address list. Scroll down the list to see the new records in rows 22 through 25, as shown in Figure 8.5. Now you need to extend the range name for your list to include the new records.

Figure 8.5
The new records are added to the bottom of the list.

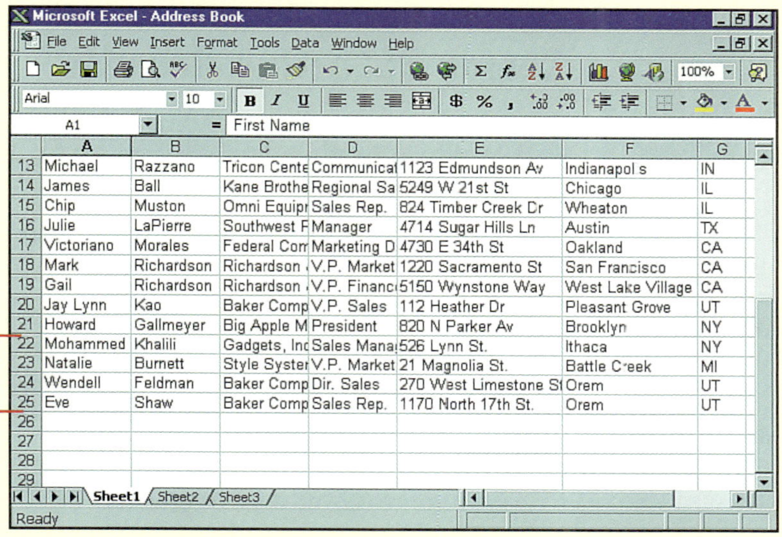

New records

9 Select the entire list, including field names (cells A1:I25).

You must redefine the list name to include the new records.

10 Choose Insert, Name, Define from the menu.

The Define Name dialog box appears.

11 Select the list name Address in the Names in workbook list box.

The list name (Address) appears in the Names in workbook text box (see Figure 8.6).

12 In the Refers to text box, change the last cell reference from row 21 to row `25`**, then choose OK.**

This redefines the Address list to include the records you just added. Deselect the list, save your work, and keep the Address Book worksheet open to use in the next lesson.

continues

To Add Records (continued)

Figure 8.6
Redefine the Address list to include the new records.

Change the cell address here

Excel

Lesson 3: Sorting Records

Sort
A function that rearranges the data in a list so that it appears in alphabetical or numerical order.

Sort fields
The fields used to determine the order in which a list is sorted.

To *sort* a list means to rearrange the list in a particular order. The sort order is determined by the *sort fields* you set for Excel. The sort fields are simply the fields you want Excel to use in sorting.

You can also choose the kind of order you want Excel to follow in sorting the field. For example, in your Address Book database, you can tell Excel to sort the Company field in *ascending order* or in *descending order*.

What if you have more than one person working at the same company? You perform a multilevel sort by using additional sort fields to break ties; in this case, you can use the last name as a second field to sort, or perhaps the title field.

Try sorting records in your list now.

To Sort Records

Ascending order
All the items appear in 0 to 9, A to Z order from beginning to end. Records with a blank sort field appear at the beginning of the list.

Descending order
All the items appear in 9 to 0, Z to A order from beginning to end.

1. **In the** `Address Book` **worksheet, open the Name box drop-down list on the Formula bar and choose Address.**

   This selects the records that you want to sort—the entire list.

2. **Choose Data, Sort from the menu.**

   The Sort dialog box appears, as shown in Figure 8.7. The Sort by text box is selected with the name of a field displayed (usually the first field, unless you've already sorted the list). By default, the sort order is Ascending, meaning A to Z or 0 to 9. You can change the sort order to Descending, meaning Z to A or 9 to 0.

3. **In the My list has area at the bottom of the Sort dialog box, make sure that the Header row option is selected.**

   This confirms that you have included the field names in the first row in the sorting range. Excel will not sort the data in the header row.

Figure 8.7
Use the Sort dialog box to specify how you want the rows in the list arranged.

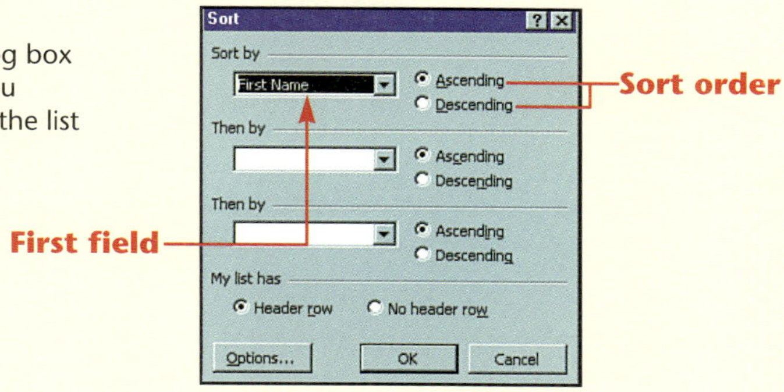

4 **Type `City` in the Sort by text box (or select it from the drop-down list), then choose OK.**

Excel sorts the records by city in ascending alphabetical order, as shown in Figure 8.8. Notice that the list records remain selected after the sort is performed. Now try resorting the list by more than one field at a time.

Figure 8.8
Records are sorted alphabetically according to the data in the City field.

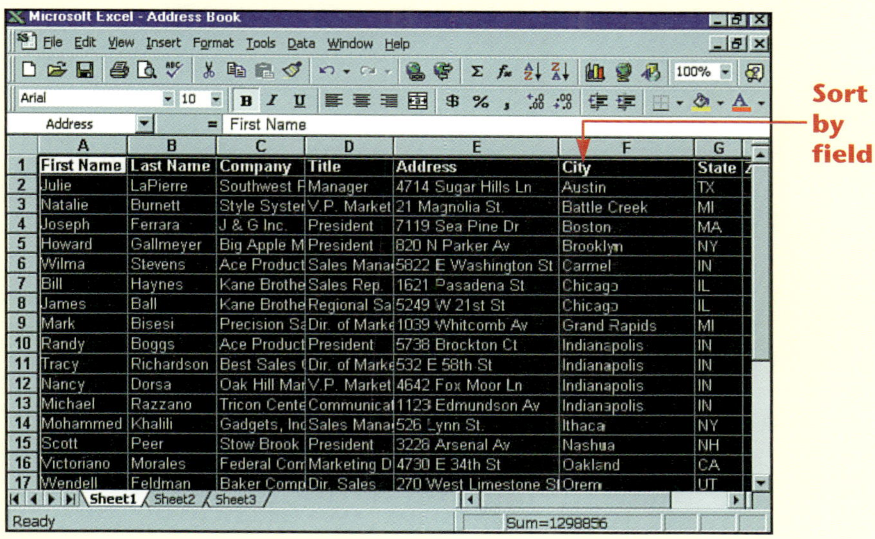

5 **With the entire list still selected, open the Data menu and choose Sort.**

The Sort dialog box appears again. Notice that `City` still appears in the Sort by text box.

6 **Click the drop-down arrow next to the Sort by text box, and select Company from the drop-down list of field names that appears.**

This enters `Company` in the Sort by text box, telling Excel you want to sort the records according to the data in the Company field.

continues

To Sort Records (continued)

However, because you know some of your records have the same data in the Company field, you also want to sort the list by last name.

7 Click the drop-down arrow next to the first Then by text box, and select Last Name from the drop-down list of field names.

Now you have added a second sort field: Last Name (see Figure 8.9). Excel first sorts by Company and then by Last Name.

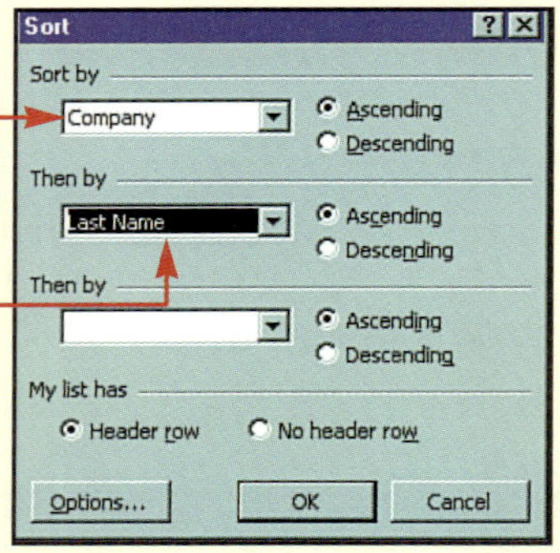

Figure 8.9
You can sort a list using up to three sort fields.

8 Choose OK.

Excel closes the dialog box and sorts the records. You may want to deselect the list to get a better look at it. Notice that the records have been alphabetized by company name. In cases where there is more than one record per company, the records are further alphabetized by last name, as shown in Figure 8.10.

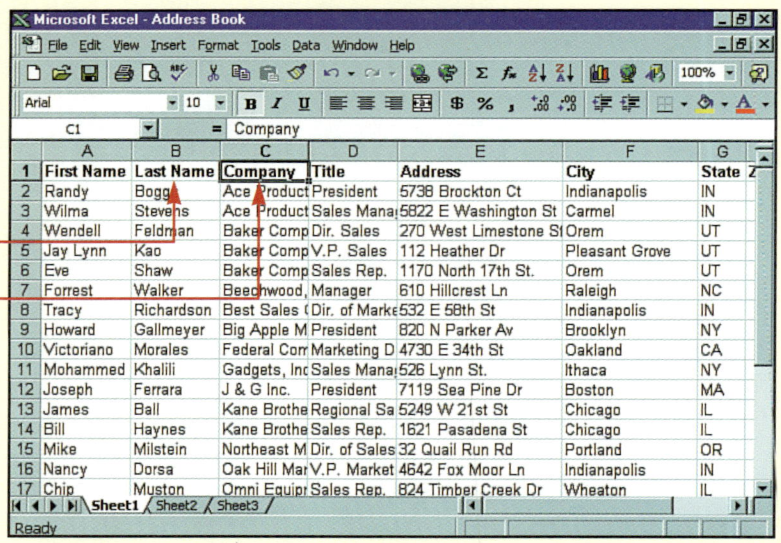

Figure 8.10
Records in the list are sorted alphabetically by Company Name, then by Last Name.

9 Save your work and keep the Address Book worksheet open to use in the next lesson.

If you have problems...

Be careful when selecting the data to sort. If you select only a column or two of data, Excel sorts only the selected data. Therefore, columns that aren't selected are not included in the sort. For example, if you selected only the Company Name and Last Name fields when sorting, you may find addresses and phone numbers paired with the wrong names. To reverse the sort, click the Undo button before performing any other action.

It's always a good idea to save your file before you perform a sort. If you make an error in sorting, you can close the file without saving, open the original file, and try again.

Inside Stuff

To quickly sort a list by the data in the current field, click the Sort Ascending or Sort Descending buttons on the Standard toolbar.

Exam Notes

If you have worksheet data that you created without thinking, you may have labels in your first column and data in subsequent columns. Choose Data, Sort and then click Options in the dialog box. In the Sort Options dialog box, select Sort left to right under Orientation. Choose OK. In the Sort dialog box, choose the row you want to Sort by, select Ascending or Descending, and choose OK.

When you need to sort your list in an order other than ascending or descending, set up a custom sort. Choose Data, Sort and then click Options in the dialog box. In the Sort Options dialog box, select the custom order you want (weekdays or months) and choose OK. Then, in the Sort by text box, select the column that has the weekday or month information.

To set up a custom sort order (such as priority), choose Tools, Options from the menu. Click the Custom Lists tab. Select NEW LIST in the Custom lists box. Type the entries for that list in the List entries box, pressing ↵Enter after each item. Click Add when the list is complete. Choose OK. The new custom order appears the next time you open the sort Options dialog box.

Lesson 4: Finding and Deleting Records

Search criteria
A defined pattern or detail used to find matching records.

One of the most useful functions of working with lists is using *search criteria* to find specific records. Using the Excel criteria data form to find specific records saves a great deal of time when you are working with dozens or hundreds of records. For example, you can use search criteria to find every person in your list with a particular job title.

You can also delete specific records in a list by using search criteria to find the records, then deleting them. For example, you can choose to delete all records containing a particular last name or all records containing a particular state. Be careful when deleting records so you don't delete records that you need.

Try finding and deleting specific records in your list now.

Excel

To Find and Delete Records

1 In the Address Book worksheet, click any cell in the list. Open the Data menu and choose Form.

A data form appears containing the data from the first record.

2 Click the Criteria button in the data form dialog box.

A blank criteria data form appears, as shown in Figure 8.11. You use the criteria data form to specify the records you want to find. Now specify criteria to find and then delete all the records for people working at Baker Computing.

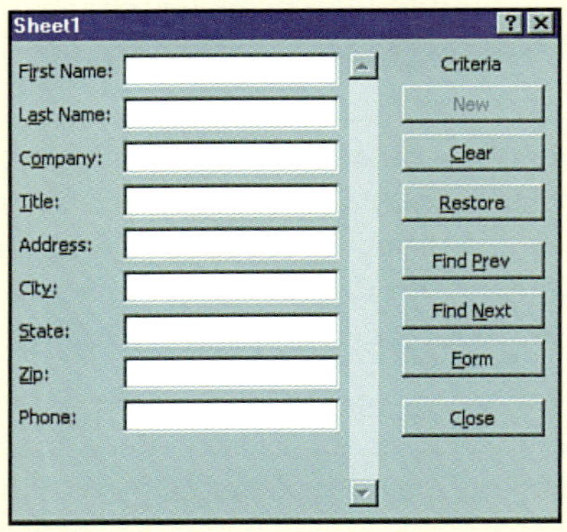

Figure 8.11 Use the blank criteria data form to find records that contain certain data.

3 Click in the Company text box and type `Baker Computing`.

This tells Excel to look through the Company field in every record to find the data Baker Computing.

4 Click the Find Next button.

Excel begins the search and displays the data form for the next record in the list that matches the specified criterion—which is the next record from the company Baker Computing, as shown in Figure 8.12.

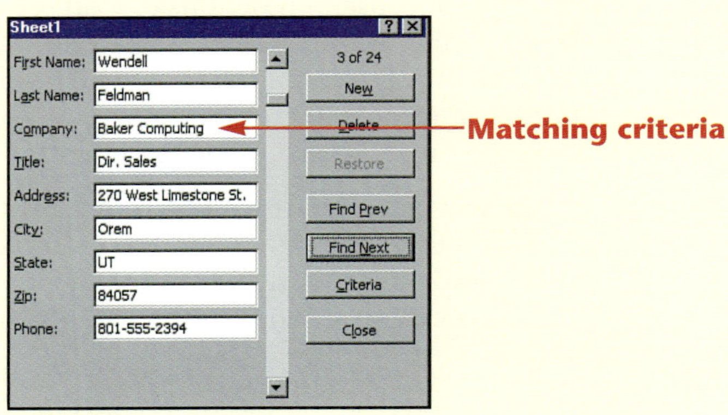

Figure 8.12 Excel displays a record that matches the criteria you entered.

5 Click the Delete button.

Excel displays a dialog box warning you that the record will be permanently deleted.

If you have problems...

Be careful when deleting records from your database. Once you choose OK in the warning dialog box, Excel deletes the record permanently. You can't retrieve the deleted record using the Undo command.

6 Choose OK.

Excel deletes the record and displays the data form for the next record in the database, whether or not it matches the search criteria. (In this case, it does match because the records are sorted by company name.) Now continue your search using the criteria data form to delete the rest of the records from Baker Computing.

7 Click the Find Next button.

Again, Excel displays the next record that matches the specified criteria.

8 Click the Delete button, then choose OK in the warning box.

Excel deletes the record. Repeat the steps to find and delete any additional records from Baker Computing. When no further records in the list match the criteria, Excel beeps.

9 Click the Close button in the data form dialog box.

This clears the dialog box and displays the Address Book worksheet.

10 Save your work and keep the worksheet open. In the next lesson, you use Excel's AutoFilter feature to extract records from the database.

Exam Notes

One way to find a particular value in a list is to use the Lookup Wizard. This feature is particularly useful when you need a formula for finding the information. Select any cell in the list and choose Tools, Wizard, Lookup. The range of the list should appear in the Where is the range to search text box (enter it if necessary). Click Next and specify the column that contains the value you want to find. Then specify the value you want to find and click Next. Choose whether you want to display just the formula or both the formula and the lookup parameters. Click Next and type or select a cell or range where you want this information to appear. Click Finish.

The Lookup Wizard may not be available on your menu. It's an add-in program, and you'll need your installation CD to install it. Ask your instructor or follow the instructions in Excel Help, under Add-in programs.

Lesson 5: Extracting Records Using AutoFilter

Filter
A method for controlling which records are extracted from the database and displayed in the worksheet.

If you want to find records that match more complex criteria, you can use Excel's AutoFilter feature. With a *filter*, you set criteria to specify the records that you want displayed in the list. Filtering does not delete the records that don't match your criteria; it just hides them until you want to display them again.

In this lesson, for example, assume that you want to send a letter to everyone in your database who works at a specific company in Chicago or Indianapolis. You want to tell them that you will be visiting those cities soon and would like to meet them. You can use the AutoFilter to extract all the records for those cities from the original list.

When you use a large database with hundreds of records, filtering data enables you to work with a more manageable set of records and fields. Always save your file before you filter data. If you have a problem extracting the records, you can close the file and revert to the saved version of the original data. Try extracting records using AutoFilter and your Address Book database now.

To Extract Records Using AutoFilter

1 In the `Address Book` worksheet, click in any cell in the list, then choose Data, Filter, AutoFilter from the menu.

Filter arrows appear next to each of the field names in the list, as shown in Figure 8.13. You specify the field that you want to use for filtering by using the filter arrow in that field. In this case, you want to filter records based on the City field.

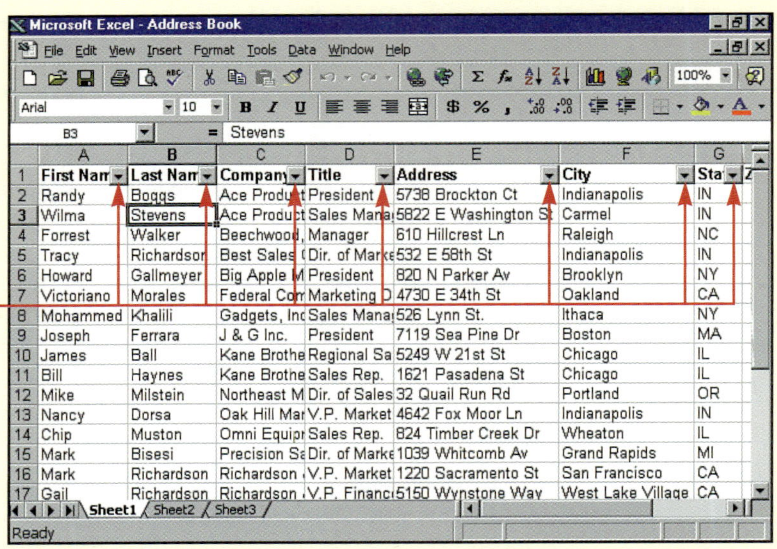

Filter arrows

Figure 8.13
Use AutoFilter to hide the records you don't want to work with.

2 Click the filter arrow in cell F1.

A drop-down list of filtering criteria appears under the arrow. Some predefined filters, including `(All)`, `(Top 10...)`, and `(Custom...)`, are displayed at the top of the list. (All), the default, shows all the records without using the field as a filter. Choose (All) when you want to remove any filtering criteria already in use for a field.

Choose (Top 10...) when you want to filter records according to the highest or lowest values in the list. For example, in a text field, such as Product Names, you would be able to filter the records by the letters A through J or Q through Z. In a numeric field, such as Price, you can filter the records by the ten highest values or the ten lowest values.

Choose (Custom...) to specify multiple selection criteria to use for filtering the field. To filter by a single criteria (such as a specific city name), simply select it from the list.

3 From the drop-down list, select (Custom...).

The Custom AutoFilter dialog box appears (see Figure 8.14). This is where you specify the criteria that Excel uses to extract records from the database. You can specify two criteria, using two operators. Operators tell Excel the type of comparison you want to use. For example, equals means to match the criteria exactly, and is less than means to find records in which the data is less than the specified criteria. Notice that `equals` appears in the first operator text box by default.

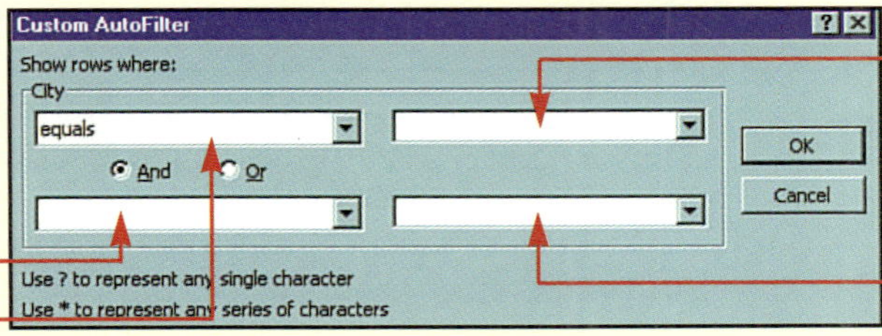

Figure 8.14
Specify the criteria for deciding which records to hide and which to display.

4 Click the drop-down arrow next to the first criteria text box, and select Chicago.

This establishes "City equals Chicago" as the first filter criterion. Remember that you want to include records either from Chicago or from Indianapolis.

5 Select the Or option in the Custom AutoFilter dialog box.

Next, you want to include Indianapolis in the criteria statement.

continues

To Extract Records Using AutoFilter (continued)

6 Click the drop-down arrow next to the second operator text box.

This displays a list of relational operators, as shown in Figure 8.15.

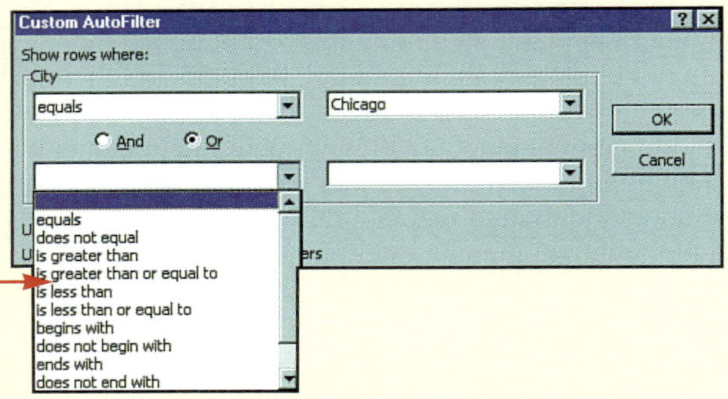

List of operators

Figure 8.15
Specify the type of comparison by selecting an operator from the drop-down list.

7 Select `equals` from the drop-down list.

This tells Excel you want to find all records that match the specified criteria exactly.

8 Click the drop-down arrow next to the second criteria text box and select Indianapolis from the list of data entries that appears.

Your dialog box should now resemble Figure 8.16. Make sure that `equals` appears in both operator text boxes and the Or option is selected.

If you have problems...

Choosing the correct option is critical. You would use the And option if you wanted to display records that contain both values in the specified field. In this case, if you specified And, all of the records would be filtered out because none of them contains both Chicago and Indianapolis in the City field. On the other hand, Or tells Excel to find records that contain either Chicago or Indianapolis.

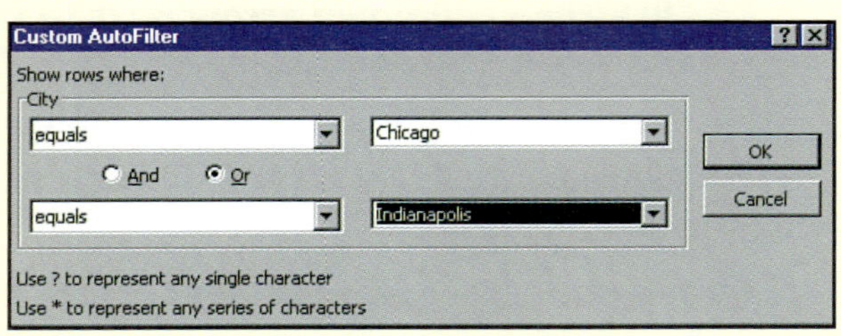

Figure 8.16
The completed Custom AutoFilter dialog box is ready to filter out records that don't meet the specified criteria.

9 Choose OK in the Custom AutoFilter dialog box.

Excel extracts all records that match the specified criteria and displays them in the list, as shown in Figure 8.17. In this case, only records where the City field contains the data Chicago or

Indianapolis are displayed. All other records are temporarily hidden. Notice that the filter arrow for the City field is colored blue to indicate that the City field has been used to filter data. Also, notice that the row numbers are blue, indicating that not all rows are displayed.

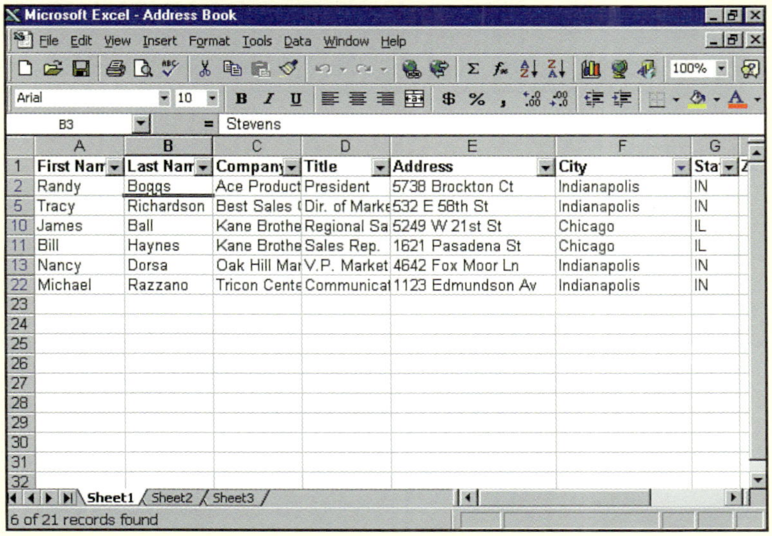

Figure 8.17
The extracted records for Chicago and Indianapolis are displayed.

10 Choose Data, Filter, AutoFilter from the menu.

This turns off the AutoFilter feature, and all records in the list are again displayed. Notice that the filter arrows disappear.

11 Save your work. If requested by your instructor, print two copies, then close the worksheet.

If you have completed your session on the computer, exit Excel 97 and Windows 95 before turning off the computer. Otherwise, continue with the "Checking Your Skills" and "Applying Your Skills" sections at the end of this project.

Inside Stuff

When specifying criteria, you can enter them directly in the box instead of selecting them from the drop-down list. To find text values that share some characters but not others, use a wildcard. Use a question mark (?) to replace a single character in the same position (`T?m` finds both Tom and Tim); use an asterisk (*) to replace a group of characters in the same position (`New*` finds both New Jersey and New York).

It's always a good idea to remove all old filtering conditions before you set new ones. Otherwise, you may forget that you have previously set a filtering condition that is still affecting a more recent search. Choose Data, Filter, Show All to clear the preceding filters.

You can clear a filter from a single column by clicking the filter button for that column and choosing (All) from the list. To turn off AutoFilter completely, simply choose Data, Filter, AutoFilter.

Exam Notes

When you need to filter your list based on more than two criteria, you need to work with a criteria range. You establish the criteria range by inserting at least three blank rows above your list. Copy the column labels from your list to the first blank row of the criteria range. Type the criteria you want to match in the rows below the criteria labels. For example, if you want to find all the records that fall into the same state, the same company, and the same title, you type the information under each of those labels. Click in any cell in your list and then choose Data, Filter, Advanced Filter. Select Filter the list, in-place to filter the list. The List range should already be specified, but you need to enter the reference for the Criteria range, which includes the criteria labels and the row of cells beneath them. Choose OK.

Project Summary

To	Do This
Name a list	Select the list and choose Insert, Name, Define. Type the name in the Names in workbook text box in the Define Name dialog box, then choose OK.
Add records	Choose Data, Form, and click New. Type data in the fields, pressing Tab to move from one field to the next.
Sort records by the current field	Click the Sort Ascending or Sort Descending buttons on the Standard toolbar.
Find records	Choose Data, Form, and click Criteria. Type the data to find in the appropriate field and click Find Next.
Delete records	Find the record you want to delete, and click Delete in the data form dialog box. Click OK in the warning dialog box.
Filter the list of records	Choose Data, Filter, then choose AutoFilter to create your own filter. Drop down the filtering criteria list in the field you want to filter, and choose the criteria you want to use, or choose (Custom...) to specify your own filtering criteria.
Display all records	Choose Data, Filter, AutoFilter.

Checking Your Skills

True/False

For each of the following, check *T* or *F* to indicate whether the statement is true or false.

__T __F **1.** The field name identifies each record in a database table.

__T __F **2.** An Excel list can be sorted only in ascending order.

__T __F **3.** A field name cannot start with a number.

__T __F **4.** If you filter records, those that do not match the criteria are deleted from the database.

__T __F **5.** If you choose equals as an operator to filter records, data must match the criteria exactly.

__T __F **6.** Naming a list is especially useful when you are working with a large amount of data.

__T __F **7.** Each collection of information in a list is divided into fields.

__T __F **8.** Excel can sort data using up to two fields.

__T __F **9.** You cannot leave any cells in a list empty.

__T __F **10.** You can retrieve a deleted record using the Undo command.

Multiple Choice

Circle the letter of the correct answer for each of the following questions.

1. To view the data for one record at a time, what should you display?

a. Criteria

b. Filter

c. Data form

d. List

2. What feature do you use to display only selected records in a list?

a. Sort

b. AutoFilter

c. Name

d. Find

3. Which option in the criteria list, displayed when you click a filter arrow, removes any filters for that field?

a. (Blank)

b. <>

c. (All)

d. None of the above

4. To display records that match both criteria entered into the Custom AutoFilter dialog box, you click which option button?

a. Or

b. And

c. And/Or

d. Either

5. How do you know when records have been filtered in the database?
   a. The word filter displays in the title bar.
   b. The column letters in the list are blue.
   c. The row numbers in the list are blue.
   d. All the above.
6. Which of the following is another name for a list?
   a. Table
   b. Worksheet
   c. Field
   d. Record
7. To find the records that match a search condition in the list, you click which button in the data form?
   a. Search
   b. Seek
   c. Criteria
   d. None of the above
8. To move to the previous field text box in the Data Form, press which of the following keys?
   a. Tab
   b. Enter
   c. ↓
   d. Shift+Tab
9. Which of the following is *not* a rule for creating a list in Excel?
   a. The field names must be in a single row.
   b. The field names must be unique.
   c. A field name can contain letters, numbers, and spaces.
   d. Leave a blank row between the row of field names and the first data record.
10. Which of the following shows all the fields in one data record?
   a. Data form
   b. Data list
   c. AutoFilter form
   d. Custom list

Completion

In the blank provided, write the correct answer for each of the following statements.

1. The best way to add records to an existing list is by using the Data ______________.
2. By default, Excel sorts in ______________ order.
3. Each individual collection of related information in a database is called a(n) ______________.
4. If you choose to sort a list in ascending alphabetical order, Excel will sort the list from ______________ to ______________.
5. To remove all filtering criteria being used in a field, choose ______________ from the drop-down list of filtering criteria.

6. To find records in a list where one criterion *or* the other is met, you use the ______________.

7. The ______________ names indicate the information contained in each record.

8. Last name is an example of a(n) ______________ in an Excel list.

9. When using the data form to find records, click the ______________ ______________ button to locate the next record matching the criteria.

10. When you ______________ records, they are hidden until you display them again.

Matching

In the blank next to each of the following terms or phrases, write the letter of the corresponding term or phrase. (Note that some letters may be used more than once.)

a. memory
b. Tab
c. Enter
d. search criteria
e. Custom AutoFilter
f. filter
g. fields
h. sort
i. Data form
j. record

_____ 1. Column headings in a list

_____ 2. Each row of worksheet data

_____ 3. A dialog box that displays only one row of your list

_____ 4. A function that rearranges data in a list so it appears in alphabetical or numerical order

_____ 5. A defined pattern or detail used to find matching records

_____ 6. A method for controlling which records are extracted from the database

_____ 7. A dialog box that lets you specify criteria for which records to display

_____ 8. Limits the number of records in a list

_____ 9. When using the data form, press this key to add the record to the list

_____ 10. When using the data form, press this key to move to the next field

Excel

Applying Your Skills

Practice

The following exercises enable you to practice the skills you have learned in this project. Take a few minutes to work through these exercises now.

Creating a List

You can use Excel's database list feature to keep track of product inventory. You can store the product names, prices, and ordering information, then work with the data using the list features, such as sorting and filtering.

To create a list, follow these steps:

Use the product information provided to create an inventory list for keeping track of products.

1. Open the file Proj0802 from the Project-08 folder on the CD and save it as `Products`.
2. Insert a row at the top of the list, then change the worksheet into a list by adding field names to the top of each column, as follows:

   Column A: `Product Name`

   Column B: `Product Number`

   Column C: `Unit Cost`

   Column D: `In Stock?`
3. Sort the list alphabetically by product name so that you can easily find any product.
4. Extract a list of all products that are not in stock so that you know what needs to be reordered.
5. Save your list. If requested by your instructor, print two copies, then close the file.

Sorting a List and Extracting Records

Create a telephone list that you can use for notifying customers of upcoming events.

To sort a list and extract records, follow these steps:

1. Open the file Proj0803 from the Project-08 folder on the CD and save it as `Phone List`.
2. Name the list `Customers`.
3. Sort the list alphabetically by customer last name.
4. Sort the list alphabetically by last name, then by first name.
5. Extract a list of customers who last attended a tasting in September.
6. Save the list. If requested by your instructor, print two copies, then close the file.

Using a Sort and AutoFilter in a Database

With Excel's list feature, you can create an employee database that can help you track vital information about staff members. You use this database to organize the work schedule and to analyze your staffing needs. In this example, use the sort and AutoFilter features of Excel to organize the employee data and evaluate salaried, hourly, and commissioned staff.

To use sort and AutoFilter in a database, follow these steps:

1. Open the file Proj0804 from the Project-08 folder on the CD and save it as `Employees`.
2. Sort the list alphabetically by three sort keys: `Last Name`, `First Name`, and `City`.
3. Extract a list of commissioned employees.
4. Extract a list of hourly employees.
5. Extract a list of salaried employees who live in Oak Hill.
6. Display all records.
7. Save the file. If requested by your instructor, print two copies of the list, including all records, then close the file.

Querying a Database

Using the worksheet provided, create a database to keep track of the music CDs you keep to play in the coffee shop.

To query a database, follow these steps:

1. Open the file Proj0805 from the Project-08 folder on the CD and save it as `CD Inventory`.
2. Change the worksheet into a list by adding field names to the top of each column, as follows: `Title`, `Artist`, `Price`, `Type`.
3. Use the data form to add the following two records:

   `Shaking the Tree, Peter Gabriel, $13.99, Rock`.

   `Rumours, Fleetwood Mac, $8.99, Rock`.
4. Sort the list alphabetically by artist so that you can easily find any CD.
5. Extract a list of all titles that cost more than $12.99 or less than $9.99 so that you can track the most expensive and least expensive titles.
6. Save the file. If requested by your instructor, print two copies, then close the file.

Using the Data Form to Add Records to a List

In this exercise, you use the data form to add records to a list.

To use the data form to add records to a list, follow these steps:

1. Open the file Proj0806 from the Project-08 folder on the CD and save it as `Billing 3`.
2. Click a cell within the list to activate it.
3. Choose Data, Form to display the data form dialog box.
4. Use the scroll bar to move to the end of the records. A blank dialog box should display on your screen.
5. Add the following record to the list:

Billing Date:	`6/1/97`
Company:	`Reliable Roofing`
Amount:	`175.00`
Date Paid:	`6/15/97`
Amt. Rec'd:	`175.00`

   You cannot enter information into the other fields because these are calculated automatically.
6. Add the following records to the list using the data form:

Billing Date:	`6/8/97`	`6/7/97`
Company:	`Craig Concrete`	`Decks & More`
Amount:	`292.00`	`87.00`
Date Paid:	`6/10/97`	`6/30/97`
Amt. Rec'd:	`292.00`	`87.00`

7. Close the data form dialog box.
8. Sort the list in ascending order by `Company` and then by `Billing Date`.
9. Use the AutoFilter. Then click the `Balance` field filter arrow and select `(Custom...)` to display the AutoFilter dialog box. In the first operator text box, select `is greater than`. Type `0` in the first criteria text box to display all the records with a balance greater than 0. The record for `Decks & More` should display on your screen.
10. Display all the companies that owe your company money. Then click the `Balance` field filter arrow and select `(Custom...)` to display the AutoFilter dialog box. In the first operator text box, select `is less than`. Type `0` in the first criteria text box to display all the records with a balance of less than 0. The records for Wilson General Contractors and Craig Concrete display on your screen.
11. If requested by your instructor, print two copies of the worksheet. Click the Balance filter arrow and select `(All)` from the list. All of the records are again displayed. Turn off AutoFilter. Save the worksheet before closing it. Exit Excel.

Challenge

The following challenges enable you to use your problem-solving skills. Take time to work through these exercises now.

Sorting Data

Open Proj0807 from the Project-08 folder on the CD and save it as `Salary`. Sort the list by Salary, from the highest to the lowest salary. This quickly tells you who is getting paid top salary and who is being paid the least. Print the worksheet. Save the workbook but leave it open for the next exercise.

Sorting by More Than One Field

Sort the list again. This time sort the list by Division and then by Department, both in alphabetical order. Save the file and leave it open for the next exercise.

Finding and Deleting Records

The Customer Service department in New York is being taken over by another company, and all the employees will be working for the new owners. You need to find everyone on the list who is in the Customer Service department in New York and delete them from the list. Save the workbook and leave it open for the next exercise.

Using AutoFilter

Your company is checking the equality of salaries for male versus female employees. Find the records of all the females earning $35,000 or less. Then find the records of all the males earning $35,000 or less. Compare this information to the printout you made earlier of the top earners in the list. Turn off the AutoFilter. Save the workbook before closing it.

Displaying Records

Open Proj0808 from the Project-08 folder on the CD and save it as `Checking Account`. Add the following checks to the list using the data form:

```
510    5/1    Jane Smith      15.00
511    5/5    Grocery Store   36.00
```

You want to see where your biggest expenditures are, so display all the checks that are larger than $100.00. Print a copy of this worksheet. Display all the records in the list. Display all the records for the Grocery Store, so that you can quickly see how much you have spent on groceries. Print the worksheet. Display all the records in the list. Turn off the AutoFilter feature. Save the file and close it.

PinPoint Assessment

PinPoint Training

You have completed the project and the associated lessons, as well as the "Checking Your Skills" and "Applying Your Skills" sections. Now use the PinPoint software evaluation mode to assess your comprehension of the specific exam tasks you have just learned. You can also use the PinPoint Trainer Mode and the Show Me tutorials to practice these specific exam tasks.

Project 9

Nine

Designing Forms with Excel

Creating an Online Order Form

In this Project, you learn how to:

Objectives	Required Activities
➤ Name a List	
➤ Add a Check Box to a Worksheet	
➤ Add an Option Button to a Worksheet	
➤ Add a Combo Box and Link to a List	
➤ Add a Spinner to a Worksheet	
➤ Enhance a Form	
➤ Protect a Form	
➤ Save a Form as a Template	Create Templates
➤ Use a Form Template	Work with Existing Templates
➤ Edit a Template	Edit Templates

Why Would I Do This?

Rather than typing information over and over again or running to the typewriter to fill in the blanks on a preprinted form, you can create an **online form** for your specific needs. The form can be filled in, printed, modified when necessary, and even routed electronically.

When you create a form, it may help to sketch a design so that you have an idea of what the form should include. You can create forms in the various Microsoft Office software packages, including Word, Access, or Excel; however, you should create the form in Excel if it collects information for calculations.

You can create sophisticated forms by adding **controls**, such as check boxes, option buttons, and list boxes to a worksheet. Controls can be linked to worksheet cells so that when a selection is made from the control, it is displayed in the worksheet cell, which then can be used in a worksheet calculation. This linking saves time for the user (who fills in the form) and reduces data entry errors. Finally, you can enhance a form by formatting the objects and controls to resemble a paper form.

In this project, you use a worksheet previously created by personnel in the Columbus Computer Store. This worksheet is your guide for creating an online form. Rectangle objects and cell borders are already added to the worksheet. You learn how to build a form using Excel's Forms toolbar to add several controls, format the objects and controls, protect the form to allow only parts to be filled-in by users, and save the form as a **template**.

Jargon Watch

An **online form** is a worksheet designed to contain frequently used, fill-in-the-blank information. The form is stored, used, and maintained on the computer (examples include an invoice, an expense report, and so on). A **template** is a workbook or worksheet created and used as a guide or pattern for completing other similar workbooks (such as budgets, payroll, and forms). A **control** is a special drawing object, used as a data entry device to enhance a worksheet and reduce errors.

Lesson 1: Adding a Check Box to a Worksheet

Check Box
A worksheet control that you select for a true answer or deselect for a false answer.

You use the Forms toolbar to draw data entry devices, known as controls, in your worksheet. Click a button on the toolbar for the control you want; then drag the mouse in the worksheet to create the control. With controls, you can present choices for data entry while reducing data entry errors by limiting the information that the user can enter in a form.

Because this worksheet is used as an online form, you decide to add several controls to assist users in completing it. In this lesson, you use the Forms toolbar to add a *check box* to the form.

To Add a Check Box to a Worksheet

1 Open the file Proj0901 from the Project-09 folder on the CD and save it as `Company Orders`.

This workbook contains two worksheets, labeled Order Form and Salesmen.

2 Click the `Order Form` sheet tab to activate that worksheet, if necessary.

3 Choose View, Toolbars and click Forms from the submenu.

The Forms toolbar is displayed as a floating toolbar, as shown in Figure 9.1.

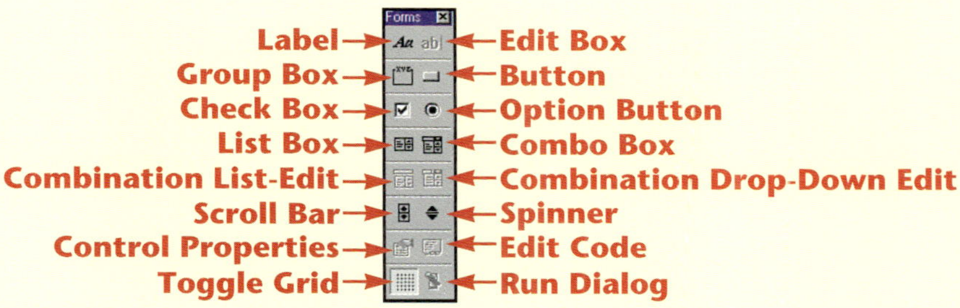

Figure 9.1
The buttons on the Forms toolbar help you add controls to the worksheet.

If you have problems...

If the Forms toolbar appears docked below the Formatting toolbar, just double-click in the space between the buttons to change it to a floating toolbar. Remember that you can drag the floating toolbar to another location on the worksheet.

4 Click the Check Box button on the Forms toolbar.

The mouse pointer changes to a small, thin cross.

5 Point to cell E15. Hold down the left mouse button and drag the mouse to create a box about the size of the cell. Release the mouse button.

The check box is created in cell E15, as shown in Figure 9.2. The label, `Check Box 4` (your system might display a different number), is displayed in the box. Change this label to Rush.

6 Click inside the selected box.

The insertion point is displayed in the box.

7 Delete the current label and number and type `Rush`.

8 Click outside of the selected box on the worksheet to deselect the box.

continues

To Add a Check Box to a Worksheet (continued)

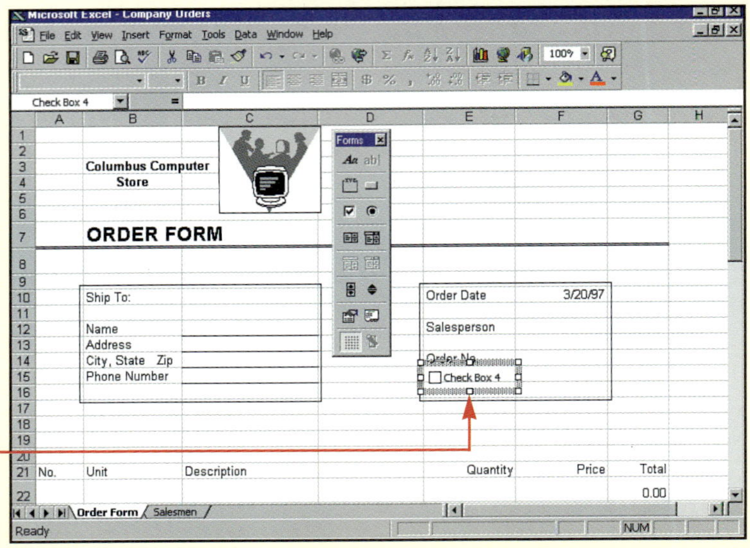

Check Box object

Figure 9.2
The check box produces a check mark when clicked.

If you have problems...

Don't be concerned if the check box is difficult to see on your worksheet or doesn't appear quite right. You format it later in this project. To use the check box, click the box; a check mark is displayed. Click the box again, and the check mark is removed.

You cannot select the check box for formatting or deleting by left-clicking the border of the check box or the label. When you left-click the border of the check box, it places a check mark in the box. To select this type of box, point the mouse to the border of the check box, hold down Ctrl and click the check box. The box is selected, and handles (white boxes) surround the border. Now you can delete, resize, or move the control. (This also applies to the other types of controls created from the Forms toolbar.)

The check box is added to your worksheet.

9. **Save the changes to the workbook and keep it open for the following lesson, where you add an option button to your form.**

Inside Stuff

The Forms toolbar contains several buttons that you can use to create controls on a worksheet and make data entry work easier. If a button cannot be used on the active sheet, it appears dimmed on the toolbar. The following buttons are not available for use on a worksheet: Edit Box, Combination List-Edit, Combination Drop-Down Edit, and Run Dialog.

Excel

Lesson 2: Adding an Option Button to a Worksheet

Option Button
A round button that selects an option from a group of options in a group box.

Another type of control is the *option button*, which is used to provide a multiple choice grouping. You can create individual option buttons. All these buttons will be in one group, no matter where they are created on the worksheet, and only one choice can be made from the group.

You also can create option buttons within different groups. The group box is drawn first, and then the option buttons are added. With this second method you can have more than one option button group, but only one choice can be made from each individual group.

In this lesson, you create an option button group with two buttons.

To Add an Option Button to a Worksheet

1. **Make sure that** `Order Form` **is the active worksheet in the** `Company Orders` **workbook.**

2. **Click the Group Box button on the Forms toolbar.**

   The mouse pointer becomes a small, thin cross.

3. **Point to the top-left corner of cell E18. Hold down the left mouse button while you drag the mouse to create the box to completely fill cells E18:F19. Release the mouse button.**

   The group box is created in cells E18 through F19. Handles surround the border, as shown in Figure 9.3.

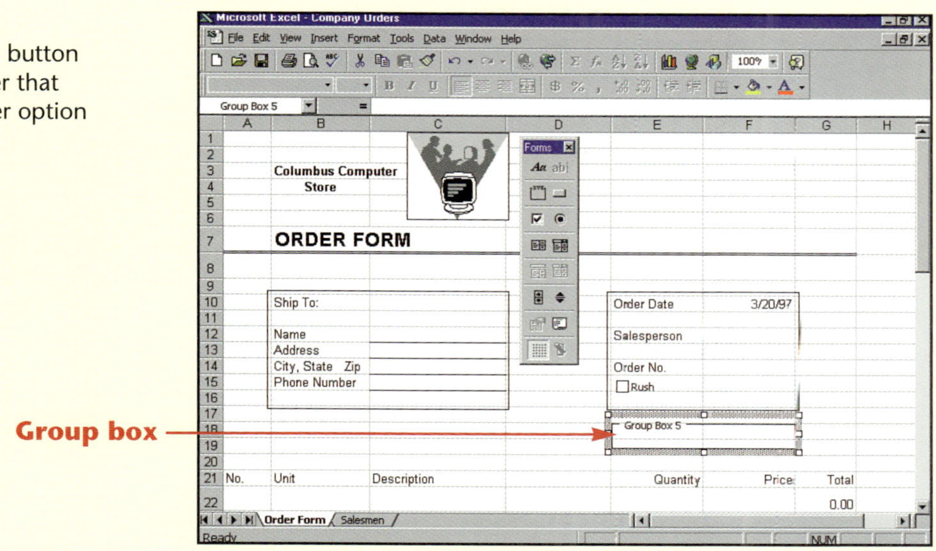

Figure 9.3
The Group Box button creates a border that groups together option buttons.

continues

To Add an Option Button to a Worksheet (continued)

4 Click in the label area (top left) inside the selected group box.

If you have problems...

If you don't click in the right place, you will deselect the group box and a cell becomes selected instead. If this happens, use Ctrl and click to select the group box and begin again.

5 Delete the current label and type `Order Information`. Click outside of the box, on the worksheet, to deselect the box.

6 Click the Option Button button on the Forms toolbar.

The mouse pointer becomes a small, thin cross.

7 Point to the left corner of cell E19. Hold down the left mouse button and drag the mouse to create a box the size of the cell. Release the mouse button.

The option button is created in cell E19, as shown in Figure 9.4. The label `Option Button`, followed by the number of the button, is displayed in the box. You change this label to Phoned In.

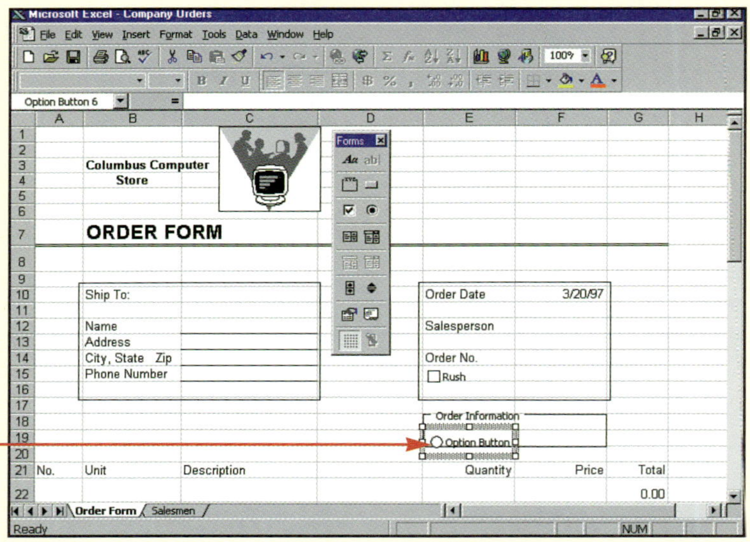

Figure 9.4
Option buttons are used to select one option from a list of two or more choices.

8 Click inside the box.

The insertion point is displayed inside the box.

9 Delete the current label and type `Phoned In`. Click outside of the box to deselect it.

10 Click the Option Button button on the Forms toolbar again.

11. **Point to the left corner of cell F19. Hold down the left mouse button and drag the mouse to create a box the full size of the cell. Release the mouse button.**
12. **Click inside the box.**
13. **Delete the current label and type `Mailed In`.**
14. **Click outside of the box to remove the selection.**
15. **Click the circle in the Phoned In option box. Now click the circle in the Mailed In option box.**

    You can only choose one option at a time; and when you click the option box, the circle will be filled. The completed group box with two option buttons is displayed (see Figure 9.5).

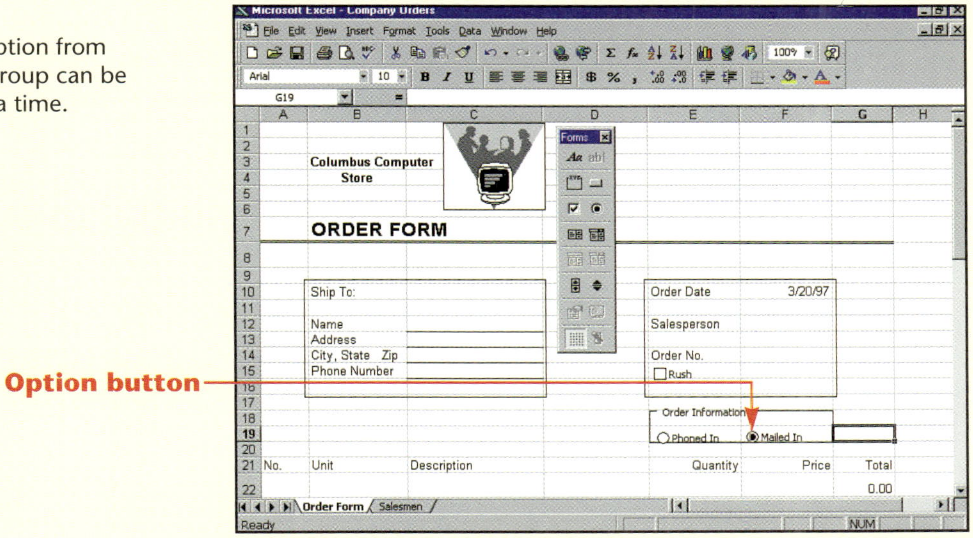

Figure 9.5
Only one option from an option group can be selected at a time.

16. **Save the changes to the workbook and keep it open for the following lesson, where you create a combo box drop-down list.**

Lesson 3: Adding a Combo Box and Link to a List

Combo Box
A list that contains text items. It displays multiple items and stays the same size. You make choices from the list, but you can't input text. The items displayed are from the data range it's linked to.

The Forms toolbar also contains buttons to draw controls, such as a *combo box*. After the control is placed on the worksheet, you can link it with a worksheet cell or range of cells. The link is used to transfer selected values from the control to a worksheet cell.

In this lesson, you add a combo box to the form to provide data entry choices.

To Add a Combo Box and Link to a List

1 Make sure that `Order Form` is the active worksheet in the `Company Orders` workbook.

2 Click the Combo Box button on the Forms toolbar.

The mouse pointer becomes a small, thin cross.

3 Point to the top-left corner of cell F12. Hold down the left mouse button while you drag the mouse to create the box the full size of the cell. Release the mouse button.

The combo box is created in cell F12. Handles surround the border, as shown in Figure 9.6. Now you can link the combo box to the Salesmen's names, which are located on another worksheet.

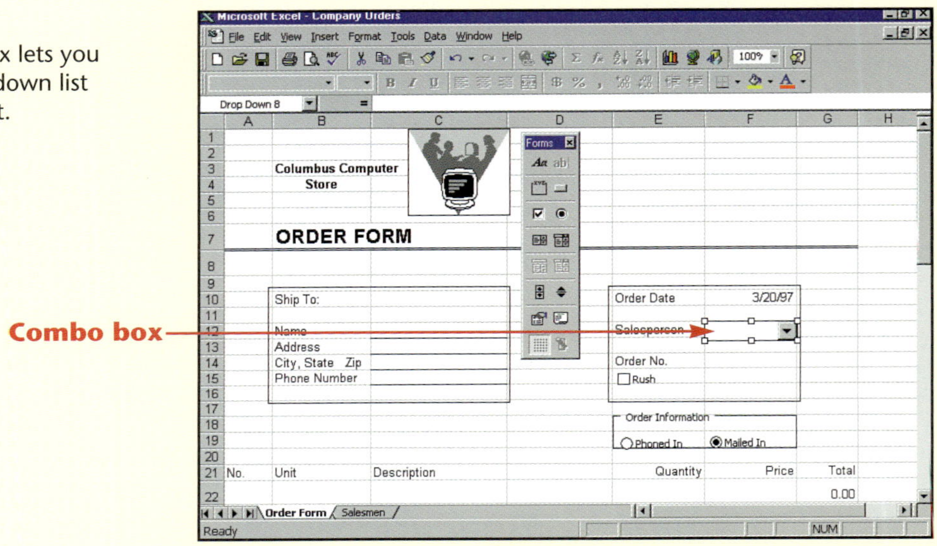

Figure 9.6
The combo box lets you create a drop-down list containing text.

4 With the combo box still selected, click the Control Properties button on the Forms toolbar.

The Format Control dialog box is displayed, as shown in Figure 9.7. Depending on the type of control, different options are available in the Control tab. For the combo box drop-down list, you need to specify the control's data limits.

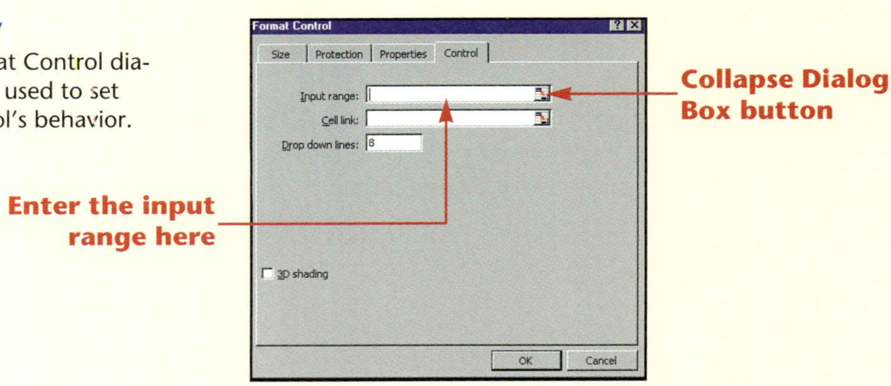

Figure 9.7
The Format Control dialog box is used to set the control's behavior.

5 On the Control tab, click the Collapse Dialog Box button on the right side of the Input range text box.

The dialog box collapses to reveal only the text box and a title bar. The Collapse Dialog Box button at the end of the text box changes to the Expand Dialog Box button. With the dialog box collapsed, you can select cells, ranges, or worksheets and have those references automatically appear in the text box.

6 Click the Salesmen sheet tab.

The company salesmen are listed in this worksheet in cells A1:A6. Cell A1 is blank so that no name appears initially in the combo box drop-down list.

7 Select the range of cells A1:A6.

The worksheet and range references appear in the text box. (If you prefer, you can type the range of cells in the text box.) This range contains the input values available for the combo box in your form.

8 Click the Expand Dialog Box button and then choose OK. Click elsewhere on the worksheet to remove the selection.

The combo box is complete.

9 Click the arrow next to the combo box in cell F12.

The salesmen's names are displayed in the list, as shown in Figure 9.8. You can click a name to fill in the list box.

Figure 9.8
The salesmen's names appear when you click the arrow next to the combo box drop-down list.

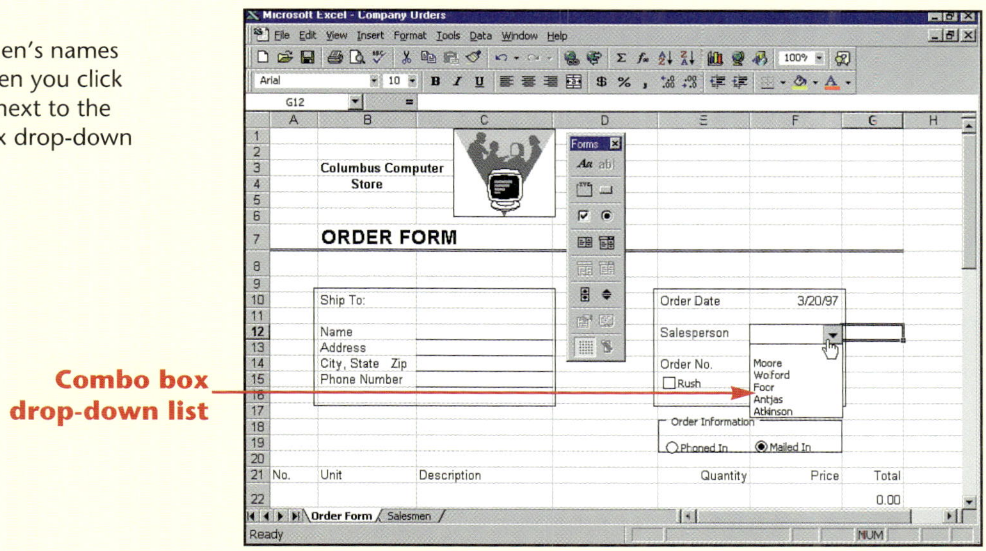

continues

To Add a Combo Box and Link to a List (continued)

10. **Click the arrow next to the combo box again.**

    The list is closed; no selection has been made.

11. **Save the changes to this workbook and keep it open for the following lesson, where you create a spinner.**

Lesson 4: Adding a Spinner to a Worksheet

Spinner
A control presented as a two-headed arrow that incrementally increases or decreases the amount in the linked cell.

A *spinner* is useful when you want to quickly increase or decrease numbers in a cell. Instead of typing in an amount, for example, you can click the control and pick a number.

In this lesson, you add a spinner to the Order No. cell in the form that you are creating.

To Add a Spinner to a Worksheet

1. **Make sure that** `Order Form` **is the active worksheet in the** `Company Orders` **workbook.**

2. **Click the Spinner button on the Forms toolbar.**

   The mouse pointer becomes a small, thin cross.

3. **Point to cell F14. Hold down the left mouse button while you drag the mouse down and across to the middle of cell F15. Release the mouse button.**

   The spinner is created in cells F14 and F15. Handles surround the border, as shown in Figure 9.9. Now you can determine default settings for the control.

Spinner

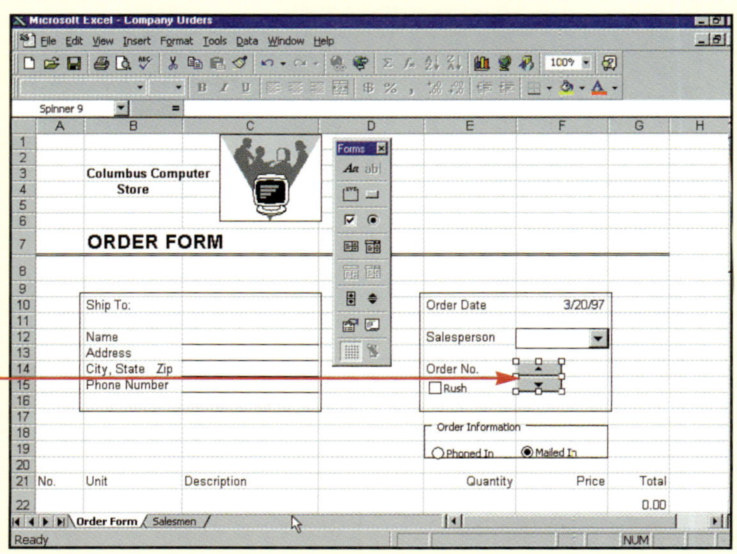

Figure 9.9
The Spinner is drawn on the worksheet.

4 Click the Control Properties button on the Forms toolbar.

The Format Control dialog box is displayed, as shown in Figure 9.10.

Figure 9.10
Control options are available for the spinner.

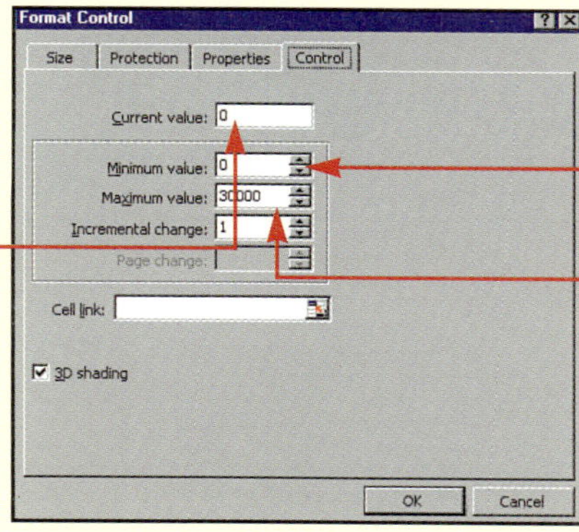

5 Type `100` **in the Current value text box.**

The number 100 is the starting number for the order forms.

6 Type `100` **in the Minimum value text box.**

With this setting, the numbers do not decrease below 100.

7 Type `1000` **in the Maximum value text box.**

With this setting, the numbers do not increase above 1,000.

8 Type `F14` **in the Cell link text box.**

Cell F14 becomes the linked cell to display the number. The Incremental change remains set at 1.

9 Click OK and then click the worksheet to remove the border.

The completed spinner is displayed, as shown in Figure 9.11. Clicking the up or down arrows of the spinner increases or decreases the number in cell F14 by 1.

10 Save the changes to this workbook and keep it open for the following lesson, where you make additional formatting changes to make the worksheet resemble a paper form.

continues

To Add a Spinner to a Worksheet (continued)

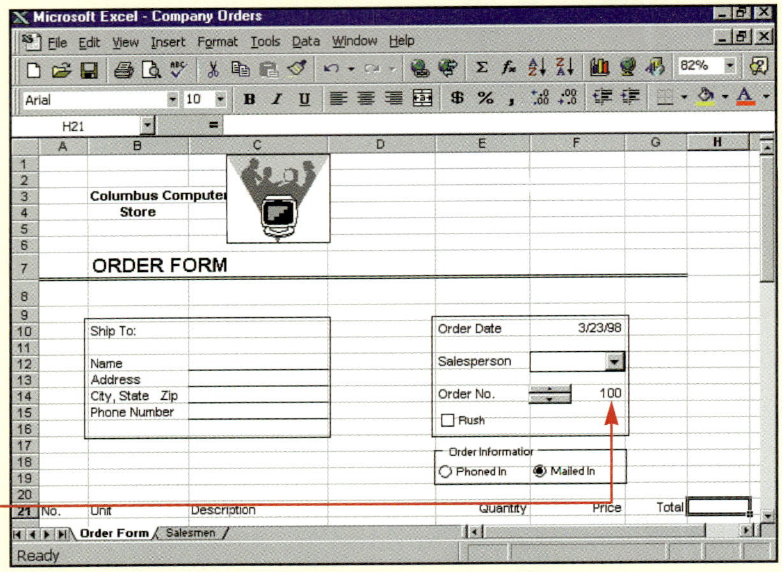

Figure 9.11
With the spinner, you can increase or decrease numbers in a cell.

Lesson 5: Enhancing a Form

You can enhance a worksheet so that it resembles a paper form by formatting the objects in the worksheet. You can format objects and some controls by changing the style and weight of a border or adding a fill pattern. You can also format some of the controls to give them a 3-D appearance. The properties of a control can also be changed so that the control graphic does not appear when the form is printed.

Because an Excel form is designed to perform calculations, formulas are included so that the data entry people don't have to create them as they enter data. You can format formula cells where appropriate so that zero values are not displayed.

In this lesson, you format the rectangles and control objects in your worksheet to emphasize specific information, to make it easy to use the form online, and to have it resemble a paper form when printed.

To Enhance a Form

1. **Make sure that** `Order Form` **is the active worksheet in the** `Company Orders` **workbook.**

2. **Click the border that surrounds the rectangle in cells B10:C16; then press Shift while you click the border surrounding the rectangle in cells E10:F16.**

   Both objects are selected.

3 Choose Format, Autoshape; then click the Colors and Lines tab.

The Format Autoshape dialog box with the Colors and Lines tab is displayed, as shown in Figure 9.12.

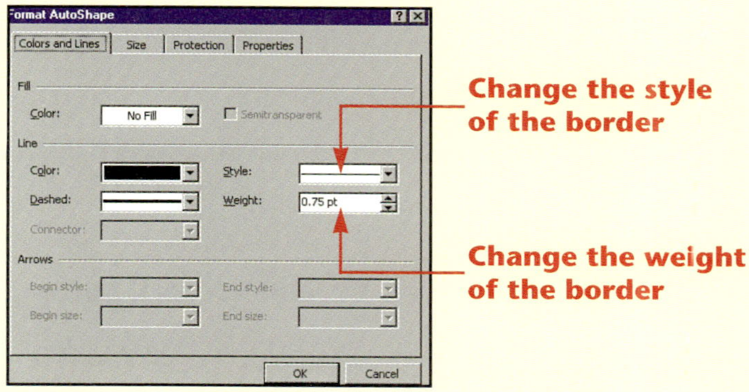

Figure 9.12
The Format Autoshape dialog box enables you to add visual effects to your form.

4 Click the drop-down arrow next to the Style option and click 1 1/2 pt. Click OK.

The rectangle objects are displayed with a new, thicker line.

5 Click outside the rectangle objects to deselect them.

6 Choose Tools, Options; then click the View tab.

The Options dialog box with the View tab is displayed, as shown in Figure 9.13.

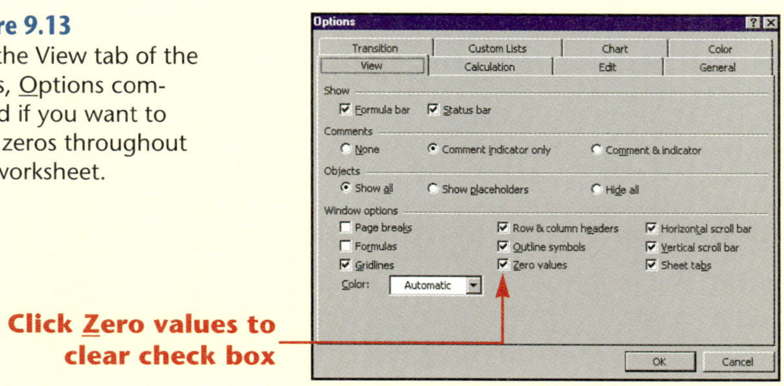

Figure 9.13
Use the View tab of the Tools, Options command if you want to hide zeros throughout the worksheet.

Cells G22:G38 on the worksheet contain formulas that multiply the quantity by the price of an item and display the total cost of the item. Cell G39 contains the SUM function to total the order. Because no data was entered in the form, zero balances are displayed in the formula cells.

continues

To Enhance a Form (continued)

7 Click Zero values to clear the check box and click OK.

The zero balances in cells G22:G39 are hidden so that the form shows an amount only when data is entered into the form. Now format the check box object.

8 Right-click cell E15.

The check box object is selected and a shortcut menu is displayed.

9 Select Format Control; then click the Control tab.

The Format Control dialog box with Control tab option is displayed.

10 Click the 3-D Shading check box and then OK.

Formatting the check box object with 3-D shading makes the box easier to see. Now format the spinner control.

11 Right-click cell F14.

Cell F14 is selected and the shortcut menu is displayed.

12 Select Format Control; then click the Properties tab.

The Format Control dialog box with Properties tab options is displayed.

13 Deselect the Print object check box and click OK.

This removes the check mark from the Print Object option. When the form is printed, the data in cell F14 prints but the spinner control graphic does not print.

14 Click the Toggle Grid button on the Forms toolbar.

This action removes the gridlines from the worksheet, which makes your form easier to read. You can click this button again to return to Grid view.

15 Click the Print Preview button on the Standard toolbar.

The completed form is displayed in the Preview window, as shown in Figure 9.14.

16 Click Close.

The Preview window is closed.

17 Close the Forms toolbar.

The form is complete, as shown in Figure 9.15.

18 Save the changes made to the workbook and keep it open for the next lesson.

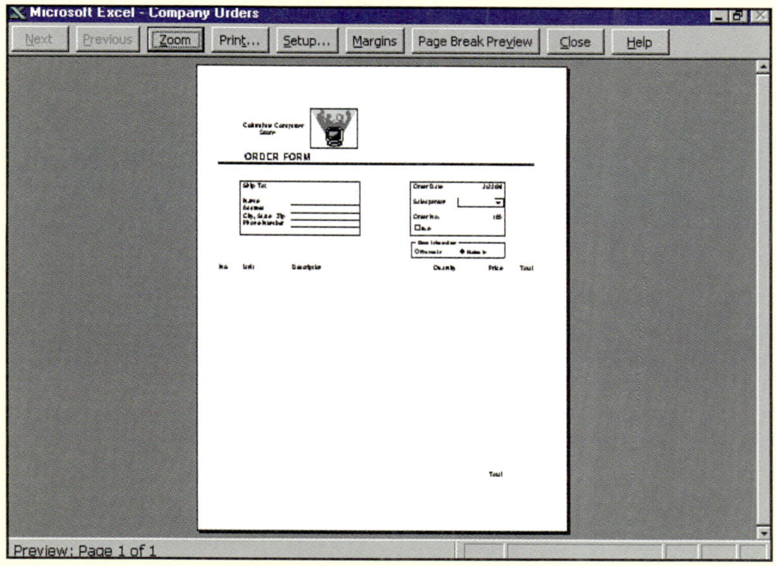

Figure 9.14
The form displayed in Print Preview does not display the spinner graphic.

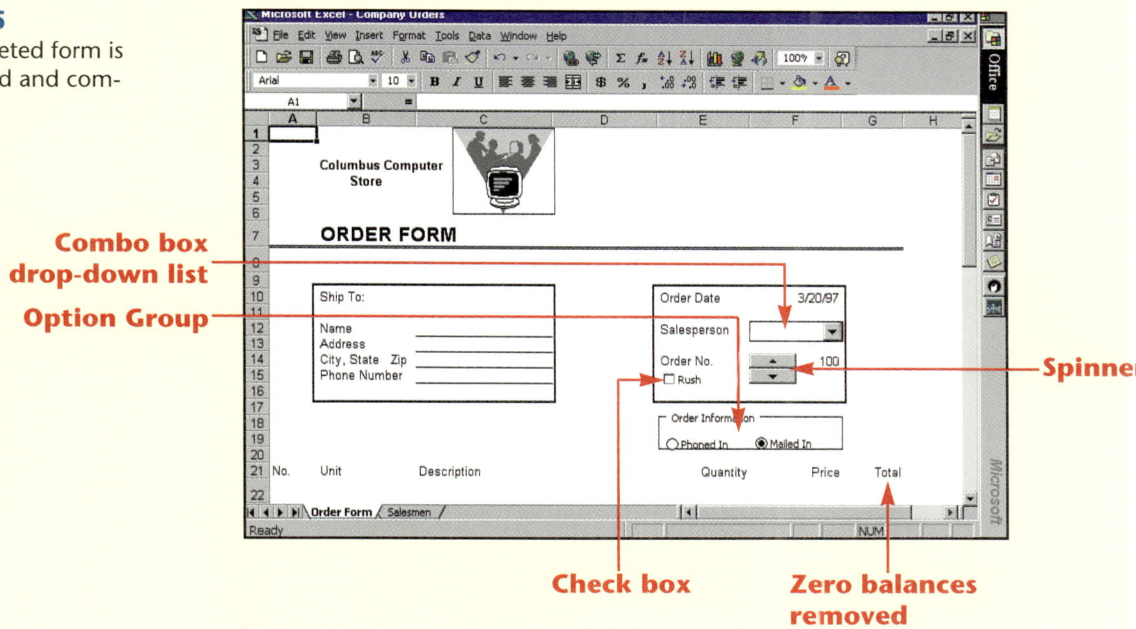

Figure 9.15
The completed form is easy to read and complete.

Inside Stuff

After you create buttons and controls, you can select them and move them for better positioning on the screen. Remember to hold down the Ctrl key as you click to select the control. Then drag the border to position the control.

Small adjustments in position can be made with the arrow keys. Select the control and then press the arrow key in the direction you want the control to move. The control will move only very small distances but it will move in a straight line in that direction, which is very hard to achieve with a mouse.

If you are trying to get two controls lined up across from each other or one on top of the other, you need to select both controls (hold down ⇧Shift+Ctrl as you click each control). Then click the Draw button on the Drawing toolbar and select Align or Distribute. Select the type of alignment you want from the submenu.

Lesson 6: Protecting a Form

In previous lessons, you created a form that can be opened and saved as a workbook file. However, you may worry that you or another user will change the formatting or formulas in the worksheet when it is being used. Excel provides a worksheet protection feature. If worksheet protection is turned on, cells are locked and cannot be edited; before turning worksheet protection on, you must unlock the cells that you allow to be changed.

In this lesson, you unlock the portions of the form to be used for data entry; then the worksheet protection is turned on to prevent any accidental or deliberate changes to formatting or formulas in the form.

To Protect a Form

1. **Make sure that** `Order Form` **is the active worksheet in the** `Company Orders` **workbook.**

2. **Select the range C10:C15.**

3. **Hold Ctrl down while you drag the mouse across the range F11:F15.**

4. **Continue holding Ctrl down and drag the mouse across the range A21:F38.**

   The selected ranges are highlighted on the worksheet.

Inside Stuff

The Ctrl key is used to select groups of noncontiguous cells in the worksheet. You can select the first range by dragging the mouse across the cells. Then to select subsequent ranges, hold down the Ctrl key while dragging across the cells.

The Shift key is used to select contiguous cells in the worksheet. Using the mouse, select the first cell in the upper-left corner of the range. Then, hold down the Shift key and click the mouse in the lower-right corner of the range. All cells in between the range address will be selected. This method works well when you are selecting a large range of cells that doesn't appear onscreen at one time.

5. **With the three ranges selected, choose Format, Cells; then click the Protection tab.**

   The Format Cells dialog box is displayed.

6. **Deselect the Locked check box and click OK.**

   When you remove the check mark from the Locked option, you unlock the cells that users are allowed to change. Now turn on the worksheet protection.

7 Choose Tools, Protection, Protect Sheet.

The Protect Sheet dialog box is displayed (see Figure 9.16).

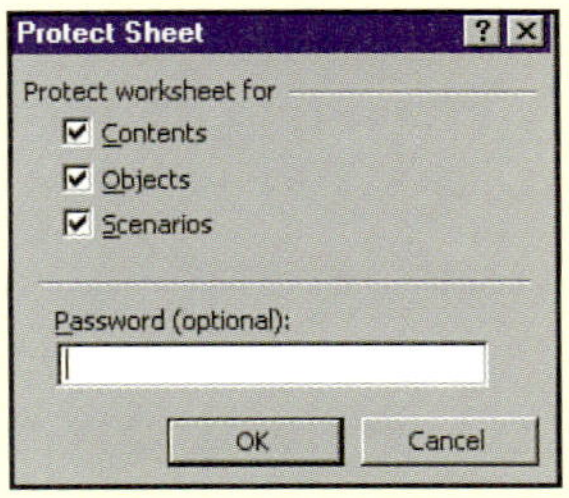

Figure 9.16
The Protect Sheet dialog box lets you enable or disable protection for a worksheet

8 Click OK to accept the default selections.

Worksheet protection is turned on for the worksheet (contents, objects, and scenarios included), and only the cells that were previously unlocked can be changed by the user. No password was assigned. Now test the protection feature.

9 Click cell G21 and press Del.

Because this portion of the form is protected, an alert box is displayed, as shown in Figure 9.17. The alert box warns you that the cell cannot be changed.

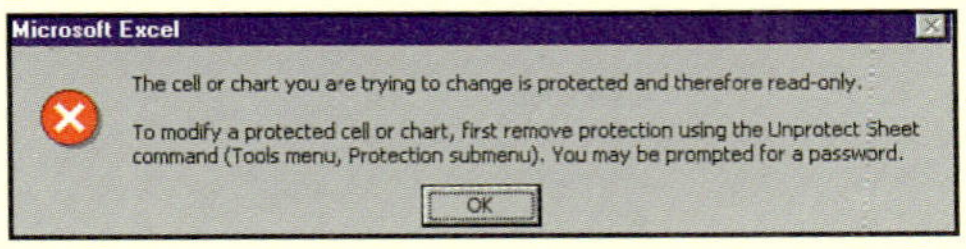

Figure 9.17
The alert box warns you when attempts are made to change a protected cell.

10 Click OK.

The alert box is removed from the screen.

11 Save the changes to the workbook and keep it open for the next lesson, where you save a form as a template.

Inside Stuff

When you turn on protection through the Tools, Protection, Protect Sheet command, an optional Password text box is shown in the Protect Sheet dialog box. You can use up to 255 characters in a password, and it can contain a combination of numbers, letters, and symbols. Be careful with passwords. They are case-sensitive, and if you forget them, you cannot access the workbook or feature to which the password was assigned. If you really must use this feature, keep a list of passwords and workbooks or workbook features, to which these passwords are assigned in a safe place.

Lesson 7: Saving a Form as a Template

Template
A workbook or worksheet that is created as a guide or pattern for completing other similar documents.

When you create a workbook that contains specific text, formulas, formatting, worksheet controls, and so on, Excel enables you to save the file as a *template*. A template file is like a workbook, but it is assigned an .XLT extension. When the template file is opened, a copy of the template is displayed. Templates are especially useful for creating forms used for data entry, such as invoices, expense accounts, and budgets.

Now that your form is created, you want users to be able to access it and create order forms when necessary. In this lesson, you save the form with its structure and formatting as a template so that users have easy access to it.

To Save a Form as a Template

1. **With the `Company Orders` workbook open, choose File, Save As.**

   The Save As dialog box is displayed.

2. **Type `Order Form` in the File Name text box.**

3. **Click the arrow next to the Save as type text box.**

   The available file types are displayed in the list, as shown in Figure 9.18.

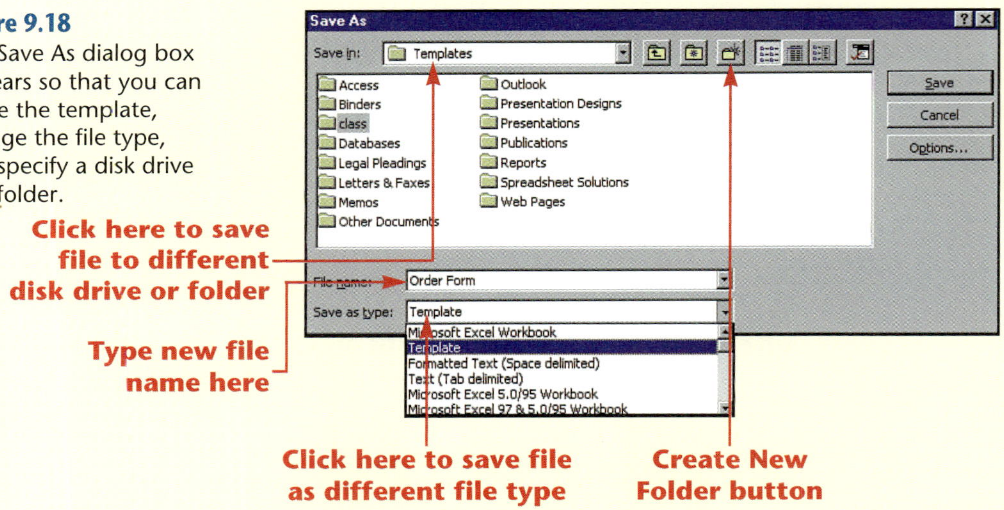

Figure 9.18
The Save As dialog box appears so that you can name the template, change the file type, and specify a disk drive and folder.

4. **In the Save as type drop-down list, click Template.**

   When Template is selected, Excel automatically displays the Templates folder, which is located on the hard drive as a subfolder to the MS Office or Excel software. This folder is automatically created on the hard drive of the computer when Excel software is installed. To be able to later access a template with the File, New command, it must be saved to the Templates folder.

   A listing of available template files is shown.

5 Click the Create New Folder button on the toolbar and type `class` **in the Name box. Choose OK.**

This creates a new folder for you to store your templates for the class.

If you have problems...

Due to possible computer network and classroom considerations, you may not be able to save your template to a new folder or even to the hard disk. Consult with the instructor to determine where this file should be saved. If necessary, insert a disk in the floppy disk drive, choose the A: drive from the Save in drop-down list, and then click Save.

6 Double-click the new class folder to open it.

7 Click the Save button.

8 Close the template.

Inside Stuff

Before creating your own templates, use the File, New command to take a look at the template files already provided by Excel. When you choose the File, New command, a dialog box opens, showing the available templates. Within the window are subfolders that are used to logically group the templates by category. Most new worksheets that you create are based on the default worksheet template, which appears in the General subfolder. In the Spreadsheet Solutions folder are several built-in templates, such as invoices, that you might want to take advantage of. There are additional templates available on the Office 97 CD, in the Excel subfolder of the Template folder, if you have none listed in the Spreadsheet Solutions folder.

Lesson 8: Using a Form Template

You can access a template through the File, New command, which opens a copy of the template into a new workbook. Changes can be made to this document, such as filling in a data entry form. Then the document is saved as a Microsoft Excel Workbook file and the template file remains intact.

Now that the order form is complete and saved as a template, you want to use it to complete a company order. In this lesson, you use the Order Form template you saved in the previous lesson as the basis for a new workbook. Then you complete the data entry, save the workbook, and print the order.

To Use a Form Template

1 Choose File, New.

The New dialog box is displayed, as shown in Figure 9.19.

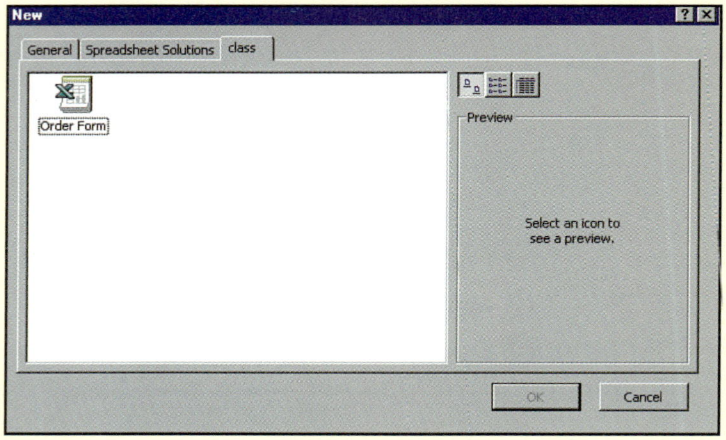

Figure 9.19
The New dialog box displays the order form template file.

2 Select the class tab.

If you have problems...

If you were not able to use the File, New command to access the template you saved in the previous lesson, choose File, Open. Make sure that 3-1/2 Floppy (A:) is selected from the Look in text box. Select Templates from the Files of type drop-down list. Double-click the Order Form file. When you finish making your changes to the form, choose File, Save As. Choose Microsoft Excel Workbook from the Save as type drop-down list and type New Orders in the File name box. Click Save.

3 Select the Order Form icon.

4 Choose OK.

A new workbook is displayed that looks like the Order Form template. Now you can type the order information to complete the form.

5 Complete cells C12:C15 with the following data:

```
Cabtel Corporation
5151 Reed Road
Columbus, OH  43220
614-555-1022
```

6 Click the arrow in cell F12 and click `Wolford`**.**

7 Click the Rush check box in cell E15 to place a check mark in the box.

8 Change the Order No. to 103.

9 Click the Phoned In option button.

10 Complete the data entry for Row 22 with the following information (skip cell D22 when entering the data):

Cell	Entry
A22	101
B22	50-pack
C22	3.5 inch formatted disks
E22	5
F22	10.99

The data entry is complete and the formula automatically calculates the Total Cost of the first item in cell G22 (54.95) (see Figure 9.20). The total is then calculated in cell G39.

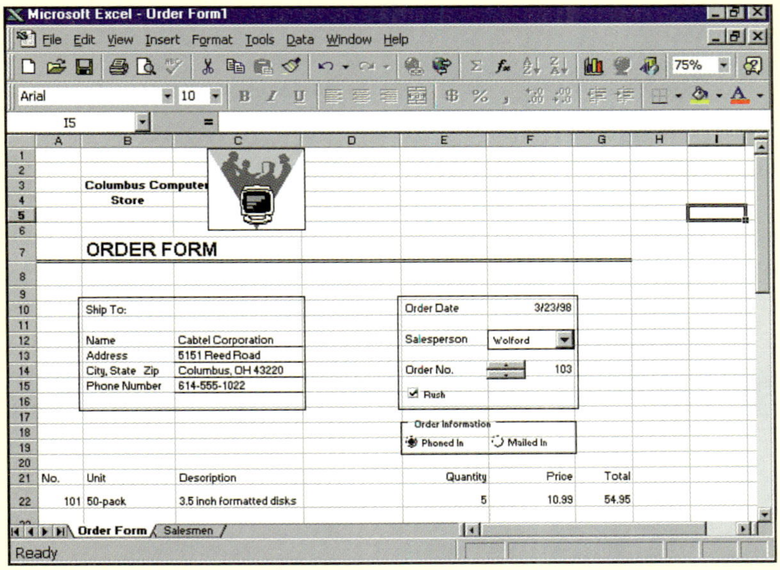

Figure 9.20
You can use a template file to fill out a form.

11 Click File, Save As.

The Save As dialog box is displayed. Because you used a template, the Save as type is Microsoft Excel Workbook. Order Form1 appears in the File name box and is highlighted. You need to change the file name.

12 Type New Orders in the File name box.

continues

To Use a Form Template (continued)

Inside Stuff

When a template file is accessed from the Templates folder on the hard drive through the File, New command, a copy of the template is placed into memory, rather than the original file. A temporary file name appears in the title bar. If the template file being accessed is named Order Form, for example, Excel assigns a temporary file name to the document, starting with Order Form1, Order Form2, and so on. When you save the new document, the Save As dialog box displays the temporary file name in the File name text box. Additionally, the file type is specified as a Microsoft Excel Workbook so that Excel can properly save the new file as a workbook.

13. **If you want to save the file to a location other than the one specified in the Save in box, click the arrow next to the box and select the appropriate location.**

14. **Click Save. The file is saved with the file name New Orders, and the Template file remains intact.**

    Print two copies of the New Orders file, if requested by the instructor. Close the file.

Lesson 9: Editing Templates

After you create a template, you may want to make adjustments as you change procedures or as different users make suggestions. Modifying a template is very similar to editing a workbook.

In this lesson, you make some formatting changes to the Order Form template.

To Edit a Template

1. **Choose File, Open.**

   The Open dialog box is displayed, as in Figure 9.21.

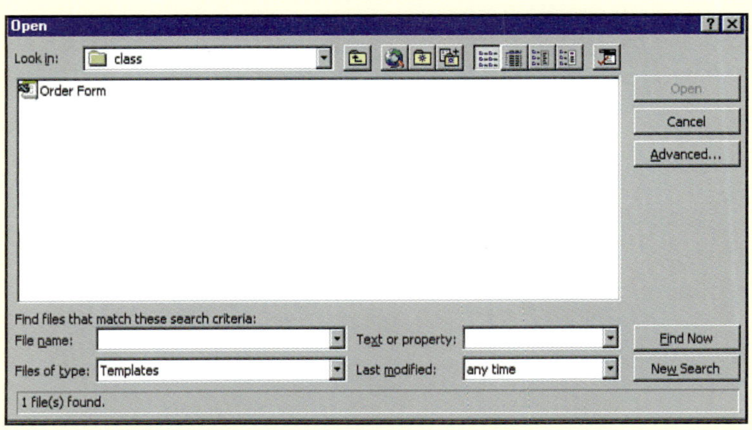

Figure 9.21
Select Templates from the Files of type drop-down list.

2. **Select Templates from the Files of type drop-down list.**

   If the Templates folder isn't automatically displayed, you can find it on your hard disk in the Microsoft Office subfolder of the Program Files folder. Ask you instructor for the location if you are using Excel on a network.

3. **Double-click the class folder to open it.**

   The Order Form template is listed. (If you saved your Order Form template in another location, select that location from the Look in drop-down list.)

4. **Select `Order Form` and click Open.**

   You are going to format the headings for the order detail area.

5. **Select the range A21:G21.**

   This range is currently protected, so most of the buttons on the Formatting toolbar are grayed out.

6. **Choose Tools, Protection, Unprotect Sheet.**

   The formatting tools are now available to you.

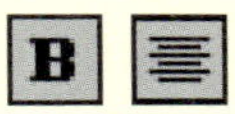

7. **Click the Bold button and then the Center button on the Formatting toolbar.**

8. **Click the down arrow next to the Font Color button on the Formatting toolbar. Select Blue (the sixth button in the second row).**

   The column labels are more distinctive because of the formatting change. Now you need to reapply the worksheet protection.

9. **Choose Tools, Protection, Protect Sheet. Choose OK to accept the defaults.**

10. **Save and close the template file.**

    The changes you made apply to future workbooks you create using the template.

Project Summary

To	Do This
Add a control to a form	Click the control on the Forms toolbar. Point the mouse to the worksheet where you want to begin drawing. Drag the mouse down and across to draw the box.
Link cells to boxes on a form	With the box selected, click the Control Properties button on the Forms toolbar. Choose the Control tab in the Format Control dialog box. Complete the Input range and Cell link.
Format an object	Select the object. Choose Format, Control.
Format a control	Select the control with the right mouse button. Choose Format Control from the shortcut menu.
Unlock ranges of a form	Select the range(s) that you will allow to be changed in the form. Choose Format, Cells; click the Protection tab and remove the check mark from the Locked option.
Turn on worksheet protection	Choose Tools, Protection, Protect Sheet.
Hide zero values in formula cells	Choose Tools, Options; click the View tab and select Zero values.
Save worksheet as a template	Choose File, Save As. In the Save As dialog box type the filename in File name text box. Click the Save as type text box and choose Template. Click the Save button.
Use a template	Choose File, New. From the General tab, double-click the Template icon.

Checking Your Skills

True/False

For each of the following, check *T* or *F* to indicate whether the statement is true or false.

__T __F **1.** An object created through the Excel drawing tools cannot be formatted.

__T __F **2.** A form that collects information with calculations is best created in Excel.

__T __F **3.** A combo box object can be linked to worksheet cells.

__T __F **4.** The first step in protecting a worksheet is to turn protection on with Tools, Protection, Protect Sheet.

__T __F **5.** A template is like a workbook but it is assigned an .XTL extension.

__T __F **6.** An option button is a square button that lets you mark a choice.

__T __F **7.** You can't add an option button until you draw the group box first.

__T __F **8.** You use a spinner box when you want to increase or decrease numbers in a cell.

__T __F **9.** To use a template as the basis for a workbook, you choose File, Open.

__T __F **10.** You can't format controls.

Multiple Choice

Circle the letter of the correct answer for each of the following.

1. An object can be formatted with which of the following?
   a. Colors and patterns
   b. A shadow
   c. Line styles and weights
   d. All of the above

2. When you want to unlock an area of the worksheet so it can be changed, first select the cells and then choose which of the following?
   a. Tools, Protection, Unprotect Sheet
   b. Format, Cells, Protection tab
   c. Format, Sheet, Hide
   d. Tools, Options

3. Which tab from the Format Control dialog box contains the option to turn off printing of the control object graphic?
   a. Patterns
   b. Protection
   c. Properties
   d. Control

4. Which of the following objects can be created by using the Forms toolbar?
   a. Check box
   b. Combo box
   c. Rectangle
   d. Both (a) and (b)

5. Which button from the Forms toolbar is used to link a check box and various types of list boxes with worksheet cells?
   a. Label
   b. Edit Box
   c. Create Button
   d. Control Properties

6. Which command do you use when you want to hide the zero values in formula cells?
   a. Window, Hide
   b. Tools, Options
   c. View, Zero Values
   d. Format, Cells

7. Type of control that you select for a true answer or deselect for a false answer.
   a. Option button
   b. Combo box
   c. Button
   d. Check box
8. To select a check box without checking it, what key do you hold down as you click?
   a. Tab
   b. Alt
   c. Ctrl
   d. Shift
9. What button in the Format Control dialog box reduces the dialog box to a text box?
   a. Shrink
   b. Collapse
   c. Reduce
   d. None of the above
10. What is the source of the list of choices in the combo box?
   a. You enter them in a dialog box.
   b. It's the names of the worksheets in the workbook.
   c. A standardized list that always appears in combo boxes.
   d. It's the data contained in a linked range.

Completion

In the blank provided, write the correct answer for each of the following statements.

1. Tools used to draw boxes, such as a check box or combo box, are accessed from the_______________ toolbar.
2. The control that presents a multiple choice of items in a group from which only one item can be chosen is known as a(n) _______________ _______________.
3. The small black boxes surrounding an object border are referred to as _______________.
4. Use the _______________ menu, _______________ option, _______________ tab to hide the zero values in formula cells.
5. Save a form as a(n) _______________ to store the structure and formatting of a worksheet for reuse.
6. Click the _______________ button on the Forms toolbar when you want to link cells to boxes on a form.
7. When you want to prevent a user from changing the formulas or formatting in a worksheet, you _______________ the worksheet.
8. The _______________ control has a two-headed arrow that incrementally increases or decreases the amount in the linked cell.

Excel

9. When you want more than one set of option boxes where only one option can be selected from the set, you need to start by drawing a _____________ _____________.

10. To use a template to create a workbook, choose the _____________, _____________ command.

Matching

In the blank next to each of the following terms or phrases, write the letter of the corresponding term or phrase. (Note that some letters may be used more than once.)

a. Forms
b. Spinner
c. Template
d. Check box
e. Print Object
f. online form
g. combo box
h. Option button
i. XLT
j. Control

_____ 1. A worksheet designed to contained frequently used, fill-in-the-blank information

_____ 2. A workbook or worksheet created and used as a guide or pattern for completing other similar workbooks

_____ 3. A special drawing object, used as a data entry device

_____ 4. A round button that selects an option

_____ 5. A list that contains text items drawn from a linked data range

_____ 6. To add check boxes and option buttons to your worksheet, you need to turn on the _____________ toolbar

_____ 7. Use this control to increase or decrease numbers in a cell

_____ 8. A worksheet control that you select for a true answer or deselect for a false answer

_____ 9. Deselect this on the Properties tab of the Format Control dialog box to keep the control from printing

_____ 10. The file extension for a template file

Applying Your Skills

Practice

The following exercises enable you to practice the skills you learned in this project. Take a few minutes to work through these exercises now.

Adding a Check Box to a Worksheet

The MIS Department of your company has a paper form that must be completed each time a department requests computer assistance. A simple Work Order worksheet was created to eliminate the paper form, but you want to make the data entry easier for employees who fill out the online form.

To begin, you want to add controls to the form. Now create two check boxes.

To add a check box to a worksheet, follow these steps:

1. Open the Proj0902 file from the Project-09 folder on the CD, and save it with the filename `Work Order`.
2. Display the `Form` worksheet.
3. Use the Forms toolbar to create a check box in B14. Label it `Hardware`.
4. Use the Forms toolbar to create a check box in C14. Label it `Software`.
5. Save your work. Keep the workbook open for the next exercise.

Adding a Combo Box to a Worksheet

A combo box is useful for data entry within a form because it presents a text list from which to choose an item and makes it easier to enter data into a cell.

Create a combo box that contains a drop-down list of departments that use this form.

To add a combo box to a worksheet, follow these steps:

1. Make sure that the `Form` worksheet of the `Work Order` workbook is displayed.
2. Use the Forms toolbar to create a combo box in the bottom half of cell B8. The box should be the full width but half the height of cell B8.
3. Now format the combo box. The input range for the control is cells A1:A6 in the Data worksheet of this workbook.
4. Save your work. Keep the workbook open for the next exercise.

Adding an Option Button to a Worksheet

The option button control can be added to your worksheet to provide several item choices, but only one selection can be made. You add an option button to your Form to choose the Hardware Type.

To add an option button to a worksheet, follow these steps:

1. Make sure the `Form` worksheet of the `Work Order` workbook is displayed.
2. Use the Forms toolbar to create a group box in cells B16 through C16. Label the group box `Hardware Types`.
3. Create three option buttons in the group box and label them

   `PC`

   `Modem`

   `Printer`
4. Save your work. Keep the workbook open for the next exercise.

Enhancing a Form and Saving It as a Template

To give the form the appearance of a paper form, you decide to format the objects on this Work Order form by changing the weight of the border; then format the controls to make the check boxes look three-dimensional.

To enhance a form and save it as a template, follow these steps:

1. Make sure that the `Form` worksheet of the `Work Order` workbook is displayed.
2. Select the two rectangle objects shown in cells C4:D4 and C11:D11.
3. Format the border of the two rectangle objects; choose the sixth style from the Style drop-down list.
4. Format the two check box objects with 3-D shading. (Remember that you need to use the right mouse button to select the object and display the shortcut menu.)
5. Remove the gridlines from view.
6. Preview the form.
7. Save the workbook as a template called `Work Orders`. Close the file.

Testing the Work Orders Template

Before notifying your department that the form is ready to use, test it by filling in requested information.

To test the work orders form template, follow these steps:

1. Start a new Excel workbook using the `Work Orders` template.
2. Click cell B6 of the Form worksheet of the form and type your name.
3. Click cell B8 and choose Finance from the drop-down list.
4. Type `Immediate` in cell E8.
5. Click the Software check box in cell C14 to add a check mark to it.
6. Click cell B18 and type a project description.
7. Your test is complete. Preview the form.
8. Save your work as a new file named `Work1`. Print two copies of the worksheet, if requested by your instructor. Close the workbook.

Editing the Work Orders Template

After looking at the work orders produced using the Work Orders template, your supervisor realized that you also need to have a check box for Training added to the Project Type.

To edit the work orders template, follow these steps:

1. Open the `Work Orders` template file.
2. Create a check box in D14 and label it `Training`.
3. Save the template and close it.
4. Test the template by creating a new work order requested by `Joe Downs` from the Human Resources department for Training.
5. Save the new workbook as `Work2` and close the file.

Challenge

The following challenges enable you to use your problem-solving skills. Take time to work through these exercises now.

Adding Check Boxes to a Worksheet

Open Proj0903 from the Project-09 folder on the CD and save it as `Student Housing`. This form is used by a local college to keep information on the students applying for rooms in the dormitories. Make sure the `Online Form` worksheet is active. Then in B10 draw a check box labeled `Yes`. In B12 draw another check box labeled `Yes`.

Adding Option Boxes to a Worksheet

In B8 draw a group box labeled `Sex`. Add two option buttons to the group box—one labeled `F` and the other labeled `M`.

Adding a Combo Box to a Worksheet

Across cells D8 through F8, draw a combo box. Link the combo box to the range A1:A13 on the `Majors` worksheet.

Adding a Spinner to a Worksheet

In cell F13 create a spinner whose current value is 100, minimum value is 100, and maximum value is 150. Link the spinner to cell F12.

Saving the File as a Template

Select the ranges B3:B12 and D3:F12. Unlock the protection for those ranges. Then apply protection to the whole worksheet. Save the worksheet as a template. Close the file. Then open a new file based on your new template and enter the following student information:

Name: `Jennifer Baker`
Address: `121 Landon Lane`
City, State, Zip: `Bristown, PA 19133`
Home Phone Number: `(610) 555-3214`
Sex: `Female`
Bed Linens: `Yes`
Housecleaning: `Yes`
Class: `Freshman`
Major: `Art`
Room Assignment: `121`

Save the worksheet as Student1.xls and close it.

Editing the Template

Open the template file. Remove the worksheet protection. Click cell A14 and type `Meal Ticket` followed by a colon. In B14 add a check box labeled `Yes`. Unlock the protection for B14 and then apply the worksheet protection again. Save the template and close it. Start a new file based on the template to see how the change affects the new worksheet. Close the new workbook without saving it.

PinPoint Assessment

PinPoint Training

You have completed the project and the associated lessons, as well as the "Checking Your Skills" and "Applying Your Skills" sections. Now use the PinPoint software evaluation mode to assess your comprehension of the specific exam tasks you have just learned. You can also use the PinPoint Trainer Mode and the Show Me tutorials to practice these specific exam tasks.

Project 10
Ten

Creating Summary Reports

Summarizing Employee Production

In this Project, you learn how to:

Objectives	Required Activities
➤ Create an Outline from an Existing Report	
➤ Chart an Outline	
➤ Create Subtotal Reports	
➤ Create Multiple Subtotal Rows	
➤ Consolidate Your Worksheets	

Why Would I Do This?

Because you have been working with Excel for a while, you probably have noticed that you keep many lists of data. Such lists often contain details that you need when you want to create reports for management. Many managers, however, don't want details; they want summaries. You might think that it would take hours to summarize the information in your detailed lists, but with just a few clicks of the mouse you can produce management summary reports in Excel.

In this project, you learn how to create an outline from a detailed worksheet, chart the outline, and use automatic subtotals to reduce your manual work. At the end of the project, you consolidate multiple worksheets into a single worksheet.

Lesson 1: Creating an Outline from an Existing Report

Outline
In Excel, a way of summarizing worksheet data by grouping rows and columns of data.

As the second-shift manager in the following example, you are interested in each employee's individual production totals. Your manager, however, is interested only in how the whole shift is performing and does not want to see individual production figures. In the past, you hid columns and rows when producing reports, but this has become a tedious task. Because your worksheet is set up in a uniform way (with subtotals below and to the right of the detailed data), you can create an *outline* that makes creating these reports less tedious and time-consuming.

To Create an Outline from an Existing Report

1. **Open the file Proj1001 from the Project-10 folder on the CD and save it as `Shift Detail`.**

2. **Make sure that the sheet tab labeled `First Quarter 97` is active.**

   The First Quarter 97 worksheet contains sales data for all three shifts, subtotaled both by shift and by month for the first quarter of 1997, as shown in Figure 10.1.

3. **Select cell A5.**

Contiguous
A contiguous block of cells has no blank rows or columns from beginning to end.

   Before you create an outline, you should select any one cell in the data area, as long as your data is *contiguous* (no blank rows or columns from beginning to end).

4. **Choose Data, Group and Outline, Auto Outline.**

   Your worksheet is now outlined, displaying all the detail, as shown in Figure 10.2.

Figure 10.1
The highlighted row and column show a summary by shift and a summary by month, respectively.

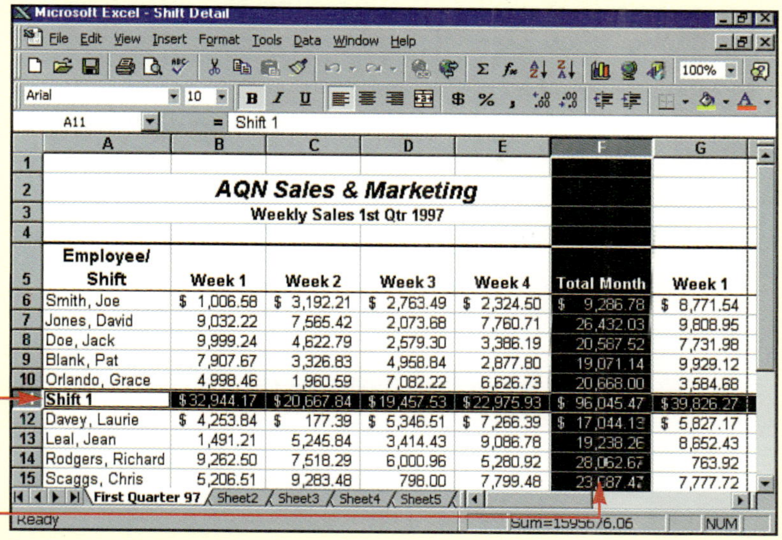

Figure 10.2
Use the Row and Column Level buttons to view different levels of detail in the outline.

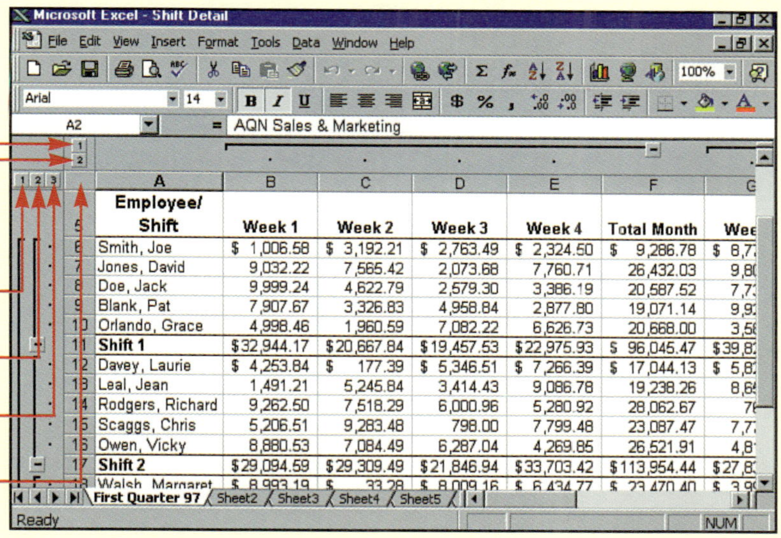

Row Level buttons
Row Level buttons are numbered sequentially, depending on the number of levels in the outline, and appear horizontally to the left of the Select All button.

Column Level buttons
Column Level buttons are numbered sequentially, depending on the number of levels in the outline, and appear vertically above the Select All button.

In the upper-left corner of the worksheet area (above and to the left of the worksheet frame) are buttons that show how many levels of detail are in the worksheet. The *Row Level buttons* appear horizontally, to indicate three levels of detail in the worksheet's rows:

1—Totals for all shifts

2—Subtotals for each shift

3—All row detail

The *Column Level buttons* appear vertically and indicate two levels of detail in the worksheet's columns:

1—Monthly totals

2—All column detail

continues

Excel

To Create an Outline from an Existing Report (continued)

The highest number for both the Row and Column Level buttons shows all the detail. The Level 1 button for both Rows and Columns shows the most summarized data. As shown in Figure 10.2, the Level 1 button for rows shows only the totals for all shifts, and the Level 1 button for columns shows only the monthly totals.

5 Click Row Level button 2.

Shift subtotals and all shift totals are now visible; all other rows are hidden.

6 Click Column Level button 1.

Only totals for the month columns are displayed; all other columns are hidden, as shown in Figure 10.3.

Figure 10.3
The worksheet now displays only totals—by month and by shift.

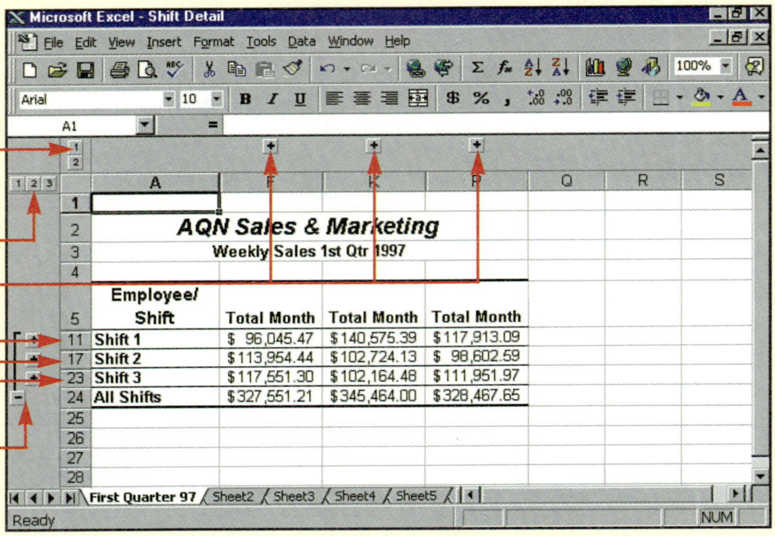

Notice that at this level of detail, it is difficult to determine which months are represented in the Total Month columns. You edit these column headings to make them more specific.

7 Edit the entries in cells F5, K5, and P5 to read `Total January`, `Total February`, and `Total March`, respectively. Adjust the column widths, if necessary.

If you have problems...

If you adjust the column widths and the weekly details appear, click Column Level button 1 to display only the totals columns.

Occasionally, you might need to see some detail—but not all. Suppose your sales manager notices that the first shift's January figures are off and wants to see the detail for that month, but wants only the summary information for the other two shifts for February and March. You can use the Collapse and Expand buttons to show selected details.

The button to the left of Shift 1 is now an Expand button containing a plus sign (+).

8 Click the Expand button for Shift 1.

The data for Shift 1 expands to show all the detail. You now see the names of all Shift 1 workers and their total sales by month.

9 The button above Total January is now an Expand button (it has a plus sign in it). Click the Expand button for Total January.

If you have problems...

If cell A5 is still selected in your worksheet and you cannot see the Expand buttons above the column letters (because the edit box is hiding them), click a cell in the middle of the worksheet.

Total January expands to show all the detail for all first-shift workers for each week in January. Notice that you still see only the monthly totals for February and March, as shown in Figure 10.4.

10 Save the workbook and keep it open for the next lesson.

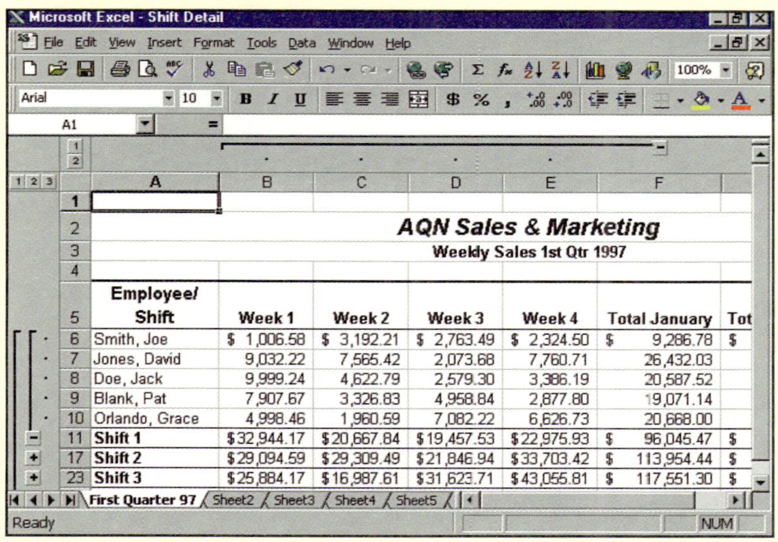

Figure 10.4
You now see the detail for all Shift 1 employees for all weeks of January.

Lesson 2: Charting an Outline

Now that you have created this report for your manager, he wants more. The report was very informative, but next week he has a presentation to give to the vice president and wants to have some visuals to show. He asks you to chart the monthly totals by shift.

Excel

To Chart an Outline

1 On the `First Quarter 97` **sheet of the** `Shift Detail` **workbook, click Row Level button 2 and Column Level button 1.**

Now only the monthly totals, individual shift totals, and totals for all shifts should be visible.

You need to create a chart based on only the summary information that currently appears in the worksheet—not the entire chart detail.

2 Select cells A5 through P24.

3 Choose Edit, Go To.

The Go To dialog box appears.

4 Click the Special button.

The Go To Special dialog box appears, as shown in Figure 10.5.

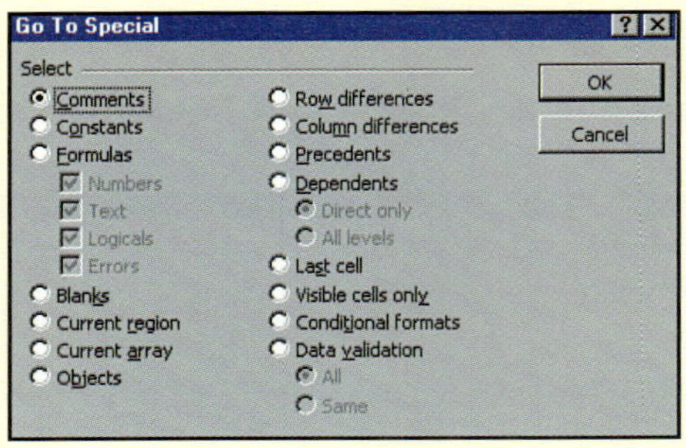

Figure 10.5
Use the Go To Special dialog box to enable the Visible cells only option.

5 Select the Visible cells only option; then choose OK.

Lines appear within the selected range, as shown in Figure 10.6, to indicate where hidden cell information is located (due to the outline setting). The separation is shown as white lines in this figure, instead of the normal gridlines, because the data is currently selected.

The Visible cells only option lets Excel know that the procedures you are to perform affect only the visible cells and not any of the hidden data.

6 Select cells A5 through P23.

This is the data range you want to chart. Be sure not to include the All Shifts totals in row 24 because you do not want to chart them.

7 Click the Chart Wizard button on the Standard toolbar.

The Chart Wizard – Step 1 of 4 – Chart Type dialog box appears. Now you can choose a chart type.

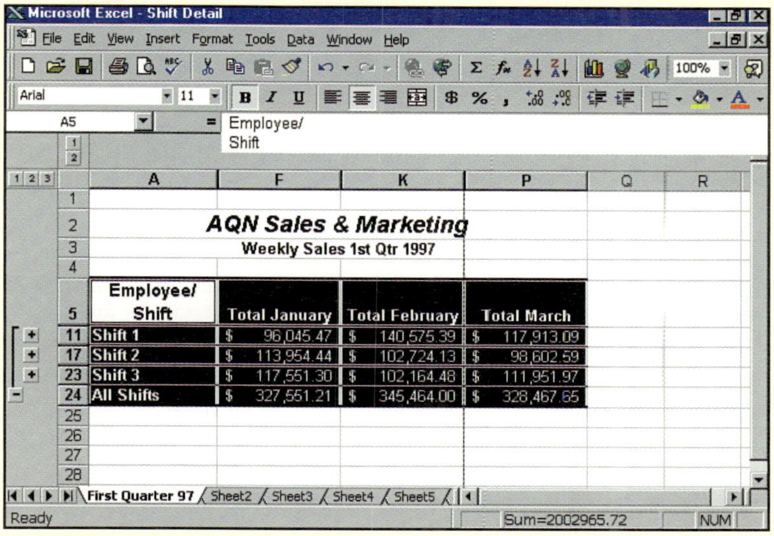

Figure 10.6
After you select the Visible cells only option, lines appear between the cells to show you where information is hidden.

8. **Select Column from the Chart type list and Clustered Column from the Chart sub-type list; then click Next.**

   The Chart Wizard – Step 2 of 4 – Chart Source Data dialog box appears. The data range is $A$5:$P$23 from the First Quarter 97 worksheet. Now you decide to change the data series to rows.

9. **Select Rows from the Series in area; then click Next.**

   The Chart Wizard – Step 3 of 4 – Chart Options dialog box displays a view of the chart and asks for a chart title and labels for the Category (x) and Value (y) axes.

10. **Click the Chart title text box and type** `Sales 1st Quarter 1997`**.**

11. **Click the Value (y) axis text box and type** `U.S. Dollars`**; then click Next.**

    The Chart Wizard – Step 4 of 4 – Chart Location dialog box appears. You want to place the chart as an object located below the data on the First Quarter 97 worksheet.

12. **Click Finish.**

    The chart appears on the worksheet with selection handles to resize and reposition the chart.

13. **Drag the chart so that the top left corner starts in cell A26; then resize the chart to fill the range A26:Q44.**

    Now improve the appearance of this chart.

continues

To Chart an Outline (continued)

14 Format the legend, Category (x) axis, and Value (y) axis to 11 point size.

Your chart is complete, as shown in Figure 10.7. (Note that the Zoom setting was temporarily changed from 100% to 75% so that you can see more of the worksheet in this figure.)

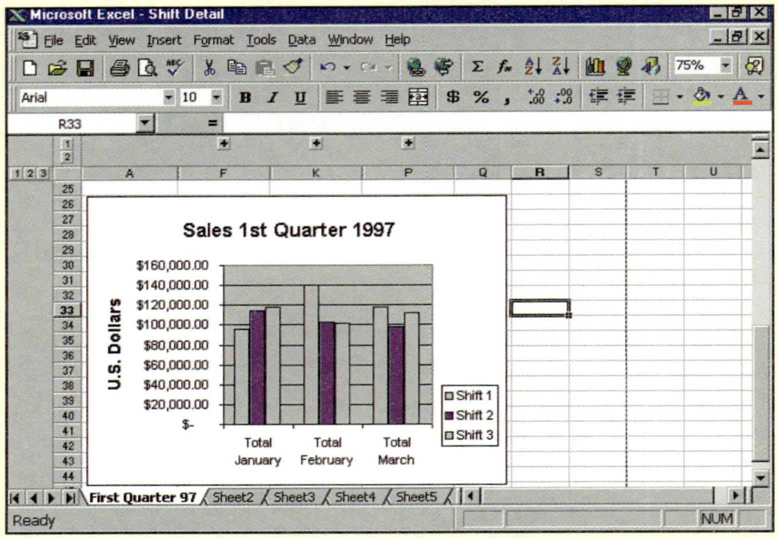

Figure 10.7
The chart you added now appears in the worksheet, below the summary table.

You have completed charting your outline. If requested by your instructor, print two copies of this worksheet, including the chart.

15 Save your changes and close the workbook.

Inside Stuff

You can chart your outline as a separate worksheet. As you are creating the chart, the Chart Wizard provides a Chart Location dialog box to prompt you for a chart location. Choose the As new sheet option in the Place Chart area; then choose OK. If your chart is already complete, right-click the chart and choose Location from the shortcut menu. The Chart Location dialog box appears; select the location and then click OK.

Lesson 3: Creating Subtotal Reports

In Lesson 1, the employee list was already sorted by shift. The list was totaled first by individual shifts and then by all shifts. This was tedious work for someone in your office. In this lesson, you take advantage of Excel's automatic subtotaling tool. The Proj1002 workbook contains a list of employees and their individual sales figures during given weeks. Your job is to analyze the daily progress of your salespeople, but your manager only wants to see the weekly progress. From your detailed list, he wants a report that shows the weekly subtotals for each employee.

To Create Subtotal Reports

1 Open the file Proj1002 from the Project-10 folder on the CD and save it as `Employee Detail`**.**

2 Click the Month 1 sheet tab.

The Month 1 worksheet contains a list of employees and their individual sales during each week in January.

3 Click any one cell in the data area, such as cell C10.

4 Choose Data, Sort.

Sort your employees alphabetically so that they are grouped together. Excel selects the entire data area for you, and the Sort dialog box appears, as shown in Figure 10.8.

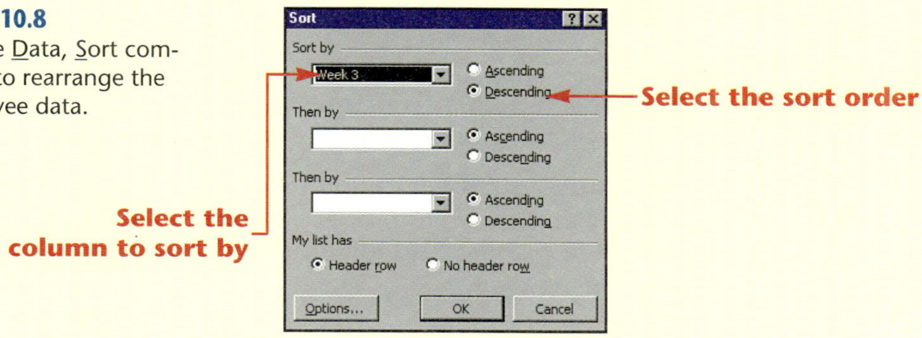

Figure 10.8 Use the Data, Sort command to rearrange the employee data.

5 From the Sort by drop-down list, choose Employee; then click the Ascending option beside the Sort by drop-down list.

This sorts your data alphabetically by employee in ascending order.

6 Choose OK.

Now that the data is sorted, you are ready to get the individual employees' subtotals.

7 Select any one cell in the data area, such as cell C10.

8 Choose Data, Subtotals.

Excel selects the entire data area for you. The Subtotal dialog box appears, as shown in Figure 10.9.

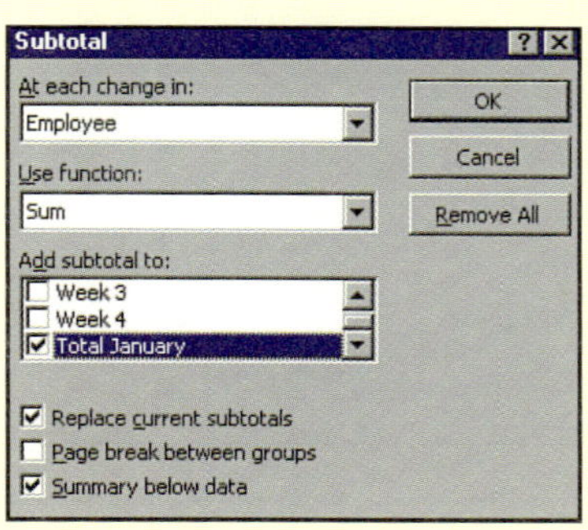

Figure 10.9 Use the Subtotal dialog box to add subtotals to your list automatically.

continues

To Create Subtotal Reports (continued)

9. **From the At each change in drop-down list, choose Employee (if it is not already selected).**

   This tells Excel that you want a subtotal each time there is a change in employee.

10. **From the Use function drop-down list, choose Sum (if it is not already selected).**

    This tells Excel that you want a sum to appear as the subtotal each time there is a change in employee (as opposed to an average, a total count, and so on).

11. **From the Add subtotal to scrolling list of check boxes, select Week 1, Week 2, Week 3, Week 4, and Total January.**

    These are the columns in your list in which you want subtotals to appear.

12. **Select the Replace current subtotals and Summary below data check boxes, if they are not already selected.**

    The Replace current subtotals option tells Excel to replace any existing subtotals with new subtotals. The Summary below data check box tells Excel to place the subtotal information below the detailed rows that are being totaled.

13. **Click OK.**

    Subtotals for the five columns have been added below each change in employee, as shown in Figure 10.10. Notice that Row Level buttons are automatically displayed for the new outline level.

14. **Save your changes to the workbook and keep it open for the next lesson.**

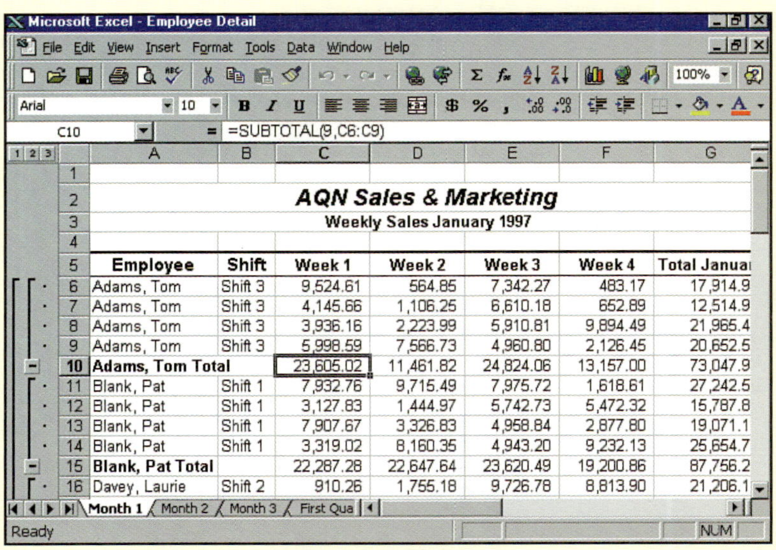

Figure 10.10
Subtotals now appear for each employee in the worksheet.

Lesson 4: Creating Multiple Subtotal Rows

Your worksheet now contains the subtotals for each employee in outline form. This report fits your needs, but your manager needs to get more information. Shift subtotals are essential to his analysis of how you are doing your job. Since you now know how simple it is to create subtotal reports, you volunteer to put this report together for him. You examine the report and notice that your list is in alphabetical order by employee with no regard to shift. You need to re-sort the data by shift, and then by employee. To do this, you need to remove the subtotals, re-sort the data, and then subtotal the report again.

To Create Multiple Subtotal Rows

1. **With the** `Month 1` **worksheet of the** `Employee Detail` **workbook still active, select any cell in the data area.**
2. **Choose Data, Subtotals.**

   Excel selects the entire data area for you, and the Subtotal dialog box appears.
3. **Click the Remove All button.**

   The Subtotal dialog box closes, and Excel removes the subtotals and outlines from the sheet.
4. **Again, select any cell in the data area.**
5. **Choose Data, Sort.**

   Excel selects the entire data area for you, and the Sort dialog box appears.
6. **In the Sort by drop-down list, choose Shift; then click the Ascending option beside the Sort by drop-down list.**
7. **In the first Then by drop-down list, choose Employee; then click the Ascending option beside the first Then by drop-down list.**
8. **Choose OK.**

   This sorts the employees by shift and then alphabetically by name.
9. **Select any cell in the data area.**

   Now it is time to create your new subtotals.
10. **Choose Data, Subtotals.**
11. **Choose Shift from the At each change in drop-down list, if it is not already selected.**

continues

To Create Multiple Subtotal Rows (continued)

12. **Choose Sum from the Use function drop-down list, if it is not already selected.**

13. **In the Add subtotal to scrolling list of check boxes, make sure that Week 1, Week 2, Week 3, Week 4, and Total January are checked.**

14. **Select the Replace current subtotals and Summary below data check boxes, if they are not already selected.**

15. **Choose OK.**

    This produces the report for your manager, showing the shift subtotals. Now you need your report to show subtotals by employee.

16. **Choose Data, Subtotals.**

17. **Choose Employee from the At each change in drop-down list.**

18. **Choose Sum from the Use function drop-down list.**

19. **In the Add subtotal to scrolling list of check boxes, make sure that Week 1, Week 2, Week 3, Week 4, and Total January are checked.**

20. **Remove the check mark from the Replace current subtotals check box; then choose OK.**

    You now have four levels of data on your outline. The worksheet is sorted by employee within each shift, with a subtotal for each employee and below each shift.

21. **Click Row Level button 2.**

    You now have your shift subtotals report for your manager, as shown in Figure 10.11.

22. **Save the changes to your workbook and keep it open for the next lesson.**

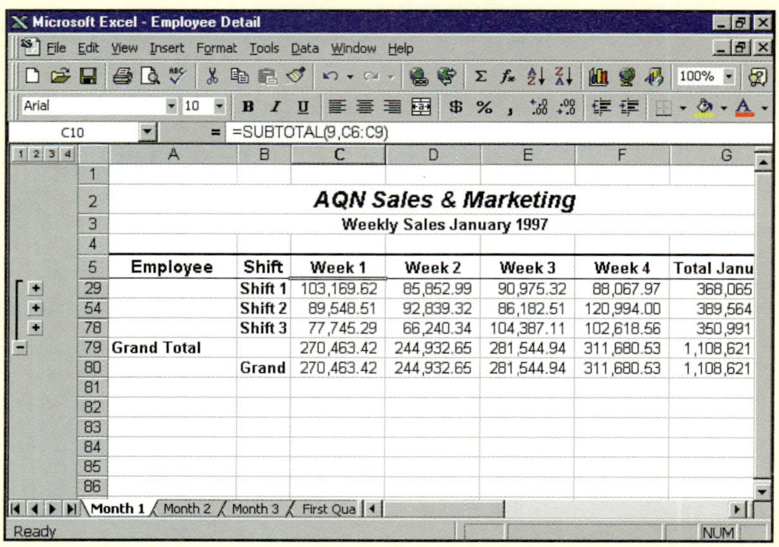

Figure 10.11
The report now shows the subtotals by week for each of the shifts, as well as a grand total for all shifts.

Inside Stuff

For some lists of data, you might want to perform more than one calculation. For example, you might want to sum the sales and get the maximum sale (using the Max function).

To display two or more summary functions for the same set of data, choose Data, Subtotals, and select the first function. Excel inserts the first set of subtotals. To insert the second function, choose Data, Subtotals and select the second function you want to use. Deselect the Replace current subtotals check box. Click OK. Excel creates a new line, inserting the second function under the first.

Lesson 5: Consolidating Your Worksheets

In Lesson 4, you worked with data from just one month. Suppose it is now April and you need to get a first quarter summary for each of your employees. This means that you need to use data from three separate months—which is stored in three separate worksheets.

In Lesson 3, you learned how to use automatic subtotals and outlining to create a report in which you could show or hide levels of detail, but all the data existed in the same worksheet. You can also create more complex summary reports by consolidating the data from multiple worksheets into one.

Consolidate
Combine values from multiple worksheets into another summary area (usually a separate worksheet).

When you *consolidate* data, you need to select a summary destination, a function (such as Sum), and the detail you want consolidated. The summary destination is usually a new worksheet or workbook. The function you use depends on what kind of report you are creating. To consolidate the three months of data in the AQN example, use the Sum function. In this lesson, you consolidate worksheets that are all contained in the same workbook, but it is also possible to consolidate worksheets from multiple workbooks.

Remember, it is necessary for your worksheets to have identical row and column headings. If not, you will end up with a detailed report instead of the summary you were aiming for.

To Consolidate Your Worksheets

1. **Make sure that the** `Month 1` **worksheet of the** `Employee Detail` **workbook is still active on your screen.**

2. **Select any cell in the data area.**

   You want to remove the subtotals added in the previous lesson.

3. **Choose Data, Subtotals; when the dialog box appears, click Remove All.**

   This removes the current subtotals from the worksheet.

continues

To Consolidate Your Worksheets (continued)

4 Click the First Quarter 97 sheet tab.

This activates the First Quarter 97 worksheet. This sheet is set up for you to consolidate your data. In the future, you must set up your own sheet.

5 Select cell A6.

This cell is your destination. That is, you want the consolidated data to appear on the First Quarter 97 worksheet, starting in cell A6.

6 Choose Data, Consolidate.

The Consolidate dialog box appears.

7 Choose Sum from the Function drop-down list, if it is not already selected.

This specifies the type of summary information that Excel will use to consolidate the data.

8 Click the Reference text box; then click the Month 1 sheet tab. Use the scroll arrows to the left of the month tab, if necessary, to view the Month 1 sheet tab.

On the Month 1 worksheet, select cells A6 through G60. You can select ranges while the dialog box is still open. The dialog box collapses automatically when you click and hold down the left mouse button and start to drag across the cells to select them. You can also click the Collapse Dialog button to collapse the dialog box and then click the button again to restore it.

9 Drag the dialog box out of the way, if necessary, to view cell A6; then select the range A6:G60.

Cells A6:G60 represent the first worksheet range to be consolidated in the First Quarter 97 worksheet. The sheet name and the range selected now appear in the Reference text box, in the First Quarter 97 worksheet. This is the information for the first worksheet and range that are consolidated in the First Quarter 97 worksheet.

10 Click the Add button.

The reference you added in the previous step is now copied to the All references text box.

11 With the Consolidate dialog box still open, click the Month 2 worksheet; then select cells A6 through G49.

This is the second worksheet range that is consolidated in the First Quarter 97 worksheet.

If you have problems...

If you prefer, you can type the range to be consolidated. First click the Sheet tab so that its name appears in the Reference text box; then scroll through the worksheet to verify the cell addresses to be included in the range. Type the range in the text box (beginning cell and ending cell separated by a colon), being sure to include the dollar sign ($) before the column and row numbers to make the range absolute.

After you select a range, it appears in the Reference text box with the insertion point following it. If you selected the wrong range, just press Backspace to erase the range and then type the correction.

12 Click the Add button.

13 Click the Month 3 worksheet; then select cells A6 through G50.

This is the third and final worksheet range that is consolidated in the First Quarter 97 worksheet.

14 Click the Add button.

15 In the Use labels in area, select the Left column check box, if it is not already selected.

This specifies which labels to use when you consolidate by category, as shown in Figure 10.12.

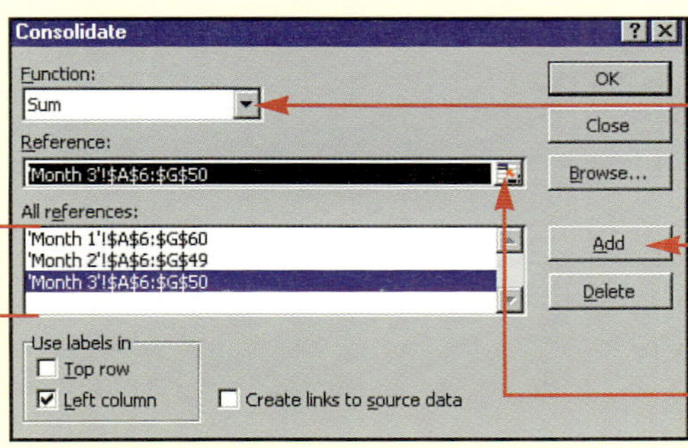

Figure 10.12
The Consolidate dialog box now includes all references to the worksheet data that you want to consolidate.

16 Choose OK to close the Consolidate dialog box and perform the consolidation.

The Month 1, Month 2, and Month 3 worksheets are now consolidated by employee and by week on the First Quarter 97 worksheet. You might need to adjust the column widths. Your First Quarter 97 report is complete, as shown in Figure 10.13.

You have completed consolidating your worksheets.

17 Save your changes and close the workbook. Print two copies of the worksheet, if requested by your instructor.

continues

To Consolidate Your Worksheets (continued)

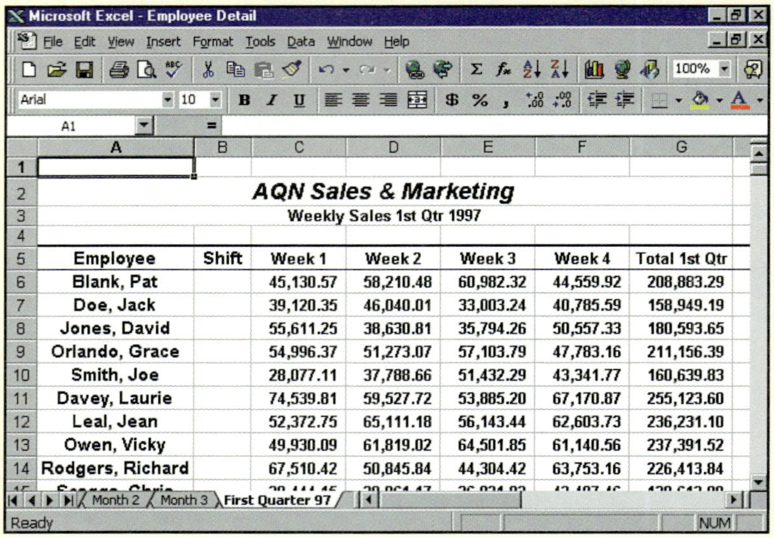

Figure 10.13
The consolidates worksheet now includes weekly totals by employee for the first quarter of 1997.

If you have completed your session on the computer, exit Excel and Windows 95 before turning off your computer. Otherwise, continue with the "Checking Your Skills" and "Applying Your Skills" sections.

Project Summary

To	Do This
Create an outline from an existing report	Select the worksheet and any cell in the range of data to be summarized. Choose Data, Group and Outline, Auto Outline.
Change the level of detail to show in the outline	Click the Row Level and Column Level buttons required to show the detail you want. Lower numbers mean less detail.
Show detail in a single element	Click the expand button above or left of the outline next to the element to be expanded.
Chart an outline	Set the level of detail you want, using the Row Level and Column Level buttons. Select the cells to be included on the chart. Choose Edit, Go To and select the Special button. Select the Visible cells only option and choose OK. Select the exact data range to chart and then click the Chart Wizard button. Follow the Chart Wizard prompts.

To	Do This
Create a subtotal report	Click any cell in the data area and choose Data, Sort; choose the appropriate options in the Sort dialog box and click OK. Select any cell in the data area and choose Data, Subtotals. Select the appropriate options in the Subtotal dialog box and click OK.
Create multiple subtotal rows	If necessary, remove all previous subtotaling. Select any cell in the data area. Choose Data, Sort, make appropriate selections, and click OK. With any cell in the data area selected, choose Data, Subtotals. Select the appropriate options in the Subtotal dialog box and click OK. Choose Data, Subtotals again as necessary to get the breakdown required. Deselect the Replace current subtotals check box to add to the current subtotals displayed instead of replacing them.
Consolidate a worksheet	Set up worksheets to be consolidated and the destination worksheet with identical row and column headings. If necessary, remove subtotals from contributing worksheets. Select the destination cell (the one on the destination worksheet where the consolidated data is to start). Choose Data, Consolidate; from the Function drop-down list, choose the summary function to consolidate the data. Complete the Reference text box by selecting the range of data to consolidate; then click Add. Repeat this step for each sheet to be included in the consolidation. If you are consolidating by category (not by position), all worksheets have the same data labels but not the same layout; be sure to include the labels in the range and select the area to Use labels in. To execute the consolidation, click OK.

Checking Your Skills

True/False

For each of the following statements, check *T* or *F* to indicate whether the statement is true or false.

__T __F **1.** The Data, Sort command performs only one sort at a time.

__T __F **2.** Creating an outline from an existing worksheet is faster than hiding columns and rows of data.

__T __F **3.** On an outlined worksheet, the lowest number for both the Row and Column Level buttons expands the worksheet to show all the detail.

__T __F 4. Excel can create only one subtotal row in a report.

__T __F 5. Click a cell in the data area before using the Data, Subtotals command or an error message will appear.

__T __F 6. You can select one cell in a data area when you create an outline, as long as your data is contiguous.

__T __F 7. The Collapse buttons are the ones with the minus (-) signs on them.

__T __F 8. To select only the cells that are showing on the worksheet, click Visible cells only from the Go To Special dialog box.

__T __F 9. Excel immediately creates subtotals rows when you choose the Data, Subtotals command.

__T __F 10. Once you create the subtotals, you have to delete each subtotal row to remove them.

Multiple Choice

Circle the letter of the correct answer for each of the following questions.

1. When a worksheet is outlined, which buttons showing levels of detail appear horizontally on the screen?
   a. Column Level
   b. Row Level
   c. Go To
   d. None of the above
2. Which Excel feature would you use to automatically place subtotals in your worksheet?
   a. Data, Consolidate
   b. Data, Group and Outline, Auto Outline
   c. Data, Sort
   d. Data, Subtotals
3. Which option in the Subtotal dialog box should not be checked in order to create a multiple-subtotal row?
   a. Page Break Between Groups
   b. Replace Current Subtotals
   c. Summary Below Data
   d. All of the above
4. What do you need to select to consolidate data from multiple worksheets into one?
   a. Summary destination
   b. A function
   c. Detail to be consolidated
   d. All of the above
5. When consolidating three months of data into one worksheet to obtain a summary total, which function would you use?
   a. Sum
   b. Max
   c. Min
   d. Product

6. Which command do you use to make Row and Column Level buttons visible?

   a. Data, Consolidate

   b. Data, Group and Outline, Auto Outline

   c. Data, Sort

   d. Data, Subtotals

7. What choice do you make in the Go To Special dialog box so your chart only includes the data currently displayed?

   a. Current region

   b. Current array

   c. Visible cells only

   d. Formulas

8. In the Subtotal dialog box, which option should you check to have the new subtotals entered in place of old ones?

   a. Replace current subtotals

   b. Page break between groups

   c. Summary below data

   d. None of the above

9. In the Subtotal dialog box, which option should you check to have the new subtotals appear immediately after the rows involved in the subtotal?

   a. Replace current subtotals

   b. Page break between groups

   c. Summary below data

   d. None of the above

10. In the Consolidate dialog box, you enter the data ranges to be consolidated in which box?

    a. Function

    b. All references

    c. Reference

    d. None of the above

Completion

In the blank provided, write the correct answer for each of the following statements.

1. In an Excel outline, click the _______________ button to show more detail in a single element.

2. The _______________ buttons appear vertically to indicate levels of detail in the worksheet _______________.

3. To see the least detail in an outline, click the Level _______________ button for rows or columns.

4. Before you create a subtotal report, make sure that you _______________ the data so that it is grouped together in the right order.

5. Use Excel's _______________ command to combine values from multiple worksheets into another summary area.

6. A _______________ block of cells has no blank rows or columns from beginning to end.

7. To create a chart in an outlined worksheet that's not showing the full details, you need to choose _______________ , click Special, and select Visible cells only.

8. Choose Data, _______________ , Auto Outline to outline your worksheet.

9. When you select the _______________ option, lines appear between the cells to how where information is hidden.

10. To add subtotal lines to groups of data within your worksheet, choose _______________.

Excel

Matching

In the blank next to each of the following terms or phrases, write the letter of the corresponding term or phrase. (Note that some letters may be used more than once.)

a. Column Level buttons
b. Data, Sort
c. Select All
d. Consolidate
e. Function
f. Row Level buttons
g. Expand
h. Data, Group and Outline, Auto Outline
i. Outline
j. Data, Subtotals

_______ 1. A way of summarizing worksheet data by grouping rows and columns of data

_______ 2. Numbered sequentially, depending on the number of levels in the outline, these buttons appear horizontally to the left of the Select All button

_______ 3. Combine values from multiple worksheets into another summary area (usually a separate worksheet)

_______ 4. Click this button to show the detail in a single element of the outline

_______ 5. Command to rearrange the order of the data

_______ 6. Command to create an outline from an existing report

_______ 7. Command to create a subtotal report

_______ 8. Button at the intersection of the row and column headers

_______ 9. Numbered sequentially, depending on the number of levels in the outline, these buttons appear vertically above the Select All button

_______ 10. Type of summary information used in the consolidation

Applying Your Skills

Practice

The following exercises enable you to practice the skills you have learned in this project. Take a few minutes to work through these exercises now.

Creating Subtotals in a Report

Pat's Pie Pantries is a small but growing chain of pie bakeries. To help figure out the buying patterns of the public (and the performance of her bakeries), Pat has started tracking pie sales by month and by store. In this exercise, you create some subtotal reports for 1996 pie sales.

To create the subtotal report, follow these steps:

1. Open Proj1003 from the Project-10 folder on the CD and save it as `1996 Pie Sales`.
2. Sort the list by product in ascending order and then by store location in ascending order. Set up a report with multiple subtotals that show Pat the sales totals of her pies and the maximum sales at any location in each month for each kind of pie. Remember to expand the column widths.
3. Now sort the list by store in ascending order and then by product in ascending order. Create a subtotal report so that Pat can review the performance of her stores by month, quarter, and for the entire year. Remember to expand the column widths.
4. This is a bit difficult to read, so create an outline. Then adjust the view so that Pat can see at a glance the performance of each store by quarter, without any product details. Save the changes to the workbook. If requested by your instructor, print two copies of this worksheet. Keep this view on-screen for the next exercise.

Charting the Performance of Pat's Stores

Pat would like an even quicker picture of how her stores compare to each other in sales performance. In this exercise, you chart the outline you just created.

To chart the performance of the stores, follow these steps:

1. Create a column chart from the outline that shows the locations grouped together by quarters to aid comparison. Place the chart below the worksheet.
2. Label the vertical Value (y) axis `U.S. Dollars`. Label the chart `Sales by Quarter`.
3. Increase the size of the chart so that the Category (x) labels are shown. Change the font to 11-point size for the Category (x) axis, Value (y) axis, and the legend.

4. Add another chart to the worksheet that shows each location's performance quarter by quarter, apart from the others. Label this chart `Sales by Location`.
5. Increase the size of the chart. Change the font to 11-point size for the Category (x) axis, Value (y) axis, and the legend.
6. Save the changes. If requested by your instructor, print two copies of the worksheet with its charts. Close the 1996 Pie Sales workbook.

Consolidating Weekly Sales Reports

Your reports have really helped Pat to see that she needs to do detailed analyses of results from the stores. So she has started tracking sales by store, by product, and by day of the week. But now she needs a faster way to consolidate these reports.

To consolidate the weekly sales reports, follow these steps:

1. Open the file Proj1004 from the Project-10 folder on the CD and save it as `Weekly Pie Sales`.
2. Consolidate the weekly reports from the three Dallas Metro Division stores onto the Weekly Summary worksheet. (Hint: The easiest way to do this is to consolidate by position.)
3. Save the workbook. If requested by your instructor, print two copies of the Weekly Summary worksheet; then close the workbook.

Challenge

The following challenges enable you to use your problem-solving skills. Take time to work through these exercises now.

Adding Subtotals to a Worksheet

Open Proj1005 from the Project-10 folder on the CD and save it as `Sales Performance`. This workbook lists the quarterly sales by salesperson for three sales territories. Look at the 1997 worksheet, which already has subtotals for the territories. Now switch to the 1998 worksheet and add territory subtotals to that data for each quarter and the total.

Save the file and leave it open for the next exercise.

Charting the 1998 Sales

Your manager would like to see a column chart of the 1998 sales, with columns representing each territory. He doesn't want to include the detail for each salesperson. You should add this chart as a separate sheet in your workbook named `1998 Chart`. The Chart title is `Sales Performance - 1998`.

In selecting the data range to chart, don't include the Grand Total row or the Total column. Make sure you only chart the visible data.

In Step 2 of the Chart Wizard, you need to exclude the Salesperson column from the chart data. Click the Series tab, select Salesperson from the Series list, and click Remove. Then continue with the Chart Wizard.

Save the workbook. Print two copies if requested by your instructor. Then close the workbook.

Consolidating Worksheet Information

Open Proj1006 from the Project-10 folder on the CD and save it as `Two Year Summary`. Select the `Two Years` worksheet, if it's not already open. Click cell A3. You are going to consolidate the data from the `1998` and `1997` worksheets onto the current worksheet. Remember to use the labels from the top row and the left column. When the consolidation is complete, adjust the width of the columns if needed. Then delete the Salesperson column.

Save the workbook. Print two copies if requested by your instructor. Close the workbook.

PinPoint Assessment

PinPoint Training

You have completed the project and the associated lessons, as well as the "Checking Your Skills" and "Applying Your Skills" sections. Now use the PinPoint software evaluation mode to assess your comprehension of the specific exam tasks you have just learned. You can also use the PinPoint Trainer Mode and the Show Me tutorials to practice these specific exam tasks.

Project 11 Eleven

Creating Custom Reports with Pivot Tables

Analyzing Employee Data from Different Views

In this Project, you learn how to:

Objectives	Required Activities
➤ Use the PivotTable Wizard	Use Data Analysis and Pivot Tables
➤ Rearrange Data in the Pivot Table	Use Data Analysis and Pivot Tables
➤ Add Data to a Pivot Table	Use Data Analysis and Pivot Tables
➤ Add and Change a Pivot Table Summary Function	Use Data Analysis and Pivot Tables
➤ Hide and Show Pivot Table Details	Use Data Analysis and Pivot Tables
➤ Format Your Pivot Table	

Why Would I Do This?

Most Excel worksheets are arranged as rows of information with each column containing a specific type of data. The employee list you will be working with in this project has seven columns of data, sorted by years of service in descending order. The list contains a significant amount of data and is difficult to review in this format.

Pivot table
An Excel table created from a source list that enables you to look at the data rearranged in three dimensions.

By using a *pivot table*, however, you can easily summarize and analyze complicated data, using different views. The pivot table appears in an Excel worksheet and looks like any other worksheet data. You can add buttons to the table that enable you to change the view of the table information with a single button click. The PivotTable Wizard walks you through the steps to make a custom report from a list of data.

In this project, you learn how to use the PivotTable Wizard to create a custom report, how to edit the report to get the best information for your situation, and how to format the report so it looks professional and is easy to read.

Lesson 1: Using the PivotTable Wizard

The Employee worksheet in this project lists all the employees who work for AQN Sales & Marketing. The list is sorted in descending order by years of service. The annual budget meeting is next month and each manager needs to know how much to budget for salaries next year. Your job is to create a report showing by department, by position, and by shift how much each department is spending on salaries.

In this lesson, you use the PivotTable Wizard to create a pivot table based on the information in the Employee worksheet. The PivotTable Wizard provides a series of dialog boxes that prompts you for information to help you set up the pivot table quickly.

To Use the Pivot Wizard Table

1. **Open the file Proj1101 from the Project-11 folder on the CD and save it as `Personnel`.**

2. **Make sure that the `Employees` worksheet is active. If it is not active, click the `Employees` tab.**

   Before you can create a pivot table, the cell pointer must be located within the data area on which the table will be based.

3. **Select cell E10.**

   You can select any one cell in the data area.

4 Choose Data, PivotTable Report.

The PivotTable Wizard – Step 1 of 4 dialog box appears, as shown in Figure 11.1. By following the wizard's dialog boxes, you can specify the data you want to use in the pivot table, set up the table, and place it in a worksheet.

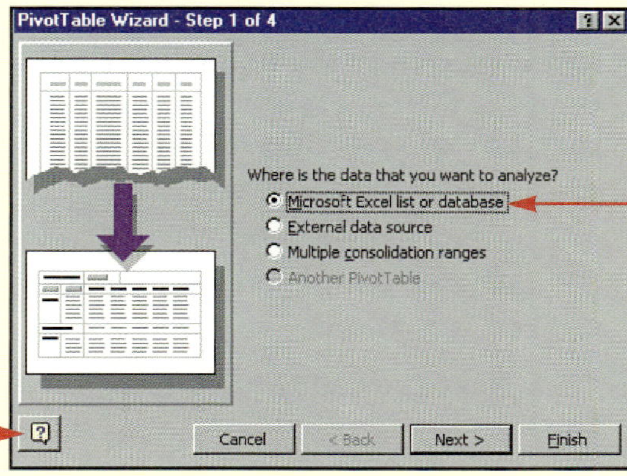

Figure 11.1
In Step 1 of the PivotTable Wizard, you select the data source for the pivot table you want to create.

If you have problems...

If you have any questions or problems while creating a pivot table, click the Help button in the PivotTable Wizard dialog box. The Office Assistant provides help for each step in creating a custom pivot table report.

5 Select the Microsoft Excel list or database option in the Step 1 of 4 dialog box.

In most cases, you want to base your pivot table on Excel worksheet data and should therefore choose the Microsoft Excel list or database option. However, you would choose the External data source option in the Step 1 of 4 dialog box if your data is contained in a program other than Excel (such as the Microsoft Query program). If you want to create a pivot table from multiple ranges in Excel worksheets, you should choose the Multiple Consolidation ranges option.

6 Click the Next button.

The PivotTable Wizard – Step 2 of 4 dialog box appears, as shown in Figure 11.2.

continues

To Use the Pivot Wizard Table (continued)

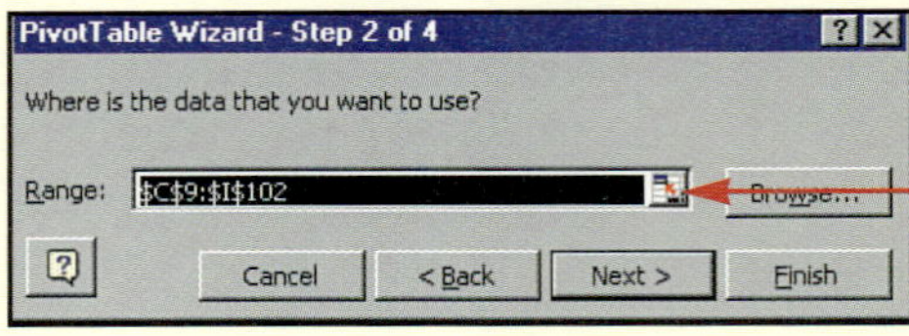

Figure 11.2
In Step 2 of the PivotTable Wizard, you select the range of data on which to base the pivot table.

7. **Make sure that the Range text box reads `$C$9:$I$102`. If your range is different, edit the range by typing it in the Range text box or selecting it from the worksheet.**

Excel has supplied this range based on the table of contiguous data in which the cell pointer was located when you started the PivotTable Wizard. Notice the moving line surrounding this range on your worksheet.

8. **Click Next (you may have to expand the dialog box to do this).**

The PivotTable Wizard – Step 3 of 4 dialog box appears, as shown in Figure 11.3.

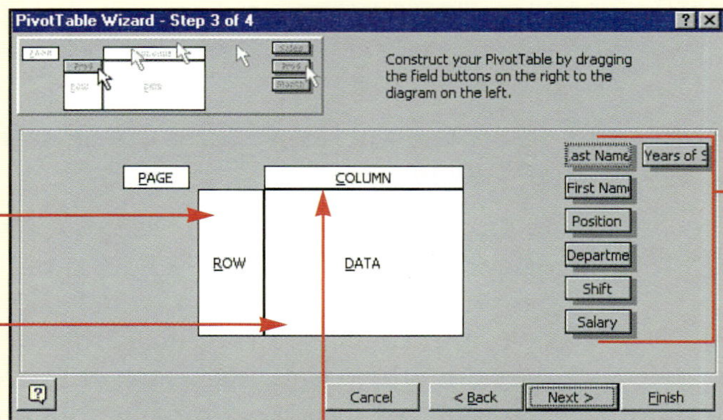

Figure 11.3
In Step 3 of the Pivot Table Wizard, you define the row and column layout of the pivot table.

In Step 3, you define the row and column layout of the pivot table, as well as the data that you want the pivot table to summarize. The column fields from your worksheet appear as buttons on the right side of the dialog box. You need to determine which of these fields contain the row, column, and table data you want to summarize in the pivot table. For this example, you want the department names to appear as row headings in the pivot table.

9. **Drag the Department button from the right side of the dialog box and drop it in the ROW area.**

Now you want the position titles to appear as subtitles (under department name) in the row headings of the pivot table.

10 Drag the Position button from the right side of the dialog box and drop it in the ROW area, placing it under the Department button.

The shift numbers should appear as column headings in the pivot table.

11 Drag the Shift button to the COLUMN area.

The salary information should appear in the body (data area) of the pivot table.

12 Drag the Salary button to the DATA area.

The data field uses Sum as the default summary function for numeric data. The Salary button changes to `Count of Salary` in this situation because several cells in the Salary column of this source contain text (Commission). Because you don't want to count how many salaries are being paid—you want the total amount of the salaries—you need to change the formula behind the button.

13 In the DATA area, double-click the Count of Salary button.

The PivotTable Field dialog box appears, as shown in Figure 11.4.

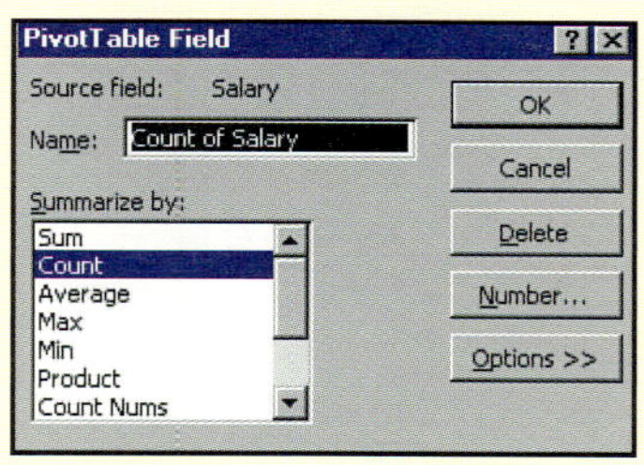

Figure 11.4
In the PivotTable Field dialog box, you specify how you want the data area of the pivot table to be summarized.

14 Click Sum in the Summarize by list box.

The Name text box changes to show Sum of Salary.

15 Click OK.

The button in the DATA area of the PivotTable Wizard dialog box now reads Sum of Salary.

16 Click Next to proceed to the next step of the PivotTable Wizard.

The PivotTable Wizard – Step 4 of 4 dialog box appears, as shown in Figure 11.5. This dialog box enables you to choose where the pivot table appears—on the existing worksheet or on a new worksheet—and what totals and other options are displayed with the pivot table. Place this pivot table on a new worksheet.

continues

To Use the Pivot Wizard Table (continued)

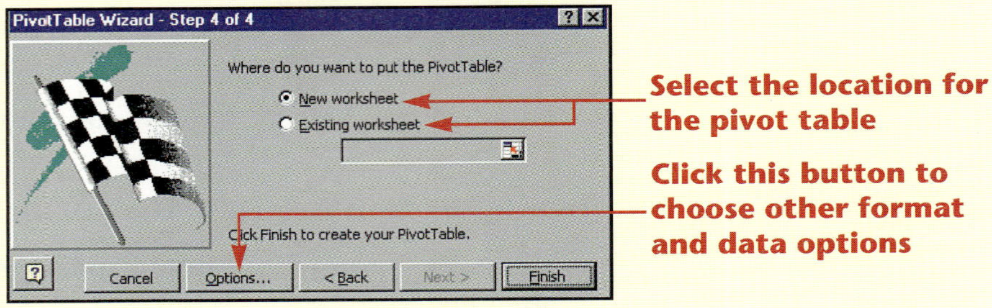

Figure 11.5
In Step 4 of the Pivot Table Wizard, you specify the location of the pivot table and other pivot table options.

⑰ Make sure that the New Worksheet option is selected; then click the Options button.

The PivotTable Options dialog box appears, as shown in Figure 11.6. If you want Excel to format your pivot table, make sure that AutoFormat Table is selected. Manual formatting changes that are made to a pivot table before or after it is automatically formatted take precedence over the changes made with AutoFormat.

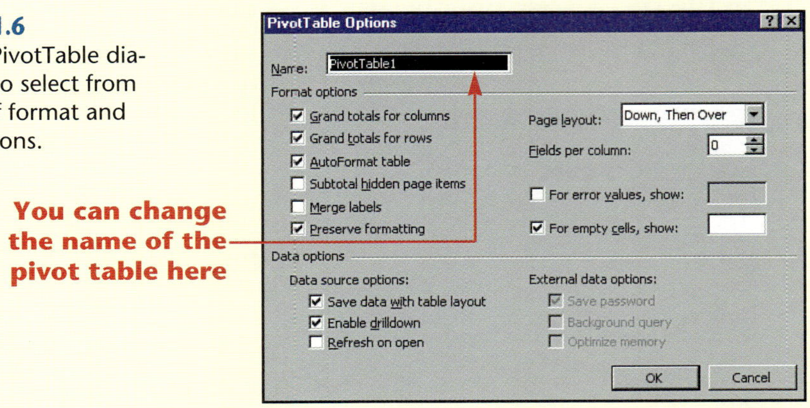

Figure 11.6
Use the PivotTable dialog box to select from the list of format and data options.

⑱ In the Format options area, make sure that the Grand totals for columns, Grand Totals for rows, AutoFormat table, and Preserve formatting check boxes are selected.

With these default options selected, your pivot table shows grand totals for both columns and rows. In addition, Excel automatically formats your table, and formatting is preserved when you change the layout of the pivot table or update it.

Note: The For empty cells, show option in the Format options area is checked, but the text box is left blank. As a default, empty cells in a pivot table report will be left blank. If you want a zero to appear in empty cells, type a zero (0) in the text box.

19 In the Data options area, make sure that the Save data with table layout and Enable drilldown options are selected.

These default options make sure that you save a copy of the source data on which the pivot table is based and enable access to pivot table detail.

20 Choose OK to accept the options; then click Finish in the Step 4 of 4 dialog box. Pivot Table toolbar opens.

21 Widen column A to fit the longest data entry in that column.

22 Rename the Sheet1 tab `Salary Budget`.

The pivot table report starts in cell A1 of the Salary Budget worksheet, as shown in Figure 11.7. Notice that the PivotTable toolbar also appears to assist you with any changes or updates to this pivot table.

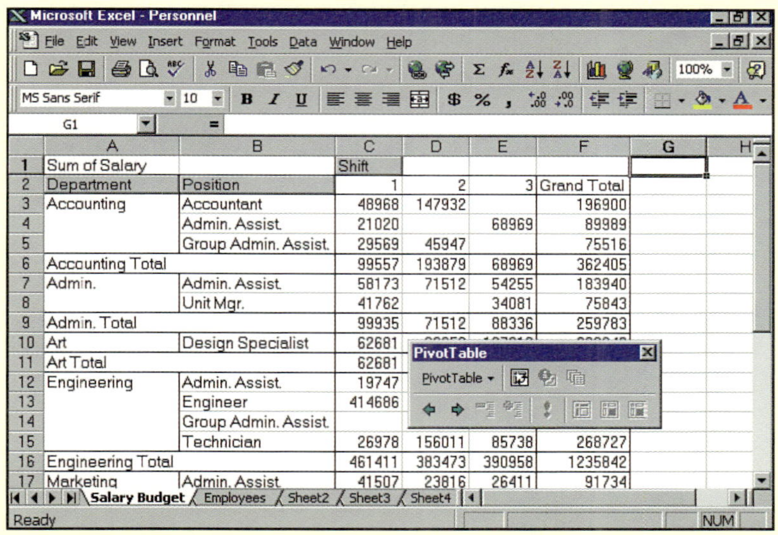

Figure 11.7
The pivot table report you created now appears in a new worksheet, Salary Budget.

You have just created your first pivot table report.

23 Save the changes to the workbook and keep it open for the next lesson.

Inside Stuff

You might need to adjust the range that appears in the Step 2 of 4 dialog box if your worksheet range should include more or fewer rows or columns than specified in the Range text box. An example of this would be a subtotals row appearing at the bottom of the range, directly beneath the last row of table data. To edit the range, you can select the Range text box and enter the correct range, or you can drag in the worksheet to select the correct range. Click the Collapse Dialog button next to the text box to move the dialog box out of the way temporarily.

continues

When telling the PivotTable Wizard in the Step 4 of 4 dialog box to put your pivot table in the existing worksheet, be careful not to select a cell in your original data list. If you tell Excel to start the pivot table in your original list, the pivot table overwrites your data and the integrity of the data is lost. If you see the warning `Do you want to replace the contents of the destination cells?`, click Cancel and start over.

You can use data lists from external workbooks as well as your active workbook. To use a data list from an external workbook, select the Microsoft Excel list or database option in Step 1 of the PivotTable Wizard. In Step 2, click the Browse button. The Browse dialog box appears, displaying a view of your files. Select the file containing the data and choose OK. The file name appears in the Range text box. Following the file name in the Range text box, you must type the range address of the data list. Click Next and follow Steps 3 and 4 as usual.

Lesson 2: Rearranging Data in the Pivot Table

The pivot table you created in Lesson 1 has two row headings (Department in cell A2 and Position in cell B2), one column heading (Shift in cell C1), and formulas (in column F, the Grand Total column) to total the salaries for each position in a department. The current pivot table includes salary information for all departments on the same report. But suppose each manager wants to see his department's information on a separate sheet. In this lesson, you rearrange the information in the existing pivot table so that you can display data for specific departments with a click of the mouse.

To Rearrange Data in the Pivot Table

1. **In the `Personnel` workbook, make sure that the `Salary Budget` worksheet is active.**
2. **Select cell A2, which contains the Department row heading.**
3. **Drag the Department button up to column letter A.**

   The mouse pointer changes as you drag it. Make sure that it changes to a pointer with three pages, as shown in Figure 11.8.

4. **Release the mouse button.**

   This step removes Department from the headings and places it in cell A1. Notice that the list of departments no longer appears on the left side of the pivot table. Instead, the department list has been removed from the table and is a separate list under the Department button in cell A1. Department now has a drop-down list box attached to it, as shown in Figure 11.9.

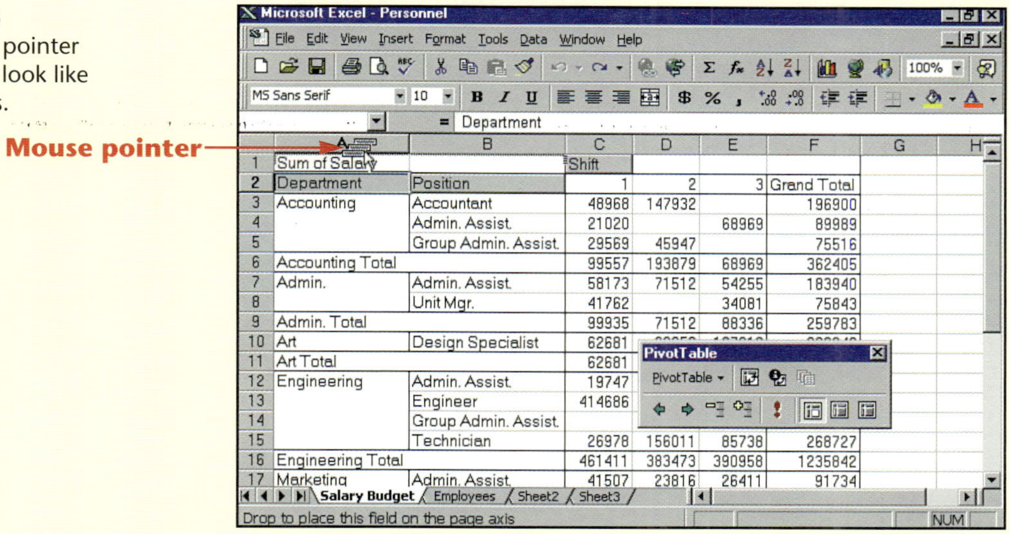

Figure 11.8
The mouse pointer changes to look like three pages.

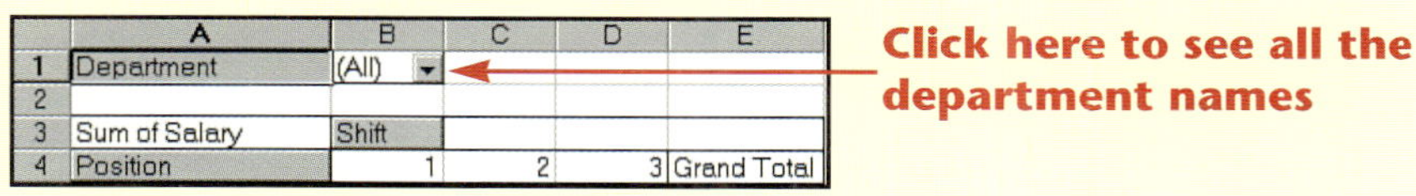

Figure 11.9
Cell B1 contains the Department drop-down list.

5 Display the Department drop-down list by clicking the arrow button.

All departments are listed.

6 Select the R and D department.

The pivot table now displays only the data related to the R and D department.

7 From the Department drop-down list, select (All).

Data for all departments is displayed again. Now you can return the Department field to a row heading.

8 Select cell A1.

9 Click the right mouse button anywhere inside the pivot table.

The shortcut menu appears.

10 Choose Wizard.

You can also click the PivotTable button on the PivotTable toolbar and choose Wizard. The PivotTable Wizard – Step 3 of 4 dialog box appears.

continues

To Rearrange Data in the Pivot Table (continued)

11. **From the PAGE area, drag the Department button to the ROW area. Place the Department button above the Position button and then click Next.**

    The PivotTable Wizard – Step 4 of 4 dialog box appears. Moving the Department heading changes where the pivot table starts on the worksheet. To position the edited pivot table report to start in cell A1, edit the cell reference in the Existing worksheet text box.

12. **Click in the Existing worksheet text box following the cell reference. Press ←Backspace to delete the 3; then type** 1.

13. **Click Finish.**

    Your pivot table should return to its original state (refer to Figure 11.7).

14. **Save the changes and keep the workbook open for the next lesson.**

Excel

Lesson 3: Adding Data to a Pivot Table

Pivot tables are seldom perfect when you first create them. Fortunately, you can make all sorts of changes to a pivot table. The department managers like the data you provided in the pivot table from Lesson 2, but they also want you to give them a count of employees in each position. This requires you to add more data to the report. This lesson shows you how to accomplish this objective.

To Add Data to a Pivot Table

1. **Select cell C7 in the** `Salary Budget` **worksheet.**

   You can select any cell as long as it is in the pivot table's data area. In this example, you can choose any cell as long as it is listed under Shift 1, Shift 2, or Shift 3.

2. **Click the PivotTable Wizard button on the PivotTable toolbar.**

   The PivotTable Wizard – Step 3 of 4 dialog box appears, displaying all the fields available on your worksheet and the current pivot table layout.

3. **Drag the Last Name button above Sum of Salary in the DATA area; then click Finish.**

   Your pivot table now includes a count of each cell containing a last name for each position, as shown in Figure 11.10.

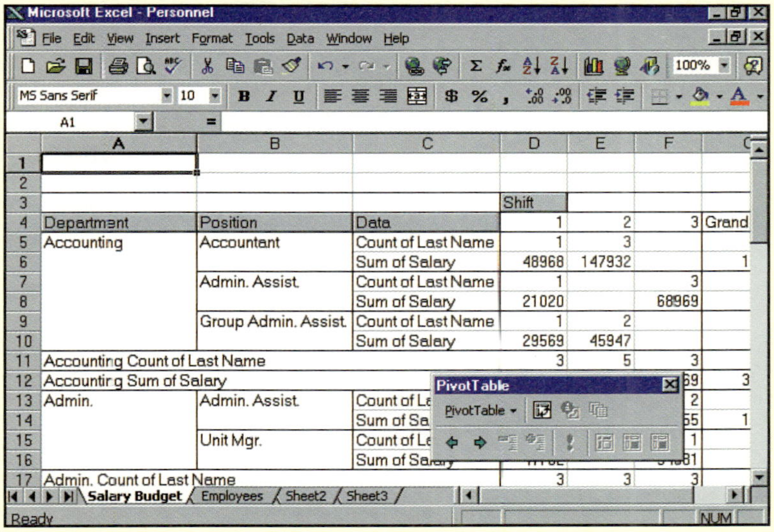

Figure 11.10
The Count of Last Name field now appears under the Data field in column C.

Now suppose you want to remove the data from the pivot table. You could accomplish this by returning to the PivotTable Wizard – Step 3 of 4 dialog box and dragging the field off the DATA area. Instead, for this example, use the shortcut menu.

4. **Right-click cell C5.**

   This step opens the shortcut menu.

5. **Choose Delete from the menu.**

   The Count of Last Name field is removed and your pivot table returns to its original form (refer to Figure 11.7).

6. **Save the workbook and keep it open for the next lesson.**

Lesson 4: Adding and Changing a Pivot Table Summary Function

In Lesson 1, you changed the summary function of the salaries from Count to Sum by double-clicking the Count of Salary button in the DATA area. There will be times when you think that you have summed up the data with the right function only to find that you want something completely different. Do not worry—there is a very simple way to change the function.

In this lesson, you add the average salary for each position by department. First you add a new function to the pivot table; then you change it to a different function.

To Add and Change a Pivot Table Summary Function

1 Click cell C5 in the `Salary Budget` worksheet of the `Personnel` workbook.

2 Click the PivotTable Wizard button on the PivotTable toolbar.

The PivotTable Wizard – Step 3 of 4 dialog box appears, showing the current pivot table layout.

3 Drag the Salary button below Sum of Salary in the DATA area.

The pivot table layout now includes a count of salaries.

4 Click Finish.

The pivot table now includes the count of salaries, but you want the average salary.

5 Right-click cell C6.

6 Choose Field from the shortcut menu.

The PivotTable Field dialog box appears, as shown in Figure 11.11.

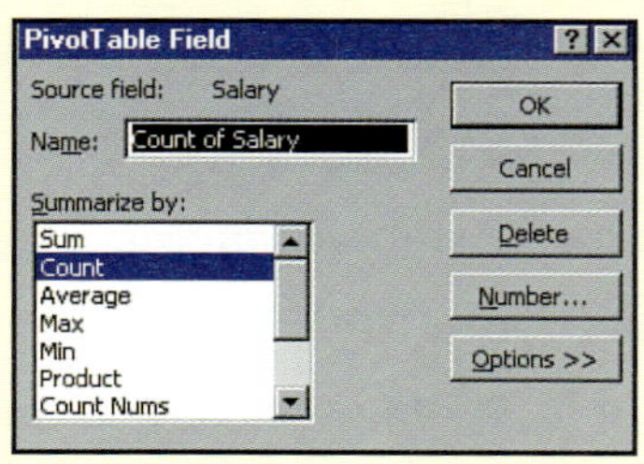

Figure 11.11
Use the PivotTable Field dialog box to change the function used to summarize data in the selected field.

7 In the Summarize by list, select Average.

The Name text box changes to show `Average of Salary`.

8 Choose OK.

Your pivot table now includes the Sum of Salary and Average of Salary headings, as shown in Figure 11.12.

9 Save the changes and keep the workbook open for the next lesson.

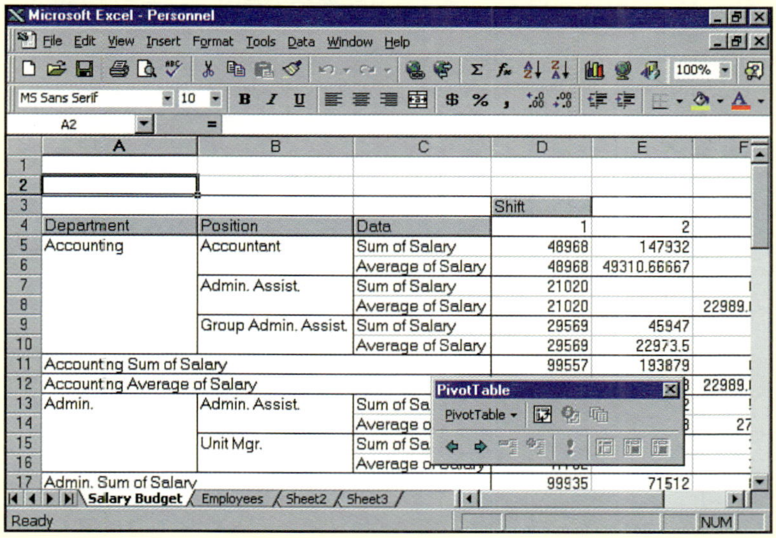

Figure 11.12
Column C now contains the headings Sum of Salary and Average of Salary.

Lesson 5: Hiding and Showing Pivot Table Details

A pivot table is a great tool to analyze your data. You can hide detail or display every item of detail. You also can hide data so no one else can view it. In this lesson, you learn how to hide data in the pivot table and then display it again without touching the original data list.

To Hide and Show Pivot Table Details

1. **Double-click cell A5 in the pivot table.**

   The detail for the Accounting department is now hidden.

2. **Double-click cell A5 again.**

   The detail for the Accounting department is now in view again.

3. **Select cell A4 and drag it to cell A1.**

   The Department data changes from a row orientation to a page orientation. To see information about a specific department, you select the department's name from the Department drop-down list.

4. **Double-click the Department button.**

   The PivotTable Field dialog box appears, as shown in Figure 11.13.

continues

To Hide and Show Pivot Table Details (continued)

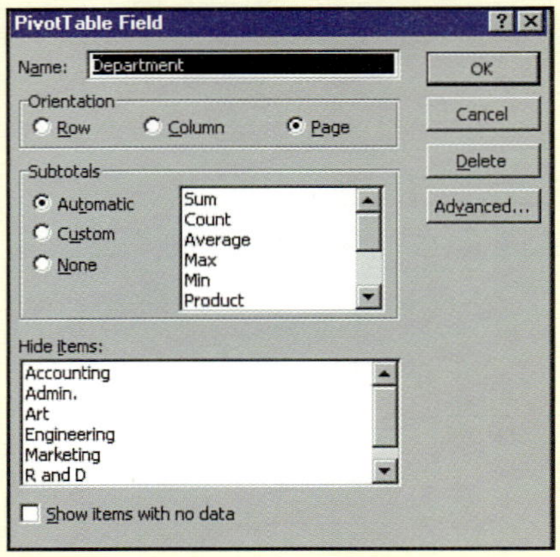

Figure 11.13
You can use the Pivot Table Field dialog box to hide items in the Department drop-down list.

5 In the Hide items list box, select both R and D and Sales.

This will hide the R and D and Sales departments in the (All) and individual department views.

6 Choose OK to close the dialog box.

7 Click the Department arrow button.

Neither the Sales department nor the R and D department is visible.

8 Select (All) if it is not already selected.

All departments are displayed except the Sales and R and D departments.

9 Double-click the Department button.

The PivotTable Field dialog box appears.

10 Click R and D and Sales again in the Hide Items list box to deselect them.

11 Choose OK to close the dialog box.

All departments are visible again.

12 Select cell A1 and drag it back to cell A4.

This step changes the department data back to row orientation.

13 Select cell G11.

This is the Sum of Salary heading for the entire Accounting department. You want to see all the detail making up this total.

14 Double-click cell G11.

A new worksheet named Sheet1 opens and all the records that make up the Accounting department Sum of Salary total are listed, as shown in Figure 11.14.

15 Save the changes and keep the workbook open for the next lesson.

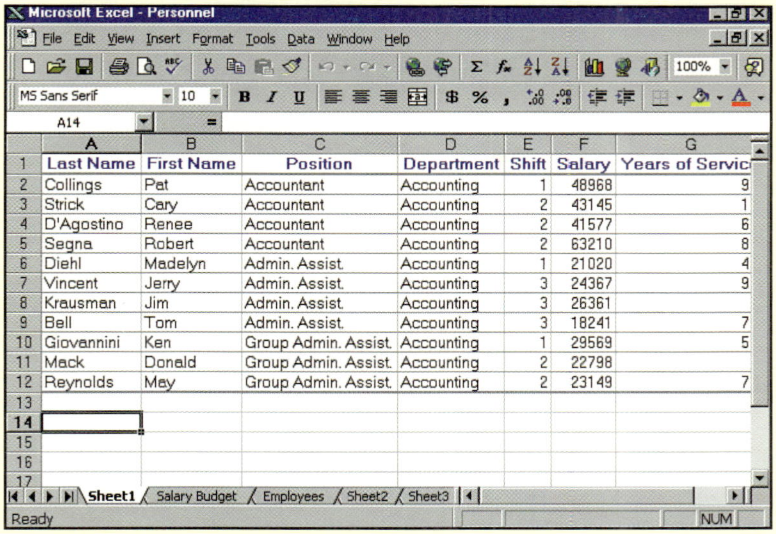

Figure 11.14
The new Sheet1 worksheet showing all the details is created when you double-click the Sum of Salary cell.

Lesson 6: Formatting Your Pivot Table

Your pivot table has not been formatted. You need to make the report a little more professional by formatting it before including it in any reports. (You want the report to make sense and be easy to read.) You can use the AutoFormat tool to format the whole pivot table, or you can format individual fields.

To Format Your Pivot Table

1. **Activate the `Salary Budget` worksheet of the `Personnel` workbook; then select cell A5 in the pivot table.**

   You do not have to select the whole pivot table; you just have to select one of its cells.

2. **Choose Format, AutoFormat.**

   The AutoFormat dialog box appears, as shown in Figure 11.15.

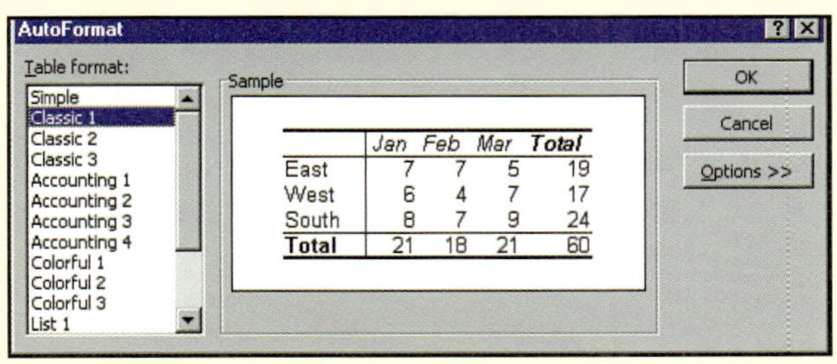

Figure 11.15
You can easily enhance the appearance of a pivot table report by using the AutoFormat dialog box.

continues

To Format Your Pivot Table (continued)

3. **Choose Classic 3 from the Table format list; then choose OK.**

   The pivot table is automatically formatted in the Classic 3 style.

4. **Select cell D5.**

   Format this Sum of Salary field, which ultimately applies the format to all Sum of Salary data cells in the pivot table report.

5. **Right-click cell D5.**

6. **Choose Field from the shortcut menu.**

   The PivotTable Field dialog box appears.

7. **Click the Number button on the right side of the PivotTable Field dialog box.**

   The Format Cells dialog box appears.

8. **In the Category list, select Currency; then select 0 Decimal places. Select the $ symbol from the Symbol drop-down list (if it is not already selected) and select the ($1,234) format displayed in red under Negative numbers.**

9. **Click OK twice.**

   Now format the Average of Salary field in cell D6, which ultimately formats all the Average of Salary data cells.

10. **Right-click cell D6.**

11. **Choose Field from the shortcut menu.**

12. **Click the Number button in the PivotTable field dialog box.**

13. **Choose Currency, 0 decimal places, $ symbol, and the ($1,234) format displayed in red.**

14. **Click OK twice.**

    All the Sum of Salary and Average of Salary data cells change to the currency format, as shown in Figure 11.16.

15. **Adjust column widths as necessary.**

16. **Close the PivotTable toolbar.**

    Your pivot table is formatted.

17. **Save the changes to the workbook. If requested by your instructor, print two copies of the Sheet1 and Salary Budget worksheets in landscape orientation; then close the Personnel workbook.**

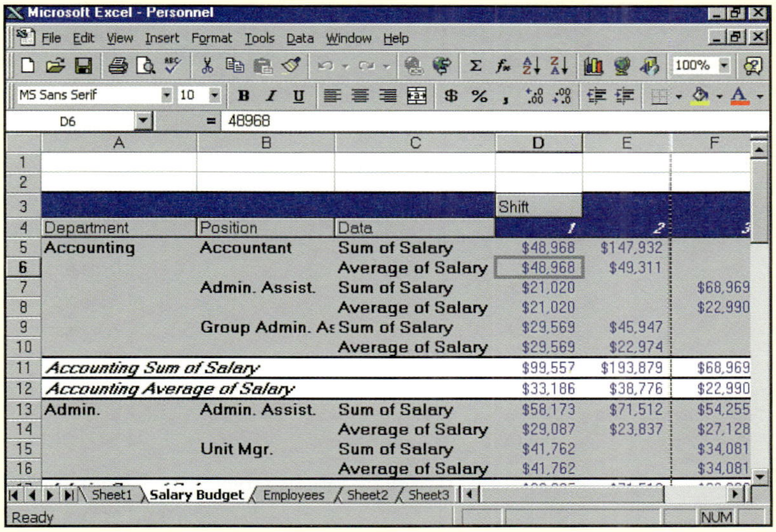

Figure 11.16
All the Sum of Salary and Average of Salary data cells are now formatted as currency, zero decimal places.

If you have completed your session on the computer, exit Excel and Windows 95 before turning off your computer. Otherwise, continue with the "Checking Your Skills" and "Applying Your Skills" sections.

Project Summary

To	Do This
Use the Pivot Table Wizard	Open the workbook, select a cell in the data area and choose Data, PivotTable Report.
Lay out a pivot table	Drag buttons from the right side of the diagram in Step 3 of the PivotTable Wizard to the area where the corresponding fields must appear.
Change the formula behind a PivotTable Wizard field	In the PivotTable Wizard – Step 3 of 4 dialog box, double-click the field in the DATA area and select the correct function from the Summarize by list box.
Rearrange elements of a pivot table	Click and drag the elements as needed.
Restore the pivot table	Click the PivotTable Wizard button on the PivotTable toolbar. In the PivotTable Wizard – Step 3 of 4 dialog box, click and drag the field buttons to their original positions.
Add data to a pivot table	Click the PivotTable Wizard button on the PivotTable toolbar. Drag the field you need to the DATA area; then click Finish.

continues

To	Do This
Change a pivot table summary function	Right-click the function in the pivot table and choose Field from the shortcut menu. Then select the desired function from the Summarize by area of the dialog box. Choose OK.
Hide PivotTable detail (and controlling restore it)	Double-click the summary cell the data or double-click a summary field name and choose the items to hide from the list box in the PivotTable Field dialog box. Repeat the process to restore the items.
Format a pivot table	Select any cell in the pivot table. Choose Format, AutoFormat and select a style from the dialog box.
Format a cell in a pivot table	Right-click the cell and choose Field from the shortcut menu. Choose the Number button and select an appropriate format. Then choose OK twice.

Checking Your Skills

True/False

For each of the following statements, check *T* or *F* to indicate whether the statement is true or false.

__T __F **1.** You select a cell inside the data area of a worksheet before starting the PivotTable Wizard.

__T __F **2.** You can base a pivot table only on Excel worksheet data.

__T __F **3.** To create a pivot table, you drag field buttons into position to lay out the table diagram.

__T __F **4.** Pivot tables are created in a new worksheet unless you specify otherwise.

__T __F **5.** You can create only one pivot table from a list of data.

__T __F **6.** You use a pivot table to easily summarize and analyze complicated data.

__T __F **7.** Once you've created the pivot table, you can't change the buttons.

__T __F **8.** The default way to summarize the data field of the pivot table is by Count of the selected field.

__T __F **9.** One of the pivot table options is to AutoFormat the table.

__T __F **10.** You lose the original data when you create a pivot table.

Multiple Choice

Circle the letter of the correct answer for each of the following questions.

1. What area of the pivot table diagram is used to summarize the information?
   a. COLUMN
   b. DATA
   c. ROW
   d. PAGE
2. Which button on the PivotTable toolbar can immediately bring you to Step 3 of the PivotTable Wizard?
   a. PivotTable
   b. PivotTable Wizard
   c. PivotTable Field
   d. Show Pages
3. How can you hide PivotTable detail?
   a. Right-click a summary cell controlling the data and choose Hide from the shortcut menu.
   b. Double-click the summary cell controlling the data.
   c. Double-click a summary field name and choose items to hide from the PivotTable Field dialog box.
   d. Both b and c.
4. In the PivotTable Options dialog box, which option allows you to see detail when you double-click a cell in the data area of a pivot table?
   a. Enable Drilldown
   b. Grand Totals for Rows
   c. Preserve Formatting
   d. Save Data with Table Layout
5. You choose from a list of automatic formats to apply a style to your pivot table by using which Excel command?
   a. Format, Cells
   b. Format, Row
   c. Format, Column
   d. Format, AutoFormat
6. What is the first step in changing the formula behind a PivotTable Wizard field?
   a. Choose Data, PivotTable Report
   b. Choose Format, AutoFormat
   c. Double-click the field in the ATA area in the PivotTable Wizard
   d. None of the above
7. How do you quickly format a cell in a pivot table?
   a. Choose Format, Cells from the menu
   b. Double-click the cell
   c. Choose Format, Auto Format from the menu
   d. Right-click the cell and choose Field from the shortcut menu and then choose the Number button
8. How do you rearrange the elements of a pivot table?
   a. Select the element and choose Format, Rearrange
   b. Click the PivotTable Wizard button
   c. Click and drag the elements
   d. None of the above

9. What do you do to quickly change the summary function of a pivot table field?
   a. Double-click the cell
   b. Right-click the cell and select Field from the shortcut menu
   c. Double-click the field in the PivotTable Wizard
   d. None of the above

10. How do you quickly reopen the PivotTable Wizard to make changes to the pivot table?
    a. Right-click anywhere inside the pivot table
    b. Click the PivotTable Wizard button
    c. Both a and b
    d. None of the above

Completion

In the blank provided, write the correct answer for each of the following statements.

1. _____________ the field button in the DATA area of the PivotTable Wizard to change the summary function.
2. When you are creating your pivot table, drag a field button to the _____________ area to create a drop-down list and show data for one item at a time.
3. Click the _____________ button in the PivotTable Wizard – Step 2 of 4 dialog box to temporarily move the PivotTable dialog box out of your way to select cells on the worksheet.
4. You can change the format of all the numbers of a source field from the _____________ dialog box.
5. You can _____________ a row, column, or page header to a new location in the pivot table and restructure its layout.
6. You use a(n) _____________ to summarize and analyze complicated data.
7. If your data source is not an Excel worksheet, choose _____________ data source in Step 1 of the PivotTable Wizard.
8. Use the _____________ button in Step 2 of the PivotTable Wizard to temporarily move the dialog box out of the way so you can select the data range.
9. To set the arrangement of the data in the pivot table, _____________ the field buttons onto the pivot table diagram in Step 3 of the PivotTable Wizard.
10. To change the formula behind the field in the ATA area, you _____________ the button.

Matching

In the blank next to each of the following terms or phrases, write the letter of the corresponding term or phrase. (Note that some letters may be used more than once.)

a. PivotTable button

b. Data, PivotTable Report

c. Field buttons

d. ROW

e. Row and column layout

f. Double-click

g. Sum

h. Pivot table

i. drag

j. Options

_______ 1. Command to create a pivot table

_______ 2. An Excel table created from a source list that enables you to look at the data rearranged in three dimensions

_______ 3. In Step 3 of the PivotTable Wizard, you define this

_______ 4. Do this to the button in the DATA area to change the formula behind the button

_______ 5. Other layout area in addition to PAGE, DATA, and COLUMN

_______ 6. The default summary function for numeric data

_______ 7. In Step 4 of the PivotTable Wizard, button to make other format and data choices

_______ 8. Do this with buttons on pivot table to rearrange the table

_______ 9. You drag these to define the pivot table layout

_______ 10. Click this button to see Step 3 of the PivotTable Wizard

Applying Your Skills

Practice

The following exercises enable you to practice the skills you have learned in this project. Take a few minutes to work through these exercises now.

Changing the Structure of Your Data

Pat's Pie Pantries, Inc. has a list of the 1997 sales of its products, sorted by store. There is a tremendous amount of information to review, and Pat wants to be able to restructure the way it is presented (to make columns into rows and vice versa). She loves the pivot table.

To change the structure of your data, follow these steps:

1. Open the file Proj1102 from the Project-11 folder on the CD and save it as `Sales Trend Analysis`.
2. Using the PivotTable Wizard, create a pivot table report in a new worksheet. Use the list in the `1997 Sales` worksheet. Lay out the products across the top instead of down the left side of the table and show Store in the ROW area. Sum only the middle months of each quarter. Rename Sheet1 as `PivotTable1`.
3. Save the changes and keep the workbook open for the next exercise.

Using the Pivot Table to Analyze Sales Trends

You can use pivot tables to analyze sales for information about patterns and trends. Pat can conveniently search for trends in the sales by product, location, or any number of other factors.

To use the pivot table to analyze sales trends, follow these steps:

1. Create a new pivot table report in a new worksheet, using the list in the `1997 Sales` worksheet.
2. Begin by setting up a new pivot table report to look for trends in the sales of products over time, from one quarter to the next. (*Hint*: Place the products in the ROW area and the Stores in the COLUMN area, with the quarters in the DATA area of the diagram.)
3. Rename the sheet tab of the new pivot table `PivotTable2`. If requested by your instructor, print two copies of the `PivotTable2` worksheet.
4. Rearrange the data in the table to show product sales by quarter. Does this change your perspective on the sales trends?
5. Make your data easier to read. Change the format of the table to List 2.
6. Save the changes to the workbook. If requested by your instructor, print two copies of `PivotTable2`; then close the workbook.

Analyzing Survey Data

An organization has commissioned a survey of the radio-listening habits of teens, young adults, and middle-aged persons in four major markets. Even though the consultants tried to keep the survey simple, a great deal of data was obtained that must now be analyzed. Use a pivot table to make this task easier!

To analyze the survey data, follow these steps:

1. Open the file Proj1103 from the Project-11 folder on the CD and save it as `Radio Listening Survey`.
2. Create a pivot table report in a new worksheet. Set it up so that the pivot table allows you to analyze the type of radio programming preferred by each gender in each market, by age group. Be sure that the table reflects average percentage, not the sum of the percentages. The table should also give an average percentage for women and men by category.
3. Widen any columns that are too narrow.
4. Format numbers so that they round off to one decimal place.
5. Since the interest in this study was listening habits by age and location, pull the Age element up so that you can look at listening habits in each market purely by age. Then restore the pivot table.
6. Save the changes to the workbook. If requested by your instructor, print two copies of the pivot table; then close the workbook.

Challenge

The following challenges enable you to use your problem-solving skills. Take time to work through these exercises now.

Changing the Structure of Your Data

Open Proj1104 from the Project-11 folder on the CD and save it as `Salesperson Performance`. This workbook provides data on the sales figures for each salesperson in the six sales territories in the United States. Your company has set up a little contest between the male and female salespeople. You need to analyze the quarterly data by territory, comparing genders.

Set up a pivot table for the range A3:I24 and put the pivot table on a separate worksheet. You need a drop-down list for the territories. *Hint:* Put the territory field in the PAGE area and the four quarters in the DATA area. Be sure to include grand totals for rows and columns and to keep the original data on its current worksheet.

Check the figures for the New York territory. Save and print the worksheet. Leave the worksheet open for the next exercise.

Rearranging the Pivot Table

Rearrange the pivot table to bring the Territory field within the ROW area, next to Salesperson. Save and print the worksheet. Leave the worksheet open for the next exercise.

Hiding Pivot Table Details

Hide the individual salespeople names, so only the territory data shows for each quarter. Choose an AutoFormat for the pivot table. Save and print the worksheet. Close the worksheet.

PinPoint Assessment

PinPoint Training

You have completed the project and the associated lessons, as well as the "Checking Your Skills" and "Applying Your Skills" sections. Now use the PinPoint software evaluation mode to assess your comprehension of the specific exam tasks you have just learned. You can also use the PinPoint Trainer Mode and the Show Me tutorials to practice these specific exam tasks.

Project 12

Twelve

Comparing Data with Advanced Pivot Tables

Analyzing Loan Officer Productivity

In this Project, you learn how to:

Objectives	Required Activities
➤ Update a List	
➤ Refresh Pivot Tables	Use Data Analysis and Pivot Tables
➤ Add Fields to a List	
➤ Edit a Pivot Table	Use Data Analysis and Pivot Tables
➤ Group Data in a Pivot Table	Use Data Analysis and Pivot Tables
➤ Create a Chart from Pivot Table Data	
➤ Change the Pivot Table View and Update a Chart	

Why Would I Do This?

One of the most useful ways to analyze data in a worksheet is to create a **pivot table**. Pivot tables summarize information from fields of a database, or **list**, and give you the ability to analyze data with different views of the same information. With the PivotTable Wizard, you specify the fields, table organization, and the calculations you want the table to perform. Using pivot tables enables you to quickly transpose columns to rows and rows to columns; this feature gives the pivot table its name.

After the pivot table is created, you may want to further customize it. Suppose that information is displayed by month, but you want to view the quarterly data. You can change fields, either within the list or in the pivot table, to provide the report layout that you need. You can even plot the data from the pivot table in a chart type of your choice to enhance a report or presentation.

In this project, you work with multiple pivot tables; each provides a different summary of your data. You update a list by using the **data form** feature, which automatically expands the **range**, which is assigned the **range name** Database. The column labels in the list become the field names in the database, and the rows become the **records**. You then update the associated pivot tables, group together information to change the view of your pivot table, and chart the pivot table data.

Jargon Watch

A **pivot table** enables you to change the layout of data into different summary views. A **list** is a worksheet set up with rows that contain similar data and have labeled columns. You can use a **range name** to define a **range** of cells, rather than using the cell addresses. A **data form** is a dialog box that you use to add one row (record) of data at a time into designated fields or to edit current data in the list. A **record** is a collection of data, stored in a row, that contains all the information about a specific item in the database.

Lesson 1: Updating a List

In Excel, it helps to give a list a range name when you're trying to keep the list of information current and up-to-date. You can add to the list and update it automatically by entering information using the Data, Form command. As you do, the named range expands and all pivot tables that are already created adjust accordingly.

To Update a List

1 Open the file Proj1201 from the Project-12 folder on the CD and save it with the new name, `Loans`**.**

If you have problems...

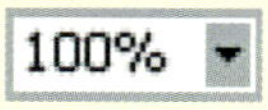

If the text is too small to read when the worksheet opens, increase the magnification by choosing a zoom percentage from the Zoom drop-down list on the Standard toolbar. Alternatively, you can type a magnification number, up to 400%, in the Zoom text box.

This workbook contains three worksheets labeled Data, Production Report, and Location Report.

2 Click the `Data` **sheet tab to display the worksheet, if necessary.**

The Data worksheet contains loan information from a mortgage company for October 1995 through March 1996.

3 Click the arrow next to the name box.

This displays the drop-down list of range names created for this worksheet (if any exist), as shown in Figure 12.1.

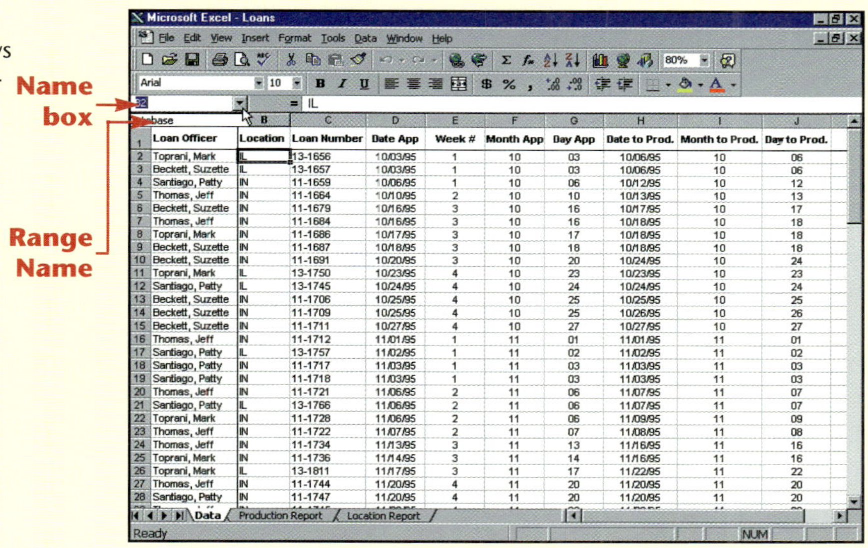

Figure 12.1
The name box displays the range name Database, which has been assigned to this list.

4 Click the range name, Database, in the name box.

The entire list in the range A1:J90 in this worksheet is selected and verifies that the range name is correct.

5 Click cell A1 on the worksheet to deselect the cells.

6 Choose Data, Form.

The Data Form dialog box displays the first record of information in the list, as shown in Figure 12.2.

continues

To Update a List (continued)

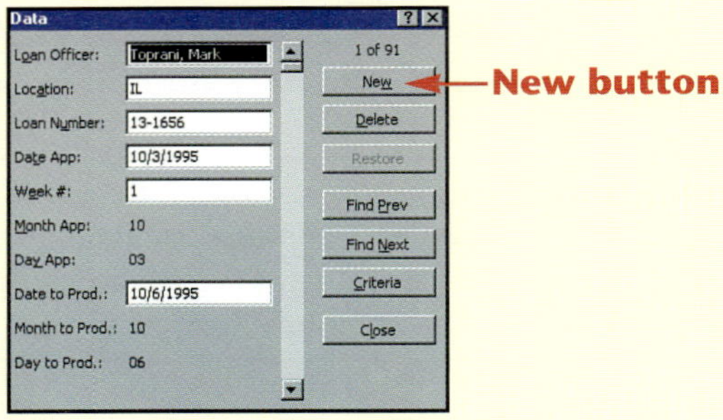

Figure 12.2
The Data Form dialog box displays the first record from the list.

7 Click New.

A blank form is displayed so that you can add a new record of information to the list. Text boxes appear next to each field name unless the column contains values calculated by formulas. In this form, the fields Month App, Day App, Month to Prod, and Day to Prod don't have corresponding text boxes for you to fill in because they contain formulas.

8 Type the following information in each of the six available text boxes (press Tab to move to the next box):

```
Thomas, Jeff

CO

31-1352

04/01/96

1

04/02/96
```

9 Click New.

Excel adds the new information (as a record) to the bottom of the list in the worksheet and displays a blank form so that you can add another record to the list. Now, type the following information, and use Tab to move through the text boxes:

```
Bayne, Betsy

IL

31-1353

04/02/96

1

04/03/96
```

10 Click the Close button.

The Data Form dialog box closes, and the list is updated.

11. **Click the arrow next to the name box and then click the range, Database.**

    Notice that the range, Database, automatically expands to include the two new rows (records) that were added using the Data Form dialog box. Also notice that the formulas located in columns F, G, I, and J were automatically entered into the new rows.

12. **Click cell A1 on the worksheet to deselect the cells.**

13. **Save the file and keep it open for the following lesson, where you update the pivot tables.**

If you have problems...

You must use the Data, Form command to add your records to the list in order to automatically expand the range name you defined with this list. If you add rows of data at the end of the list directly on the worksheet, the range name does not automatically expand, and you must redefine the range name to include the new rows of data.

Inside Stuff

Range names can be used whenever Excel requires that a range be specified in a command, formula, or macro. (Macros are covered in Project 7, Automating Tasks with Macros.) Because range names are easier to remember than cell addresses, you can use them with the Edit, Go To command or the name box to move to any area of the worksheet. Follow these steps to name a range: Select the range of cells you want to name. Choose Insert, Name, Define and enter the name of the range in the Names in workbook text box. Click OK. Range names can be a maximum of 255 characters. The first character must be a letter or underscore and no spaces may be used.

Lesson 2: Refreshing Pivot Tables

Source Data
The list of information from which the pivot table is derived.

Refresh Data
Option used to update a pivot table after source data is changed.

In Lesson 1, you added records to a list by using the Data, Form command and automatically expanded the range, named Database. This named range is the *source data* for the pivot tables in this workbook, which means the data in the list is linked with the pivot tables.

Because pivot tables do not automatically update when new information is added to the source data, you will use the *Refresh Data* option to update the multiple tables in this workbook. This saves you time as you keep summary reports current.

Now you use the Refresh Data option to update the multiple pivot tables in this workbook.

To Refresh Pivot Tables

1 Click the `Production Report` sheet tab in the `Loans` workbook.

This report summarizes the number of loans produced by each loan officer by week for each month. Currently, the month of March is being summarized as shown in Figure 12.3.

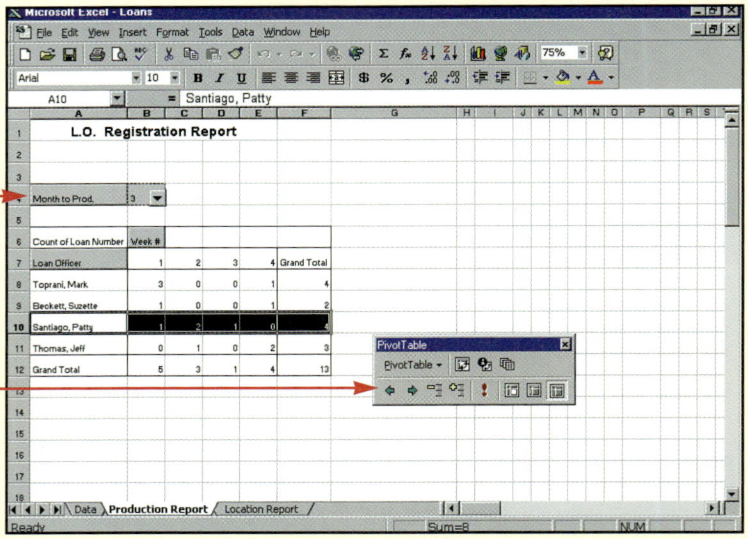

March is being summarized

PivotTable toolbar

Figure 12.3
The Production Report sheet displaying a pivot table.

2 Make sure that the PivotTable toolbar is displayed onscreen. If it isn't, choose View, Toolbars and click PivotTable from the submenu.

If you have problems...

If the PivotTable toolbar obstructs your view of the report, you can move it to another location onscreen by dragging the toolbar title bar or dock it in place by double-clicking the toolbar title bar.

3 In cell B4, click the down arrow.

The drop-down list displays the months included in this pivot table from the source list (10, 11, and 12 of the first year and 1, 2, and 3 of the second).

4 Click the down arrow again to close the drop-down list and click cell A10.

This action selects the range A10:F10, the record for Patty Santiago, in the pivot table and activates the PivotTable toolbar, as shown in Figure 12.4. At this point, the pivot table contains data from only October 1995 through March 1996 because the pivot table data was not refreshed after you added the April 1996 records to the Database in Lesson 1.

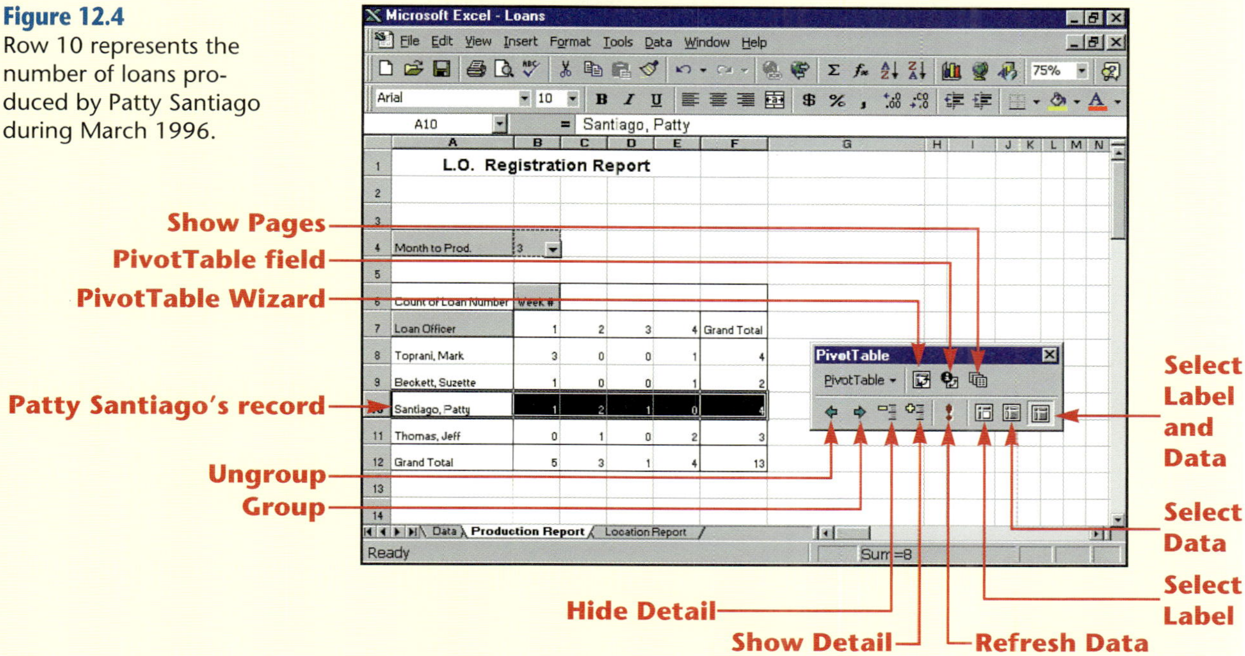

Figure 12.4
Row 10 represents the number of loans produced by Patty Santiago during March 1996.

5 Click the Refresh Data button on the PivotTable toolbar.

You can also right-click a cell inside the pivot table and choose Refresh Data from the shortcut menu. Refresh Data retrieves the most current data into the pivot table.

An alert box displays the message `Pivot table was changed during Refresh Data operation`.

6 Click OK.

The alert message is removed, and even though no data has visibly changed in the table, the pivot table is updated with the April data.

7 In cell B4, click the arrow and click the number 4.

The updated pivot table now shows a page for April (see Figure 12.5). Rows 8 and 9 display the April data you entered in Lesson 1 for Jeff Thomas and Betsy Bayne.

8 Click the Location Report sheet tab.

The Location Report, as shown in Figure 12.6, shows the total number of loans produced by the loan officer per month by office location. The pivot table needs to be updated to include April in the summary report.

continues

To Refresh Pivot Tables (continued)

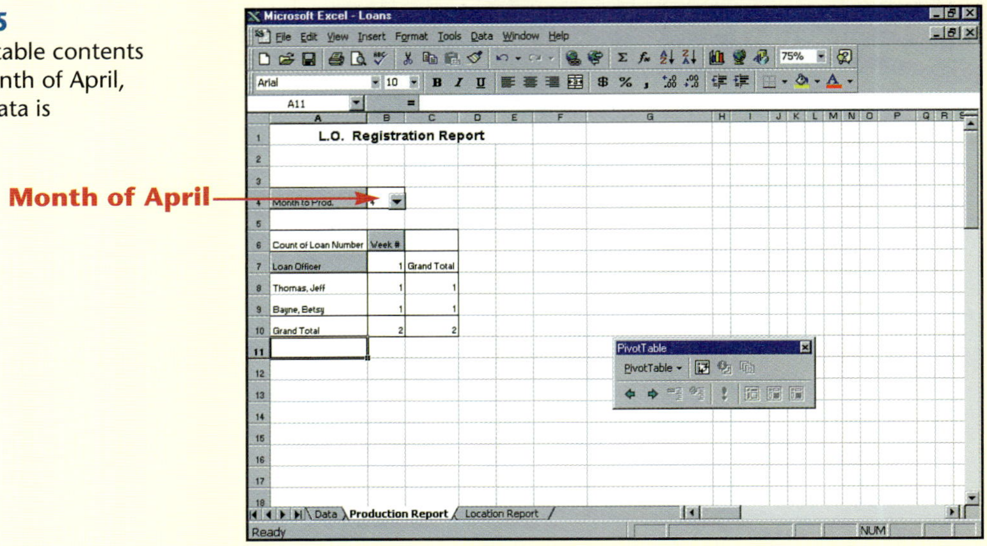

Figure 12.5
The pivot table contents for the month of April, after the data is refreshed.

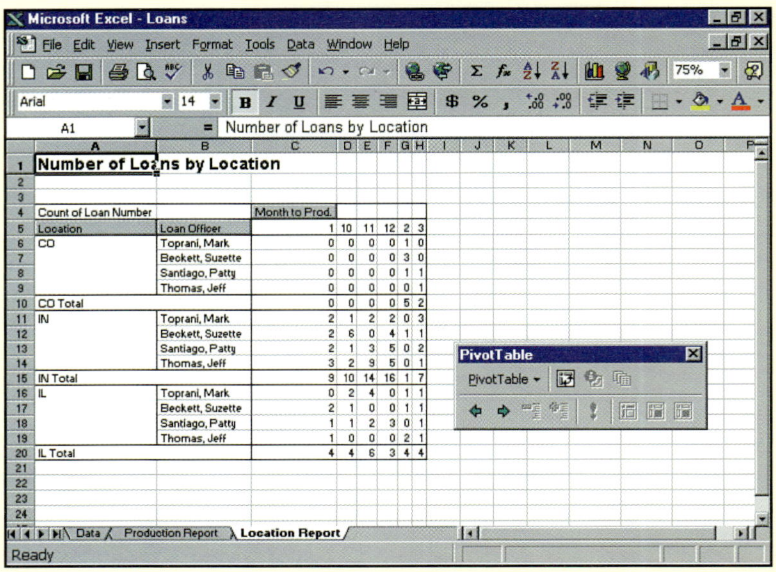

Figure 12.6
The Location Report sheet, before the pivot table is updated.

Before refreshing a pivot table, you must click a cell inside the table.

9 Click cell A6.

This highlights cells A6:H9, which is the row for the state of Colorado. Normally, clicking a row header only highlights that row, but in a pivot table it highlights the merged cell for that row and all the related data.

10 Click the Refresh Data button.

An alert box displays the message `Pivot table was changed during Refresh Data operation.`

11 Click OK.

The pivot table is updated and Column I shows the April results, as shown in Figure 12.7.

If you have problems...

The Refresh Data button becomes dimmed or unavailable when a cell in the pivot table isn't selected, and if you click this button, nothing happens to the pivot table. Make sure that you click a cell inside the pivot table before you click the Refresh Data button.

Figure 12.7
The pivot table contents, after the data is refreshed.

April results appear after the pivot table is updated

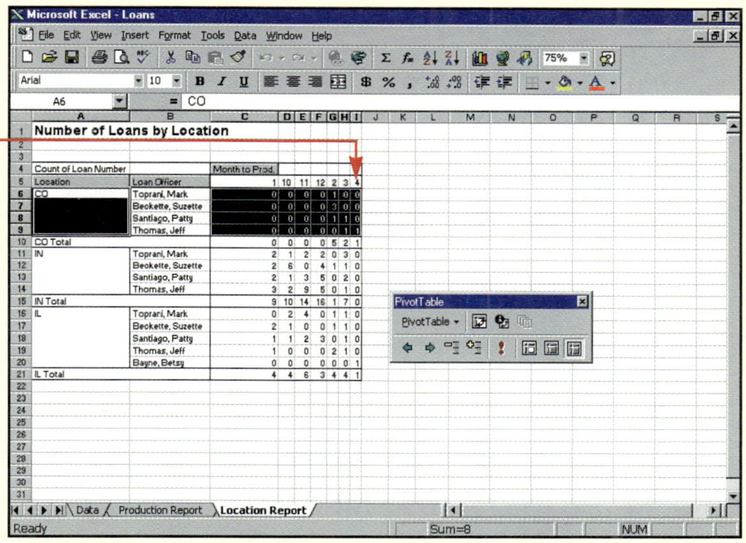

12 Save the workbook and leave it open. You use it in the next lesson, where you learn about adding fields to a list.

Lesson 3: Adding Fields to a List

In Excel, you can add new fields to a list by inserting columns in the worksheet within the original list range. As long as the columns are inserted within the list range, the range name expands to incorporate the new information and the pivot table can be updated.

You now add a new field, named Year App, to the list range. This field contains the YEAR() function from the Time and Date function category.

To Add Fields to a List

1. **Click the `Data` sheet tab of the `Loans` workbook; scroll to the top of the list and click column heading F.**

   The entire column is selected.

2. **Choose Insert, Columns.**

   Excel inserts a new column where the original column F data was located and moves all the data over one column to the right. A blank column now appears for column F.

3. **In cell F1, type `Year App` and press Enter.**

4. **Click column heading J to select where another new column will be inserted.**

5. **Choose Insert, Columns.**

   A blank column now appears for column J.

6. **In cell J1, type `Year to Prod.` and press Enter.**

7. **In cell F2, type `=YEAR(D2)` and press Enter.**

   This step enters the formula to extract the year from the date in cell D2. In cell F2, `1995` appears.

8. **In cell J2, type `=YEAR(I2)` and press Enter.**

   In cell J2, `06/17/95` appears, rather than a year, because the number format for this column is the Date format. It needs to be changed to the General format.

9. **Select Column J and right-click the selection.**

10. **Choose Format Cells.**

11. **Click the Number tab and click the General category. Click OK.**

    The results of the formulas are displayed in cells F2 and J2, as shown in Figure 12.8.

12. **Select cell F2 and drag the fill handle to row 92.**

    The formula is copied to the end of the list.

13. **Select cell J2 and drag the fill handle to row 92.**

    The formula is copied to the end of the list.

14. **Click the arrow next to the name box and click `Database` in the list.**

    Notice that the entire list, including the two new inserted columns, is selected.

Figure 12.8
Column F and Column J represent the new fields inserted within the original list range.

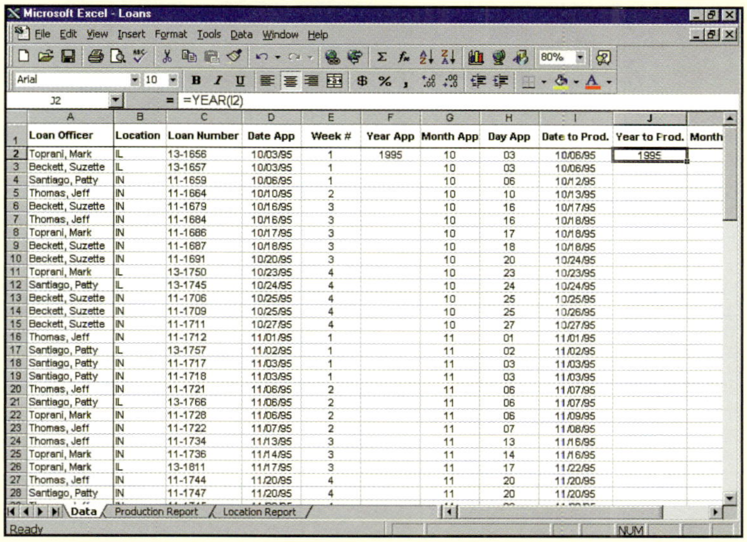

	A	B	C	D	E	F	G	H	I	J	
1	Loan Officer	Location	Loan Number	Date App	Week #	Year App	Month App	Day App	Date to Prod.	Year to Prod.	Month
2	Toprani, Mark	IL	13-1656	10/03/95	1	1995	10	03	10/06/95	1995	
3	Beckett, Suzette	IL	13-1657	10/03/95	1		10	03	10/06/95		
4	Santiago, Patty	IN	11-1659	10/06/95	1		10	06	10/12/95		
5	Thomas, Jeff	IN	11-1664	10/10/95	2		10	10	10/13/95		
6	Beckett, Suzette	IN	11-1679	10/16/95	3		10	16	10/17/95		
7	Thomas, Jeff	IN	11-1684	10/16/95	3		10	16	10/18/95		
8	Toprani, Mark	IN	11-1686	10/17/95	3		10	17	10/18/95		
9	Beckett, Suzette	IN	11-1687	10/18/95	3		10	18	10/18/95		
10	Beckett, Suzette	IN	11-1691	10/20/95	3		10	20	10/24/95		
11	Toprani, Mark	IL	13-1750	10/23/95	4		10	23	10/23/95		
12	Santiago, Patty	IL	13-1745	10/24/95	4		10	24	10/24/95		
13	Beckett, Suzette	IN	11-1706	10/25/95	4		10	25	10/25/95		
14	Beckett, Suzette	IN	11-1709	10/25/95	4		10	25	10/26/95		
15	Beckett, Suzette	IN	11-1711	10/27/95	4		10	27	10/27/95		
16	Thomas, Jeff	IN	11-1712	11/01/95	1		11	01	11/01/95		
17	Santiago, Patty	IL	13-1757	11/02/95	1		11	02	11/02/95		
18	Santiago, Patty	IN	11-1717	11/03/95	1		11	03	11/03/95		
19	Santiago, Patty	IN	11-1718	11/03/95	1		11	03	11/03/95		
20	Thomas, Jeff	IN	11-1721	11/06/95	2		11	06	11/07/95		
21	Santiago, Patty	IL	13-1766	11/06/95	2		11	06	11/07/95		
22	Toprani, Mark	IN	11-1728	11/06/95	2		11	06	11/09/95		
23	Thomas, Jeff	IN	11-1722	11/07/95	2		11	07	11/08/95		
24	Thomas, Jeff	IN	11-1734	11/13/95	3		11	13	11/16/95		
25	Toprani, Mark	IN	11-1736	11/14/95	3		11	14	11/16/95		
26	Toprani, Mark	IL	13-1811	11/17/95	3		11	17	11/22/95		
27	Thomas, Jeff	IN	11-1744	11/20/95	4		11	20	11/20/95		
28	Santiago, Patty	IN	11-1747	11/20/95	4		11	20	11/20/95		

15 **Click in cell A1 to deselect the cells.**

16 **Save the workbook and leave it open. You use it in the following lesson, where you learn about editing the pivot table.**

Lesson 4: Editing a Pivot Table

When you add a new field within the original list range, the range name expands to include the new columns. If, however, you want to change the view of your report by using these new fields, you must edit the pivot table.

Now you edit a pivot table to include the new fields you added in Lesson 3.

To Edit a Pivot Table

1 **Click the `Production Report` sheet tab of the `Loans` workbook.**

The `Loan Officer Report` pivot table is displayed.

2 **Click cell A8 and click the Refresh Data button on the PivotTable toolbar.**

The pivot table is refreshed to make the new fields (columns) that were added to the source data available. However, there is no visible change to the table yet.

continues

To Edit a Pivot Table (continued)

3 Click the PivotTable Wizard button on the PivotTable toolbar.

You will use the PivotTable Wizard to edit the pivot table. The PivotTable Wizard – Step 3 of 4 dialog box is displayed onscreen. Two new buttons were added that represent the new fields, `Year App` and `Year to Prod.`, as shown in Figure 12.9.

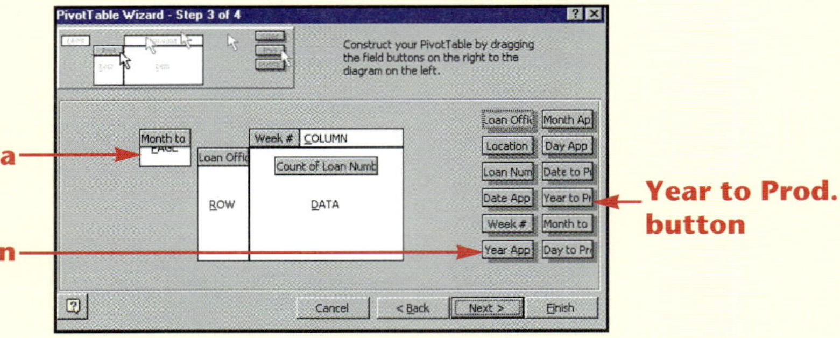

Figure 12.9
Two new field buttons have been added, as shown in the PivotTable Wizard.

4 Drag the Year to Prod. button to the PAGE area, above the Month to button, and click Finish.

It is important that the Year to Prod. button appear just above the Month to button in the diagram before you click Finish (see Figure 12.10).

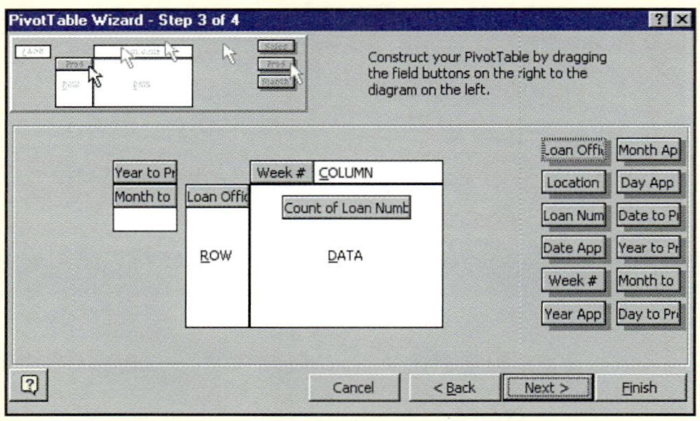

Figure 12.10
Drag the Year to Prod. field button from the right to its new position above the Month to button.

If you have problems...

If you don't drop the field button in exactly the right position in the pivot table, the button will not appear in the diagram. Simply drag and drop again. If you place the wrong field onto the pivot table, you can remove it by dragging it anywhere outside the table.

The new field Year to Prod. is added to the report in cell A3, as shown in Figure 12.11. You now can change your summary report view for each month and year.

Figure 12.11
The Year to Prod. field is added to the Loan Officer Report.

New field

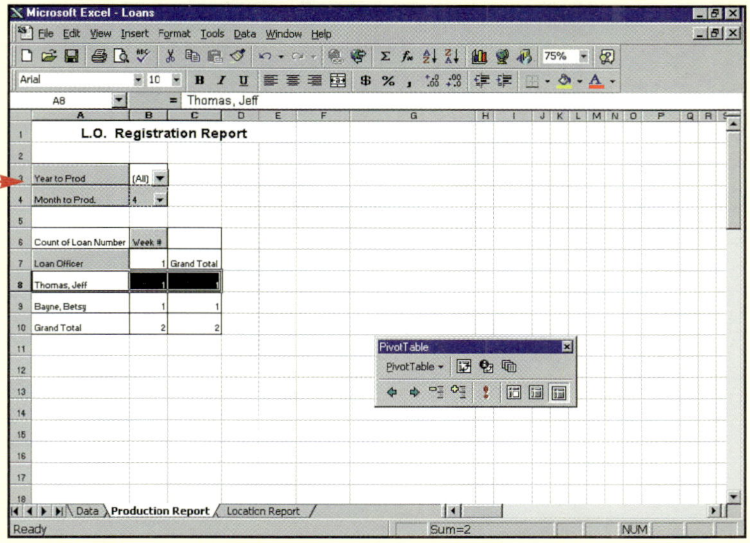

❺ **Click the** `Location Report` **sheet tab and verify that A6:I9 is selected.**

❻ **Click the Refresh Data button on the PivotTable toolbar.**

The pivot table is refreshed to make the new fields (columns) that you added to the source data available, even if there is no visible change to the table.

❼ **Click the PivotTable Wizard button on the PivotTable toolbar.**

❽ **Drag the Year to Prod. button to the Page area, as shown in Figure 12.12, and click Finish.**

Figure 12.12
The Year to Prod. button is added to the pivot table.

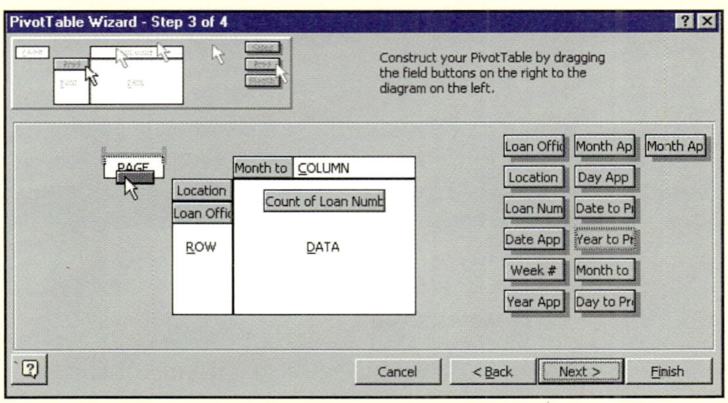

The new field `Year to Prod.` is added to the report in cell A2, as shown in Figure 12.13. Rather than displaying part of 1995 and the first four months of 1996 in the report as currently shown, you now can change your summary report view for each year.

continues

To Edit a Pivot Table (continued)

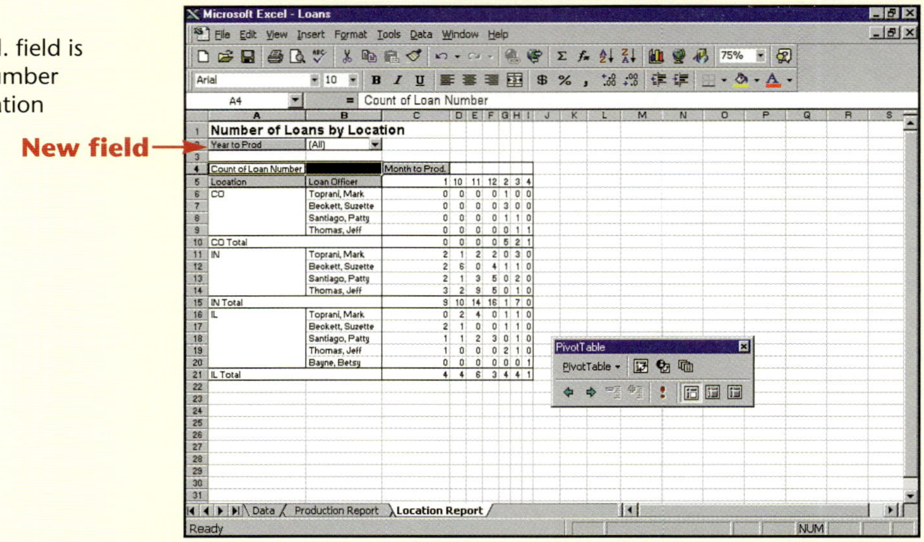

Figure 12.13
The Year to Prod. field is added to the Number of Loans by Location Report.

9 **Save the workbook and keep it open. You use it in the next lesson, where you learn about grouping data in a pivot table.**

Lesson 5: Grouping Data in a Pivot Table

When you create a pivot table from a list, it may include more detail than you need for a particular report. In this lesson, you learn how to group a *series* in the pivot table and change the view of your data. This has no effect on the source data in the worksheet.

Series
A series is a range of cells that contain data represented by incremented dates, numbers, or text.

To Group Data in a Pivot Table

1 **Click the** `Location Report` **sheet tab, if necessary, to display that worksheet.**

This worksheet consolidates information by location, the loan officer who handled the loan for that location, and the total number of loans to production for the month. You want to change the view of this report and group and count the loans by quarters for the year 1995.

2 **Click the arrow in cell B2 to display the drop-down list of choices. Click** `1995`**.**

Months 10, 11, and 12 are displayed in the pivot table. Remember that this report was started in October of 1995, so the first three quarters are not available.

3 Select cells C5:I15. Click the Group button on the PivotTable toolbar.

Cells C5:I15 contain the months 10 through 12, which represent a series. Group1 is displayed in cell C5, as shown in Figure 12.14.

Figure 12.14
The series of months 10, 11, and 12 of 1995 are grouped.

Group1

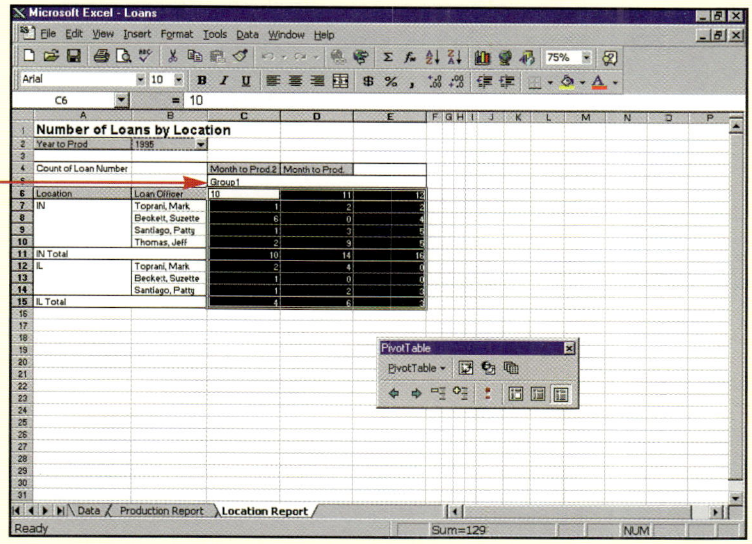

4 Click cell C5; then click the Hide Detail button on the PivotTable toolbar.

This hides the details of the group.

5 In cell C5, type `Qtr 4` and press Enter.

`Qtr 4` replaces `Group1` in cell C5. This is a change to the pivot table only.

The Location Report now provides you with a Quarterly Loan count for 1995, for each location, and by Loan Officer, as shown in Figure 12.15.

6 Select cells A7:A15 and click the Hide Detail button on the PivotTable toolbar.

7 Click in cell D1 to remove the selection.

The Loan Officer information is hidden from view and the report summarizes the data by location for the fourth quarter of 1995, as shown in Figure 12.16.

8 Click cell C5 and click the Show Detail button on the PivotTable toolbar.

The details for the three months in 1995 are displayed.

continues

To Edit a Pivot Table (continued)

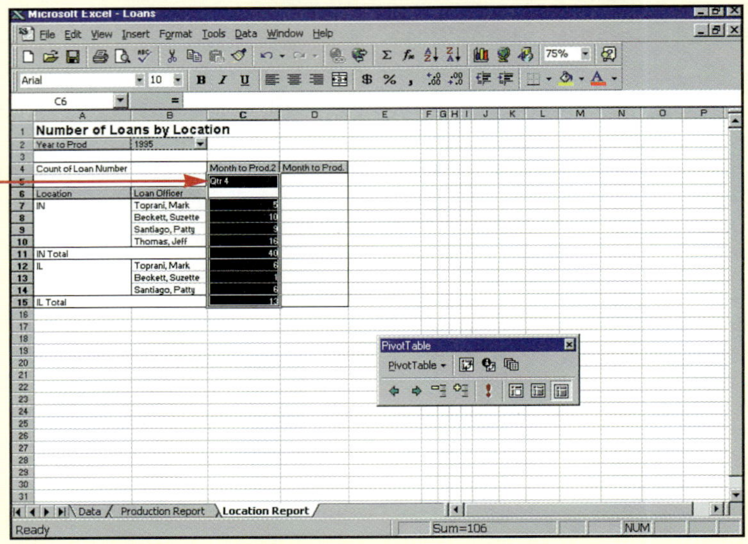

Figure 12.15
The report shows quarterly counts for 1995.

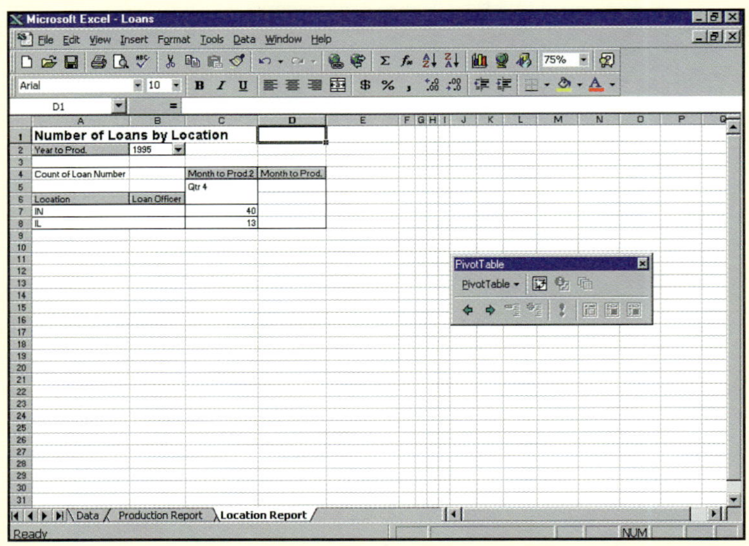

Figure 12.16
The Loan Officer information and monthly details are hidden.

9 **Save the workbook and leave it open. You use it in the following lesson, where you learn how to create a chart from pivot table data.**

Inside Stuff

You can either hide or show details in a group by double-clicking the cell that contains the group name (such as Qtr 4).

Also, changing the name of a field or item does not change the name in your source list.

Lesson 6: Creating a Chart from Pivot Table Data

In earlier lessons, you added fields and changed the view of a pivot table to create various reports. Remember that a chart can be a useful enhancement to a report and can add impact to a presentation.

In this lesson, you learn to plot the data from a pivot table view into a column chart to show the loans produced by location for the first four months of 1996.

To Create a Chart from Pivot Table Data

1 Click the `Location Report` sheet tab to display that worksheet, if necessary.

The data from this pivot table is used to create the column chart.

2 Click the arrow in cell B2 and click 1996.

The pivot table view changes to 1996 loan information, as shown in Figure 12.17.

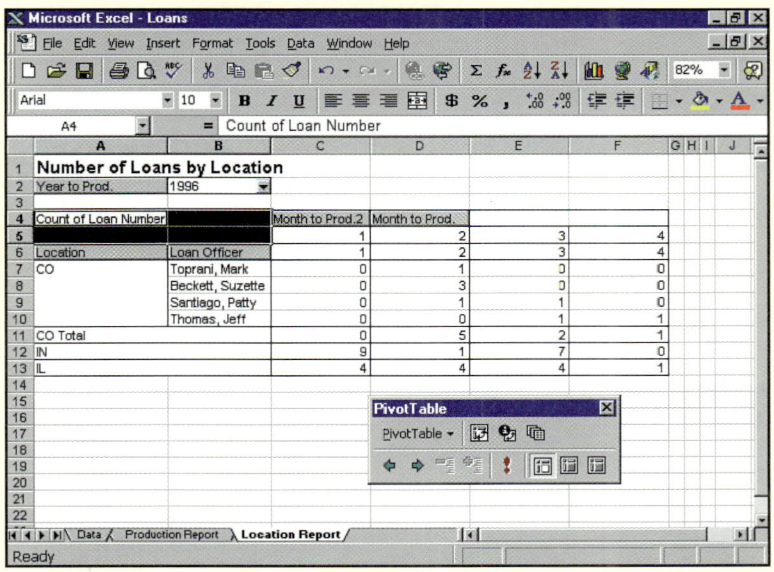

Figure 12.17 The pivot table displays 1996 loan information.

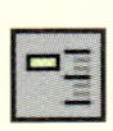

3 Select cells A7:A13 and click the Hide Detail button on the PivotTable toolbar.

Only the locations are now displayed in column A. You decide to chart this view with only the locations and monthly information showing.

continues

To Create a Chart from Pivot Table Data (continued)

Inside Stuff

You can sort items in a pivot table. After you sort an item, the labels are rearranged in ascending or descending order. Click the field name; choose Data, Sort; then choose the order. Choose the Labels option in the Sort box and click OK. For example, the Location field in this pivot table has labels that you can sort in alphabetical order.

4 Click the Chart Wizard button on the Standard toolbar.

The Chart Wizard – Step 1 of 4 dialog box is displayed on the screen so that you can choose a chart type, as shown in Figure 12.18.

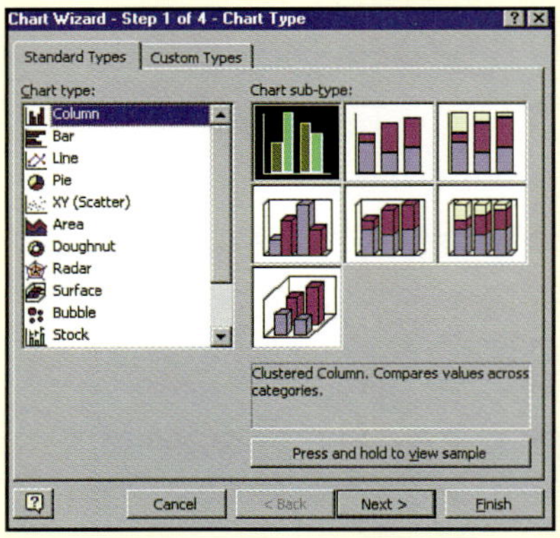

Figure 12.18
The first dialog box of the Chart Wizard lets you choose from many basic chart types.

5 By default, the Column chart type and Clustered Column chart sub-types are selected. Click Next.

The Chart Wizard – Step 2 of 4 dialog box is displayed, verifying the data source to be charted.

6 Select cells A7:A9 in the worksheet and type a comma.

If you have problems...

If the Chart Wizard dialog box is covering the pivot table, move it out of your way by dragging the title bar of the dialog box to another location on the worksheet.

The dialog box changes to the Source Data dialog box when the comma is added to the formula in the Data Range text box.

7 Select cells C7:F9.

The nonadjacent cells to be charted are displayed in the Data Range text box as `='Location Report'!$A$7:$A$9,'Location Report'!$C$7:$F$9`.

8 Click Next.

The ChartWizard – Step 3 of 4 dialog box is displayed, as shown in Figure 12.19, so that you can type the Chart and Axis titles.

Figure 12.19
Use the Titles tab to add a chart and category title.

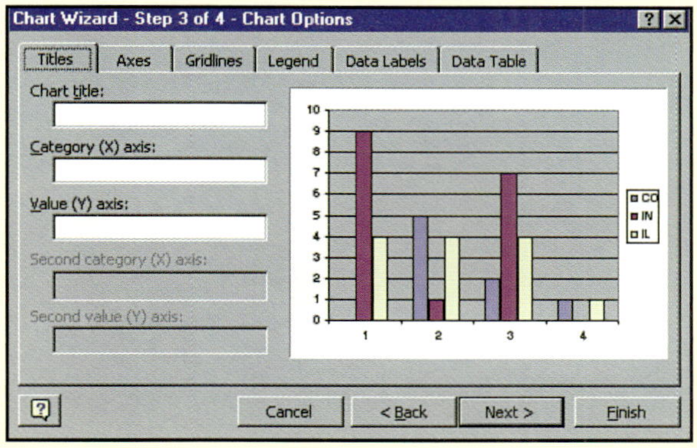

9 Type `Loans Produced` **in the Chart title text box and press Tab to move to the next text box.**

10 Type `Months` **in the Category (x) axis text box and click Next.**

The Chart Wizard – Step 4 of 4 dialog box is displayed so that you can choose where to place the finished chart (see Figure 12.20).

Figure 12.20
Choose either an embedded chart or a chart sheet for the Chart Location.

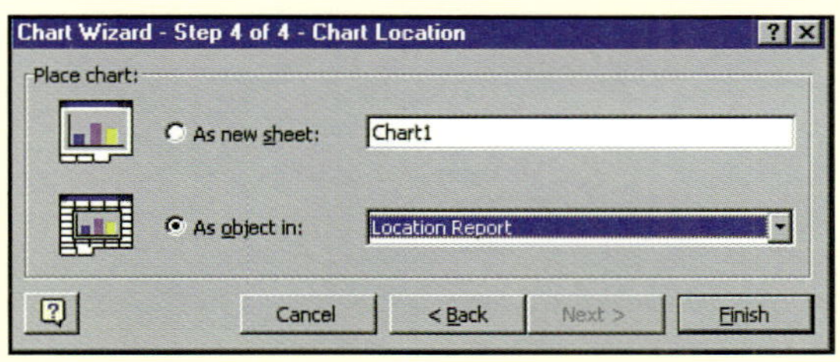

11 Click Finish to accept the default to place the chart in the Location Report sheet.

The chart is displayed onscreen.

If the chart obstructs your view of the pivot table as shown in Figure 12.21, simply drag the chart (and the Chart toolbar if necessary) to another location on the screen.

12 Save the workbook and keep it open for the next lesson, where you learn to edit the pivot table and update the chart.

continues

To Create a Chart from Pivot Table Data (continued)

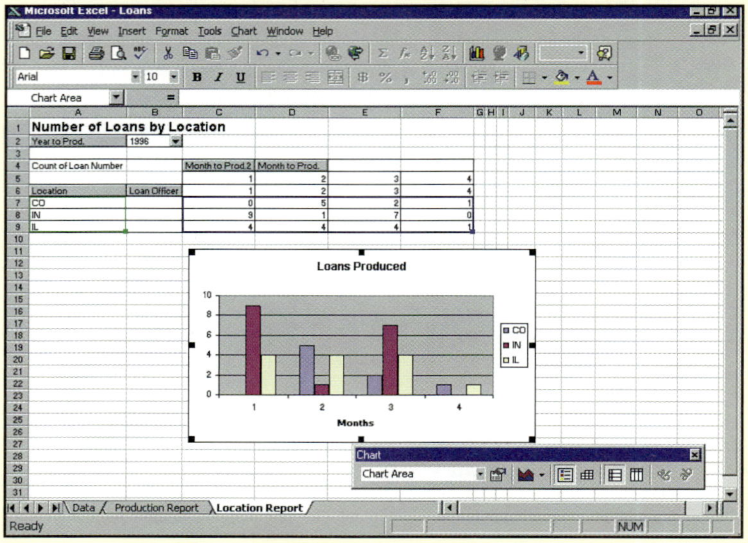

Figure 12.21
The completed chart shows the loans produced in 1996.

Lesson 7: Changing the Pivot Table View and Updating a Chart

Not only can you change the information in the list and update your pivot table, you also can update a chart created from the pivot table. In this lesson, you change the pivot table view and let Excel update the chart.

To Change the Pivot Table View and Update a Chart

1. **Click the** `Location Report` **sheet tab to display that worksheet, if necessary.**

   You change this pivot table view, and the chart reflects the changes.

2. **Click the arrow in cell B2 of the pivot table and click 1995.**

   This pivot table has multiple pages for each year. Because the main section of the pivot table was selected as the range to be plotted, the chart automatically updates when you click a different page view. In this chart, the three months of 1995 data are plotted.

3. **Click the arrow in cell B2 and click 1996.**

   You decide to change the pivot table view to plot the Loan Officer data for the first three months of 1996.

4 Select cells A7:A9 and click the Show Detail button on the PivotTable toolbar.

The Location and Loan Officer detail is displayed in the pivot table. Now that the detail rows are displayed, the original range selected for the chart has changed, and the chart is no longer appropriate. The chart needs to be updated to include the new ranges.

5 Select the chart.

The handles appear around the chart to show that it is selected.

6 Click the Chart Wizard button on the Standard toolbar.

The Chart Wizard – Step 1 of 4 dialog box is displayed. Click Next.

If you have problems...

If the Chart Wizard dialog box is covering the pivot table, move it out of your way by dragging the title bar of the dialog box to another location on the worksheet.

---

7 Select cells A17:E21 on the worksheet. The Source Data dialog box displays `='Location Report'!$A$17:$E$21`**.**

8 Click Next.

The Chart Wizard – Step 3 of 4 dialog box is displayed so that you can add or change the Chart and Axis titles.

9 Change `Loans Produced` **in the Chart title text box to** `Loans Produced for Illinois` **and click Finish.**

The chart is updated to reflect the new ranges, as shown in Figure 12.22. If requested by your instructor, print two copies of the Location Report worksheet in landscape orientation.

10 Save and close the workbook.

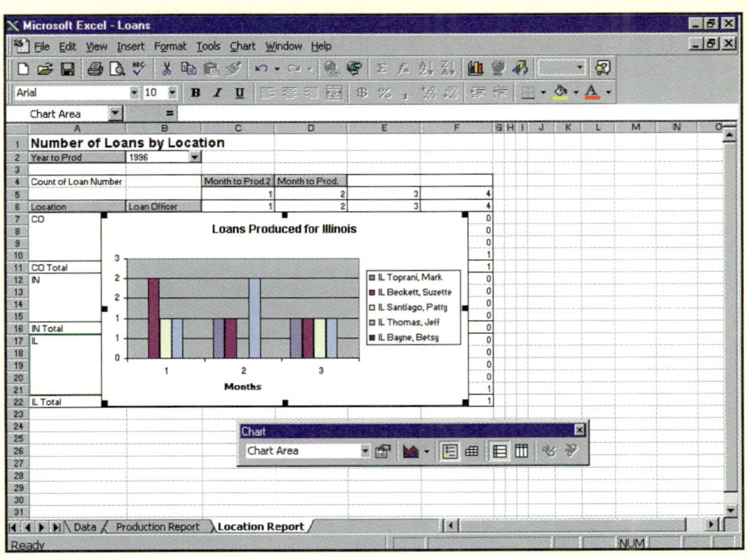

Figure 12.22
The completed column chart shows loans produced for Illinois.

Inside Stuff

Because your pivot table contains a page field, you must change the page each time you want to see a different view. Instead of individually viewing each page of your report, you may want to save each page view in its own worksheet in the workbook for viewing or printing. To accomplish this, click the sheet tab of the pivot table report you want to use. Click a cell inside the pivot table. From the Page view drop-down list, choose (All). Click the Show Pages button on the Pivot Table toolbar so that each report page can be displayed in its own worksheet with a separate chart created and saved for this report view.

If you have completed your session on the computer, exit Excel and Windows 95 before turning off your computer. Otherwise continue with the "Checking Your Skills" and Applying Your Skills" sections.

Project Summary

To	Do This
Add to a list and expand	Choose Data, Form. Click the New the Database range button and type the data into the fields. Close the data form.
Update pivot tables	Click inside the pivot table and click the Refresh Data button on PivotTable toolbar, or right-click inside the pivot table and choose Refresh Data from the shortcut menu.
Add a field to a list	Select the appropriate location in the list range and then choose Insert, Columns. Type the title of the field and enter new information into the appropriate cells.
Update pivot table to reflect a new field	Click inside the pivot table and click the Refresh Data button on the PivotTable toolbar or right-click inside the pivot table and choose Refresh Data from the shortcut menu.
Edit the pivot table and use a new field	Click inside the pivot table. Click the PivotTable Wizard button on the PivotTable toolbar. Drag the new field to the position you desire on the pivot table.
Group data series in the pivot table	Click inside the pivot table. Select the series to be grouped. Click the Group button on the PivotTable toolbar.
Hide or show details of group	Double-click the cell that identifies the group.
Create a chart	Click the Chart Wizard button.

Checking Your Skills

True/False

For each of the following comments, check *T* or *F* to indicate whether the statement is true or false.

__T __F 1. You can update your list and automatically expand the named range by entering data directly into the worksheet below the last record.

__T __F 2. If you add fields (columns) to your list within the named range, the range name is automatically expanded.

__T __F 3. The Hide Details button is used to group a series of data into smaller categories.

__T __F 4. Only one pivot table can be created from a worksheet list.

__T __F 5. An alert message is displayed when you try to change a field name in the pivot table.

__T __F 6. Pivot tables automatically update when new information is added to the source data.

__T __F 7. If you want to change the view of your report based on new fields you added, you must edit the pivot table.

__T __F 8. Before refreshing a pivot table, you must click a cell inside the table.

__T __F 9. To edit the pivot table layout, click the PivotTable Wizard button.

__T __F 10. You can right-click a cell inside the pivot table and choose Refresh Data to update the pivot table.

Multiple Choice

Circle the letter of the correct answer for each of the following.

1. Which commands are used to add information to a table or list?
   a. Data, Enter, Form
   b. Format, Add, Data
   c. Data, Form
   d. Update, Data

2. Which option is used to update a pivot table when the source data has been changed?
   a. Pivot Table
   b. Hide Details
   c. Refresh Data
   d. Update Data

3. To group a series on the pivot table, you use the following button:
   a. Show Detail
   b. Group
   c. Insert
   d. Show Pages

4. You can save and print the multiple pages of a pivot table by using the following button:
   a. Group
   b. Ungroup
   c. Show Pages
   d. Refresh Data
5. The following labels are available when you are designing or editing a layout for the pivot table:
   a. Row
   b. Column
   c. Data
   d. All of the above
6. If your pivot table includes a page field, which button do you click to see each page view on a separate sheet?
   a. Show All
   b. Show Pages
   c. Insert Worksheet
   d. Split Pages
7. To sort items in a pivot table, which option should you choose in the Sort dialog box?
   a. Ascending
   b. Descending
   c. Labels
   d. None of the above
8. What do you double-click to hide or show details in a group?
   a. Show Details button
   b. Show Pages button
   c. Cell that contains the group name
   d. Row header
9. What is another name for "database" in Excel?
   a. Range name
   b. Pivot table
   c. Worksheet
   d. List
10. What do you call a collection of data that contains all the information about a specific item in a database?
   a. Field
   b. Column
   c. Record
   d. List

Completion

In the blanks provided, write the correct answer for each of the following statements.

1. Use the ______________ option to add new data to your list and automatically expand the database range.
2. If a list has been changed, you can update the pivot table by using the ______________ option.
3. You can quickly hide or show details for a grouped series by ______________ the cell that contains the group name.
4. To edit the pivot table, you need to click inside the pivot table; then click the ______________ button on the PivotTable toolbar.
5. In the PivotTable Wizard, you can move a field to create a new layout. Just ______________ the field button with the mouse.

6. A(n) ______________ enables you to change the layout of data into different summary views.

7. Giving the database a ______________ eliminates the need to use cell address to define a block of cells.

8. A(n) ______________ is a dialog box that you use to add one row of data at a time into designated fields.

9. A record is a collection of data about a specific item in a database that is all stored in a(n) ______________ of the worksheet.

10. A(n) ______________ is a range of cells that contain data represented by incremented dates, numbers, or text.

Matching

In the blank next to each of the following terms or phrases, write the letter of the corresponding term or phrase. (Note that some letters may be used more than once.)

a. Name
b. Insert, Columns
c. PivotTable Wizard button
d. Group button
e. Data, Form
f. Source data
g. PivotTable Wizard - Step 3 of 4
h. Chart Wizard button
i. Refresh Data button
j. Show Details button

_____ 1. Use this command to add to a list

_____ 2. Use this dialog box to set the layout of the pivot table

_____ 3. Click this to update the pivot table

_____ 4. Choose this command first to add a field to a list

_____ 5. Click this to create a chart for a selected range

_____ 6. Click this to rearrange the layout of a pivot table

_____ 7. To quickly select the entire list, click the range name in this box

_____ 8. Click this to define a series as a group

_____ 9. The list of information from which the pivot table is derived

_____ 10. To see the hidden details of a group, select the cell containing the group name and then click this

Applying Your Skills

Practice

The following exercises enable you to practice the skills you learned in this project. Take a few minutes to work through these exercises now.

Analyzing Sales by Type of Product

A pivot table was created to analyze the sales of each product of the Reliable Tool Company by region for the first six months of the year. Using the Group feature in an Excel pivot table, group a series of information into categories for further trend analysis.

To analyze sales by type of product, follow these steps:

1. Open Proj1202 from the Project-12 folder on the CD and save it as `Six Month Sales Analysis`.
2. Click the `Production Report` sheet tab to display the pivot table.
3. Group the Products by series numbers into three categories (100-101, 200-201, 300-301).
4. Hide the detail for each of the three groups.
5. Edit the Group headings to read `100 Series`, `200 Series`, `300 Series`.
6. Save the workbook and leave it open for the next exercise.

Plotting a Production Report in a Chart

Use the information from the Production Report to create a column chart for a presentation.

To plot the production report in a chart, follow these steps:

1. In the `Production Report` worksheet of the `Six Months Sales Analysis` workbook, plot the range A4:D7 in a column chart (any type you choose), using the Chart Wizard. The Region labels should be on the x-axis.
2. Place the chart on this same sheet, starting in cell A12.
3. Resize the chart, if necessary, to display the x-axis titles.
4. If requested by your instructor, print two copies of the `Production Report` worksheet. Save the workbook and close it.

Editing a Pivot Table

A pivot table was created to analyze dessert sales by Store No. and type of dessert. Add a page field to this pivot table so you can change the view of the report.

To edit a pivot table, follow these steps:

1. Open the Proj1203 workbook from the Project-12 folder on the CD and save it as `Dessert Sales`.
2. Click the `Sales Report` sheet tab where the pivot table is located.
3. Click inside the pivot table and use the PivotTable Wizard to change the report so that the Store No. is a page field instead of a row field
4. After making this change, you need to add new data to the list for the month of July. Click the Desserts tab. Choose Data, Form; then update the list with the following new information for July for Store No. 101 only:

July	Key Lime Pie	101	850
July	Carrot Cake	101	700
July	Fudge Brownies	101	500

5. Check the range, Database, to be sure that the range expanded to include the new entries in the list.
6. Click the `Sales Report` sheet tab. Now click inside the pivot table and refresh the data in the pivot table.
7. Save the workbook and keep it open to create a chart from the pivot table in the next exercise.

Creating a Chart from a Pivot Table

The pivot table is located in the Sales Report sheet. Now you can use this report view to create a line chart for your presentation.

To create a chart from a pivot table, follow these steps:

1. Make sure that the `Sales Report` worksheet of the `Dessert Sales` workbook is active. Using the Chart Wizard, create a chart from the current view of the pivot table and place it below the pivot table. Plot the range A5:H7 in a line chart. Resize the chart to make it larger.
2. Click the arrow in cell B1 to change to Store No. 101, which is the only store updated for July. Note that the chart view changes, based on the page selected.
3. Click the `Desserts` sheet tab. Insert a new column where column B is currently located. Type `Year` in cell B2. Then fill in the year `1997` in cells B3:B59. The named range, Database, automatically expands and incorporates the new records.

4. Click the `Sales Report` tab. Click inside the pivot table and refresh the data.
5. Use the PivotTable Wizard to drag the Year button to the page layout area above Store No. Future reports can be summarized by year.
6. The new field was added in cell A1; select the chart and use the Chart Wizard to change the range to be plotted. It now should be A6:H8.
7. If requested by the instructor, print two copies of the Sales Report sheet. Save the workbook and close it.

Challenge

The following challenges enable you to use your problem-solving skills. Take time to work through these exercises now.

Analyzing Real Estate Salespeople

Open Proj1204 from the Project-12 folder on the CD and save it as `Real Estate`. Select A3:H24 and name that range `Database`. Click in one of the cells in the Database range and create a pivot table. The pivot table should appear in a separate worksheet. Move the Total field to the DATA area, Region and Salesperson in the ROW area, and Level in the COLUMN area. Name the pivot table worksheet `Table` (double-click the sheet tab, type the name, then press ↵Enter). Name the worksheet where the original data is kept `Original`. Save the workbook and print it.

Editing and Refreshing the Pivot Table Data

Add two salespeople to the list on the Original worksheet using the Data Form:

```
Rhonda Feinstein 1      Chicago 0      0      0      1
Harry Worthy 2    Atlanta 0      0      1      0
```

If necessary, when you return to the worksheet, copy the total equation from another cell to total the number of houses sold for these two salespeople. Then switch to the Table worksheet and refresh the data for the pivot table. Save the worksheet and print it.

Grouping Data on a Pivot Table

Select the Level 1 and 2 data and group it. Change the name of the group to `Novice`. Hide the Novice details. Save the worksheet and print it.

Rearranging the Pivot Table View

Drag the Region field label to A1. Select the Chicago region from the drop-down list. Show the details for the Novice group. Save the workbook and print it.

Charting the Pivot Table

Rearrange the layout of the pivot table to move Region from the PAGE area to the ROW area above Salesperson. Select A6:F11 and create a bar chart. In Step 2 of the Chart Wizard, specify that the Series are in columns. Click the Series tab and remove all the Series except Series5, which includes the range F6:F11 (see the Values box). Title the chart `Houses Sold by Territory`. Turn off the legend. Move the completed chart just below the pivot table. Save and print the workbook. Close the workbook.

PinPoint Assessment

You have completed the project and the associated lessons, as well as the "Checking Your Skills" and "Applying Your Skills" sections. Now use the PinPoint software evaluation mode to assess your comprehension of the specific exam tasks you have just learned. You can also use the PinPoint Trainer Mode and the Show Me tutorials to practice these specific exam tasks.

Project 13 Thirteen

Using Advanced Data Analysis Techniques

Checking Errors and Making Business Projections

In this Project, you learn how to:

Objectives	Required Activities
➤ Use Auditing Tools to Interpret Error Messages	Find Errors Use Data Analysis and Pivot Tables
➤ Use Auditing Tools to Check Worksheet Formulas	Check and Review Data Find Cells Referred to in a Specific Formula Find Formulas that Refer to a Specific Cell Use Data Analysis and Pivot Tables
➤ Use Goal Seek to Forecast Revenues	Use Data Analysis and Pivot Tables
➤ Use Solver to Maximize Profits	Use Data Analysis and Pivot Tables
➤ Create a Histogram	Use Data Analysis and Pivot Tables
➤ Create a Moving Average	Use Data Analysis and Pivot Tables
➤ Use Data Validation	Use Data Validation

Why Would I Do This?

Business decisions often involve making projections for the future or solving problems based on current data. One advantage of using a spreadsheet program is that it gives you the capability to make changes easily to the data and view various alternatives to see the positive or negative results that occur. You probably are familiar with Excel analysis techniques, including Goal Seeking and Solver.

Audit
To perform an audit, you cross-check formulas in a worksheet for possible errors.

In this project, you learn to *audit* your worksheets to make sure that the formulas are correct, and you learn to use Excel's data analysis tools to look at the statistical data and make business projections.

Lesson 1: Using Auditing Tools to Interpret Error Messages

Error value
An error value displayed in a cell identifies a problem in a formula. Excel uses seven error values (such as #NAME?), which always begin with the pound (#) symbol.

It's easy to make a mistake as you create or modify a worksheet. You can introduce errors when you enter or edit formulas or when you copy or move formulas. When Excel cannot interpret a formula that you enter in a worksheet, an *error value* is displayed in the formula cell. See Table 13.1 at the end of this lesson for a list of error values. Fortunately, when you see an error value in your worksheet, the Trace Error auditing tool can help you find the source of that error.

In this lesson, you use a worksheet created for a motel that shows the motel's revenues and expenses for the current year, as well as projections for the coming three years.

To Use Auditing Tools to Interpret Error Messages

1. **Open the file Proj1301 and save it as `Welcome Inn Income`.**

   This workbook contains three worksheets labeled `Revenue & Expenses`, `Chart`, and `Guests`.

2. **Click cell A1 in the `Revenue & Expenses` worksheet.**

3. **Choose Tools, Auditing, Show Auditing Toolbar.**

   The Auditing Toolbar is displayed as a floating toolbar on your worksheet, as shown in Figure 13.1.

If you have problems...

If the Auditing toolbar on your screen is docked below the Formatting toolbar, you can return it to a floating toolbar by double-clicking in the space between toolbar buttons.

Figure 13.1
The Auditing Toolbar contains buttons to control the cell tracers, comments, and validations.

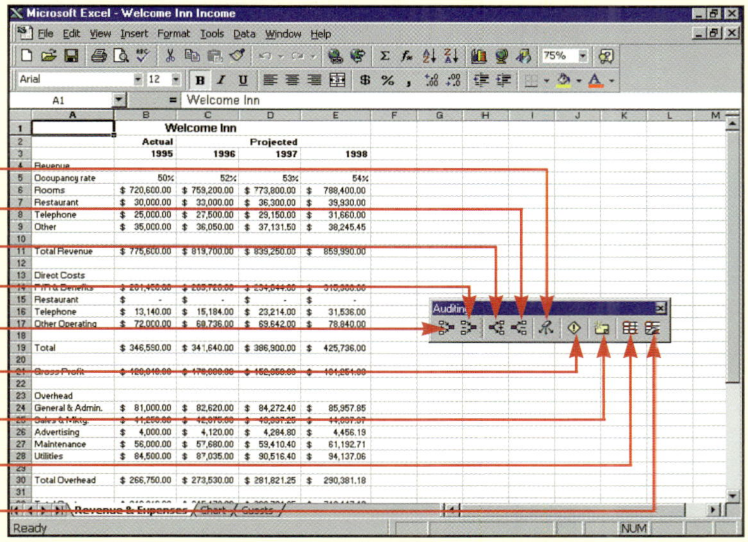

As you work through this lesson, it is easier to see the arrows and borders displayed on your screen by the auditing tools if you remove the gridlines from your worksheet. Choose Tools, Options and click the View tab. Click the Gridlines option to remove the check mark and then choose OK.

4 Click cell B34.

The `#VALUE!` error message is displayed in cells B34:E34 and B39:E39.

5 Click the Trace Error button on the Auditing toolbar.

A blue border surrounds the cells (B21:B30) that contain the error. A blue tracer line with an arrow that points to cell B34 also appears (see Figure 13.2).

Figure 13.2
Excel displays the cells that contain the error in the selected formula cell.

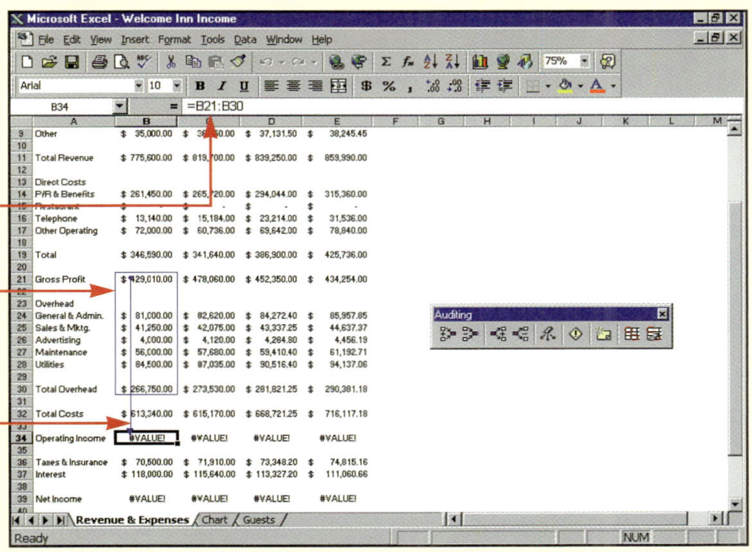

continues

To Use Auditing Tools to Interpret Error Messages (continued)

Table 13.1 (at the end of this lesson) indicates that the #VALUE! error means that the wrong type of operand or argument was used in the formula. In reviewing the formula, you notice that rather than typing a minus sign between the cell references to designate subtraction, you typed a colon (:), which identifies a range.

6. **Click the Formula bar; delete the colon and replace it with a minus sign or hyphen (-). Press Enter.**

   The hyphen designates subtraction and this corrects the error in cells B34 and B39.

7. **Copy the formula from cell B34 to cells C34:E34.**

   The formulas in cells C34:E34 and C39:E39 are corrected.

8. **Save the changes to the worksheet and keep the workbook open for the following lesson, where you use the Trace Precedents and Trace Dependents auditing tools.**

If you have problems...

Depending on the type of error value you are tracing, a red tracer arrow may be displayed. A red tracer arrow points to a formula that is the source of an error rather than the values involved in creating an error.

Table 13.1 A List of Excel Error Values

Error Value	Description
#DIV/0!	The formula is attempting to divide by zero.
#N/A	No value is available in the formula.
#NAME?	Excel doesn't recognize a name used in the formula.
#NULL!	An incorrect cell reference or range operator is used in the formula.
#NUM!	There is a problem with a number in the formula.
#REF!	The formula refers to a cell that is not valid.
#VALUE!	The wrong type of operand or argument is used in the formula.

Lesson 2: Using Auditing Tools to Check Worksheet Formulas

The Trace Precedents and Trace Dependents auditing tools can assist you in checking for obvious errors in the formulas that you developed in your worksheets, as well as errors that aren't immediately apparent. Beyond your usual routine of planning and developing a worksheet, you can add cross-checking the worksheet as a final step before making important decisions based on the information that is provided.

Using the Excel Trace Precedents and Trace Dependents tools, you can determine errors in formulas prior to looking at profit alternatives or business solutions.

To Use Auditing Tools to Check Worksheet Formulas

1 Click cell B11 in the `Revenue & Expenses` worksheet (in the `Welcome Inn Income` workbook).

You want to trace the cells that are used in this formula.

2 Click the Trace Precedents button on the Auditing toolbar.

A border surrounds the cells used in the formula and a blue tracer line connects the active cell with related cells, as shown in Figure 13.3. Scroll to the top of the worksheet if you don't see these lines onscreen. The tracer line ends with an arrow, pointing to the formula in cell B11. Following the line and the cells included in the border, you can see that cell B9 was excluded from the SUM function by mistake.

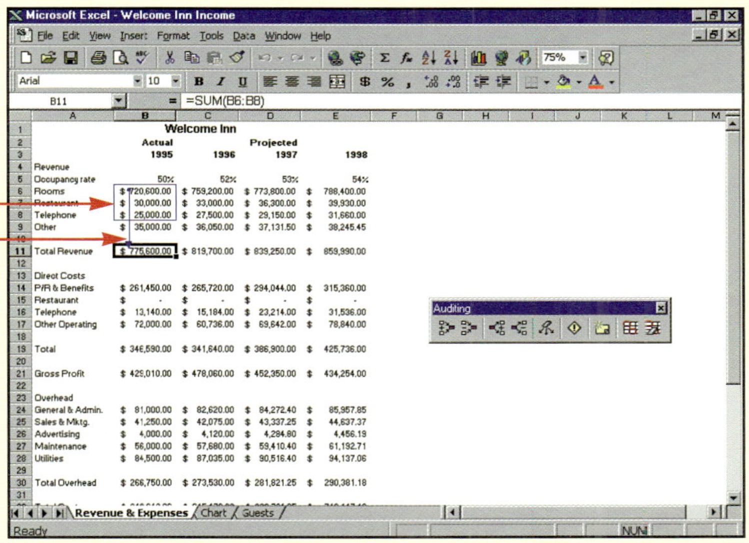

Figure 13.3 The worksheet after you trace the precedents for cell B11.

3 Click cell C11 and click the Trace Precedents button on the Auditing toolbar.

You can see, by following the line and the cells included in the border, that cell C9 was excluded from the total.

4 Click cell D11 and click the Trace Precedents button.

5 Click cell E11 and click the Trace Precedents button.

It is important that you display the precedent arrows for cells one at a time. If you select multiple cells and click the Trace Precedents button, you see the border and arrows for the only first cell in the selected range.

continues

To Use Auditing Tools to Check Worksheet Formulas (continued)

All of the formulas in row 11 are incorrect because the values in row 9 weren't included in the SUM formula (see Figure 13.4). The same error was made because the formula was copied from cell B11 to cells C11:E11.

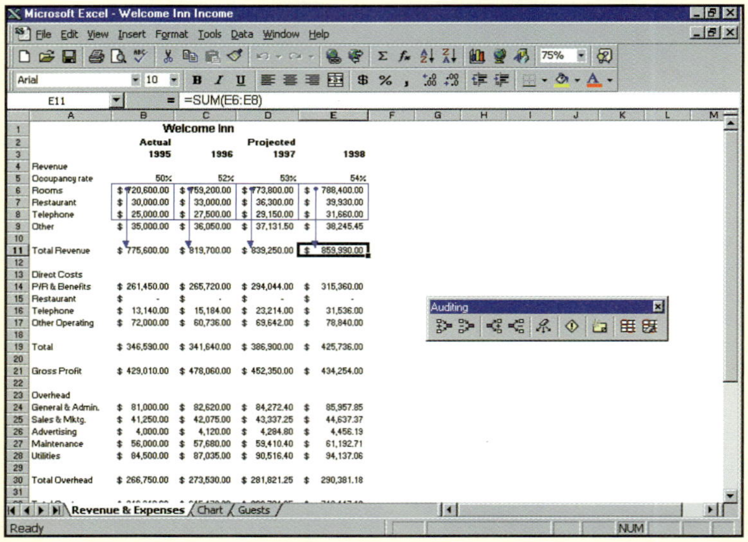

Figure 13.4
The worksheet after you trace the precedents of four cells.

6 Click cell B11. Correct the formula to sum the range B6:B9.

The correction is made, and the tracer lines and arrow are automatically removed from cell B11. It is important to note, however, that the corrected formula has to be checked for accuracy. The tracer lines are removed automatically because the formula has been changed, not because the formula is correct.

7 Copy the formula from cell B11 to cells C11:E11.

The correction is made and the tracer lines and arrows are automatically removed from cells C11:E11.

8 Click cell B32 and then the Trace Precedents button in the Auditing toolbar.

A blue tracer line with an arrow points from cell B19 to the formula in cell B32. Tiny blue dots in cells B19 and B30 show that the selected cell is dependent on these two cells.

9 Click the Trace Precedents button again.

Each time you click the Trace Precedents button, the next level of cells, with values used by the formula, is displayed.

10 Click the Remove All Arrows button in the Auditing toolbar.

All tracer lines and arrows are removed from the worksheet.

11 Click cell B21.

You would like to see which formulas reference the Gross Profit data in cell B21.

12 Click the Trace Dependents button on the Auditing toolbar.

The tracer arrow indicates that cell B21 is directly referred to by the formula in Cell B34.

13 Click the Trace Dependents button on the Auditing toolbar again.

Another arrow is displayed in cell B39 to show the next level of dependency (see Figure 13.5).

Figure 13.5
The worksheet, after you click the Trace Dependents button.

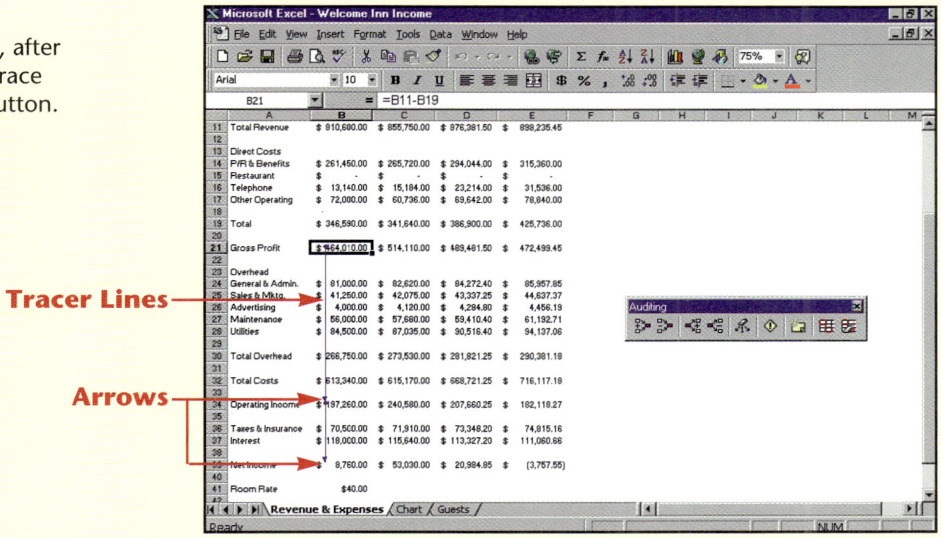

14 Click the Remove All Arrows button; then close the Auditing toolbar.

15 Save the changes to the workbook and keep it open for the following lesson, where you use Goal Seek.

Lesson 3: Using Goal Seek to Forecast Revenues

Goal Seek
A command that lets you find the value for a variable that will make the result of a formula equal to a specified value.

Input value
The adjustable cell value, used by Goal Seek to provide the requested solution.

After cross-checking formulas and correcting errors in your worksheet, you can use the worksheet to explore profit alternatives. Excel's data analysis tools can assist you. Use the *Goal Seek* tool when you know the result you want but need Excel to find the *input value* to get you that result.

In this lesson, you use the worksheet and chart, which show revenues and costs for a four-year period (one year of actual data and three years of projected data). After reviewing the report, you feel that the revenue projections are too conservative, and you decide to use Goal Seek to explore business alternatives.

To Use Goal Seek to Forecast Revenues

1 Click the `Chart` sheet tab in the `Welcome Inn Income` workbook.

The Revenue data series is shown in the chart by column bars; the Costs are shown by line markers. You want to see how you can increase the revenue projections by making changes to the worksheet.

2 Click the `Revenue & Expenses` sheet tab and click cell D6.

This cell contains the projected revenue for rooms for the year 1997, based on a 53% occupancy rate.

3 Choose Tools, Goal Seek.

The Goal Seek dialog box is displayed, as shown in Figure 13.6. Cell D6 is the cell to be adjusted.

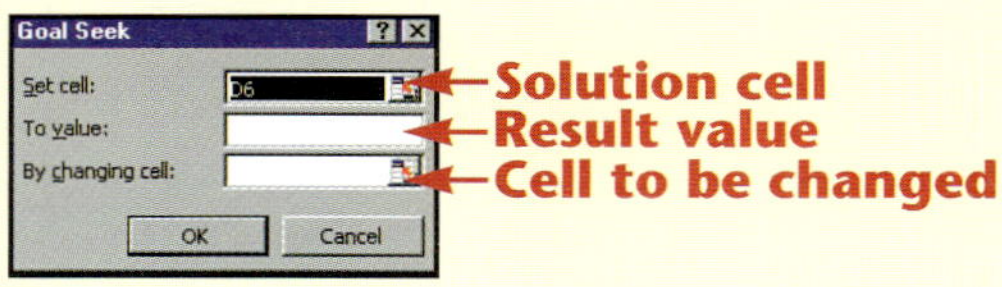

Figure 13.6
The Goal Seek dialog box lets you specify which cell value you want to remain constant and which you want to vary.

4 Click the To value text box and type `800000`.

This number is the new target value you want to solve for.

5 Click the By changing cell text box and click cell D5 in the worksheet.

The address, `$D$5`, is displayed in the text box. This address indicates the cell that contains the value you want to change while the Goal Seek solves for the target value.

6 Click OK.

The Goal Seek Status dialog box indicates that a solution was found that reaches the target value of 800,000 (see Figure 13.7).

7 Click OK again to close the Goal Seek Status dialog box.

The worksheet is updated with the changes. Cell D5 now shows that an occupancy rate of 55% is needed to reach room revenues of $800,000.

To use the Goal Seek option correctly, the cell that you identify in the Goal Seek dialog box as the By changing cell, must be a value and not a formula. In the preceding exercise, cell D5 contained the occupancy rate percentage as a value, and the Goal Seek feature was able to change it. However, if D5 contained a formula instead of a value, an alert box would display the message `Cell must contain a value.`

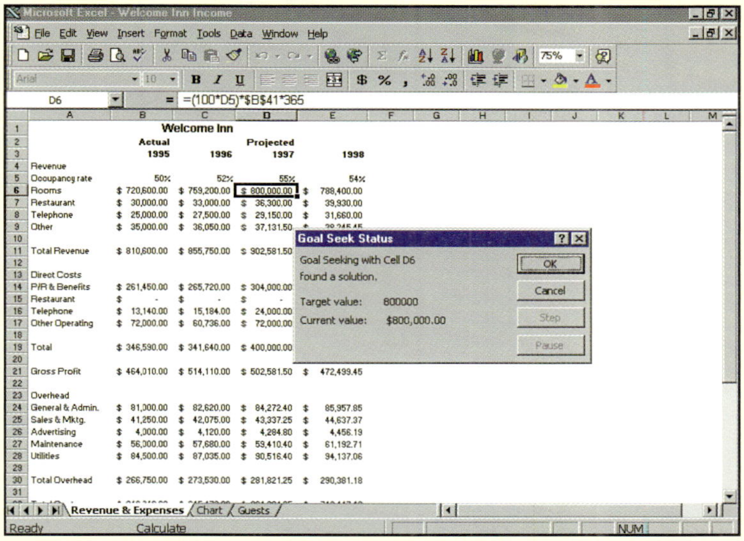

Figure 13.7
The Goal Seek Status dialog box shows that a solution has been found. Cell data in cells D5 and D6 has changed.

If you have problems...

If you change your mind after clicking OK and want to return to the previous view of your worksheet, click the Undo button on the Standard toolbar.

8 Click the Chart sheet tab.

The chart is updated with the Goal Seek changes. The total revenue for the third column in the chart (1997 data) has increased.

Now you want to change the revenue projections for year 1998. Your goal is to reach $950,000 in revenues in 1998. You can use the chart to activate Goal Seek.

9 Click the last column of the chart, which represents 1998.

Black squares appear in the Revenue column markers.

10 Click the last Revenue column marker again.

Black handles are displayed around only the last column, as shown in Figure 13.8.

11 Drag the handle at the top of the column to the $950,000 mark.

While dragging the handle, the value is displayed in the name box.

12 Release the mouse button.

Excel returns you to the `Revenue & Expenses` worksheet, and the Goal Seek dialog box appears with the Set cell text box displaying `E11` and a suggested To value change of `950000`.

continues

To Use Goal Seek to Forecast Revenues (continued)

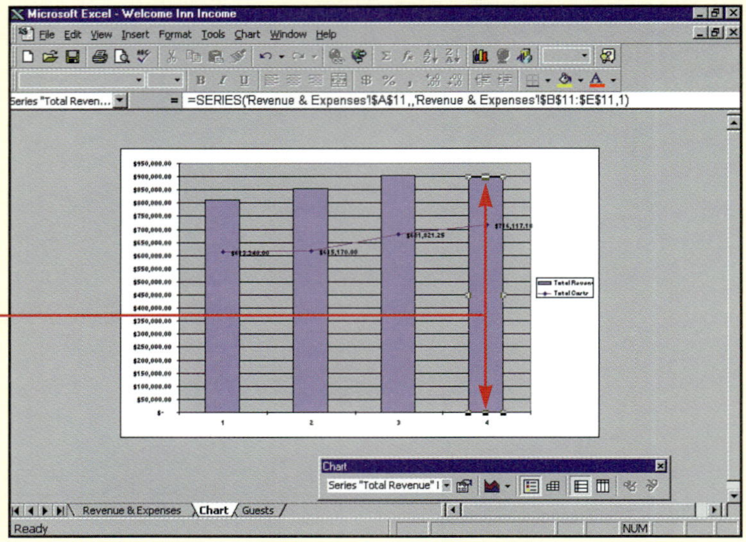

Figure 13.8
Black handles surround the column marker.

If you have problems...

If the Goal Seek dialog box does not display 950000 in the To value text box, you can click the Cancel button and readjust the column marker or just click the text box and type the number.

⓭ **Type** E5 **in the By changing cell text box; then click OK.**

The Goal Seek Status dialog box reports that a solution was found. Cell E5 on the worksheet displays an occupancy rate of 58% to meet the desired goal of total revenues of $950,000. The change in cell E5 updates the formulas in cells E6 and E11, as shown in Figure 13.9.

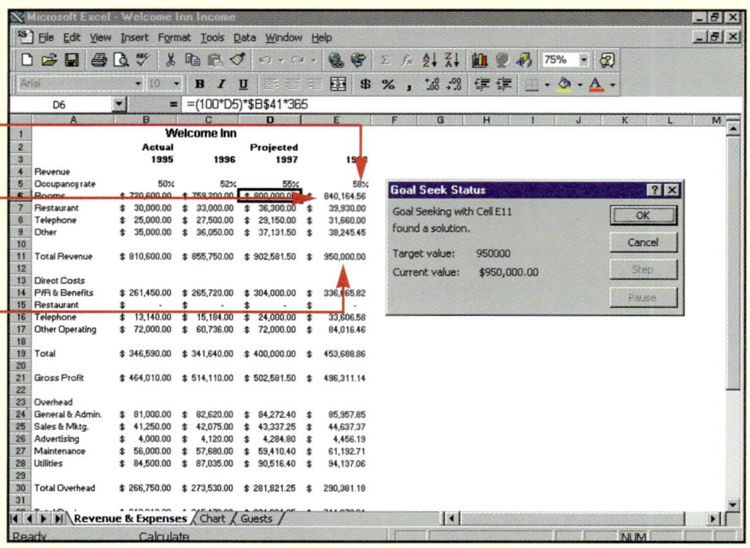

Figure 13.9
The worksheet, after you complete Lesson 3.

If you have problems...

If the dialog box is hiding the cells you want to view, drag the title bar of the Goal Seek Status window and move it to another location on the worksheet.

14. **Click OK.**

The Goal Seek Status window closes and the chart is displayed, reflecting the change of $950,000 for the total 1998 revenues.

15. **Save the changes in the workbook and keep it open for the following lesson, where you use the Solver tool.**

Inside Stuff

The Goal Seek command is activated from a chart only if the data series you are dragging is linked to a formula cell in the worksheet. In this example, the data series is linked to the formulas in row 11.

Lesson 4: Using Solver to Maximize Profits

Solver
A tool that helps you solve certain kinds of problems involving changing multiple cells.

Constraints
In Excel, constraints are limits set to control the changes made to a cell.

Like the Goal Seek command, the *Solver* command is designed to help you target the result of a formula. However, with the Solver option, you can explore more complicated business situations and find the best solution to a problem—in this case, maximizing profit. You can change more than one input cell and place *constraints* on the value of the cell to control the changes made to it.

In this lesson, you project a higher profit for 1998 by decreasing Welcome Inn's direct expenses.

To Use Solver to Maximize Profits

1. **Click the** `Revenue & Expenses` **sheet tab in the** `Welcome Inn Income` **workbook and click cell E32.**

This cell represents Projected Total Costs for 1998.

2. **Choose Tools, Solver.**

The Solver Parameters dialog box is displayed, as shown in Figure 13.10.

Inside Stuff

The Tools, Solver command is a special add-in feature of Excel. If it doesn't appear on the menu, choose Tools, Add-Ins to see if the Solver add-in is listed in the dialog box as being available. If it is listed but the box is not checked, check the box and click OK to make the add-in available on the menu. If it isn't listed or it doesn't appear on the menu, it means that it has not been installed. If this is the case, check with your instructor.

continues

To Use Solver to Maximize Profits (continued)

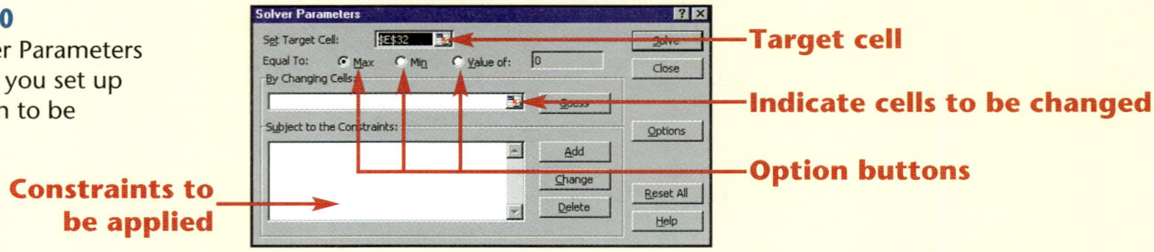

Figure 13.10
In the Solver Parameters dialog box, you set up the problem to be resolved.

3 Click the Value of option button and type `700000` in the text box.

This number indicates that the Target Cell (cell E32) should be equal to a value of 700000.

4 Click the By Changing Cells text box; then click cell E14. (You can also type `$E$14` in the text box.)

A *marquee* surrounds the selected cell.

Marquee
A flashing border that displays around a cell or group of cells.

If you have problems...

If the Solver Parameters dialog box obstructs your view of cell E14, you can drag the window title bar to move the dialog box to another location on the worksheet.

5 Type a comma in the By Changing Cells text box after $E$14.

Typing the comma enables you to add another cell address to the text box.

6 Click cell E26.

A marquee surrounds the selected cell.

7 Click the Add button to add a constraint.

The Add Constraint dialog box is displayed, as shown in Figure 13.11.

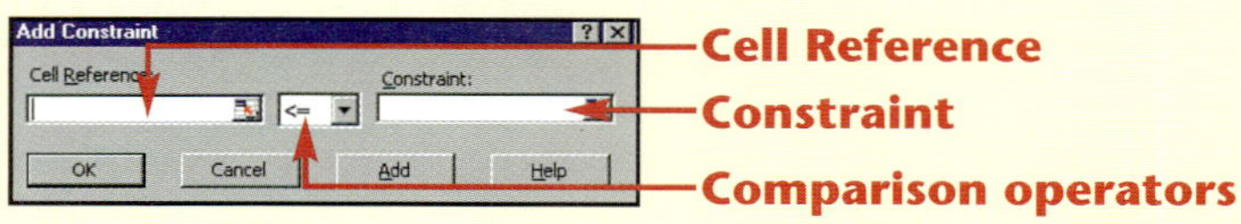

Figure 13.11
In the Add Constraint dialog box, you add your problem's constraints one at a time.

8 Type `E14` in the Cell Reference text box.

The cell reference E14 is displayed in the Cell Reference text box. Now you need to create a relationship between the referenced cell and the constraint. The Constraint is already set to <= (less than or equal to), which is exactly what you need.

9 Type `320000` **in the Constraint text box.**

The first constraint is complete. You want to lower the P/R & Benefits costs to see how it affects the revenue.

10 Click the Add button in the Add Constraint dialog box.

11 Type `E26` **in the Cell Reference text box.**

The Constraint is already set to <= (less than or equal to), which is what you need.

12 Type `4000` **in the Constraint text box and click OK.**

The Solver Parameters dialog box displays the two constraints you specified (see Figure 13.12).

Figure 13.12
The Solver parameters are set.

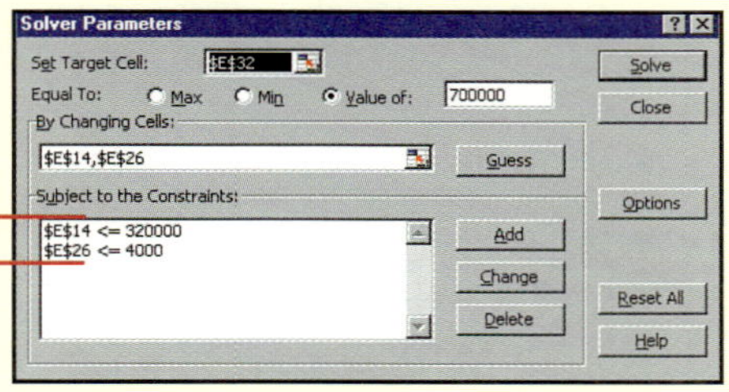

13 Click the Solve button.

The Solver Results dialog box is displayed, as shown in Figure 13.13.

Scenario
A named group of values assigned to variables in a what-if model.

Now you decide whether to keep the solution or restore the original values. Also note that the *scenario* you just created can be saved for future use. Because it's difficult to determine what changes Solver made to the worksheet, you can create a report that details the changes.

Figure 13.13
In the Solver Results dialog box, you can choose to keep the results or restore the original values.

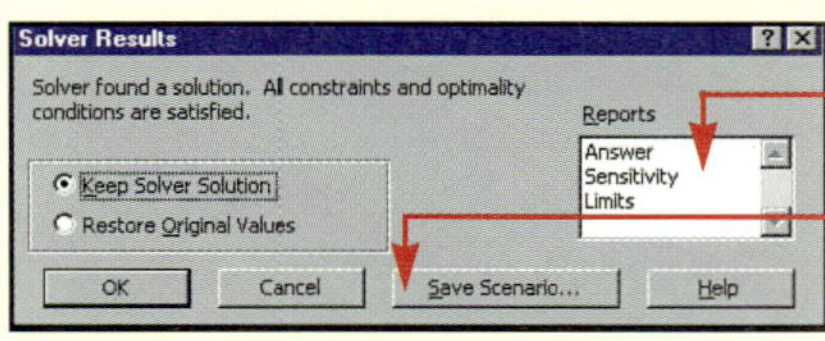

If you have problems...

It is important to note that if you accept the default Keep Solver Solution option button in the Solver Results dialog box, the worksheet is updated. This change is permanent, and the Undo feature will not work to restore the original values to your worksheet. Therefore, you may choose to save your worksheet prior to using the Solver tool, so you can return to a previous copy, if needed.

continues

To Use Solver to Maximize Profits (continued)

14 Click Answer in the Reports list box and click OK.

The dialog box closes, and the Answer Report is saved to a separate sheet as Answer Report 1.

15 Click the Answer Report 1 sheet tab.

The details in the report (see Figure 13.14) show the changes made to your worksheet in cells E14 and E26 to reduce your Total Costs to $700,000.

16 Save the changes to the worksheet and keep it open for the following lesson, where you use options from the Data Analysis Toolpak.

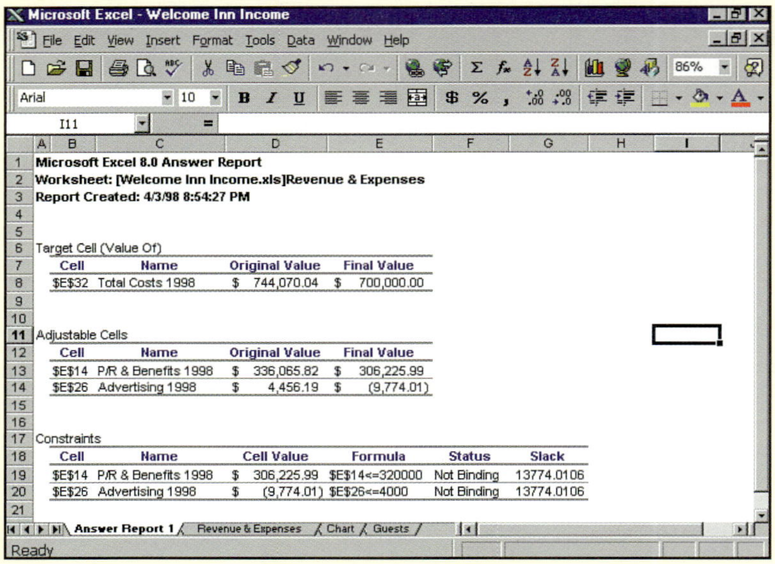

Figure 13.14
The completed Solver report is stored in a separate sheet named Answer Report 1.

Inside Stuff

To use the Solver option, the cells to be changed to meet your solution must be related through formulas. After the solver parameters are set, you can save them as a scenario for future use.

Lesson 5: Creating a Histogram

Another powerful analysis tool for working with large amounts of data is the *histogram*. A histogram (sometimes called *frequency distribution*) is a table that counts the number of entries belonging to a specific numeric category and plots the *frequency* with which the number occurs in certain intervals. The intervals are generally referred to as *bins* and are set up in a separate section of the worksheet. The bin values must be in alphabetical order. You can let Excel set up the bins, based on the data you are analyzing. The Histogram command creates a table from the worksheet data, showing the frequency of the worksheet values for each bin.

Histogram
Calculates cumulative frequencies for a cell range of data and data bins.

Frequency
The number of occurrences for each value in the worksheet data being analyzed.

Bins
A series of numbers, sorted in ascending order, used to group the occurrences of the values in the worksheet data being analyzed.

In this lesson, you create a histogram (from data that you accumulated this year) on the number of motel rooms rented each week. You want to determine the frequency of the number of rooms rented per week.

To Create a Histogram

1 Click the `Guests` sheet tab of the `Welcome Inn Income` workbook.

This worksheet contains a sample of the data you keep on the motel room occupancy each week at the Welcome Inn.

2 Choose Tools, Data Analysis.

The Data Analysis dialog box displays a list of the available Analysis Tools, as shown in Figure 13.15.

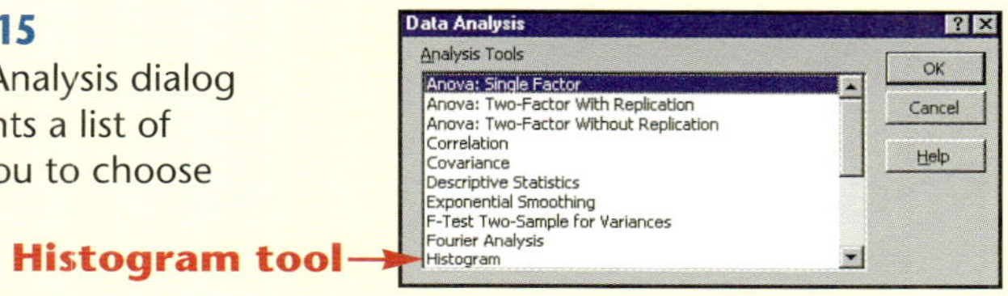

Figure 13.15
The Data Analysis dialog box presents a list of tools for you to choose from.

If you have problems...

The Tools, Data Analysis command is a special add-in feature of Excel. If it doesn't appear on the menu, choose Tools, Add-Ins to see if the Solver add-in is listed in the dialog box as being available. If it is listed but the box is not checked, check the box and click OK to make the add-in available on the menu. If it isn't listed or it doesn't appear on the menu, it means that it has not been installed. If this is the case, check with your instructor.

3 Click Histogram from the Analysis Tools list box and click OK.

The Histogram dialog box is displayed (see Figure 13.16).

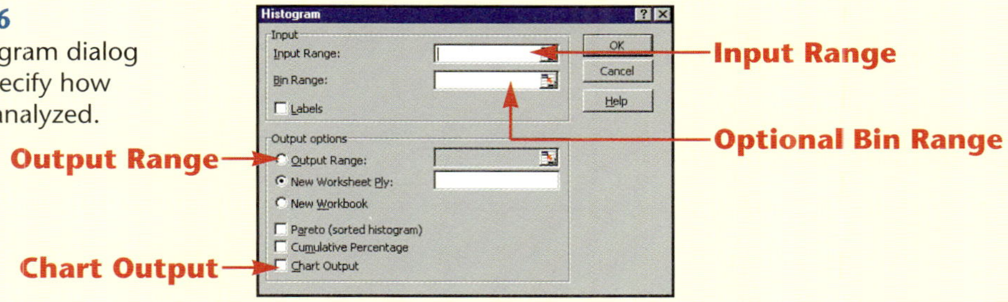

Figure 13.16
In the Histogram dialog box, you specify how the data is analyzed.

continues

To Create a Histogram (continued)

4 The insertion point, by default, should be in the Input Range text box. If it isn't, click in this text box and use the mouse to select the range B2:B40 on the worksheet.

The Input Range is displayed in the dialog box, and a marquee surrounds the selected cells. (If you prefer, you can type the range `B2:B40` in the text box.)

If you omit the Bin Range, Excel creates ten equal interval bins automatically. In this lesson, you leave the text box blank so that Excel creates a set of evenly distributed bins between the minimum and maximum values that you show in the worksheet.

5 Click the Output Range option button; in the Output Range text box, type `D2`.

This designates cell D2 as the starting point of the output range. The output fills down and to the right of this cell. Be sure to specify a blank area of the worksheet so that you won't overwrite any existing data.

6 Click the Chart Output check box.

This action generates a chart along with the output table. The Histogram dialog box is now complete (see Figure 13.17).

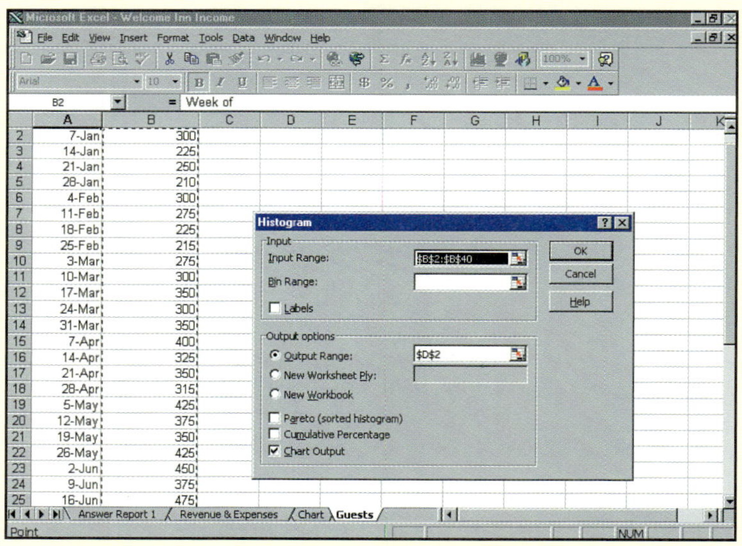

Figure 13.17
The completed Histogram dialog box specifies input and output ranges and a chart.

7 Click OK.

The Bin and Frequency distribution is displayed on the worksheet, starting in cell D2. A Histogram chart shows the frequency of the number of rooms rented per week (see Figure 13.18).

If you have problems...

You might need to use the scroll arrows to bring the output range and Histogram chart into full view.

The chart needs to be resized to display all the data.

8 **Click the border of the chart to select the chart and drag the bottom-left handle to row 21 (approximately) in the worksheet. This lengthens the chart (see Figure 13.19).**

At a glance, the Histogram table and chart help you get a picture of the weekly room rentals for the nine-month period being analyzed. The category of the number of room rentals per week (the Bin category in the chart) shows you the highs and lows of your motel business.

9 **Save the changes to the workbook and keep it open for the following lesson, where you use Moving average to smooth the time-series data and see trends in weekly room rentals.**

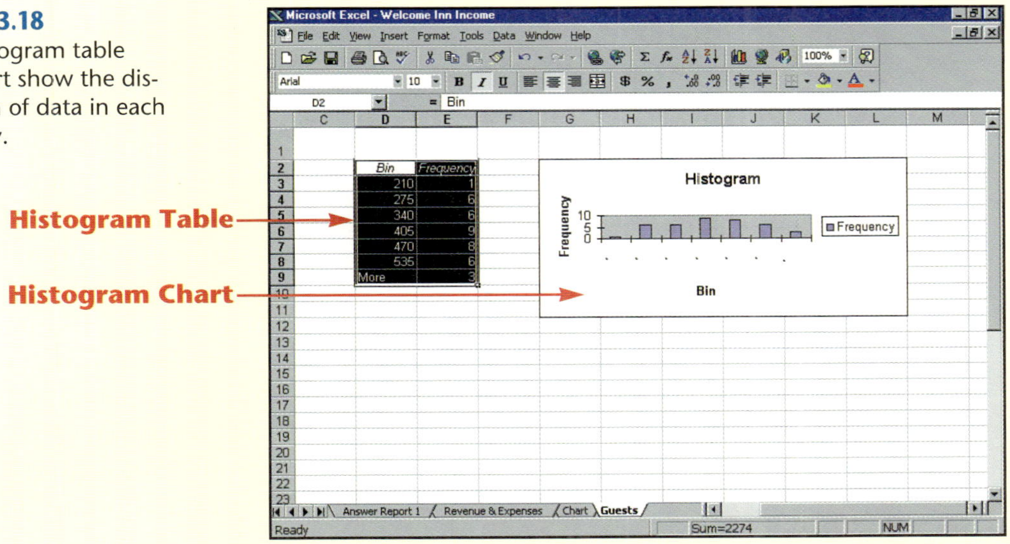

Figure 13.18
The Histogram table and chart show the distribution of data in each category.

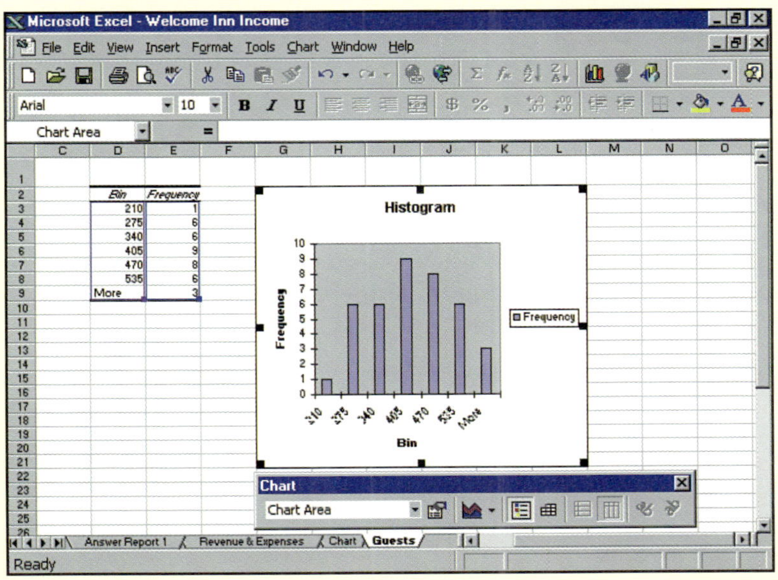

Figure 13.19
The revised chart clearly displays the Bin and Frequency categories.

Lesson 6: Creating a Moving Average

Moving Average
A command used to smooth time-series data. Each period in the Moving Average is the average of several previous periods.

If your business uses an Excel worksheet to keep track of company data over a period of time, you may want to analyze the data to see business trends. If the data fluctuates frequently, it is hard to see underlying trends; so Excel provides the *Moving Average* command, which assists you by smoothing out the data variations.

In this lesson, you create a Moving Average chart to help you see any trends based on the weekly room rentals for the past nine months. At what time of year, for example, is weekly room rental the highest and lowest? These trends can help you project the future occupancy rate for your motel.

Exam Notes

The Data Analysis Toolpak contains 17 statistical commands and 2 engineering commands. You provide the data and specify parameters, and the data analysis tools perform the appropriate functions and generate the output. Some of the most useful data analysis tools are explained here.

Excel generates random numbers, with the Random Number Generation tool to assist you in creating realistic sample data for a statistical model. You can choose the type of distribution for these random numbers that then can be graphically represented in a Histogram. The Histogram evaluates performance by showing the distribution of the values in your data set in a frequency table and chart. Similar to a histogram, the Rank and Percentile tool also can be used for evaluating performance. It creates a table showing Ordinal and Percentage rank of the values in a data set.

The Moving Average and Exponential Smoothing tools assist you in analyzing data that is tracked over time. Time-series data may fluctuate, making it difficult to see underlying trends. A Moving Average smoothes data by averaging the last few periods of data; Exponential Smoothing smoothes data but places more weight on the recent data.

To Create a Moving Average

1. **Click the `Guests` sheet tab of the `Welcome Inn Income` workbook.**

   You use the data in this worksheet to create the Moving Average chart.

2. **Choose Tools, Data Analysis.**

   The Data Analysis dialog box is displayed.

3. **Select the Moving Average option from the Analysis Tools list and click OK.**

   The Moving Average dialog box is displayed. You need to complete the Input Range, Output Range, and Chart Output options.

4. **The insertion point, by default, should be in the Input Range text box. If not, click in this text box and select cells B2:B40.**

   The Input Range displays `$B$2:$B$40`.

5 Click the Output Range text box and click cell A45.

This cell address designates the top-left corner of the output range. Select a location that won't overwrite existing data.

6 Click the Chart Output check box to place a check mark in the box.

This action generates a chart with the output table. The Moving Average dialog box is complete, as shown in Figure 13.20.

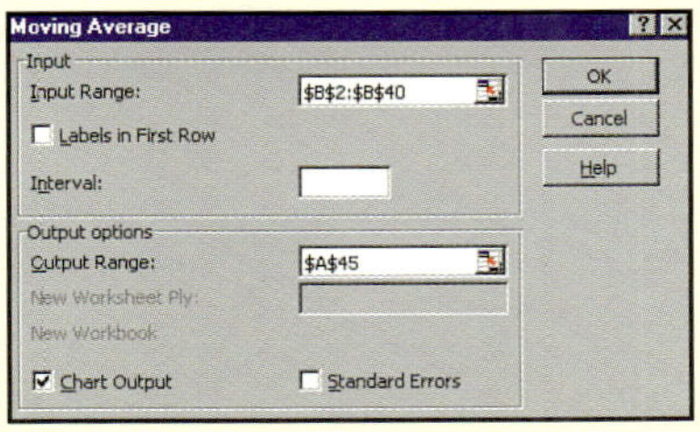

Figure 13.20
The completed Moving Average dialog box specifies input and output ranges and a chart.

7 Click OK.

The Moving Average data and chart is displayed in the Guests worksheet beginning in cell A45 (see Figure 13.21).

If you have problems...

You might need to use the scroll arrows to bring the output range and Moving Average chart into full view.

The chart needs to be resized to display all the data.

8 Click the border of the chart to select the chart and drag the bottom-left handle to row 63 (approximately) in the worksheet; this lengthens the chart, as shown in Figure 13.22.

In the Moving Average chart, the data is smoothed to show a trend in room rentals over the 39-week period. Note that the early weeks of January show the lowest room rentals. Room rentals gradually increase over the weeks and peak in Weeks 33 and 34 in August (summer season). Room rentals then drop from Week 35 to 39 to show a downward trend when summer is over.

9 Save your work and leave the workbook open for the next lesson.

continues

To Create a Moving Average (continued)

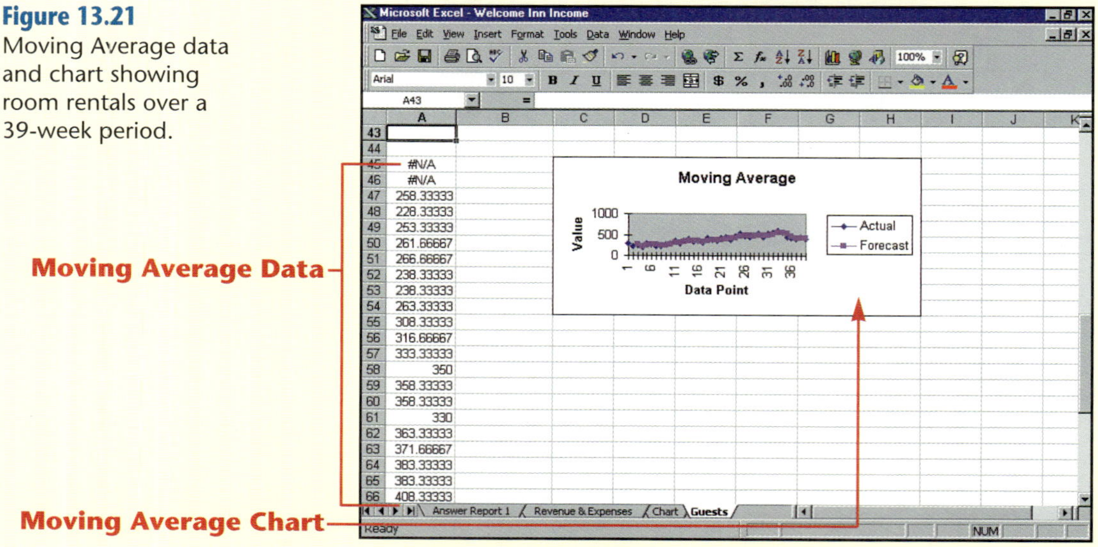

Figure 13.21
Moving Average data and chart showing room rentals over a 39-week period.

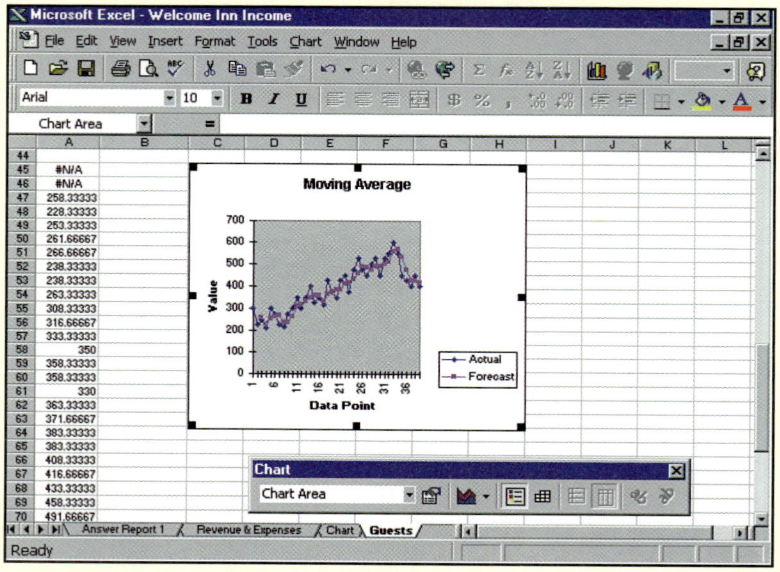

Figure 13.22
The revised Moving Average data and chart is easier to read.

Inside Stuff

You'll notice #N/A displayed in cells A45 and A46. The Moving Average command did not have enough data to average; until there is enough data, the data cannot be smoothed.

The majority of the data analysis tools provided by Excel are used for sophisticated analyses performed by scientists, engineers, and researchers. Before you use a data analysis tool, you need to understand the specific statistical or engineering area for which you are developing the analysis, so you know how to accurately interpret the resulting information.

Lesson 7: Using Data Validation

When you are not the only person entering data in a worksheet, or if you designed a worksheet for use by others, how do you guarantee that the data they entered is valid or correct? Microsoft Excel provides tools to validate the data.

In this lesson, you define what constitutes a valid entry and then you check the data already entered to see if it is valid.

To Define and Check Valid Entries

1. **Open the** `Revenue & Expenses` **worksheet of the** `Welcome Inn Income` **workbook.**

2. **Select the range B5:E5.**

   You are about to define the valid entry parameters for the selected range.

3. **Choose Data, Validation from the menu.**

   The Data Validation dialog box opens (see Figure 13.23). Your dialog box may differ from the one you see in Figure 13.23, depending on the validation criteria you set.

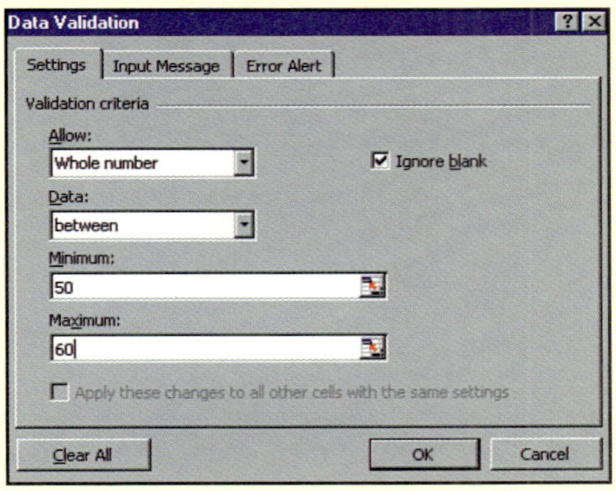

Figure 13.23
Select the type of data you want to allow in the selected range, and the dialog box changes so you can set the parameters for that type of data, which in this case is Whole number.

4. **Select the Settings tab if it's not already active.**

   On the Settings tab, you set up the validation criteria to define what data is considered valid for the selected range.

5. **From the Allow drop-down list, select Whole number.**

   By selecting Whole number, you are not allowing any decimal places, or fractions, to be entered. (Table 13.2 describes the available choices from this list.) Now you need to choose a comparison operator from the Data list.

continues

To Define and Check Valid Entries (continued)

Table 13.2 Types of Data Restrictions

Type	Description
Any Value	Places no restrictions on the valid entries. Use this setting if you want to display an input message without checking for valid entries.
Custom	Lets you enter a formula, use an expression, or refer to a calculation in another cell to determine valid entries. Enter a formula in the Formula text box, starting with an equal sign (=); the formula must evaluate True or False.
Date	Specifies that entries must be dates. Select an operator from the Data drop-down list and then fill in the options. Enter a date for the operator, a start date, or an ending date as required by the Data choice.
Decimal	Specifies that entries must be numbers or fractions.
List	Lets you specify a list of the valid entries. In Source, enter a reference to the range in the workbook where you have entered the valid entries, enter a reference to a defined name, or type the valid entries, separated by commas (for example, low, medium, high). Select In-cell drop-down to display a drop-down arrow that provides the list to select from when the person entering data clicks the cell.
Text Length	Specifies the number of characters for entries. Select a comparison operator, such as equal to, from the Data drop-down list. Enter a number in the Length box.
Time	Specifies that entries must be times. Select a comparison operator from the Data drop-down list. Enter a time for the operator in the Time box, as well as a Start time and an End time.
Whole Number	Specifies that entries must be integers. Select a comparison operator from the Data drop-down list. Enter the number for the operator in Value. Enter the smallest number for the operator in Minimum and the largest number in Maximum.

6 Select between from the Data drop-down list.

This choice lets you set a minimum and maximum for the values entered in the selected range.

7 Type `50` in the Minimum text box and `60` in the Maximum text box.

This limits the values that can be entered to whole numbers between 50 and 60.

8 Deselect Ignore blank.

When you deselect the Ignore blank option, you enforce the restrictions you set for blank cells, treating those cells as if they contain zeroes.

9 Click the Input Message tab and make sure there is a check mark in the option to Show input message when cell is selected.

Check this option when you want a prompt message displayed for entries.

10 In the Title box, type `Limits`**. Then type** `You may only enter whole numbers between 50 and 60` **in the Input message box.**

When someone attempts to enter a value in one of the cells, the input message appears. Now you need to enter a message to appear when an incorrect value is entered.

11 Click the Error Alert tab and make sure a check mark appears in the option Show error alert after invalid data is entered.

12 Select Warning from the Style drop-down list. Type `Invalid Data` **in the Title box and then type** `You may only enter values between 50 and 60` **in the Error message box. Choose OK.**

Now you need to test your settings to see how they work.

13 Click B5.

Your input message should appear by the cell, as shown in Figure 13.24.

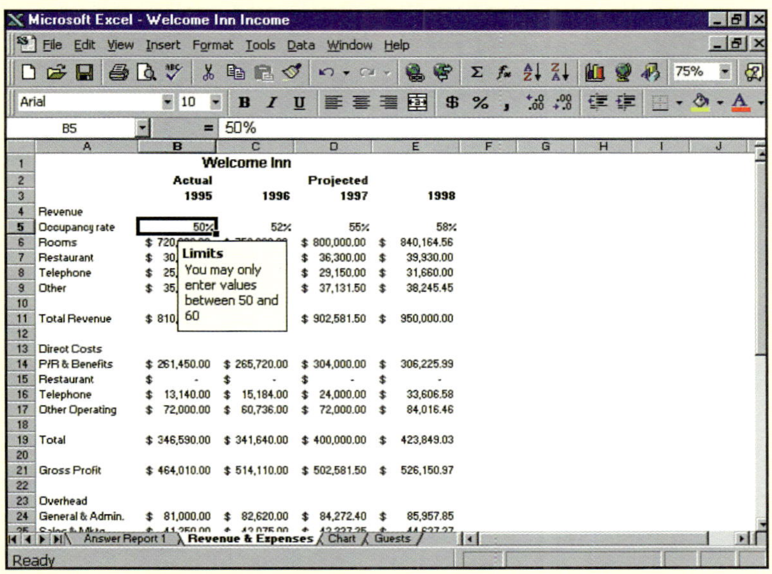

Figure 13.24
The input message you entered appears when you click one of the cells.

14 Enter a value of `62` **in cell B5 and press enter.**

An Invalid Data alert box appears, warning you that you may only enter values between 50 and 60 and asking if you want to continue. You can ignore a warning and continue.

continues

To Define and Check Valid Entries (continued)

15 **Click Yes.**

When you only have a warning, the user may override your input restrictions. Don't be surprised if you even get 6200%. Because it is possible for incorrect entries to be made or for incorrect entries to have existed before you set the validation restrictions, you may need to check your worksheet for any invalid entries.

16 **Display the Auditing toolbar by choosing Tools, Auditing, Show Auditing Toolbar from the menu.**

17 **Click the Circle Invalid Data button on the Auditing toolbar.**

All the values in cells B5, C5, D5, and E5 are circled. The values in those cells are percentages, which are actually decimal numbers (50% is 0.5 numerically). You need to edit your validation settings.

18 **Select the range B5:E5 and choose Data, Validation to reopen the Data Validation dialog box. Click the Settings tab.**

19 **Change the Allow setting to Decimal, the Minimum to `0.5` and the Maximum to `0.6`. Click OK.**

Now only the value in B5 is circled because it is truly an invalid entry.

20 **Save your work and print two copies of the workbook, if requested by your instructor. Close the workbook.**

If you have completed your session on the computer, exit Excel 97 and Windows 95 before turning off the computer. Otherwise, continue with the "Checking You Skills" and "Applying Your Skills" sections at the end of this project.

Project Summary

To	Do This
Show cells which are causing the error value in your worksheet	Click the Trace Error button on the Auditing toolbar or choose Tools, Auditing, Trace Error.
Show cells that are referred to in the active cell formula	Click the Trace Precedents button on the Auditing toolbar or Choose Tools, Auditing, Trace Precedents.
Show which formulas reference the active cell	Click the Trace Dependents button on the Auditing toolbar or choose Tools, Auditing, Trace Dependents.
Remove one level of trace precedent arrows	Click the Remove Precedent Arrows button on the Auditing toolbar.

To	Do This
Remove one level of trace dependent arrows	Click the Remove Dependent Arrows button on the Auditing toolbar.
Remove all tracer arrows	Click the Remove All Arrows button on the Auditing toolbar or choose Tools, Auditing, Remove All Arrows.
Activate Goal Seek	Click target cell. Choose Tools, Goal Seek.
Activate Solver	Click target cell. Choose Tools, Solver.
Create a histogram	Create the data set on your worksheet. Choose Tools, Data Analysis, Histogram.
Create a moving average	Create the data set on your worksheet. Choose Tools, Data Analysis, Moving Average.
Set data validation restrictions	Select the range for which you want to set restrictions and choose Data, Validation.

Checking Your Skills

True/False

For each of the following, check *T* or *F* to indicate whether the statement is true or false.

__T __F **1.** The Trace Dependents tool is used to show the cells to which a formula refers.

__T __F **2.** Excel uses seven different error values to indicate that it cannot interpret a formula.

__T __F **3.** The Goal Seek tool is automatically activated if you adjust a data series on your chart that is linked to a formula cell in your worksheet.

__T __F **4.** When completing the Histogram dialog box Input options, the Bin Range must be specified.

__T __F **5.** Solutions found through the Solver tool cannot be saved for future use.

__T __F **6.** To restrict the data that can be entered in a cell you use data validation.

__T __F **7.** When a #VALUE() error message appears in a group of cells, you click Trace Dependents to put a blue border around the cells that contain the error.

__T __F **8.** If you see a #NUM! error message in a cell, an incorrect cell reference or range operator is used in the formula.

__T __F **9.** To use Goal Seek correctly, the cell you designate as the By changing cell must be a formula and not a value.

__T __F **10.** To see the underlying trends of frequently fluctuating data, use the Moving Average command.

Multiple Choice

Circle the letter of the correct answer for each of the following.

1. When the Trace Precedents tool is used, a blue arrow shows
   a. The cells being referred to in the active cell formula.
   b. The cells with formulas that reference the active cell.
   c. The errors in the formula in the active cell.
   d. None of the above.

2. Which error value suggests that the wrong type of operand or argument is used in the formula?
   a. #NAME?
   b. #REF!
   c. #VALUE!
   d. #N/A

3. Which Data Analysis tool provides trend information by smoothing a time-series of data?
   a. Histogram
   b. Moving Average
   c. Sampling
   d. Regression

4. Choose Tools, Auditing to access the following auditing options:
   a. Trace Precedents
   b. Trace Dependents
   c. Remove All Arrows
   d. All of the above

5. When a solution is found with Solver,
   a. the worksheet is automatically updated with the designated changes.
   b. you can keep the Solver solution or restore the original values.
   c. you can create a report.
   d. Both (b) and (c) are correct

6. Which auditing tool locates all cells referenced by a formula that results in an error?
   a. Trace Precedents
   b. Trace Dependents
   c. Trace Error
   d. Circle Invalid Data

7. Which error message appears when the wrong type of operand or argument is used in the formula?
   a. #NAME?
   b. #REF!
   c. #N/A
   d. #VALUE!

8. When you know the result you want but you need to know what value to input in the formula to get it, which feature should you use?
   a. Data Validation
   b. Goal Seek
   c. Auditing
   d. Histogram

9. Which feature should you use if want a certain result but you want to change the input in more than one cell and place constraints on the value of the cell?

    a. Goal Seek

    b. Solver

    c. Data Validation

    d. Error Tracing

10. Which tool would you use to plot the frequency distribution of data?

    a. Goal Seek

    b. Solver

    c. Data Validation

    d. Histogram

Completion

In the blank(s) provided, write the correct answer for each of the following statements.

1. Use the ______________ tool when you have a solution in mind and need Excel to find the input value to give you this solution.
2. A(n) ______________ provides a frequency distribution for a range of data.
3. The Histogram and Moving Average tools can be accessed through the ______________ menu, ______________ option.
4. The ______________ tool allows Excel to change more than one cell and add constraints to the changing cells to assist you in reaching your desired solution.
5. To remove all tracer arrows that are displayed when using auditing tools, click the ______________ button.
6. A(n) ______________value displayed in a cell identifies a problem in a formula.
7. Clicking the ______________ button identifies all cells that contain values that are outside the limits you set by using the Data, Validation command.
8. The ____________ tool creates a table showing Ordinal and Percentage rank of the values in a data set.
9. A(n) ______________ error message in a cell means there is a problem with a number in the formula.
10. To smooth data by averaging the last few periods of data, select the ______________ option from the Data Analysis dialog box.

Matching

In the blank next to each of the following terms or phrases, write the letter of the corresponding term or phrase. (Note that some letters may be used more than once.)

- a. Scenario
- b. Trace Precedents
- c. Constraints
- d. Trace Dependents
- e. Goal Seek
- f. Moving Average
- g. Data, Validation
- h. Trace Error
- i. #NULL!
- j. Histogram

_______ 1. Click this button to show cells that are causing the error value in your worksheet

_______ 2. Shows the distribution of the values in your data set in a frequency table and chart

_______ 3. Tool that smoothes time-series data by averaging the last few periods of data

_______ 4. Click this button to show cells that are referred to in the active cell formula

_______ 5. Use this command to set restrictions on the data to be entered in selected cells

_______ 6. A named group of values assigned to variables in a what-if model

_______ 7. Click this button to show which formulas reference the active cell

_______ 8. Limits set to control the changes made to a cell

_______ 9. This tool lets you find the value for a variable that will make the result of a formula equal to a specified value

_______ 10. Indicates an incorrect cell reference or range operator is used in the formula

Applying Your Skills

Practice

The following exercises enable you to practice the skills you learned in this project. Take a few minutes to work through these exercises now.

Using Solver to Maximize Profit

Your company's revenues and expenses for the next four quarters are projected in a worksheet. The expenses are based on the percentages shown. You want to increase 4th Quarter profits by reducing expenses.

Use the Solver tool to meet your company's profit goal for the 4th Quarter by reducing expenses.

To use solver to maximize profit, follow these steps:

1. Open the Proj1302 file from the Project-13 folder on the CD and save it with the file name `Company Profit`.
2. Click the `Profit` sheet tab.
3. You want to try to reach a projected 4th Quarter profit of $120,000. Use the Solver tools with the following parameters:

   F17 is the target cell

   Equal to a Value of 120000

   F8 is the cell that you allow to be changed to reach a solution

   Constraints are F10<=392000
4. Keep the Solver solution.
5. Save the changes. Keep the workbook open for the next exercise.

Using Goal Seek to Forecast Revenues

You want to change your company's revenue projection for the 4th Quarter to $1,000,000. Adjust the data series on the column chart, which activates the Goal Seek tool, in order to specify the solution parameters.

To use goal seek to forecast revenues, follow these steps:

1. Click the `Chart1` sheet tab of the `Company Profit` workbook.
2. Click the last column in the Revenue data series. Click it again to select just that column.
3. Drag the column marker to 1,000,000 to activate Goal Seek. Complete the Goal Seek dialog box as follows: the Set cell already shows `F5` and the By changing cell is `F4`.
4. Accept the solution, and the Profit worksheet is updated to reflect the change.
5. Save the changes and print two copies of the workbook, if requested by your instructor.
6. Close the workbook.

Creating a Histogram

You completed the grades for the students in your Advanced Excel class and would like to see a frequency distribution based on the data. Use the skills you learned to create the histogram.

To create a histogram, follow these steps:

1. Open the Proj1303 workbook from the Project-13 folder on the CD and save it as `Student Grades`.

2. Create a bin range with the following numbers in cells D4:D8 of the Grades worksheet (numbers represent the letter grades):

   Cell D4 0

   Cell D5 1

   Cell D6 2

   Cell D7 3

   Cell D8 4

3. Using the Histogram data analysis tool, designate cells B4:B23 as the input range for the histogram, cells D4:D8 as the bin range, and cell F4 as the output range.

4. Choose the Chart Output option, and then complete the analysis.

   Note: Notice an extra bin value, named More. The bin More is for any item that is above the last bin. In this example, the last bin is in cell D8 (4). If a grade greater than 4 was entered in error, this is where it would appear. You could say that More is a nice way to track errors.

5. Save the changes and print two copies of the workbook, if requested by your instructor.

6. Close the workbook.

Create a Moving Average

You have tracked service calls placed over the past month. Because this data fluctuated throughout the month, it is difficult to see any trends in the number of service calls received. Smooth the data by creating a moving average with chart output.

To create a moving average, follow these steps:

1. Open the Proj1304 workbook from the Project-13 folder on the CD and save it as `Service Calls`.

2. Create a moving average from the data in this worksheet. Use the Input Range B4:B24 to create a chart in the Output Range, A30.

3. Save the changes and print two copies of the workbook, if requested by your instructor.

4. Close the workbook.

Audit a Worksheet

There are some errors in the Total Sales worksheet that you need to find and correct.

To audit a worksheet, follow these steps:

1. Open the Proj1305 file from the Project-13 folder on the CD and save it as `Total Sales`.

2. Click cell E9. Note that the total represents too large a number for the values contained in cells E6 through E8. Identify the cells that are involved in the formula in E9 by using the Auditing toolbar.
3. Identify other cells that contain formulas referring to cell E9.
4. Click cell E21 and trace the error in that cell.
5. Select the range B6:E23. Set validation restrictions to allow only whole numbers between 1 and 20,000. Have an error message appear noting that an incorrect number has been entered.
6. Circle all invalid numbers.
7. Save the changes and print two copies of the workbook, if requested by your instructor.

Close the workbook.

Challenge

The following challenges enable you to use your problem-solving skills. Take time to work through these exercises now.

Checking and Reviewing Data

Your supervisor has received a workbook completed by someone in another office. He would like you to check out the data to see if it is correct and to mark the errors so he can send it back for correction. Open Proj1306 from the Project-13 folder on the CD and name it `Review`.

Your supervisor claims the Q1 Total for Lee Wong looks too low. Find the cells that contribute to that total. Mark the cells that contribute to that formula.

The commissions are incorrect. Click on cell B17 and draw arrows to the formulas where that cell reference is used.

An error message appears in G6 through G15. Trace the error to see what is wrong, starting with G6.

Save the workbook and print the worksheet. Close the workbook.

Using Goal Seek to Plan Your Budget

Open Proj1307 from the Project-13 folder on the CD and name it `Projection`. In planning the budget for a new store your company is opening, you need to know how much income you need to make in the 4th Quarter to make a profit in the first year of $200,000. Print the worksheet.

Use the chart on the Chart 1 worksheet to try to adjust the Q1 profits to $0, the Q2 profits to $20,000, the Q3 profits to $60,000, and the Q4 profits to $80,000. This will change the values in the cells in row 4. Check to see what the total profit changes to in cell F14. Save the workbook and print it. Close the workbook.

Using Solver to Plan Your Fundraising

Your nonprofit organization is raising funds to build a children's wing on the local library. Although your activities were successful last year, your projected costs for next year mean the net won't be much greater. You would like to have a net of at least $10,000. Open Proj1308 from the Project-13 folder on the CD and save it as `Library Funds`. Use the Solver to find how to achieve this $10,000 net by changing the Printing and Advertising costs. Set the Printing so it can be no more than $12,000 and the Advertising no more than $7,500. Save the solver results. Save and print the worksheet. Close the worksheet.

Create a Histogram to Study Grooming Habits

Your daughter's third grade class is doing some projects on hygiene that are to be done with their parents. For her project, your daughter is studying dental hygiene. She surveyed the members of her class about their tooth brushing habits. For a period of seven days, each of the 20 students in the class kept a record of how many times they brushed each day. Your part of the project is to prepare a chart or diagram. Open Project1309 from the Project-13 folder on the CD to see the worksheet where you recorded the data from the survey. Save the workbook as `Tooth Brushing`. Create a histogram that displays the frequency of brushings over the one-week time period (hint: use input range I5:I24). Save the worksheet and print it. Close the worksheet.

Set Data Validation for an Expense Report

The employees in your company submit their expenses on worksheets. Your manager wants to be sure that they are entering the correct data. Open Proj1310 from the Project-13 folder on the CD and save it as `Expense Report`. Make sure that Laundry entries are limited to no more than $5.00 and that Meals entries are limited to $25.00. Limit the Personal Auto Miles entries to whole numbers up to 500. Have warning messages appear for out of limit entries, but allow the user to override them. Save the workbook. Then enter the following expenses for the week ending July 24:

Hotel:

Tuesday `$125.00`

Wednesday `$125.00`

Laundry:

Wednesday `$5.50`

Meals:

Tuesday `$18.95`

Wednesday `$26.31`

Thursday `$5.01`

Tips:

Tuesday `$3.00`

Wednesday `$4.00`

Thursday `$.75`

Personal Auto Miles:

Tuesday `305`

Thursday `305`

Circle the invalid data. Save the worksheet and print it. Close the workbook.

PinPoint Assessment

You have completed the project and the associated lessons, as well as the "Checking Your Skills" and "Applying Your Skills" sections. Now use the PinPoint software evaluation mode to assess your comprehension of the specific exam tasks you have just learned. You can also use the PinPoint Trainer Mode and the Show Me tutorials to practice these specific exam tasks.

Project 14

Fourteen

Sharing Workbooks on the Network

Maintaining a Project List

In this Project, you learn how to:

Objectives	Required Activities
➤ Set Up Workbook Sharing	Share Lists
➤ Work with a Shared Workbook	
➤ Track Changes	Track Changes Show History Resolve Conflicts
➤ Merge Workbooks	
➤ Discontinue Workbook Sharing	

Why Would I Do This?

Network
Hardware and software that connect computers, giving users access to shared data.

Shared List or Workbook
A workbook that allows multiple users on a network to view and make changes to the workbook simultaneously. Users who save the workbook can view the modifications made by others.

Do you have an Excel workbook that receives input from more than one person in your workgroup or department? Have you ever tried to open a workbook while someone else was already using it and wished that you could update it at the same time? Users of Microsoft Excel 97 on a *network* now have this ability. If you set up a workbook as a *shared list or workbook*, it can be viewed and modified simultaneously by multiple users. When saving the workbook, users view the modifications made by the other users. All users who want to make changes to the shared workbook must be working in Microsoft Excel 97 (either the Macintosh or Windows version).

Here is an example. You are a department manager who wants to maintain better control of your staff's outstanding and completed projects. You have set up a workbook containing your department's project list and project assignments. With workbook sharing, you and your staff can view the project list simultaneously. In addition, you can be updating the project list while other staff members are adding comments or completion dates to their projects. When a staff member saves the project workbook, he or she will see the changes made by the other staff members. Everyone in the department is kept up-to-date.

Lesson 1: Setting Up Workbook Sharing

To use workbook sharing, a workbook must be set up as a shared workbook, giving other users the authority to view and edit it. Workbook sharing is set up with the Tools, Share Workbook command.

To Set Up Workbook Sharing

1. **Start Excel.**

2. **Open the Proj1401 workbook from the Project-14 folder on the CD and save it as `Project List`.**

   This is the workbook you allow to be shared. Next, make changes to it and save it to a shared network drive. If you are not on a network, consult the instructor.

3. **Choose Tools, Share Workbook. Make sure that the Editing tab is displayed.**

   The Share Workbook dialog box appears, as shown in Figure 14.1.

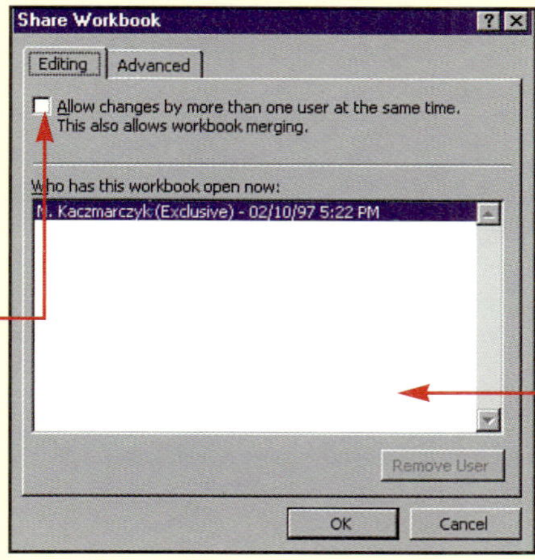

Figure 14.1
Use the Share Workbook dialog box to set up your workbook so that it can be shared simultaneously by multiple users.

4. **Select Allow changes by more than one user at the same time, if it is not already selected.**

A 30-day history of all changes to the workbook is kept so that you can reject changes made by a user and return to a previous version, if necessary. You can view this change history on the worksheet or on a separate History worksheet.

To increase the number of days saved in the change history, use the Advanced tab.

5. **Click the Advanced tab.**

The Advanced tab of the Share Workbook dialog box is shown in Figure 14.2. Each user can individually set options for receiving changes made by other users.

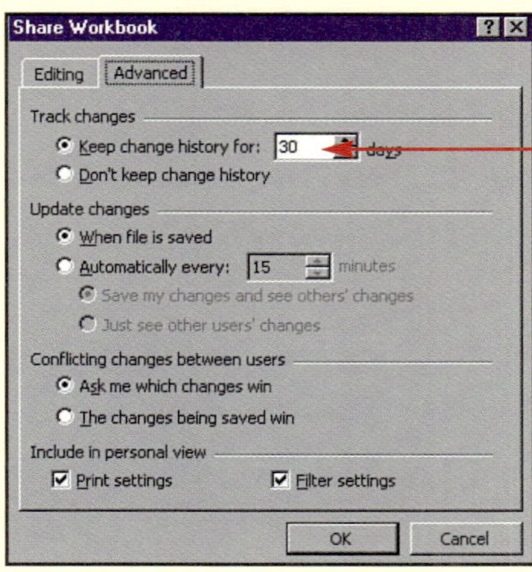

Figure 14.2
Use the Advanced tab to change the number of history days, when changes are updated, how to handle conflicting changes, and the personal workbook view for each user.

6. **Choose OK.**

You have accepted the settings. The Share Workbook dialog box closes and a warning box alerts you with the message `This action will now save the workbook. Do you want to continue?`

continues

To Set Up Workbook Sharing (continued)

7 Choose OK.

The workbook is saved. Close the workbook.

Lesson 2: Working with a Shared Workbook

Read-only file
A file that you can view but cannot make changes to or save using the same filename.

Excel identifies changes in a shared workbook by user name. Your user name should have been entered when Excel was installed on your computer. To be certain, choose Tools, Options from the menu, click the General tab, and type your user name in the User name box. Then choose OK.

When your computer is on a network, you can open your files and any other files for which you have been granted access rights. If you try to open a file on a network and it is already in use by someone else, you will open it as a *read-only file*.

With workbook sharing in Excel 97, users can simultaneously open a shared workbook. Open the shared document by choosing File, Open and change to the disk drive and folder containing the file. If the workbook is shared, the word `[Shared]` appears in the workbook's title bar, next to the filename.

To Work with a Shared Workbook

1 Open the file `Project List`; make sure that `Sheet1` is activated.

The workbook is open on your screen. Notice that the word `[Shared]` appears in the title bar, next to the filename. As a user of this shared workbook, you can enter data, change formatting, add and edit formulas, and insert rows and columns in the shared workbook.

2 Click cell E4. Type the current date and then press ↵Enter.

You have now entered the date that you started this project.

3 Choose File, Save.

Your changes to the workbook are saved. At this point, you would receive any saved changes made by the other users of this shared workbook.

If you have problems...

If you saved your shared workbook to a network location instead of your own hard disk, make sure that any links to other workbooks or documents are still intact. Choose Edit, Links from the menu and make any corrections to the link definitions.

Inside Stuff

The Excel actions in the following list cannot be performed in a shared workbook. If you implement an action before setting up the sharing feature in your workbook, however, that action is available after sharing the workbook. You also can discontinue workbook sharing to make the changes.

- Deleting worksheets
- Inserting or deleting blocks of cells (you can insert or delete entire rows and columns, however)
- Inserting or modifying charts, pictures, objects, or hyperlinks
- Merging cells
- Defining or applying conditional formats
- Setting up or modifying data validation restrictions and messages
- Assigning passwords to individual worksheets or to the entire workbook; changing or removing passwords
- Saving, viewing, or modifying scenarios
- Using drawing tools
- Grouping or outlining data
- Inserting automatic subtotals
- Creating data tables
- Creating pivot tables or modifying the layout of an existing pivot table
- Modifying dialog boxes or menus
- Writing, modifying, viewing, recording, or assigning a macro

Lesson 3: Tracking Changes

With a shared workbook, you can turn on the change history and highlight changes that are subsequently made to your workbook. If you allow changes to be made, it is important to show the details about these changes—who made them and when. These changes can be highlighted onscreen by displaying them in a different color for each user and can also be listed on a separate History worksheet.

To Track Changes

1 Choose Tools, Track Changes.

Two commands appear in this submenu: Highlight Changes and Accept or Reject Changes. For this example, you want all changes made by everyone to be highlighted on the screen and on a new sheet.

2 Choose Highlight Changes.

The Highlight Changes dialog box appears, as shown in Figure 14.3.

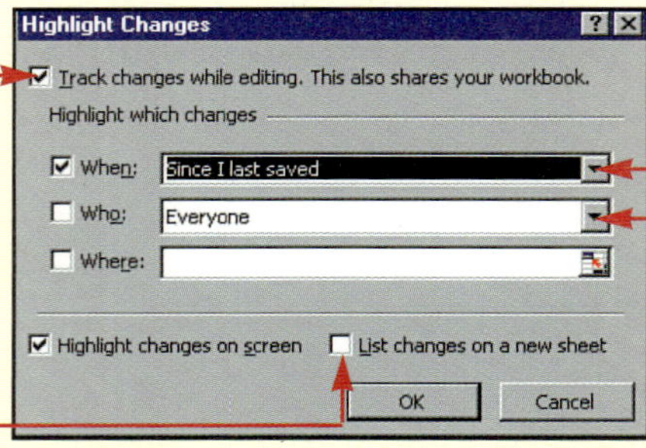

Figure 14.3
Use the Highlight Changes dialog box to specify how changes are tracked and highlighted.

3 Make sure that the Track changes while editing check box is selected.

4 Make sure that the When check box is selected; then choose All from the drop-down list.

The default is to highlight changes since you last saved.

5 Make sure that the Who check box is selected; then choose Everyone from the drop-down list.

Everyone is the default for this option.

6 Make sure that the Highlight changes on screen and List changes on a new sheet check boxes are selected.

A History sheet is displayed to show a list of all the changes made to the shared workbook.

7 Choose OK.

A separate History worksheet is created for this workbook, with data-filtering capabilities.

8 Activate `Sheet1` and point to cell E4.

The details of a change appear as a comment when you point to a cell, as shown in Figure A.4. Changes are highlighted in separate colors for each user. Additional comments can be added to a cell by choosing Insert, Comment.

Figure 14.4
Details of a cell change appear as a comment.

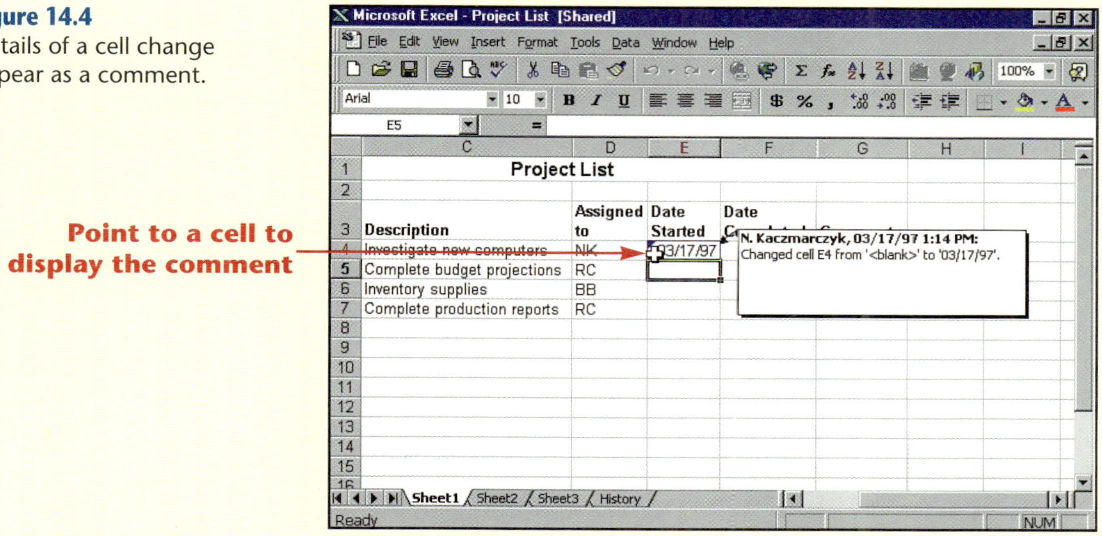

9 Click cell G6 and type Rush**. Press** Enter**.**

The change made in cell G6 is highlighted in the same user color.

10 Choose File, Save.

The changes to the workbook are saved except for the History worksheet. When you need one, you can request a History sheet showing an updated list of all the user changes.

11 Choose Tools, Track Changes, Highlight Changes, and select List changes on a new sheet; then click OK.

The new History sheet appears with detailed information about the two changes made to this workbook, as shown in Figure 14.5. (Note that this screen was changed to an 80 percent zoom to be able to see all the columns in this figure.)

From this History sheet, you can determine the number of changes that were made; the date, time, and author of a change; and where it appears on the worksheet. From the New Value and Old Value columns, you can see the change that was made. The Action Type and Losing Action columns show you how conflicting changes were resolved.

12 Review the changes on the History sheet.

The History sheet can be filtered or printed. Notice the arrows next to each column heading. These filtering arrows enable you to find specific change information based on a column heading. For example, if you want to see only the changes made on a specific date, click the arrow next to the Date heading and select that date from the list. Only the rows including that date appear on the screen; all others are hidden.

continues

To Track Changes (continued)

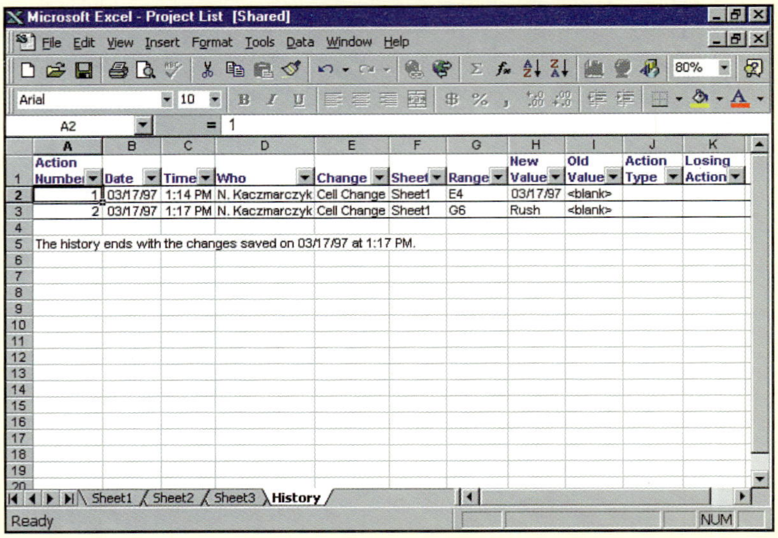

Figure 14.5
The History sheet shows detailed information about the changes made to the workbook.

13. **Print the History sheet.**
14. **Save the changes; then close the workbook.**

Inside Stuff

You specify how you want to see the changes of other users in the Share Workbook dialog box, on the Advanced tab. The default option for updating changes is When file is saved. As an alternative, you can select Automatically every and enter the number of minutes. When you choose this option, there are two further options: Save my changes and see others' changes, or Just see other users' changes.

When you set up workbook sharing, you should select Print settings under the Include in personal view area of the Advanced tab in the Share Workbook dialog box. This allows you to save your own personal print settings you specified in the shared workbook, including page breaks, print areas, and page setup. If each user does the same, each person can print the shared workbook differently without affecting how others print it.

Exam Notes

Unless you specify otherwise, you see the changes made by other users whenever you save the workbook. If more than one user adds a comment to the same cell, the notations from all users appear when each user saves the shared workbook.

If the modifications you made are in conflict with those saved by another user, the Resolve Conflicts dialog box appears, giving you the opportunity to save your changes or keep the changes made by the other user. To have the changes you save always win, choose Tools, Share Workbook from the menu, click the Advanced tab, and select The changes being saved win under Conflicting changes between users. Then choose OK.

To further identify which changes to accept or reject, choose Tools, Track Changes, Accept or Reject Changes. In the Select Changes to Accept or Reject dialog box, you can further qualify changes as to When, Who, and Where created. When you click OK, the first change found is listed in a dialog box, where you may choose Accept or Reject. Once you choose, the dialog box displays the next change. You continue to accept or reject the changes (choose Accept All or Reject All to accept or reject all the changes at one time) until you have seen the entire list.

When two or more users made conflicting entries in the same cell, a list of all the entries appears in the dialog box. You select the change you want to keep and click Accept. Then continue reviewing the remaining changes.

When you finish reviewing the last change, the dialog box automatically closes. Click Close to close the dialog box without reviewing the rest of the changes.

Lesson 4: Merging Workbooks

When you have several copies of the shared workbook being used by different people, you have to merge all the versions together at some point. To do this, users must maintain the change history from the date the copies were created until the date of the merge.

If the number of days you specified to keep the history has been exceeded, you can no longer merge the copies. Therefore, when you aren't sure how long the review process will take, you should maintain the change history for a sufficient number of days or enter a large number, such as 1,000.

To Merge Workbooks

1. **Open the `Project List` workbook.**

   This is the workbook into which you want to merge all the other versions of the workbook.

2. **Choose Tools, Merge Workbooks from the menu. If prompted, save the current workbook.**

   The Select Files to Merge Into Current Workbook dialog box appears.

3. **Select the location and the name of the file(s) you want to merge with the current workbook.**

   To select adjacent files, click the first file you want in the list, hold down Shift, and then click the last file in the list. To select files that aren't next to each other, click the first file, hold down Ctrl, and then click each additional file.

4. **Click OK.**

   The changes merge into one workbook.

5. **Save and close the workbook.**

Lesson 5: Discontinuing Workbook Sharing

There are two specific times when you need to discontinue workbook sharing. You may decide that you no longer want to share the workbook with other users, or you may need to use a feature that cannot be used while workbook sharing is active.

To Discontinue Workbook Sharing

1. **Open the `Project List` workbook and activate the `Sheet1` worksheet.**

2. **Choose Tools, Share Workbook; then click the Editing tab.**

   The Share Workbook dialog box appears, as shown in Figure 14.6.

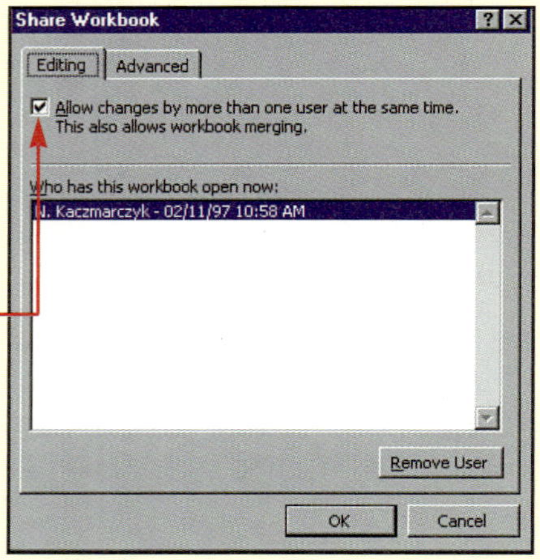

Figure 14.6
Use the Editing tab of the Share Workbook dialog box to start or stop workbook sharing.

Click here to remove the check mark and discontinue workbook sharing

3. **Make sure that no users other than you are shown in the Who has this workbook open now list box.**

   You want to be sure that you are the only user currently using the workbook. Before discontinuing the Share Workbook feature, notify any users who currently have the workbook open of your intention so that they can save and close the file; otherwise, they may lose their unsaved changes. Note that you can also remove individual users from workbook sharing by selecting the user and clicking the Remove User button.

4. **Click the Allow changes by more than one user at the same time box to remove the check mark.**

5. **Choose OK.**

   Excel warns you that this action removes the workbook from shared use. To make the workbook exclusive, you must choose Yes.

6. **Click Yes.**

   Workbook sharing is discontinued. When you stop workbook sharing, the change history is erased and can no longer be viewed.

7. **Save the changes to the workbook; then close it.**

If you have completed your session on the computer, exit Excel 97 and Windows 95 before turning off your computer. Otherwise, continue with the "Checking Your Skills" and "Applying Your Skills" sections at the end of this project.

Project Summary

To	Do This
Share a workbook	Choose Tools, Share Workbook. On the Editing tab, select Allow changes by more than one user at the same time and click OK.
Track changes	Choose Tools, Track Changes, Highlight Changes. Check Track Changes While Editing. Specify When and Who. Select Highlight changes on screen and click OK.
See a History sheet	Choose Tools, Track Changes, Highlight Changes. Select List Changes on a New Sheet and then click OK.
Merge workbooks	Choose Tools, Merge Workbooks. Select the names of the files you want to merge into the current workbook and click OK.
Discontinue workbook sharing	Choose Tools, Share Workbook. Click the Editing tab. Deselect Allow changes by more than one user at the same time. Click OK.

Checking Your Skills

True/False

For each of the following, check *T* or *F* to indicate whether the statement is true or false.

__T __F **1.** When working with a shared workbook, all users must use the same print settings.

__T __F **2.** All the users of a shared workbook must work in Microsoft Excel 97.

__T __F **3.** By default, a history of changes is kept 30 days.

__T __F **4.** Other users won't lose their work if you turn off the shared workbook feature.

__T __F **5.** You can't delete worksheets from a shared workbook.

__T __F **6.** All users of the shared workbook must be on the same network.

__T __F 7. You can't insert automatic subtotals in a shared workbook.

__T __F 8. You can delete columns and rows in a shared workbook.

__T __F 9. Conditional formatting works well in a shared workbook.

__T __F 10. You can't create or modify a macro in a shared workbook.

Multiple Choice

Circle the letter of the correct answer for each of the following.

1. In the Highlight Changes dialog box, you can specify which of the following?
   a. When changes should be highlighted.
   b. Whose changes can be highlighted.
   c. What color the highlighting should be.
   d. Only b and c
   e. Only a and b

2. When you accept the defaults, changes made by other users only appear in your worksheet __________
   a. At 15 minute intervals.
   b. When the other user logs off.
   c. When you save the file.
   d. When you click the Update button.

3. Which actions can you perform in a shared workbook?
   a. Insert or delete columns and rows.
   b. Save, view, or modify scenarios.
   c. Group or outline data.
   d. Assign passwords.

4. When another user changes a cell in a shared workbook, it appears as a(n) __________
   a. Shaded cell.
   b. Flashing cell.
   c. Comment.
   d. None of the above

5. What happens if the modifications you make are in conflict with the changes made by another user?
   a. Your change gets wiped out by the other user.
   b. The Resolve Conflict dialog box appears, and you accept or reject the change.
   c. Your change wipes out the entry by the other user.
   d. Nothing happens.

6. Which of the choices below is not necessary for sharing workbooks?
   a. All users are on a network.
   b. All users must have Microsoft Excel 97.
   c. All users must have the password.
   d. All users must have network access to the file.

7. Any changes you make to the shared workbook are identified by:
   a. Your computer name.
   b. The name you enter in the workbook.

c. Your network logon.

d. The user name in the Options dialog box.

8. How do you find out who is using the shared workbook?

a. Check the login list.

b. Call your network administrator.

c. Choose Tools, Share Workbook and look on the Editing tab.

d. Choose Tools, Share Workbook and look on the Advanced tab.

9. You specify how you want to see others' changes in a shared workbook. What are your choices?

a. When the file is saved.

b. Every specified interval (in minutes); then show me only other users' changes.

c. Every specified interval (in minutes); then show me my changes and those of other users.

d. All of the above

10. When more than one user makes a comment in the same cell, what happens?

a. The last user's comment is the only one seen.

b. The first user's comment is the only one seen.

c. All of the comments are displayed.

d. A reference appears to another worksheet where the comments are stored.

Completion

In the blank(s) provided, write the correct answer for each of the following statements.

1. The History sheet can be ______________ or printed.
2. Your ____________ __________ identifies any changes you make to a shared workbook.
3. You ____________ use the drawing tools in a shared workbook.
4. To see the changes others make to the workbook, you choose Tools, ________________, ______________.
5. To have a History sheet appear to display everyone's changes to a workbook, select ___________________ in the Highlight Changes dialog box.
6. You can view but not make changes to or save a ______________ file with the same filename.
7. You can't delete ___________ or blocks of cells in a shared workbook but you can delete rows and columns.
8. To specify how changes will be tracked in the shared workbook, you choose Tools, Track Changes, _______________.

9. When you have several copies of a shared workbook being used by different people, you have to ____________ all the versions at some point.

10. The record of changes made to the workbook since you started tracking changes is called the ____________.

Matching

In the blank next to each of the following terms or phrases, write the letter of the corresponding term or phrase. (Note that some letters may be used more than once.)

a. Filtering

b. User name

c. Read-only file

d. Network

e. Highlight Changes

f. Merging

g. 30

h. When file is saved

i. Tools, Share Workbook

j. Rows and columns

_____ 1. Combining all versions of a shared workbook

_____ 2. Command used to share a workbook

_____ 3. Default number of days history of changes is kept

_____ 4. A file you can view but cannot make changes to or save using the same file name

_____ 5. Use this to find specific information in the change history

_____ 6. To set up who, when, and where specifics of tracking changes, open this dialog box

_____ 7. Hardware and software that connect computers, giving users access to shared data

_____ 8. Choices for updating changes by other users include automaically and this

_____ 9. How Excel identifies who made the changes in a worksheet

_____ 10. You can delete these in a shared workbook

Applying Your Skills

Practice

The following exercises enable you to practice the skills you learned in this project. Take a few minutes to work through these exercises now.

Sharing a Workbook

You have a personnel database that you want to share with other people in your department, so each of you can add or modify entries in the workbook.

To share a workbook, follow these steps:

1. Open the Proj1403 file from the Project-14 folder on the CD and save it as `Personnel`.

2. Share the workbook, allowing more than one user at the same time.

3. Set the track changes option to save the history for `1,000` days.
4. Save the workbook and leave it open for the next exercise.

Tracking Changes and Showing a History of Changes

Now that you are sharing the workbook with other users, you want to track the changes made by each user. You also need to see a complete history of changes so you can filter them.

To track changes and show a history of changes, follow these steps:

1. Click D6 and change the division to `New York`.
2. Click B17 and change the last name to `Foster-Smythe`.
3. Click H18 and change the salary to `$27,500`.
4. Save the workbook.
5. Turn on the tracking of changes by highlighting the changes. Track all the changes that have ever been made to the workbook for everyone using the workbook. Make sure you create a history sheet to record the changes.
6. Point at each of the cells that you changed and read the comments. View the history sheet.
7. Save the workbook and leave it open for the next exercise.

Merging Workbooks and Resolving Conflicts

Another user has a copy of the shared workbook and has made changes in the copy. You need to merge the two versions of the shared workbook and resolve any conflicts.

To merge workbooks and resolve conflicts, follow these steps:

1. Merge the `Personnel` workbook with the Proj1404 file in the Project-14 folder on the CD.
2. Resolve all the conflicts which appear in the merged workbook. Accept any changes you or another user made without conflict. Where conflicts occur, accept the ones made by Jane Calabria.
3. Save the workbook. If requested by your instructor, print two copies of the workbook. Close the workbook.

Challenge

The following challenges enable you to use your problem-solving skills. Take time to work through these exercises now.

Setting Up a Workbook for Sharing

Your company maintains a client list that is updated by everyone in the company. Right now, each customer service person keeps an index card file on their own customers and leaves a carbon in a central file (which doesn't always get updated as soon as it should). Your boss would like to keep the list in a central place on the computer and has chosen for now to keep it in Excel. Open Proj1405 from the Project-14 folder on the CD and save it as `Client List`. The beginning of the list has been entered. Now save the file as a shared workbook. Keep the change history for 60 days and update changes when the file is saved. Include the print settings in your personal view, and have Excel ask you which changes win any conflicts. Close the workbook.

Adding or Changing Data in a Shared Workbook

Open the Client List shared workbook. Click in I1 and type today's date. Add the following new client to the file:

```
Juanita Estevez

44 Benjamin Franklin Pkwy., Apt. 309

Philadelphia, PA 19108

(215) 981-7823

Last ordered 3/13/98
```

Save the file.

Tracking Changes

Set up the Client List workbook to track changes by highlighting them. Track all the changes to the worksheet for everyone. List the changes on a new sheet, and make sure you highlight the changes onscreen. Save the workbook.

Merging Versions

Merge the Client List file with Proj1406 to combine the changes made by other users. Resolve any conflicting entries. Save the merged file and print it.

Discontinuing Workbook Sharing

Discontinue sharing the Client List file. Save the workbook and close it.

PinPoint Assessment

PinPoint Training

You have completed the project and the associated lessons, as well as the "Checking Your Skills" and "Applying Your Skills" sections. Now use the PinPoint software evaluation mode to assess your comprehension of the specific exam tasks you have just learned. You can also use the PinPoint Trainer Mode and the Show Me tutorials to practice these specific exam tasks.

appendix A

Working with Windows 95

Objectives

In this Appendix, you learn how to:

- ➤ Start Windows 95
- ➤ Use the Mouse
- ➤ Understand the Start Menu
- ➤ Identify the Elements of a Window
- ➤ Manipulate Windows
- ➤ Exit the Windows 95 Program

Why Would I Do This?

Graphical user interface (GUI)
A computer application that uses pictures, graphics, menus, and commands to help users communicate with their computers.

Desktop
The background of the Windows screen, on which windows, icons, and dialog boxes appear.

Icon
A picture that represents an application, a file, or a system resource.

Shortcut
Gives you quick access to frequently used objects so you don't have to look through menus each time you need to use that object.

Microsoft Windows 95 is a powerful operating environment that enables you to access the power of DOS without memorizing DOS commands and syntax. Windows 95 uses a *graphical user interface* (GUI) so that you can easily see onscreen the tools that you need to complete specific file- and program-management tasks.

This appendix, an overview of the Windows 95 environment, is designed to help you learn the basics of Windows 95.

Lesson 1: Starting Windows 95

The first thing you need to know about Windows is how to start the software. In this lesson, you learn how to start Windows; however, before you can start Windows, it must be installed on your computer. If you need to install Windows, refer to your Windows 95 manual or ask your instructor for assistance.

In most cases, Windows starts automatically when you turn on your computer. If your system is set up differently, you must start Windows from the DOS prompt (such as C:\>). Try starting the Windows program now.

To Start Windows 95

Taskbar
Contains the Start button, buttons for each open window, and the current time.

Start button
A click of the Start button opens the Start menu.

1. **Turn on your computer and monitor.**

   Most computers display technical information about the computer and the operating software installed on it.

   If Windows starts, you can skip step 2. Otherwise, you will see the DOS prompt C:\>.

2. **At the DOS prompt, type `win` and press Enter.**

   When you start the Windows program, a Microsoft Windows 95 banner displays for a few seconds; then the *desktop* appears (see Figure A.1).

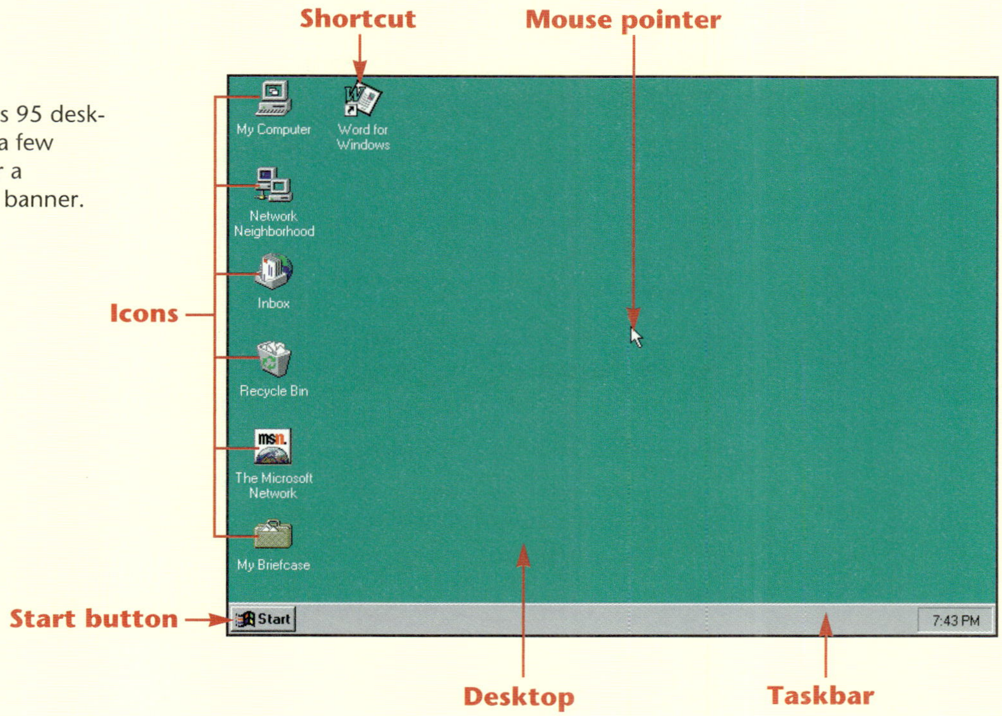

Figure A.1
The Windows 95 desktop appears a few seconds after a Windows 95 banner.

Inside Stuff

Program *icons* that were created during installation (such as My Computer, Recycle Bin, and Network Neighborhood) are displayed on the desktop. Other icons might also appear, depending on how your system is set up. Shortcuts to frequently used objects (such as documents, printers, and network drives) can be placed on the desktop. The *Taskbar* appears along the bottom edge of the desktop. The *Start button* appears at the left end of the Taskbar.

Pull-down menus
Menus that cascade downward into the screen whenever you select a command from the menu bar.

Dialog box
A window that opens onscreen to provide information about the current action or to ask the user to provide additional information to complete the action.

Mouse
A pointing device used in many programs to make choices, select data, and otherwise communicate with the computer.

Mouse pad
A pad that provides a uniform surface for the mouse to slide on.

Lesson 2: Using the Mouse

Windows is designed to be used with a *mouse,* so it's important that you learn how to use a mouse correctly. With a little practice, using a mouse is as easy as pointing to something with your finger. You can use the mouse to select icons, to make selections from *pull-down menus* and *dialog boxes*, and to select objects that you want to move or resize.

In the Windows desktop, you can use a mouse to

- Open windows
- Close windows
- Open menus
- Choose menu commands
- Rearrange onscreen items, such as icons and windows

The position of the mouse is indicated onscreen by a *mouse pointer*. Usually, the mouse pointer is an arrow, but it sometimes changes shape depending on the current action.

Mouse pointer
A symbol that appears onscreen to indicate the current location of the mouse.

Onscreen, the mouse pointer moves according to the movements of the mouse on your desk or on a *mouse pad*. To move the mouse pointer, simply move the mouse.

There are four basic mouse actions:

- *Click.* To point to an item, and then press and quickly release the left mouse button. You click to select an item, such as an option on a menu. To cancel a selection, click an empty area of the desktop. Unless otherwise specified, you use the left mouse button for all mouse actions.
- *Double-click.* To point to an item, and then press and release the left mouse button twice, as quickly as possible. You double-click to open or close windows and to start applications from icons.
- *Right-click.* To point to an item, and then press and release the right mouse button. This opens a Context menu, which gives you a shortcut to frequently used commands. To cancel a Context menu, click the left mouse button outside the menu.
- *Drag.* To point to an item, then press and hold down the left mouse button as you move the pointer to another location, and then release the mouse button. You drag to resize windows, move icons, and scroll.

If you have problems...

If you double-click but nothing happens, you may not be clicking fast enough. Try again.

Lesson 3: Understanding the Start Menu

Program folder
Represented by an icon of a file folder with an application window in front of it, program folders contain shortcut icons and other program folders.

The Start button on the Taskbar gives you access to your applications, settings, recently opened documents, the Find utility, the Run command, the Help system, and the Shut Down command. Clicking the Start button opens the Start menu. Choosing the Programs option at the top of the Start menu displays the Programs submenu, which lists the *program folders* on your system. Program folders are listed first, followed by shortcuts (see Figure A.2).

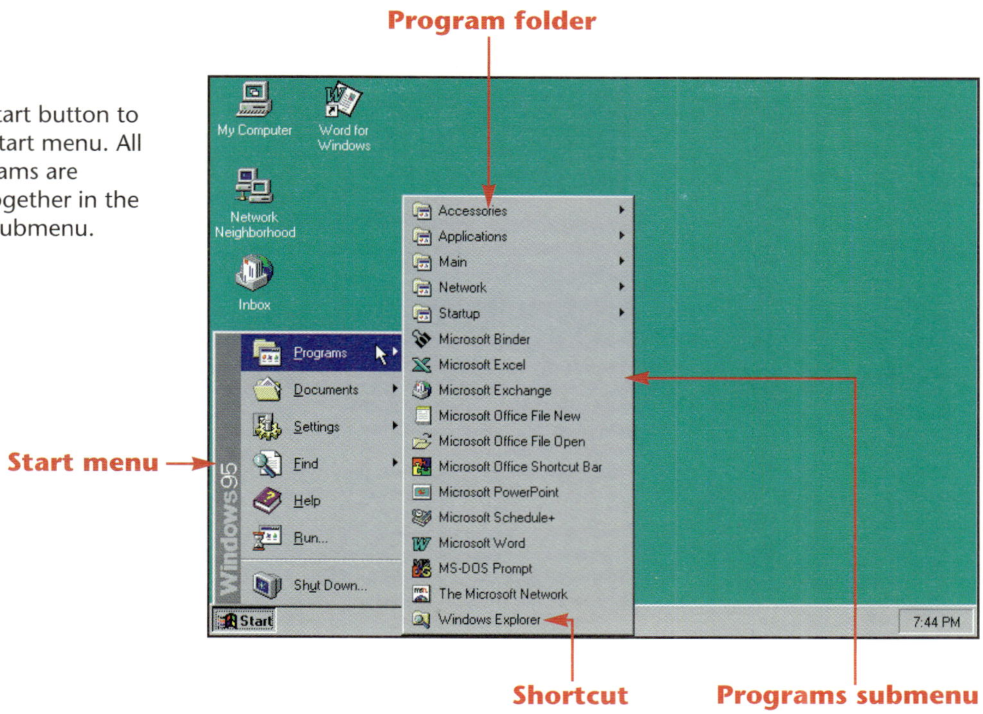

Figure A.2
Click the Start button to open the Start menu. All your programs are grouped together in the Programs submenu.

When the Start menu is open, moving the mouse pointer moves a selection bar through the menu options. When the selection bar highlights a menu command with a right-facing triangle, a submenu opens. Click the shortcut icon to start an application. If a menu command is followed by an ellipsis, clicking that command opens a dialog box.

Lesson 4: Identifying the Elements of a Window

In Windows 95, everything opens in a window. Applications, documents, and dialog boxes all open in windows. For example, double-clicking the My Computer icon opens the My Computer application into a window. Because window elements stay the same for all Windows applications, this section uses the My Computer window for illustration.

Title Bar

Across the top of each window is its title bar. A title bar contains the name of the open window, as well as three buttons to manipulate it. The Minimize button reduces the window to a button on the Taskbar. The Maximize button expands the window to fill the desktop. The Close button closes the window.

Menu Bar

The menu bar gives you access to the application's menus. Menus enable you to select options that perform functions or carry out commands (see Figure A.3). The File menu in My Computer, for example, enables you to open, save, and print files.

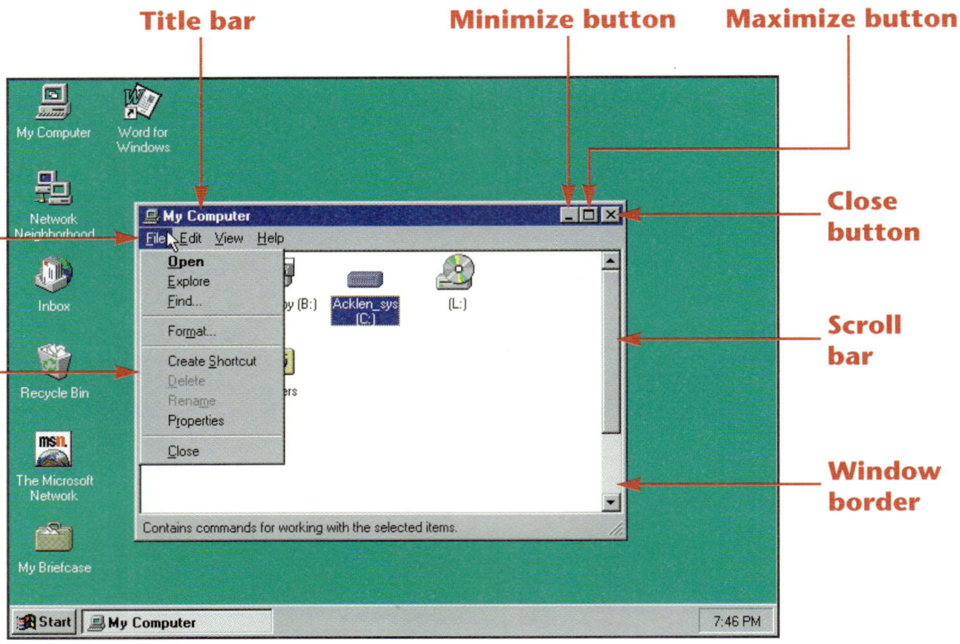

Figure A.3
The My Computer window has window elements found in all Windows applications.

Some menu options require you to enter additional information. When you select one of these options, a dialog box opens (see Figure A.4). You type the additional information, select from a list of options, or select a button. Most dialog boxes have a Cancel button, which closes the dialog box without saving the changes; an OK button, which closes the dialog box and saves the changes; and a Help button, which opens a Help window.

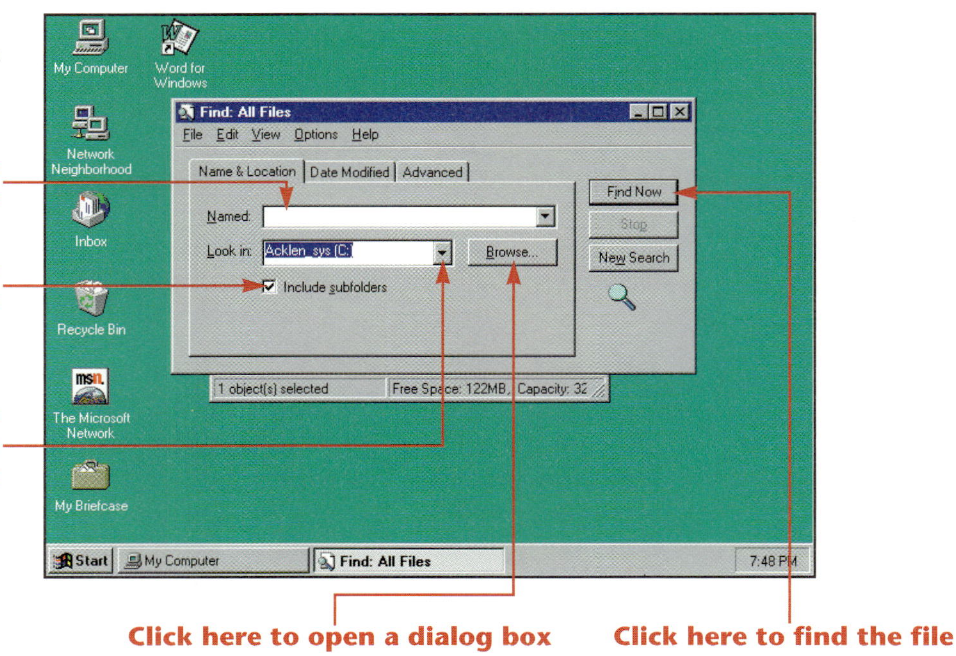

Figure A.4
You can use the options in the Find dialog box to search for a file.

Scroll Bar

Scroll bars appear when you have more information in a window than is currently displayed onscreen. A horizontal scroll bar appears along the bottom of a window, and a vertical scroll bar appears along the right side of a window.

Window Border

The window border identifies the edge of the window. In most windows, it can be used to change the size of a window. The window corner is used to resize a window on two sides at the same time.

Lesson 5: Manipulating Windows

When you work with windows, you need to know how to arrange them. You can shrink the window into an icon or enlarge the window to fill the desktop. You can stack windows together or give them each an equal slice of the desktop.

Maximizing a Window

Maximize
To increase the size of a window so that it fills the entire screen.

You can *maximize* a window so that it fills the desktop. Maximizing a window gives you more space to work in. To maximize a window, click the Maximize button on the title bar.

Minimizing a Window

Minimize
To reduce a window to an icon.

When you *minimize* a window, it shrinks the window to an icon on the Taskbar. Even though you can't see the window anymore, the application stays loaded in the computer's memory. To minimize a window, click the Minimize button on the title bar.

Restoring a Window

When a window is maximized, the Maximize button changes into a Restore button. Clicking the Restore button restores the window back to the original size and position before the window was maximized.

Closing a Window

When you are finished working in a window, you can close the window by clicking the Close button. Closing an application window exits the program, removing it from memory. When you click the Close button, the window (on the desktop) and the window button (on the Taskbar) disappear.

Arranging Windows

Changing the size and position of a window enables you to see more than one application window, which makes copying and pasting data between programs much easier. You can also move a window to any location on the desktop. By moving application windows, you can arrange your work on the Windows desktop just as you arrange papers on your desk.

Tile
To arrange open windows on the desktop so that they do not overlap.

Cascade
To arrange open windows on the desktop so that they overlap, with only the title bar of each window (behind the top window) displayed.

Use one of the following options to arrange windows:

- Right-click the Taskbar and choose Tile Horizontally.
- Right-click the Taskbar and choose Tile Vertically. See Figure A.5 for an example.
- Right-click the Taskbar and choose Cascade. See Figure A.6 for an example.
- Click and drag the window's title bar to move the window around on the desktop.
- Click and drag a window border (or corner) to increase or decrease the size of the window.

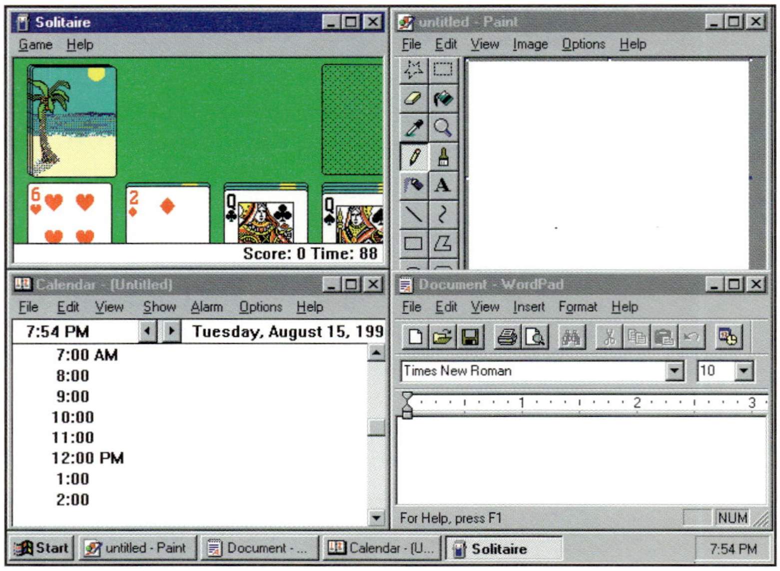

Figure A.5
The windows are tiled vertically across the desktop.

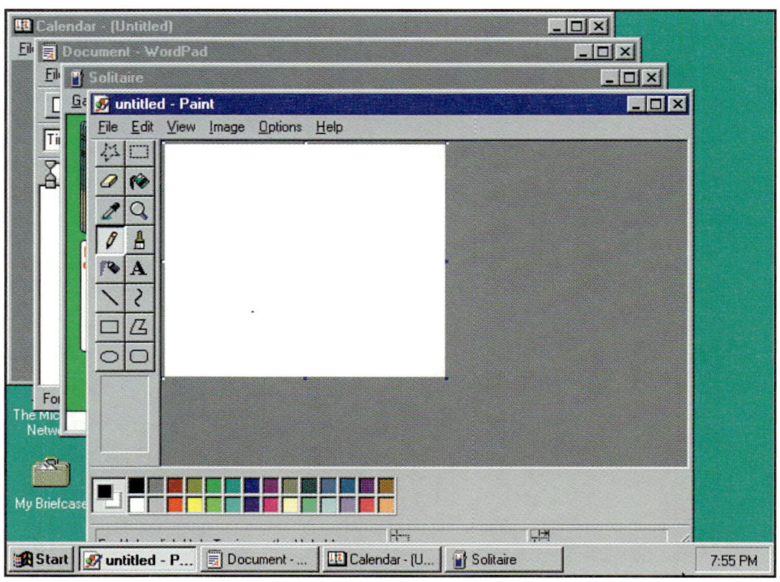

Figure A.6
The windows are cascaded on the desktop.

Lesson 6: Exiting the Windows 95 Program

In Windows 95, you use the Shut Down command to exit the Windows 95 program. You should always use this command, which closes all open applications and files, before you turn off the computer. If you haven't saved your work in an application when you choose this command, you'll be prompted to save your changes before Windows shuts down.

To Exit Windows 95

1. **Click the Start button on the Taskbar.**
2. **Choose Shut Down.**
3. **Choose Shut down the computer.**
4. **Choose Yes.**

   Windows displays a message asking you to wait while the computer is shutting down. When this process is complete, a message appears telling you that you can safely turn off your computer.

appendix B

Glossary

Absolute reference An absolute reference is a cell reference in a formula that does not change when copied to a new location.

Active cell The currently selected cell (a thick border appears around that cell when you click in it).

Ascending order Sorts records from beginning to end, from A to Z or 1 to 100. (Records with a blank sort field appear in front of other records.)

AutoFormat A built-in collection of formats (such as font size, patterns, and alignment) that you can quickly apply to a range of data. Microsoft Excel determines the levels of summary and detail in the selected range and applies the formats accordingly.

Axis A line that serves as a major reference for plotting data on a graph. In a two-dimensional chart, there are two axes: the vertical axis is the y-axis, or Value Axis, and the horizontal axis is the x-axis, or Category Axis (except in bar charts where the Category Axis is the vertical and the Value axis is horizontal). In a three-dimensional chart, the z-axis represents the vertical plane, and the x-axis (distance) and y-axis (width) represent the two sides on the floor of the chart. Pie charts do not have axes.

Browser A program that translates the HTML codes in a web page to a layout that is viewed by the user.

Category One item against which Excel plots the data series. It may be a time (month, year, quarter), a product name, a location, and so on. A chart may only have one category, or it may have several.

Cell Rectangle formed by the intersection of a column and a row.

Cell address Each cell (or rectangle) in the spreadsheet has a unique address by which you may reference that cell in formulas. That address consists of the letter of the column the cell is in and the row number.

Clip art Pictures you can use without copyright restrictions.

Clipboard A temporary memory holding area where Windows stores items that you Cut or Copy from a document. The items remain in the Clipboard until a different item is cut or copied or until your computer is shut down; the new item then replaces it. As long as an item remains in the Clipboard, you may Paste it into an Excel worksheet. Pasting places a copy of the Clipboard contents into the active cell or selected range.

Comparison operator A sign used to compare two values, such as = (equal to), > (greater than), < (less than), >= (greater than or equal to), <= (less than or equal to), or <> (not equal to).

Conditional format A format, such as cell shading or font color, that Microsoft Excel automatically applies to cells if a specified condition is true.

Data labels Optional labels that appear at the data points on the chart. They may show the value, category, or percentage of the data point.

Data marker A bar (in column and bar charts), shape (in area or pie charts), dot, or symbol (in line and Scatter charts) that marks a single data point or value. Related markers in a graph represent the same data series.

Data point A single cell value, representing a single category in a data series.

Data series A row or column of data used to plot one line, one pie, or one set of bars or columns in a chart.

Database A collection of related information organized into fields and records. You use a database to store, organize, and retrieve information. A mailing list is a type of database.

Descending order Sorts records from end to beginning, from Z to A or from 100 to 1.

Dynamic Data Exchange (DDE) A communications protocol that lets you share data between two open applications.

Embedded charts A chart that is placed on the same worksheet that contains the data used to create the chart. A chart can also be placed on a chart sheet in the workbook so that the worksheet and chart are separate. Embedded charts are useful for showing the actual data and its graphic representation side-by-side.

Embedding Places an "object" created by another program directly into your worksheet. You edit the object contents by activating the source application directly from your worksheet. Changing an embedded object does not change the source document.

Field A piece of information unique for each record in the database. In a mailing list, the name of the city would be stored in a "city" field, and each individual in the database would also have data in that "city" field.

Filter An action Microsoft Excel performs to select a subset of your list. All the rows in the subset meet specific criteria, and all other rows are "filtered out."

Font A set of characters that have the same typeface, which means they are of a single design (such as Times New Roman).

Formula An algebraic expression using numbers, functions, mathematical operators, and cell addresses that tells Excel what operations to perform on numbers or the contents of the designated cells.

Function Ready-made formula that performs a series of operations on a specified range of values.

Gridlines Optional lines that extend from the tick marks on an axis through the plot area to make it easier to evaluate data points (*see also Major and Minor Gridlines*).

Histogram analysis tool Calculates individual and cumulative frequencies for a cell range of data and data bins. It generates data for the number of occurrences of a value in the data set.

Hyperlink Colored and underlined text or graphics on web pages that you click to go to another location on the current page, another Web page, an HTML page on the World Wide Web, or an HTML page on an intranet.

Hypertext Markup Language (HTML) HTML is a collection of instructions, or *tags*, that tell a browser program how to display a document—when the text is bold, italic, and so on.

Internet A worldwide conglomeration of computer networks that can talk to each other.

Intranet A company's computer network working with software that lets it route HTML documents. The documents can be read on the network using a browser.

Legend A key that identifies the patterns, colors, or symbols associated with the markers of a data series. Shows the data series name that corresponds to each marker.

Linking Utilizes the Clipboard (via the Cut and Copy commands) to bring data from a source document and place it into your document. Any updates to the source information will also appear in your worksheet. The location of the source file cannot change or the link will fail.

Macro A set of commands and instructions that are recorded and played back when you command it to run.

Major and minor gridlines Major gridlines help you pinpoint exact locations in a chart without cluttering the chart. On the value axis, the value labels appear next to the major gridlines. When major gridlines don't provide enough detail, you can use minor gridlines as well. Minor gridlines fall between the major intervals on the axis.

Mixed reference A reference that is only partially absolute, such as A$2 or $A2. When a formula that uses a mixed reference is copied to another cell, part of the cell reference (the relative part) is adjusted.

Number format Determines how a number appears in the format, such as a Currency format which adds a dollar sign, a comma as a thousands separator, and two decimal places to the number you entered in the cell.

Object Linking and Embedding (OLE) Extends your ability to dynamically share information between programs and program files. Because of OLE, you can embed or link files from another application into your worksheet; or you can embed a new object and use the object's source application to enter data into your worksheet.

PivotTable An interactive table that summarizes large amounts of data. To see different summaries of the source data, you rotate its rows and columns.

Plot area The area in which Excel plots the data for a graph. It includes the axes and all markers that represent data points.

Query A question you ask about data stored in an external database.

Range A group of adjacent cells joined horizontally or vertically.

Record An individual set of information consisting of the data for each field in a database that relates to one individual or company or thing. In a mailing list, a record would be one person's name, address, city, state, and zip code.

Relative reference A *relative reference* is a cell reference in a formula that is adjusted when the formula is copied.

Series names The names that identify each row or column of data. These names appear in the legend.

Shared list or workbook A workbook that allows multiple users on a network to view and make changes to the workbook simultaneously. Users who save the workbook can view the modifications made by others.

Style A collection of formats (such as font size, patterns, and alignment) that you define and save as a group.

Template A preformatted workbook or worksheet that contains text, formulas, and automating features that help you set up consistent workbooks for specific tasks.

Tick mark A small line that intersects an axis and marks off a category, scale, or data series.

Tick mark labels The names that appear along the Category axis where the tick marks are.

URL The Web uses a type of address called a uniform resource locator (URL) to identify specific documents and locations.

Web The World Wide Web (or just Web) is a component of the Internet. It's a collection of documents accessible through the Internet.

Workbook An Excel file. Each workbook consists of three worksheets (although you can add and remove worksheets as needed). The tabs at the bottom of the workbook window (labeled Sheet1, Sheet2, and Sheet3) let you flip through the worksheets by clicking them with the mouse.

Worksheet Consists of columns and rows that intersect to form boxes called cells into which you enter values (numbers) or labels (text).

appendix C

Student Preparation Guide

The purpose of this appendix is to provide you with information you'll need about the certification tests—how to register, what is covered in the tests, how the tests work, and so on.

Studying for the Tests

Although you aren't required to take a training course to pass the Microsoft Office User Specialist exams, you certainly need to be sure you can successfully complete the tasks that are covered by the exams. Although a training class provides guidance, support, and practice, it may not be convenient or necessary for you.

This book provides the tutorial, review questions, and practice to help you complete your exams successfully. It can be used in a classroom situation, or you can work through the projects on your own. You don't have to work through the book from front to back, as each project stands on its own. The "Checking Your Skills" and "Applying Your Skills" sections at the end of each project give you a chance to become familiar with the tasks. The Kelly PinPoint CBT trainer located on the accompanying CD has end-of-project computer-based training and evaluation, as well as a final practice examination.

Levels of Certification

For the Microsoft Office User Specialist exam for Microsoft Excel 97, there are two levels of certification:

- **Microsoft Excel Proficient Specialist** You are able to handle a wide range of everyday tasks without difficulty.
- **Microsoft Excel Expert Specialist** In addition to the everyday tasks at the Proficient level, you are able to handle complex assignments involving advanced formatting and functionality.

Microsoft also has a special Office 97 certification, the Microsoft Office Expert. To attain this level, you must be an Expert User in each of the Microsoft Office applications (Access, Excel, Word, PowerPoint, and FrontPage) and have taken the Office Integration Exam to prove you can integrate these applications.

The specific topics covered at each level are listed in the "Required Tasks" section of this appendix. In this book, these tasks are broken down into projects. At the beginning of each project is a list of which tasks are covered and which subject area they fall under in the tests.

Required Tasks

Each exam involves a list of required tasks that you may be asked to perform. The list of possible tasks is categorized by skill area.

Proficient User

A Proficient User should be able to do the following:

- Basic financial statements
- Budgets

- Expense reports
- Invoices and purchase orders
- Marketing and sales reports
- Spreadsheet information for use on the Internet and intranet

The skill areas covered in the exam and the required tasks for those skill areas are listed in Table C1.

Table C.1 Proficient User Skills

Skill Set	Required Activity
Create workbooks	Open electronic workbooks Enter text and numbers Enter formulas Save workbooks Close workbooks
Modify workbooks	Delete cell contents Delete worksheets Revise text and numbers Rotate and indent text Revise formulas Copy and move data Insert, modify, and delete rows and columns Use references (absolute, relative, and mixed) Sort data
Print workbooks	Preview and print worksheets Print the screen and ranges Print headers and footers
Format worksheets	Modify cell size and alignment Apply general numbers formats Apply font formats Apply outlines
Create and apply ranges	Create and name ranges Clear and format ranges Copy and move ranges
Use functions	Use the AVERAGE, MIN, and MAX functions Use worksheet functions
Use draw	Create and modify lines and objects Create and modify 3D shapes
Use charts	Create, format, and modify charts Preview and print charts
Save spreadsheets as HTML	Save spreadsheets as HTML documents

Expert User

You are not required to pass, or even take, the Proficient User exam before taking the Expert User test. If you feel confident of your skill level, you can take the Expert User exam without taking the Proficient User test and receive the Expert User certification when you pass.

An Expert User should be able to do the following:

- Accounting and other financial statements
- Amortization schedules
- Data Analysis
- Forecasts
- Lists
- Personnel records
- Statistical tables

The skill areas covered in the exam and the required tasks for those skill areas are listed in Table C2.

Table C.2 Expert User Skills

Skill Set	Required Activity
Format worksheets	Apply formats (accounting, fraction, and scientific) Create custom formats Use styles and AutoFormats
Use lists	Sort data Query from a list
Print workbooks	Preview workbooks Print workbooks
Audit a worksheet	Check and review data Find cells referred to in a specific formula Find formulas that refer to a specific cell Find errors
Use advanced functionality	Query databases Extract data Use filters Use data analysis and pivot tables Use data map Use data validation Use conditional formatting Perform multilevel sorts
Use macros	Create and record macros Edit macros Run macros
Import and export data	Import from other applications Export to other applications

Skill Set	Required Activity
Use templates	Work with existing templates Create templates Edit templates
Use multiple workbooks	Link workbooks Use multiple workbooks
Use workgroup functions	Cell tips Share lists Track changes Resolve conflicts Show history of changes Merge workbooks

Registering for the Exams

Microsoft Office User Specialist exams are administered by Authorized Testing Centers (ATC). To find out where the nearest ATC center is, call (800) 933-4493. Contact the ATC center to find out what their test policies and schedules are, whether they accept walk-ins or must register the candidates in advance, how the exams are conducted, and what they are charging for the tests. The estimated retail price of each exam is $50.00 in the United States, but that can vary based on the center's sales policies. Payment for the tests must be paid in advance. There is no refund for missed or failed exams.

Exams are currently available only in English, although Microsoft plans to offer the Office 97 exams in other languages as soon as the courseware in those languages becomes available.

Taking the Tests

Microsoft Office User Specialist exams are not multiple-choice or true-false tests. Instead, they are based on the types of tasks you may encounter in the everyday world. When you take the test, you sit at a computer that uses Windows® 95 or Windows NT® Workstation, work with a Microsoft Word 97 document, and use the features of Word to perform the tasks outlined for you.

You can't use notes, manuals, laptops, tape recorders, or other aids during the tests. Word Help is available, but using it cuts down on the time you have available to complete the exam tasks.

Exams are one hour or less (some as short as 30 minutes). Your score is based on the number of tasks you successfully perform in the allotted time. This measures your productivity and efficiency, as well as your skill and knowledge.

Each test has a minimum score. If your score meets or exceeds that minimum, you pass the test. If not, you may take the test as many times as you need to until you pass. There is no refund if you don't pass the test.

You see your test results as soon as you complete the exam. Successful candidates receive a certificate a week or two after the testing. Test scores are confidential; only you and Microsoft see them.

To keep up to date on the Certified Microsoft Office User exams, check Microsoft's Web site:

http://www.mous.net

http://www.microsoft.com/office/train_cert/

INDEX

Symbol

A

B - C

D

E

F